Lecture Notes in Computer Science   **14553**

Founding Editors

Gerhard Goos
Juris Hartmanis

The series Lecture Notes in Computer Science (LNCS), including its subseries Lecture Notes in Artificial Intelligence (LNAI) and Lecture Notes in Bioinformatics (LNBI), has established itself as a medium for the publication of new developments in computer science and information technology research, teaching, and education.

LNCS enjoys close cooperation with the computer science R & D community, the series counts many renowned academics among its volume editors and paper authors, and collaborates with prestigious societies. Its mission is to serve this international community by providing an invaluable service, mainly focused on the publication of conference and workshop proceedings and postproceedings. LNCS commenced publication in 1973.

Iouliia Skliarova · Piedad Brox Jiménez ·
Mário Véstias · Pedro C. Diniz
Editors

Applied Reconfigurable Computing

Architectures, Tools, and Applications

20th International Symposium, ARC 2024
Aveiro, Portugal, March 20–22, 2024
Proceedings

 Springer

Editors
Iouliia Skliarova ⓘ
University of Aveiro
Aveiro, Portugal

Piedad Brox Jiménez ⓘ
University of Seville
Seville, Spain

Mário Véstias ⓘ
Instituto Superior de Engenharia de Lisboa
Lisbon, Portugal

Pedro C. Diniz ⓘ
University of Porto
Porto, Portugal

ISSN 0302-9743   ISSN 1611-3349 (electronic)
Lecture Notes in Computer Science
ISBN 978-3-031-55672-2   ISBN 978-3-031-55673-9 (eBook)
https://doi.org/10.1007/978-3-031-55673-9

This Springer imprint is published by the registered company Springer Nature Switzerland AG
The registered company address is: Gewerbestrasse 11, 6330 Cham, Switzerland

Paper in this product is recyclable.

Preface

The 20th International Symposium on Applied Reconfigurable Computing (ARC 2024) was organized by the University of Aveiro, Portugal, and took place in Aveiro from March 20th – 22nd, 2024.

As with previous years, the ARC 2024 edition covered a broad spectrum of applications of reconfigurable computing, from fault-tolerance, data and graph processing acceleration to computer security.

This year's successful program was made possible by the contribution of many talented individuals and world-class research groups. First, and foremost, we would like to thank all submission authors who responded to the call for papers, the members of the program committee and the additional external reviewers who, with their opinion and expertise, ensured a program of the highest quality.

This year's symposium program included 16 regular papers selected from 24 regular paper submissions, from various continents, the Americas, Europe and Asia. The selection process was very competitive with each submission receiving between three to five (double-blind) peer reviews with an average of 3.9 reviews per paper. The symposium also included one special session devoted to *Collaborative Research Projects*, which focused on the application and development of reconfigurable computing techniques.

We extend our sincere gratitude to the authors, reviewers, sponsors, and the organizing committee for their invaluable contributions to making this symposium a resounding success. The collective efforts of the community have made the 20th International Symposium on Applied Reconfigurable Computing a milestone event, and we look forward to the continued growth and impact of reconfigurable computing in the years to come.

Thank you for being part of this exciting journey, and we hope you find the proceedings both informative and inspiring.

Thank you all.

March 2024

Iouliia Skliarova
Piedad Brox Jiménez
Pedro C. Diniz

Organization

General Chair

Pedro C. Diniz   University of Porto, Portugal

Program Committee Chairs

Iouliia Skliarova   University of Aveiro, Portugal
Piedad Brox Jiménez   Instituto de Microelectrónica de Sevilla
                                (CSIC/University of Sevilla), Spain

Steering Committee

Hideharu Amano   Keio University, Japan
Jürgen Becker   Karlsruhe Institute of Technology, Germany
Mladen Berekovic   Lübeck University, Germany
Koen Bertels   QBee.eu, Belgium
João M. P. Cardoso   University of Porto, Portugal
Katherine (Compton) Morrow   University of Wisconsin-Madison, USA
George Constantinides   Imperial College of Science, Technology and
                                Medicine, UK

Pedro C. Diniz   University of Porto, Portugal
Philip H. W. Leong   University of Sydney, Australia
Walid Najjar   University of California Riverside, USA
Roger Woods   Queen's University of Belfast, UK

Program Committee

Hideharu Amano	Keio University, Japan
Caaliph Andriamisaina	Commisariat á l'Énergie Atomique et aux Énergies Alternatives, France
Zachary Baker	Los Alamos National Laboratory, USA
Lars Bauer	Karlsruhe Institute of Technology, Germany
Mladen Berekovic	University of Lübeck, Germany
Piedad Brox Jiménez	Instituto de Microelectrónica de Sevilla (CSIC/University of Sevilla), Spain
Alejandro Cabrera	Tampere University, Finland
João Canas Ferreira	University of Porto, Portugal
João M. P. Cardoso	University of Porto, Portugal
Ray Cheung	City University of Hong Kong, P. R. of China
Daniel Chillet	University of Rennes 1 - IRISA/Inria, France
Pedro C. Diniz	University of Porto, Portugal
Roberto Giorgi	University of Siena, Italy
Diana Göhringer	TU Dresden, Germany
Jim Harkin	University of Ulster, UK
Christian Hochberger	TU Darmstadt, Germany
Michael Hübner	TU Brandenburg Cottbus-Senftenberg, Germany
Maksim Jenihhin	Tallinn University of Technology, Estonia
Krzysztof Kepa	GE Global Research, USA
Georgios Keramidas	Aristotle University of Thessaloniki, Greece
Andreas Koch	TU Darmstadt, Germany
Angeliki Kritikakou	University of Rennes 1 - IRISA/Inria, France
Tomasz Kryjak	AGH University of Science and Technology, Poland
Antonio Miele	Politecnico di Milano, Italy
Dimitris Nikolos	University of Patras, Greece
Rihards Novickis	Institute of Elect. and Computer Science, Latvia
Andrés Otero	Universidad Politécnica de Madrid, Spain
Francesca Palumbo	University of Cagliari, Italy
Thilo Pionteck	Otto-von-Guericke Univ. Magdeburg, Germany
Marco Platzner	University of Paderborn, Germany
Jaan Raik	Tallinn University of Technology, Estonia
Francesco Regazzoni	University of Amsterdam, The Netherlands
Fernando Rincón	Universidade de Castilla-La Mancha, Spain
Yukinori Sato	Toyohashi University of Technology, Japan
Yuichiro Shibata	Nagasaki University, Japan
Nicolas Sklavos	University of Patras, Greece
Iouliia Skliarova	University of Aveiro, Portugal

Tomyslav Sledevič	Vilnius Gediminas Technical University, Lithuania
Srdjan Stankovic	University of Montenegro, Montenegro
Artūras Serackis	Vilnius Gediminas Technical University, Lithuania
Dimitrios Soudris	National Technical University of Athens, Greece
George Souliotis	University of the Peloponnese, Greece
George Theodoridis	University of Patras, Greece
Chao Wang	Univ. of Science and Tech. of China, P. R. of China

Additional Reviewers

Rainer Buchty

Vitalii Burtsev

Claire Jin

Ahmed Kamaleldin

George Lentaris

Vasileios Leon

Ashraf Muhammad

Daniele Passaretti

Marco Procaccini

Harry Ran

Henrik Strunck

Cornelia Wulf

Contents

Design Methods and Tools

Applications and Architectures

Special Session: Collaborative Research Projects

Applications

Applications

SNN vs. CNN Implementations on FPGAs: An Empirical Evaluation

Patrick Plagwitz$^{(\boxtimes)}$ ⓘ, Frank Hannig ⓘ, Jürgen Teich ⓘ, and Oliver Keszocze ⓘ

Hardware/Software Co-Design, Department of Computer Science,
Friedrich-Alexander-Universität Erlangen-Nürnberg (FAU), Erlangen, Germany
{patrick.plagwitz,frank.hannig,juergen.teich,oliver.keszoecze}@fau.de

Abstract. Convolutional Neural Networks (CNNs) are widely employed to solve various problems, e.g., image classification. Due to their compute- and data-intensive nature, CNN accelerators have been developed as ASICs or on FPGAs. The increasing complexity of applications has caused resource costs and energy requirements of these accelerators to grow. Spiking Neural Networks (SNNs) are an emerging alternative to CNN implementations, promising higher resource and energy efficiency. The main research question addressed in this paper is whether SNN accelerators truly meet these expectations of reduced energy demands compared to their CNN equivalents when implemented on modern FPGAs. For this purpose, we analyze multiple SNN hardware accelerators for FPGAs regarding performance and energy efficiency. We also present a novel encoding scheme of spike event queues and a novel memory organization technique to improve SNN energy efficiency further. Both techniques have been integrated into a state-of-the-art SNN architecture and evaluated for MNIST, SVHN, and CIFAR-10 data sets and corresponding network architectures on two differently sized modern FPGA platforms. A result of our empirical analysis is that for complex benchmarks such as SVHN and CIFAR-10, SNNs do live up to their expectations.

1 Introduction

Spiking Neural Networks (SNNs) and traditional Artificial Neural Networks (ANNs) represent two diverging research directions. While, e.g., Convolutional Neural Networks (CNNs) and transformer-based networks have come a long way from the initial idea of algorithmically imitating the activities of a biological brain, SNN research still strives to find architectures based on biologically plausible neuron models [1,2]. They are defined by their non-temporal representation of neurons as weight matrices. We use the term "traditional ANNs" when referring to neural network counterparts of SNNs that are non-spiking. In general, the use of traditional ANNs is justified by their vast success in various application domains like image or audio processing or generative models for natural language. Advances in this field have also been driven by ever more powerful hardware for parallelized matrix-matrix multiplications, which is the central compute-intensive component of both learning and inference in these

I. Skliarova et al. (Eds.): ARC 2024, LNCS 14553, pp. 3–18, 2024.
https://doi.org/10.1007/978-3-031-55673-9_1

types of networks. Platforms, including Graphics Processing Units (GPUs) but also Field-Programmable Gate Arrays (FPGAs), have proven to be viable targets for specialized ANN accelerators.

On the other hand, SNNs feature properties that make them particularly interesting for hardware acceleration. For example, they are inherently event-driven, rendering them suitable for applications where sensor data is generated in an event-driven manner [2]. Another consequence of this fact is that only spiked neurons need to be evaluated, i.e., a network input that generates only a few or even no spikes can be evaluated in a very short amount of time. This is in contrast to ANNs, where all neurons must be computed unless optimization techniques like pruning are employed. In SNNs, pruning is achieved implicitly. Moreover, occurring spikes can be evaluated multiplier-less, providing an obvious potential for cost and energy savings.

Finally, the biological focus can also be reduced, creating a hybrid approach of hardware-friendly SNNs. For example, the neuron model does not need to be entirely biologically accurate to produce a good network quality for classification tasks. The popular integrate-and-fire model [3] allows spikes to be represented as bits and all neuron computations to be performed completely multiplier-free, a property explained later in more detail.

An important question to be tackled is whether hardware implementations for SNNs indeed outperform traditional ANN accelerators in terms of performance, resource cost, and energy demands. To the best of our knowledge, this work is the first to quantitatively assess and compare these properties of CNN and SNN accelerator implementations, thus answering the question of whether "to spike or not to spike?" for a representative set of networks with a focus on FPGA implementations. Herein, we focus on CNNs and SNNs that include convolutional layers and investigate the subject by employing image classification as the use case. To make comparisons fair, various FPGA-specific and NN-related properties must be taken into account and evaluated. These include FPGA resource usage, classification accuracy, target platform, and network architecture.

2   Background

2.1   Spiking Neural Networks

Spiking neural networks encode activations not using real-valued numbers but sequences of binary spikes. An extensive set of SNN models has emerged to trade-off between biological plausibility and model complexity. On the one hand, the *Hodgkin-Huxley* model describes the complex electrochemical processes of biological neurons, but is prohibitively expensive in its computational cost [4]. On the other hand, the *Integrate-and-Fire (IF)* model only loosely models biological neurons, but can be implemented more efficiently in hardware [3].

Apart from the neuron model, the *spike encoding* (i.e., how spikes encode numbers) is a defining characteristic of SNN accelerators. Objectives affected by it are training time, accuracy, and classification latency because some encodings allow for similar accuracy to be achieved in fewer so-called *algorithmic time steps* but are more complicated to implement. The IF model as well as the used spike encoding shall now be explained in more detail.

The Integrate-and-Fire (IF) Model: In the IF model, neuron activations are represented by binary spikes. Contrary to ANNs where neuron activations are real-valued: a large activation is represented by a large numeric value and vice versa. In the IF model, neurons have an internal state called the *membrane potential V_m*. Their activation is dependent on their membrane potential, in contrast to neurons of an ANN that are not stateful, i.e., their output only depends directly on their inputs. The *IF model* depends on neurons being evaluated repeatedly in discrete *algorithmic time steps t*. If a spike arrives at neuron via a synapse at time step t, the weight of the synapse is added to the neuron's membrane potential $V_m(t)$. Whenever $V_m(t)$ crosses the membrane potential V_τ, the neuron will (a) reset its membrane potential V_m to 0, and (b) generate a spike, which travels to all neurons connected to its output. As a result, costly weight-input multiplications are avoided due to the binary spikes. On the other hand, the membrane potentials have to be stored in memory and may be updated multiple times before the neuron is firing a spike. In Sect. 5, we will answer the legitimate and currently open question as to whether SNNs can indeed offer any substantial energy, hardware resource cost and latency reductions over CNNs as motivated by multiplier-less and sparse processing of neuron activities despite the additionally needed membrane potential memories and respective update activities.

Spike Encodings: Another essential characteristic of an SNN implementation is how spikes are encoded. Two commonly used encoding schemes are *rate coding* [5] and *Time-To-First Spike (TTFS)* coding [6]. Rate coding requires neurons to estimate the *firing rate* of connected neurons by averaging spikes over a time window. The size of this window has a significant impact on the hardware resources and execution time needed to arrive at a stable value for the firing rate until feed-forward computations can be performed. Likewise, a larger window allows for higher SNN accuracy after training. Therefore, a trade-off exists between timing error robustness, latency, and accuracy when choosing the time window [5].

On the other hand, in TTFS encoding, not the firing rate of a neuron but the time it generates a spike for the first time is considered. The earlier this happens, the more important the spike is (see Fig. 1 for an example). The consequences of this are vastly increased processing speed for the evaluation of one neuron [7] and also for an entire SNN as long as the sparsity of spikes is exploited. Also, a neuron can only fire once, which leads to the fact that to reach acceptable accuracies using this method, SNNs need to be evaluated multiple times [8]. Han and Roy [9] introduced a TTFS variant that continuously emits spikes after reaching the membrane threshold V_τ. Following the notation introduced in [8], we call this variant *m-TTFS*.

2.2 Related Work

Extensive research work has been published regarding the topics of implementation and acceleration of SNNs in hardware. The approaches distinguish

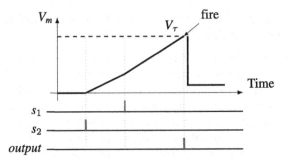

Fig. 1. Spiking behavior of an IF neuron with two inputs s_1 and s_2 using TTFS encoding. The membrane potential V_m rises up to the threshold V_τ. Then, a spike is emitted and the membrane potential is reset to zero.

themselves by considering different design objectives, including inference latency, required hardware resources, achieved classification accuracy, and energy requirements. An extensive literature review reveals that most works use image classification data sets such as MNIST, SVHN, or CIFAR-10 for benchmarking and typically condense performance objectives into a single metric denoting energy efficiency in terms of frames per second per Watt (FPS/W). Usually, only the average or maximal achievable frame rate and FPS/W are reported.

We show that the SNN's inference latency, and thus also corresponding energy, considerably depends on the input data. We therefore explicitly do not compute average values but present the full ranges instead. In the following, we review works most closely related to ours: SIES [10] is an accelerator designed explicitly for convolutional SNNs closely following the architecture of traditional CNN accelerators. The difference is that membrane potential changes can be calculated with only adders, requiring no Multiply Accumulate (MAC) operations. With a 64×64 array of PEs, this, however, also does not exploit the spike sparsity in SNNs due to the spike encoding and fixed PE array. Fang et al. [11] propose an accelerator that is implemented using High-Level Synthesis (HLS) and standard MAC-based matrix multiplications but supports temporal spike encoding. This leads to a much lower classification latency but is quite expensive in terms of hardware resources and energy. FireFly [12] is an accelerator design implemented in SpinalHDL[1], featuring a Processing Element (PE) array for membrane potential updates. A key advantage is the efficient usage of DSP resources for parallelized accumulate operations, yielding efficient resource usage on Xilinx UltraScale devices. The training and deployment method via PyTorch [13] and BrainCog [14] leads to high flexibility but also reduced efficiency for specific workloads like MNIST. SyncNN [15] is an HLS-based implementation of a queue-processing accelerator involving mixed-precision quantization and several other hardware optimizations. It achieves a very high energy efficiency on various data sets and can be synthesized for different network models. In SyncNN, spikes are

---

[1] https://github.com/SpinalHDL/SpinalHDL.

not represented as binary values but as integers representing how often a neuron has spiked. These values are then multiplied with kernel weights to produce membrane potential slopes. As such, this approach can be regarded as hybrid in that it sequentially processes layers using multiplications but with sparse and very low-precision activations.

Cerebron [16] is an FPGA-based accelerator for SNNs that uses a systolic array. Its specialty is its support for depthwise separable convolutions where a single filter output can be broadcast to multiple compute units. This reduces the memory requirements and improves energy efficiency as long as suitable network architectures and training methods are used. However, a significant scheduling overhead is involved in gaining these advantages, in addition to suffering from increased hardware complexity. Spiker [17] is an approach using Spike-Timing-Dependent Plasticity (STDP) as its training method instead of converting from CNNs to SNNs. It implements an MNIST classifier using a single layer only, resulting in a relatively low accuracy of 77%. Moreover, the design cannot be easily adapted to deeper networks or other data sets. Corradi et al. [18] present an FPGA-based accelerator for SNNs whose Gyro architecture is restricted to fully connected layers arranged in a pipeline with weight memories in between. The SNN architecture has exclusively been evaluated for the specific task of pixel-wise farmland classification into different types of crops using fused optical-radar data — no results for other benchmarks (data sets), especially the commonly used benchmarks MNIST, SVHN, or CIFAR-10, are reported. Further, key performance indicators are provided as a function of the number of synaptic operations. Therefore, the approach can hardly be compared with other accelerators. For a good overview of the field of SNN accelerators, the interested reader is referred to the work by Chen et al. [1].

3 Neural Network Hardware Architectures

For our comparative analysis, we investigate a recently published, state-of-the-art work: the unnamed approach of Sommer et al. [8]. This architecture is chosen

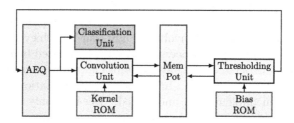

Fig. 2. Overview of the SNN accelerator architecture as proposed in [8]. Incoming spikes are stored in an Address Event Queue (AEQ), and the membrane potentials in a memory Mem Pot. After all spikes in the AEQ have been processed, newly emitted spikes are fed into the AEQ for being processed. The classification unit implements the output layer. Figure reproduced from [8, Fig. 3].

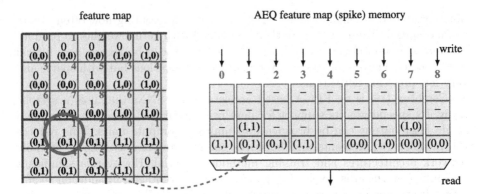

Fig. 3. Concept of Address Event Queues (AEQs). Left: A given feature map is partitioned into tiles of kernel size 3×3 each and each spike is identified by a intra-tile coordinate (red number) and a tile coordinate (tuple (x, y)). Right: The AEQ is implemented by $3 \times 3 = 9$ independent queues. Each enqueues those spikes (storing the tile coordinates) that share the same kernel coordinate. As an example, the spike highlighted by a red circle is stored in queue 1.

as it exploits the sparsity in SNNs as well as multiplier-less implementations of convolutional layers as concepts to achieve high expected energy efficiency. It also features a high degree of configurability, allowing us to match resource usage and frequency on a given platform and measure the resulting changes (see Fig. 2 for an overview of the architecture). As the accelerator targets convolution operations (e.g., in image classification tasks), its design centers around two-dimensional matrices: the spatial arrangement of the incoming spikes (called a *feature map*) and the kernel matrix used in the convolution. Consequently, spikes are understood as events associated with a location within the feature map and are consequently named Address Events (AEs). These events are then stored in so-called Address Event Queues (AEQs) [8] and processed in-order.

Using an addressing scheme that divides these memories into segments depending on the algorithmic time step t, input and output channel, and layer, they allow the convolutional kernel operation of the neighborhood of one pixel to be processed within one clock cycle. By pipelining the computations, a throughput of one spike per cycle per convolution unit can be achieved as long as the queues are filled [8]. The spike processing can be parallelized by replicating convolution units and associated AEQ and membrane potential memories and distributing spike events across them. In this work, parallelization factors between 1 and 16 have been implemented and tested. Because only one word can be read from and written to a BRAM simultaneously, memories are laid out using multiple BRAMs to parallelize accesses to both feature maps (storing the spikes still to be processed) and membrane potentials. For example, nine separate AEQ BRAM memory cells are instantiated so the neighborhood of an incoming spike can be updated simultaneously as shown in Fig. 3. Here, a 3×3 convolution is performed, involving consequently a neighborhood of nine neurons. Dividing feature maps into tiles of size 3×3 enables input neurons to be identified by their tile coordinates x, y and intra-tile positions (red numbers). By using the shown numbering scheme, no two input spikes within all possible 3×3 neighborhoods in a feature map will share the same BRAM cell. Thus, multiple accesses to the same cell, which would have to be sequentialized, are avoided. For membrane potentials, the same strategy is applied, although with the purpose of enabling parallel read instead of write accesses, see [8] for more details. Regarding training, the approach follows the method of converting a trained traditional CNN to an SNN. In [8], the `snntoolbox` [19] is used for this purpose. As a result, accuracy drops of less than 0.4% can be achieved when comparing the converted net to the original CNN for the MNIST benchmark.

Convolutional Neural Network Architectures: Hardware implementations for CNNs have been proposed in a large number for which several surveys and overviews exist, see, e.g., [20, 21]. Currently, the state-of-the-art consists of entire compiler toolchains such as FINN [22]. In the following, we emphasize dedicated hardware accelerators for CNNs instead of reprogrammable overlay architectures as these have not yet been considered for comparison with SNN accelerators. For reasons of scalability in terms of network complexity and support of a variety of target FPGAs, we decided to employ the FINN framework [22] for our comparative analysis to generate efficient, dedicated CNN accelerators. FINN creates so-called streaming dataflow architectures where each layer is instantiated as an array of PEs with FIFO buffers in between. In FINN accelerators, all network layers execute in parallel. The complete computation is pipelined with layers being implemented as IP cores connected using self-synchronizing protocols and FIFOs in between for storing intermediate results.

4   Experimental Evaluation

In this section, we compare SNN and CNN accelerator designs to answer the major question of the paper whether SNNs surpass CNNs in terms of performance and energy efficiency. We use the Keras framework[2] to model and train the networks employed for both accelerator types. For fair comparison, we thereby try to match the FPGA resource requirements of the designs in terms of LUTs, registers, Block RAMs (BRAMs), and DSPs. For synthesis, we use the Xilinx xc7z020-1clg400c part found on the PYNQ-Z1 board as well as the ZCU102 board with a larger FPGA chip (xczu9eg-ffvb1156-2-e) to evaluate the scalability of the approach. On the other hand, we also tried to achieve comparable clock rates in order to assess the execution time in terms of the achievable latencies (in clock cycles). The objectives we evaluated are execution time, power, and energy per performed classification.

First, we identify the corresponding configuration options to match FPGA resources. For the SNN accelerator architecture proposed by Sommer et al. [8], this is the parallelization factor P as well as the AEQ depth D. There is one

---

[2] https://keras.io.

Table 1. Architectures used for MNIST, SVHN, and CIFAR-10. nCk denotes a convolutional layer with n kernels of size $k \times k$, Pn a pooling layer with a window size of n, and just n a fully connected layer with n neurons. The last two columns show Keras's classification accuracy, including quantization effects before and after conversion using the `snntoolbox` [19].

Dataset	Architecture	#Params	Accuracy	
			Keras	snntoolbox
MNIST	32C3-32C3-P3-10C3-10	20,568	98.2%	97.8%
SVHN	1C3-32C3-32C3-P3-64C3-64C3-P3-128C3-128C3-10	297,966	91.7%	72.1%
CIFAR-10	32C3-32C3-P3-64C3-64C3-P3-128C3-128C3-128C3-10	446,122	80.1%	60.2%

AEQ per PE, which is replicated P times from (P ranging from 1 to 16). The depth D indicates the number of spikes each of the queues of an AEQ can store. For the NN implementations, we chose configurations resulting in comparable resource requirements. For the experiments, we use the MNIST, SVHN, and CIFAR-10 data sets for training and evaluation for both SNNs and the corresponding traditional CNNs implementations. We chose these data sets as they are commonly used as benchmarks in the literature. The nets we use for classification also have the same architecture on the SNN and CNN accelerator. The difference is that for SNN, the models are translated via `snntoolbox` [19] to a spiking net using m-TTFS encoding. This incurs an accuracy loss. For MNIST, this is small (0.4%) but becomes larger for the correspondingly deeper architectures for SVHN and CIFAR-10. Table 1 gives an overview of the used model architectures. The architectures were chosen to analyze the trade-off between size and classification accuracy.

The Spiking Neural Network accelerator in [8] uses m-TTFS spike encoding and the IF neuron model with the constraint that neurons can only spike once and are not reset to zero afterward. The number of algorithmic time steps is set to four. None of the provided designs requires any off-chip memory transfer of weights. Only activations (sample images) are streamed into the architectures, and the classification result is fed back via AXI interfaces. Each SNN design is characterized by the applied parallelization factor P as well as its memory configuration. For the discussed designs, only BRAMs are used as memories, but we show in Sect. 5 that using other means of storing memory potentials and spikes can be beneficial. Based on our observations, BRAMs can be identified as the resource that tends to be the limiting factor, while only roughly half of the available LUT and register resources are used. To determine the latency for sample classification, we run both FINN and SNN accelerators in a simulator (Vivado). FINN designs always require the same number of cycles to complete, given the same streaming control signals, regardless of the input sample. However, due to the nature of SNNs, the latency cannot be measured as a single

Table 2. Latency and power comparison: SNN vs. CNN.

Design	Data Set	Latency	Power [W]
CNN_1	MNIST	38.7k	0.119
CNN_2	MNIST	42.8k	0.107
CNN_3	SVHN	624.8k	0.450
CNN_4	SVHN	382.9k	0.623
CNN_5	CIFAR-10	1171.5k	0.587
CNN_6	CIFAR-10	741.1k	0.687
SNN4	MNIST	[21.9k; 80.2k]	[0.263; 0.305]
SNN8	MNIST	[11.8k; 43.3k]	[0.445; 0.530]
SNN4	SVHN	[319.3k; 996.1k]	[0.290; 0.364]
SNN8	SVHN	[172.6k; 538.4k]	[0.468; 0.612]
SNN4	CIFAR-10	[334.1k; 1172.9k]	[0.474; 0.627]
SNN8	CIFAR-10	[180.6k; 634.0k]	[0.590; 0.743]

number, as different samples generate different numbers of spikes. Since sparse SNN acceleration, put simply, processes spikes from queues until the queues are depleted, the latency can vary a lot in dependence of the input. To measure this effect and enable a fair comparison of SNN and CNN approaches, we run the accelerator with 1,000 input images from the benchmark data sets to get a good picture of the distribution of latencies. Exemplary results are depicted in Table 2. For the SNNs, the latency greatly varies. Some results look very promising. For example, the design SNN8 is faster than CNN_1 for almost all input samples.

To determine the required electrical power of a design, we used the Vivado Power Estimator and focused on evaluating the dynamic power. As the power consumption per inference naturally depends on the input data for both the CNN and the SNN designs, we performed estimations for multiple MNIST samples. For the CNN designs, we recorded power consumptions varying by less than 0.01W. By contrast, the SNN counterparts show significant variations depending on input data.

When analyzing the breakdown of power among different categories as shown in the Power Estimator, BRAMs can be identified as a major contributor. In the case of SNN8 for instance, it is 2/3 of the shown power which is due to BRAMs. Hence, in the following, we focus on optimizing the power requirements introduced by BRAMs.

5   Optimized Memory Architecture

In this section, we explore options to reduce BRAM usage and, therefore, power consumption by using a more efficient memory organization for spikes and weights.

5.1 FPGA Memory Scalability Study

Memory usage for SNNs can be divided into (a) membrane potentials, (b) data structures for storing spike sequences, and (c) the read-only kernel and dense layer weights. For all, there is the option of synthesizing memories as BRAMs or LUTRAMs, depending on the granularity and the settings of the FPGA toolchain. For Xilinx devices, BRAMs store 36K bits and can be configured to be accessed using 36-, 18-, 9-, 4-, 2-, or 1-bit words. Also, it is possible to use halves of BRAMs, storing 18K bits. If parallelized memory accesses are desired, BRAMs must be split for the sake of latency reduction, even though they might be sparsely occupied as a result. For this reason, the number of BRAMs is determined not only by the amount of data to store but also by the parallelism in access patterns. On the other hand, LUTRAMs are not fixed to 18K or 36K bits but are not as energy-efficient per bit. Where is the point when it becomes more efficient to opt for LUTRAM rather than BRAM? As an experiment, we created a BRAM test design that uses an array of R BRAM-based memories to store 8192 words of bit width w. The output of the individual BRAMs is XOR'ed to compute an output word of width w without incurring a measurable impact on energy. For the conducted experiments, the setting was to read from all memories at every clock cycle. We synthesized variants using (a) actual BRAMs or (b) LUTRAMs to investigate when to choose which type of memory. We varied the bit-width w from 1 to 36 and measured the power. LUTRAMs scale linearly with the bit width w, while BRAMs tend to have an increase in power whenever #words(w) increases. In BRAMs, 10-bit words can, for instance, be synthesized to be composed of 2 3-bit words and 1 4-bit word, resulting in 3 BRAMs with a more favorable configuration than a single BRAM storing 10-bit words. A major factor in deciding whether to use LUTRAMs or BRAMs is the depth D of each memory row. LUTRAMs perform better than BRAMs whenever words do not fit exactly into the available aspect ratios of BRAMs. For instance, $D = 256$ is not favorable for BRAMs as it leads to multiple half BRAMs being synthesized, which are not fully used. In the following, we use both of these insights to improve the memory architecture of the examined SNN accelerator: Reduce inefficient BRAM usage for small depths and drop word lengths below the aspect ratio thresholds.

5.2 Optimized Spike Encoding

A major cause for badly utilized memory is the gap between the word sizes of Xilinx BRAM primitives. This is most pronounced in the AEQ implementations. Using a word width of 10 bits, for example, causes each BRAM to hold only 2048 words, whereas it can hold $4,096$ 9-bit words. This is an issue that can be overcome by reducing the word width by compressing spike events. Therefore, we propose the use of an improved encoding of spikes as compressed coordinates (i_c, j_c). In the original work [8], two additional status bits were used to signify the segmentation of the AEQs. These can be done away with when recognizing that for a feature map of 28×28, since it is divided into windows of 3×3 due to the kernel size $K = 3$ in this case, actual coordinates can be encoded as the *explicit* number as well as the *implicit* window position given by the queue data structure the event is stored in. Let $W = 28$ be the feature map width. For quadratic sizes, the required bit width for i_c is $\lceil \log_2 \frac{W}{K} \rceil = 4$. There exist 6 unused bit-patterns for both i_c and j_c. These can be used to encode status information with minimal logic overhead. When W/K is close to a power of two, not enough bit patterns are available, and we have to fall back to the original encoding.

5.3 Evaluation of the Optimization Techniques

When accelerating SNNs on FPGAs, we identified the membrane potentials as a source of inefficiency. Unlike in CNNs, where all neurons are computed sequentially by way of performing matrix multiplications, in SNNs, all neuron potentials must be held in memory. However, due to the high degree of parallelization, these are distributed across many memories. For instance, we determine the number of words of membrane potential memory never to exceed 256 in our experiments. Since BRAMs can hold 4096 8-bit words, this means an actual usage of only 6.25%, which is very wasteful. By changing the memory architecture to implement required memory blocks with low usage as LUTRAMs, the energy efficiency can be improved. Referring to Table 3, notice the reduction of, e.g., power by 15% between the original SNN8 and the SNN8$_{\text{LUTRAM}}$ design.

Table 3. Resource usage and power estimation of base and designs with optimized memory architecture for MNIST on the PYNQ platform.

Design	LUTs	Regs.	BRAMs	Power [W]	
				BRAMs	Total
CNN$_1$	20368	26886	14.5	0.012	**0.122**
CNN$_2$	16793	17810	11	0.012	**0.107**
SNN4	4967	5019	76	0.185	**0.283**
SNN4$_{\text{LUTRAM}}$	9256	5669	40	0.099	**0.242**
SNN4$_{\text{COMPR.}}$	9436	5669	22	0.056	**0.200**
SNN8	9649	9738	116	0.277	**0.480**
SNN8$_{\text{LUTRAM}}$	18311	11080	44	0.106	**0.405**
SNN8$_{\text{COMPR.}}$	18311	11080	44	0.106	**0.405**

Another side effect is the shift of resource usage from BRAMs to LUTs. The effect of the spike compression strategy is also shown in Table 3. Again, a reduction of about 17% in power can be observed. Note that SNN8$_{\text{LUTRAM}}$ and SNN8$_{\text{COMPR.}}$ show no difference because the memory parallelism required here already leads to a minimum of BRAMs being used per PE in SNN8$_{\text{LUTRAM}}$.

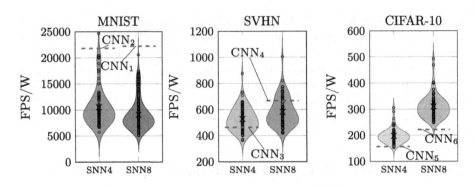

Fig. 4. Energy efficiency (FPS/W) comparison of various CNN and optimized SNN implementations (SNN4$_{COMPR.}$and SNN8$_{COMPR.}$for datasets MNIST, SVHN, and CIFAR-10).

Figure 4 shows the distribution of the energy efficiency in FPS/W for different NN implementations and data sets. As can be seen, the SNNs' energy efficiency varies with the input data while the CNNs' energy efficiency is constant (dashed red lines). For the MNIST data set, the CNNs clearly outperform the SNNs in terms of FPS/W. The measurements for the SVHN data sets show a different picture. Here, SNN8$_{COMPR.}$ often classifies images with a better FPS/W than CNN$_4$, while SNN4$_{COMPR.}$ clearly outperforms CNN$_3$ on average. For CIFAR-10, the FPS/W of the SNN implementations are better in even the vast majority of cases. Detailed resource usage and power comparisons on the PYNQ and ZCU boards using the SVHN data set are given in Table 4.

The NN architecture used for SVHN has more than 14 times as many weights and requires larger membrane potential memories as the network for the MNIST data. This is why both power and latency numbers are higher than in the MNIST case. The same holds true for CIFAR-10. The CNN designs considered have been chosen to have almost equal estimated power values as the SNNs. Similar to the MNIST data set, CNNs use more registers and fewer BRAMs for storing intermediate values between layers. However, this leads to corresponding decreases and increases in the BRAM and Signal categories of the estimated power. Likewise, CNNs use more LUTs because they are instantiated as part of MAC units, while for SNNs, LUTs are employed predominantly as memory, which is also restricted, e.g., 17,400 LUT slices being available on the xc7Z020 FPGA. Also, one significant difference between the FINN-generated CNN implementations and the synthesized SNN implementations is that FINN uses a dedicated streaming dataflow architecture. This means that one IP block is instantiated on the FPGA per layer. The more layers there are in a network, the fewer options remain for configuring and optimizing the throughput of bottleneck parts of the network. This can be seen when looking at the latencies needed to process one input sample shown in Table 2.

Table 4. Resource usage and power evaluation of SNNs and CNNs for the SVHN data set.

Design	Platform	LUTs	Regs.	BRAMs	Power [W] BRAMs	Total
CNN_3	PYNQ	32765	50968	50	0.087	**0.450**
CNN_4	PYNQ	39927	59187	47.5	0.063	**0.623**
CNN_3	ZCU102	32656	52964	46	0.053	**0.743**
CNN_4	ZCU102	40172	59258	47	0.136	**0.903**
$SNN2_{COMPR.}$	PYNQ	4733	2961	91	0.174	**0.264**
$SNN4_{COMPR.}$	PYNQ	9393	5652	92	0.175	**0.322**
$SNN8_{COMPR.}$	PYNQ	18487	11024	104	0.200	**0.500**
$SNN16_{COMPR.}$	PYNQ	37674	22077	140	0.265	**0.914**
$SNN2_{COMPR.}$	ZCU102	4896	2961	82	0.096	**0.230**
$SNN4_{COMPR.}$	ZCU102	9293	5645	82	0.103	**0.344**
$SNN8_{COMPR.}$	ZCU102	18135	11013	100	0.163	**0.652**
$SNN16_{COMPR.}$	ZCU102	36038	21976	136	0.282	**1.242**

For more than half of the input samples, $SNN8_{COMPR.}$ needs less energy than CNN_4. In the case of the larger CIFAR-10 network model, $SNN8_{COMPR.}$ has a higher energy efficiency than CNN_6. Moreover, SNNs with $P = 8$ yield the best energy efficiency. Since the ZCU102 board has a different chip technology and architecture than the PYNQ board, BRAMs use less power. However, clock routing is more expensive in terms of energy compared to the PYNQ platform. With increasing parallelization factor P, the ZCU102 scales slightly worse than the PYNQ. For example, $SNN16_{COMPR.}$ consumes more power on the ZCU102 than on the PYNQ due to the larger clock tree. The FINN-based CNN implementations witness an increased dynamic power on the larger ZCU102 board when compared to the PYNQ platform. This is due to the use of LUTs and registers for MAC operations, whereas in the SNN accelerator, they are used to a much larger degree for keeping intermediate results or storing read-only weights.

In Table 5, existing SNN implementations are compared with our implementations in terms of classification accuracy and FPS/W for the MNIST, SVHN, and CIFAR-10 data sets. Works discussed in Sect. 2.2 but not listed in Table 5 either did not provide any FPS/W data or reported results for networks/data sets not considered in this work. We used SyncNN [15] with a scaled down LeNet-S configuration requiring 16,326 LUTs and 16,228 registers, along with 69 DSPs and 253 half BRAMs. For comparability, we then used the vector-less Vivado Power Estimator tool to measure a dynamic power of 0.405 W. Together with the reported 800 FPS for the ZedBoard [15], this yields an energy efficiency of $1,975$ FPS/W on the PYNQ-Z1. We likewise read the throughput for the same network architecture applied to the SVHN data set as 90 FPS, arriving at 222

Table 5. Overview of SNN accelerator approaches for multiple data sets regarding accuracy and FPS/W. Empty cells in the related work indicate that these values are not available. The accelerators SNN4$_{\text{LUTRAM}}$ and SNN8$_{\text{LUTRAM}}$ have not been used for the SVHN and CIFAR-10 benchmarks as they are not optimized. For the CIFAR-10 data set, the SNN16$_{\text{COMPR.}}$ has a resource requirement that the Pynq board cannot meet; hence, no results are reported.

Work	MNIST		SVHN		CIFAR-10	
	Accuracy	FPS/W	Accuracy	FPS/W	Accuracy	FPS/W
Fang et al. [11]	98.9%	472	–	–	–	–
FireFly [12]	98.8%	799	–	–	91.36%	379
Sommer et al. [8]	98.3%	9,615	–	–	–	–
Spiker [17]	77.2%	77	–	–	–	–
Cerebron [16]	99.4%	25,641	–	–	91.9%	64
SyncNN [15]	99.3%	1,975	91%	222	87.9%	7.2
$P = 4$, LUTRAM	98.2%	[5,409; 18,869]	–	–	–	–
$P = 4$, Compr.	98.2%	[5,721; 24,682]	72.1%	[366; 877]	60.2%	[154; 306]
$P = 8$, LUTRAM	98.2%	[6,244; 18,163]	–	–	–	–
$P = 8$, Compr.	98.2%	[5,080; 20,569]	72.1%	[419; 1007]	60.2%	[249; 493]
$P = 16$, Compr.	98.2%	[4,759; 15,711]	72.1%	[434; 1005]	–	–

FPS/W. For CIFAR-10, we synthesized the SyncNN with an 8-bit NiN network [23] configuration, and obtained a power consumption estimate of 0.553 W. The values for the other SNNs have been taken from the respective publications. As can be seen, together with the applied improvements, the examined architecture is a state-of-the-art accelerator for SNNs on embedded platforms. Regarding SVHN and CIFAR-10, only FireFly achieves an energy efficiency that falls into the intervals measured for CIFAR-10 and the SNN8$_{\text{COMPR.}}$ accelerator. From Table 5, we can finally recognize a drop in accuracy of our SNN implementations for the two larger networks SVHN and CIFAR-10 when using the snntoolbox. In the future, we would therefore like to investigate alternative ways for SNN training, such as done by Cerebron [16], with which we hope to obtain similarly high accuracies.

6 Conclusion

In this work, we tried to answer the question whether SNNs really offer a promised higher energy efficiency in comparison to conventional CNNs due to the sparse processing of spikes. For this purpose, comparisons between different CNN and SNN implementations have been carried out to find a confirmation of this hypothesis when targeting different FPGA devices. It was shown that SNNs can be faster in some cases but can fall short in average power consumption for smaller classification tasks such as MNIST. As candidates, we compared

CNN architectures synthesized using the FINN-based streaming dataflow architecture [22] with a parameterizable SNN architecture introduced in [8] for two FPGA platforms of different sizes and the three benchmark data sets MNIST, SVHN, and CIFAR-10.

We also investigated potential techniques to reduce the power footprint of SNN designs. This was achieved first by instantiating LUTRAMs instead of BRAMs to store spike address events and, second, by employing an improved encoding scheme for spike events. These concepts have led to a total increase in energy efficiency (FPS/W) by a factor of 1.41 for the MNIST case. For the comparison of different pairs of CNN and SNN nets for a given benchmark and FPGA platform, we matched solutions of equal power and at equal clock rate. We showed that for small-scale benchmarks such as MNIST, matching SNN designs provide rather no or little energy efficiency improvements. The trend reverses for larger networks such as those used for the SVHN and CIFAR-10 data sets. The rationale is that MAC units and FIFO buffers, instantiated for each layer for CNN implementations synthesized using the FINN-based streaming dataflow architecture principle, incur a high power consumption such that the SNN implementations provide higher energy efficiency values in terms of FPS/W.

Acknowledgments. The paper has been partially funded by the Deutsche Forschungsgemeinschaft (DFG, German Research Foundation) - 450987171.

Disclosure of Interests. The authors have no competing interests to declare that are relevant to the content of this article.

References

1. Chen, L., Xiong, X., Liu, J.: A survey of intelligent chip design research based on spiking neural networks. IEEE Access **10**, 89663–89686 (2022)
2. Smithson, S.C., Boga, K., Ardakani, A., Meyer, B.H., Gross, W.J.: Stochastic computing can improve upon digital spiking neural networks. In: Proceedings of International Workshop on Signal Processing Systems (SiPS), pp. 309–314. IEEE (2016)
3. Bouvier, M., et al.: Spiking neural networks hardware implementations and challenges: a survey. ACM J. Emerg. Technol. Comput. Syst. **15**(2), 22:1-22:35 (2019)
4. Izhikevich, E.M.: Which model to use for cortical spiking neurons? IEEE Trans. Neural Netw. **15**(5), 1063–1070 (2004)
5. Guo, W., Fouda, M.E., Eltawil, A.M., Salama, K.N.: Neural coding in spiking neural networks: a comparative study for robust neuromorphic systems. Frontiers Neurosci. **15**, 1–14 (2021)
6. Rueckauer, B., Liu, S.-C.: Conversion of analog to spiking neural networks using sparse temporal coding. In: Proceeding of International Symposium on Circuits and Systems (ISCAS), 27–30 May 2018, pp. 1–5. IEEE (2018)
7. Panzeri, S., Brunel, N., Logothetis, N.K., Kayser, C.: Sensory neural codes using multiplexed temporal scales. Trends Neurosci. **33**(3), 111–120 (2010)
8. Sommer, J., Özkan, M.A., Keszocze, O., Teich, J.: Efficient hardware acceleration of sparsely active convolutional spiking neural networks. IEEE Trans. CAD **41**(11), 3767–3778 (2022)

9. Han, B., Roy, K.: Deep spiking neural network: energy efficiency through time based coding. In: Vedaldi, A., Bischof, H., Brox, T., Frahm, J.-M. (eds.) ECCV 2020. LNCS, vol. 12355, pp. 388–404. Springer, Cham (2020). https://doi.org/10.1007/978-3-030-58607-2_23

10. Wang, S.-Q., et al.: SIES: a novel implementation of spiking convolutional neural network inference engine on field-programmable gate array. J. Comput. Sci. Technol. **35**, 475–489 (2020)

11. Fang, H., et al.: Encoding, model, and architecture: systematic optimization for spiking neural network in FPGAs. In: Proceedings of the 39th International Conference on Computer- Aided Design (ICCAD), November 2–5, 2020, pp. 62:1–62:9. ACM (2020)

12. Li, J., Shen, G., Zhao, D., Zhang, Q., Yi, Z.: FireFly: a high-throughput and reconfigurable hardware accelerator for spiking neural networks. In: The Computing Research Repository (CoRR), January 2023. arXiv: 2301.01905 [cs.NE]

13. Paszke, A., et al.: PyTorch: an imperative style, high-performance deep learning library. In: Proceedings of the Annual Conference on Neural Information Processing Systems (NeurIPS), December 8–14, 2019, pp. 8024–8035 (2019)

14. Zeng, Y., et al.: BrainCog: a spiking neural network based brain-inspired cognitive intelligence engine for brain-inspired AI and brain simulation. In: The Computing Research Repository (CoRR), July 2022. arXiv: 2207.08533 [cs.NE]

15. Panchapakesan, S., Fang, Z., Li, J.: SyncNN: evaluating and accelerating spiking neural networks on FPGAs. ACM Trans. Reconfig. Technol. Syst. **15**(4), 48:1-48:27 (2022)

16. Chen, Q., Gao, C., Fu, Y.: Cerebron: a reconfigurable architecture for spatiotemporal sparse spiking neural networks. IEEE Trans. Very Large Scale Integr. (VLSI) Syst. **30**(10), 1425–1437 (2022)

17. Carpegna, A., Savino, A., Di Carlo, S.: Spiker: an FPGA-optimized hardware accelerator for spiking neural networks. In: Proceedings of IEEE Computer Society Annual Symposium on VLSI (ISVLSI), July 4–6, 2022, pp. 14–19. IEEE (2022)

18. Corradi, F., Adriaans, G., Stuijk, S.: Gyro: a digital spiking neural network architecture for multi-sensory data analytics. In: Proceedings of the Drone Systems Engineering (DroneSE) and Rapid Simulation and Performance Evaluation (RAPIDO): Methods and Tools, January 18, 2021, pp. 9–15. ACM (2021)

19. Rueckauer, B., Lungu, I.-A., Hu, Y., Pfeiffer, M., Liu, S.-C.: Conversion of continuous-valued deep networks to efficient event-driven networks for image classification. Frontiers Neurosci. **11**, 1–17 (2017)

20. Plagwitz, P., Hannig, F., Ströbel, M., Strohmeyer, C., Teich, J.: A safari through FPGA-based neural network compilation and design automation flows. In: Proceedings of International Symposium on Field-Programmable Custom Computing Machines (FCCM), May 9–12, 2021, pp. 10–19. IEEE (2021)

21. Shawahna, A., Sait, S.M., El-Maleh, A.: FPGA-based accelerators of deep learning networks for learning and classification: a review. IEEE Access **7**, 7823–7859 (2018)

22. Blott, M., et al.: FINN-R: an end-to-end deep-learning framework for fast exploration of quantized neural networks. ACM Trans. Reconfig. Technol. Syst. **11**(3), 16:1-16:23 (2018)

23. Lin, M., Chen, Q., Yan, S.: Network in Network. In: The Computing Research Repository (CoRR), December 2013. arXiv: 1312.4400 [cs.NE]

Open-Source SpMV Multiplication Hardware Accelerator for FPGA-Based HPC Systems

Panagiotis Mpakos[1]([✉]), Ioanna Tasou[1], Chloe Alverti[3], Panagiotis Miliadis[1], Pavlos Malakonakis[2], Dimitris Theodoropoulos[1], Georgios Goumas[1], Dionisios N. Pnevmatikatos[1], and Nectarios Koziris[1]

[1] Computing Systems Laboratory, National Technical University of Athens, Athens, Greece
pmpakos@cslab.ece.ntua.gr
[2] Technical University of Crete, Chania, Greece
[3] University of Illinois at Urbana-Champaign, Champaign, USA

Abstract. The Sparse Matrix Vector (SpMV) multiplication kernel is a key component of many high-performance computing applications, but at the same time one of the most challenging to optimize, primarily due to its low flop-per-byte ratio and irregular memory accesses. As such, modern FPGAs, combined with High-Bandwidth Memory (HBM) modules, are much better-suited to the memory-bound nature of this kernel, compared to general purpose CPUs. Current FPGA-based approaches on SpMV support only single-precision floating point arithmetic. Moreover, they target for highly-streamed implementations that, although enhance performance, facilitate custom matrix storage formats, which (i) can increase the matrix footprint up to 3x, and (ii) drop the burden of input matrix transformation to developers. Towards widening the spectrum of FPGA-supported floating point formats for sparse algebra, this paper presents a first set of effective optimizations for double-precision SpMV hardware kernels using High-Level Synthesis (HLS) tools on HBM-equipped FPGAs. Results show that our work can provide 52.4x on average better performance compared to state-of-practice SpMV double-precision multiplication implementations on FPGAs for applications with volatile matrices, and up to 5.1x better performance-per-Watt compared to server-class CPUs.

Keywords: Open-Source · SpMV · Sparse Matrix · HLS

1 Introduction

Sparse Matrix-Vector multiplication (SpMV) is a fundamental operation in various scientific applications, including computational physics, machine learning, and graph analytics. Extensive research has been conducted on SpMV for CPU and GPU systems, resulting in numerous storage formats, which aim to achieve either high performance across a broad range of matrices or specialize in specific matrix patterns. However, SpMV performance is limited by its low flop-per-byte ratio, i.e., it carries out a small amount of computations relative to the total memory accesses required.

I. Skliarova et al. (Eds.): ARC 2024, LNCS 14553, pp. 19–32, 2024.
https://doi.org/10.1007/978-3-031-55673-9_2

In recent years, a more energy-efficient approach is noticed in the design of HPC systems, with FPGA-based solutions becoming increasingly popular due to their energy efficiency and high performance. In particular, FPGAs equipped with High Bandwidth Memory (HBM) provide a unique opportunity for memory-bound applications, with increased memory bandwidth compared to conventional DDR memories.

Specifically for SpMV, several works [2,3,9,11,17] have proposed designs for HBM-FPGAs, mainly targeting graph applications with support for single floating-point or fixed-point precision arithmetic. For scientific applications though, it is essential to use double precision in the computational kernels. Xilinx has proposed its own accelerator, called Vitis SPARSE Library (VSL) [18], with this work being the only implementation available for double-precision SpMV. However, the proposed design is available for one FPGA only and its storage format incurs large memory overheads, with a pre-processing cost that is not feasible for some matrices. Finally, the work presented in [1] also supports double-precision SpMV multiplication, however it targets the Virtex5 FPGAs generation, thus cannot be considered as a ready-to-use solution for applications executed on HBM-equipped FPGAs.

Unlike other works that support integer and/or single precision floating point format arithmetics for sparse algebra [3,17], the goal of this work is to explore and propose a simpler design for double-precision SpMV, that can be easily deployed on FPGA-based systems with HBM support. As such, evaluation of other platforms (e.g. GPUs) is out of this work's scope. To achieve this, we use the Compressed Sparse Row (CSR) format, which is the most commonly used storage format for sparse matrices, and incorporate optimizations based on previous research. Our initial design, called 'Simple-CSR', is used as a baseline. We then introduce a design called 'Index Concatenation', which slightly reduces the memory footprint of our representation and improves performance by 9%. Finally, we propose a design called 'Stream-X', that trades increased memory usage for performance. At the cost of 30% additional memory usage, Stream-X achieves higher utilization of HBM bandwidth. This results in an 83% improvement in performance over 'Simple-CSR' (and 67% improvement over 'Index Concatenation'), with a stable performance pattern across all tested FPGAs.

Overall, the paper contributions are as follows:

- We explore three different approaches for mapping double-precision floating point SpMV onto reconfigurable hardware using High-Level Synthesis (HLS) tools (Sect. 3).
- We map 'Stream-X' to three Xilinx Alveo FPGAs (U280, U50, U55C) and compare results against a highly-optimized multi-threaded software implementation on an Intel 14-core Xeon-class CPU (Sect. 4).
- We compare 'Stream-X' against related work that can be considered as ready-to-use by developers, in terms of performance, and energy, as well as portability; as shown, our work achieves 52.4x on average better performance compared to state-of-practice SpMV multiplication implementations on FPGAs for applications with volatile matrices, and 3.6x (up to 5.1x) better performance-per-Watt compared to a server-class CPU (Sect. 5).

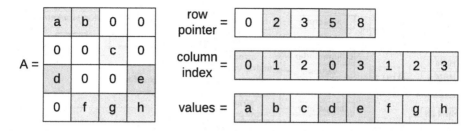

Fig. 1. CSR representation of a sparse matrix

2 Background

2.1 Sparse Matrix-Vector Multiplication (SpMV)

Sparse Matrix-Vector multiplication (SpMV) is a fundamental operation in a wide range of scientific and engineering applications, including graph algorithms, linear solvers, and finite element simulations. SpMV involves multiplying a sparse matrix A with a dense vector x, resulting in a dense output vector y $(y = A * x)$. Due to its irregular memory access pattern, it still remains a computational bottleneck, limiting the maximum performance that can be achieved on modern high-performance computing architectures. To enhance the performance of SpMV, numerous storage formats and algorithms have been proposed, each with its unique advantages and disadvantages. In this work, we focus on the Compressed Sparse Row (CSR) format and propose optimizations to further improve its performance.

The Compressed Sparse Row (CSR) format stores a sparse matrix as three arrays: the values array, the column-index array and the row-pointer array. The values array contains the non-zero values of the matrix, the column-index array contains the column indices of each non-zero element and the row-pointer array contains the indices of the first non-zero element of each row. Figure 1 shows an example. Overall, the CSR format strikes a good balance between storage efficiency and computational performance, making it a popular choice for representing sparse matrices in a variety of applications.

2.2 Vitis SPARSE Library (VSL)

Xilinx has introduced a specialized format called VSL [18] for the Alveo U280 FPGA. This format applies 2D blocking on the matrix, with each block being split in 16 partitions and assigned to an equal number of Compute Units. Each Compute Unit represents an independent computation path. In order to achieve high throughput and properly utilize the available HBM bandwidth of the U280 FPGA, the VSL format applies extensive zero padding to the matrix. Specifically, each row of each 2D block of the matrix needs to have a multiple of 32 nonzeros. Section 4.3 includes a performance comparison of our implementation with the VSL format, as well as a discussion of the limitations of each design.

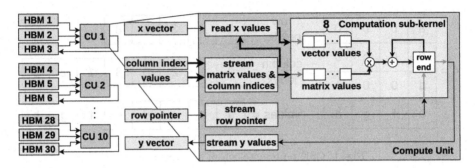

Fig. 2. 'Simple-CSR' accelerator design. Bold arrows represent vectorized data movement.

3 Architecture Overview

In this section we present the development path towards our final design, with the CSR format as our starting point. All kernels are written

3.1 Initial Design - Simple CSR

Compute Unit Internals. We begin by presenting the internal workings of a single Compute Unit, as depicted in the right part of Fig. 2. The structures of a sparse matrix stored in CSR format, i.e., row-pointer, column-index and values are 'streamed' to the FPGA, since there is no reuse of their elements. On the contrary, the x vector is accessed randomly, depending on the values of the column-index structure. The x vector is not stored on the FPGA's BRAM, to avoid limiting the maximum problem size or requiring vertical splitting of the matrix and the vector. In order to enable computation vectorization, values and their corresponding column indices are transferred in packets of 8 elements. The row pointer is streamed separately, due to the differing rates at which it is required. The x vector values that are requested after processing a packet of column indices, are packed similarly to the values, in packets of 8 elements for computation vectorization. The matrix values, the vector values and the row pointer are then streamed internally to the computation sub-kernel. Once all nonzeros of a row have been processed, the resulting value is streamed back to the host, and the computation proceeds with the subsequent row. Among the internal modules of a single Compute Unit, streaming interfaces are utilized to allow for parallel execution of the respective functions in a dataflow manner.

Choice of Vectorization Factor. The vectorization factor is chosen to be 8, in order to fully utilize the available High-Bandwidth Memory (HBM) bandwidth. More specifically, 8 double values match the interface width (set at 512 bits) of the HBM channels. As a result, it is necessary to pre-process each row of the matrix to contain a multiple of 8 nonzeros.

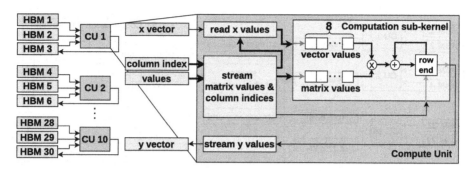

Fig. 3. 'Index Concatenation' accelerator design. Bold arrows represent vectorized data movement.

HBM Channel Mapping. In order to achieve maximum parallelism, it is necessary to take into account the scaling to multiple Compute Units, when mapping variables from a single Compute Unit to the HBM channels. To this end, we impose a restriction of three HBM channels per Compute Unit. After evaluating various configurations the following mapping of variables is selected, illustrated in Fig. 2:

- The x vector is assigned to the first HBM channel, as constant random accesses to this structure require a dedicated channel.
- The values and the column indices are mapped to the second HBM channel. Despite being the variables that generate the most memory traffic in the kernel, they can be mapped to a single channel, because data from both variables are processed at the same rate. Both variables are transferred as 'wide' structures, i.e., in packets of 8 elements.
- The row pointer and the y (result) vector are mapped to the third HBM channel. Both of these variables generate low traffic.

Scaling to Multiple Compute Units. The proposed design can be scaled up to 10 Compute Units. As 32 HBM channels are available and 3 HBM channels are allocated per Compute Unit. Given that the matrix is stored in CSR format, row-traversal can be performed efficiently. Therefore, this allows for the application of row-splitting (1D-blocking), and the assignment of a portion of the matrix to each Compute Unit. The assignment is carried out such that each Compute Unit operates independently from the others and is assigned an equal number of rows. Load balancing of the nonzeros assigned per Compute Unit was also tested, but no significant improvement in performance was observed.

3.2   Index Concatenation

In an effort to reduce the memory footprint of the CSR representation, and at the same time alleviate the load on the HBM channels, it was observed that the row-pointer structure can be omitted, by merging its useful information into the

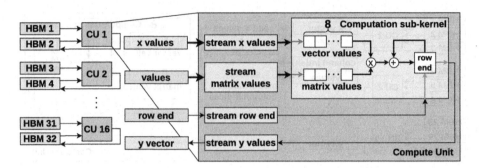

Fig. 4. 'Stream-X' accelerator design. Bold arrows represent vectorized data movement.

column index structure. The new design uses one bit of the column index structure to identify the last element of each row, as 31 bits are sufficient for column indexing for the supported matrices. The revised design is illustrated in Fig. 3. Nothing changes in the computation part of the kernel. The allocation of three HBM channels per Compute Unit also remains unchanged, with the only difference being that only the y (result) vector is now transferred through the third channel.

3.3   Stream-X

The final design that we implement, presented in Fig. 4, requires pre-processing from the host side (CPU), but promises to provide performance gains. The proposed conversion of the 'x vector' to 'x values' takes place during pre-processing and aims to eliminate random accesses to the x vector. Instead, all values that are required from the x vector are streamed to the FPGA, discarding the column index structure. The only indexing structure that is streamed is the row-end structure, which is identified by the 1-bit marker that indicates the last nonzero of a row, introduced in the previous design.

This design allows us to better utilize the available bandwidth from the HBM memory, which favors streaming data transfers over random accesses. However, this design results in an increased memory footprint of the workload (total size of matrix + x vector), since we replace a 32-bit structure (column index) with a 64-bit structure (x values) of equal number of elements, minus the original size of the 64-bit x vector. The pre-processing cost and memory overhead associated with this approach are examined in Sect. 4.2.

Regarding the HBM channel mapping, we choose to use two HBM channels per Compute Unit. One channel is allocated to the x values and the y (result) vector, while the other channel is allocated to the matrix values and the row-end structure. This configuration is selected as the optimal, since the x values and the matrix values are the two structures transferred as 'wide' structures, while row-end and result vector are the structures that generate low traffic. With this mapping we increase the parallelism of the design, scaling up to 16 Compute Units, instead of 10.

Table 1. Evaluation Matrix Dataset

Matrix Name	Rows	Nonzeros	Size (MB)
StocF_1465	1.4M	21M	245.98
Fault_639	638K	28.6M	329.90
PFlow_742	743K	37M	427.85
Emilia_923	923K	41M	472.79
Heel_1138	1.1M	51.7M	595.75
Geo_1438	1.4M	60.2M	694.84
Hook_1498	1.5M	61M	702.86
Serena	1.4M	64.5M	743.81
Flan_1565	1.6M	117.4M	1349.57
Bump_2911	2.9M	127.7M	1472.86

4 Evaluation

The initial stage of the evaluation involves a comparative performance analysis of our implementations on a Xilinx Alveo U280. In the next part of the evaluation, we compare our best-performing implementation against the Vitis SPARSE Library (2021.1) [18] (VSL), which has been designed for the Alveo U280, and is the only currently available work that supports double precision floating point format for sparse algebra. The final part of our evaluation involves comparing the performance (GFLOPs) and energy efficiency (GFLOPs/Watt) of our best implementation across three different Xilinx Alveo FPGAs (U280, U50, U55C) against a server-class CPU.

As mentioned, this work focuses solely on exploring and providing a ready-to-use SpMV software solution for applications with volatile matrices that leverage the double precision floating point format, and are executed on HBM-based FPGAs. Consequently, evaluating any other acceleration platform (e.g. GPUs) is out of this work's scope. Finally, as discussed in Sect. 5, the only related work that supports double precision SpMV using HLS tools on HBM-based FPGAs is the Vitis Sparse Library (VSL) kernel, provided by Xilinx [18]; all others support either fixed point or single precision, thus cannot be included in our evaluation.

4.1 Experimental Setup

We implement our designs using Xilinx Vitis tools, version 2020.2 for the U280 and U50 FPGAs, and 2022.1 for the more recent U55C. The CPU used for comparison is a 14-core Intel Xeon Gold 5120 CPU operating at 2.2 GHz, and the CSR implementation is provided by the Intel Math Kernel Library (MKL) (version 2018.1) [10].

Evaluation matrices are presented in Table 1 and sourced from M3E [14]. They originate from various physics applications and simulations, with varying

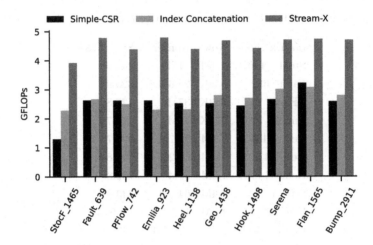

Fig. 5. Performance comparison of proposed implementations on the Xilinx Alveo U280.

input matrices, hence pre-processing is mandatory. Each matrix underwent 128 iterations, and performance (GFLOPs) and power consumption (Watts) were recorded, with the arithmetic mean of five experiments being calculated. We note that the reported performance is calculated on the original number of nonzeros of each matrix, disregarding the zero-padding that each implementation may have applied to facilitate better performance, ensuring a more equitable comparison among different implementations. Power readings for the CPU and for the FPGA were collected using the `turbostat` (measuring *PkgWatt* and *RAMWatt*) and `xbutil` tools respectively.

4.2   Comparison of Our Implementations

The performance evaluation of our implementations on the Xilinx Alveo U280 is presented in Fig. 5. The 'Simple-CSR' design shows limited performance, which is improved by the 'Index Concatenation' design, although not for all matrices. The only noticeable difference is the first matrix (StocF_1465), where the memory savings from discarding the row pointer structure are larger than on average. Overall, although the average reduction in the memory footprint of the matrix is only 0.8%, the improvement in performance is 9% on average.

The last design (Stream-X) provides the largest performance gains, with an average improvement of 83% compared to the 'Simple-CSR' implementation (67% compared to 'Index Concatenation'). The elimination of random accesses to the x vector, and the streaming of x values instead, leads to a significant performance boost. On the other hand, this conversion results in an increased memory footprint of the total workload, 30% on average, which can be amortised due to the high bandwidth offered from the HBM channels. Apart from the larger footprint, the conversion of the 'x vector' to 'x values' involves some

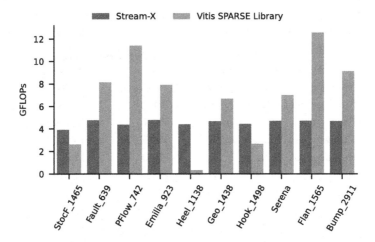

Fig. 6. Performance comparison of the 'Stream-X' implementation and the Vitis SPARSE Library on the Xilinx Alveo U280 without padding overhead.

additional preprocessing, in order to create the proper stream of x values. This preprocessing requires time equal to 125–150 'Simple-CSR' SpMV iterations.

4.3   Comparison with State-of-practice Implementations

Evaluation Against the Vitis SPARSE Library. Towards listing a comprehensive set of results, evaluation against the Vitis SPARSE library (VSL) is done without and with the overhead of matrix padding. Figure 6 presents the performance comparison against VSL without considering the matrix padding overhead. The majority of the matrices exhibit better performance with VSL, outperforming our implementation by an average of 1.5x. However, our design outperforms VSL for three matrices (StocF_1465, Heel_1138, Hook_1498), which possess structural patterns that limit the throughput of VSL. This is also attributed to the significant padding applied by VSL to these matrices, as reported in Table 2. We can also assert that our implementation displays greater performance stability and is less affected by the pattern of the sparse matrix, compared to VSL.

However, as mentioned, this work focuses on applications with volatile input matrices (i.e. multiple varying input matrices that require pre-processing), hence taking into account the padding overhead is mandatory for our work's evaluation. Table 2 presents the comparison of the two implementations, in terms of time and padding overhead. Results show that matrix pre-processing dominates the overall execution time, ranging from several minutes to almost an hour. As a result, 'Stream-X' can speedup SpMV multiplication on average 52.4x for applications with volatile matrices. Additionally, VSL applies extensive zero-padding, where a matrix is split in 2D blocks, and each row of each block is padded to hold a multiple of 32 nonzeros. This results in exhaustive padding up to 8x and

Table 2. Performance comparison of Stream-X against VSL, including pre-processing overhead and actual execution time

Matrix	Stream-X		Vitis SPARSE Library	
	Time (s)	Padding Overhead	Time (s)	Padding Overhead
StocF_1465	10.21	15.02 %	791.60	639.53 %
Fault_639	11.53	6.97 %	525.75	172.14 %
PFlow_742	15.28	9.8 %	654.55	136.51 %
Emilia_923	16.91	7.05 %	774.04	179.03 %
Heel_1138	24.48	7.42 %	2082.63	817.16 %
Geo_1438	25.11	8.05 %	1315.08	211.27 %
Hook_1498	26.13	9.18 %	1527.43	331.09 %
Serena	26.30	7.23 %	1283.96	196.42 %
Flan_1565	48.20	7.89 %	2074.85	125.96 %
Bump_2911	51.49	7.22 %	2386.66	155.35 %
Average	**25.59**	**12.58 %**	**1341.70**	**296.45 %**
Average pre-processing + runtime speedup				**52.4x**

an average of almost 3x (296.45%) compared to the original matrices, enforcing developers to allocate substantially more storage resources. Moreover, its current implementation supports only the U280 FPGA. In contrast, 'Stream-X' uses a conservative scheme, where each row is padded to hold a multiple of 8 nonzeros, resulting in an average overhead of only 12.58%, whereas it can be deployed in U280, U50 and U55C FPGAs.

Evaluation Against CPU. In the final part of our evaluation, we compare the performance of the 'Stream-X' implementation across three Xilinx Alveo FPGAs (U280, U50, U55C) versus an Intel Xeon CPU running the CSR implementation of Intel's MKL. Figure 7 shows that the FPGA implementation is able to achieve 47–52% of the CPU performance on average, with all FPGAs showing a similar performance pattern across all matrices. On the other hand, as shown in Fig. 8, the 'Stream-X' implementation on the U280, U50 and U55C FPGAs deliver an energy-efficient solution that outperforms the CPU in terms of performance-per-Watt by 2.90x, 3.48x and 4.26x respectively.

4.4   Discussion

The following points summarize our observations from the evaluation:

– VSL SpMV multiplication processing is 50% more efficient compared to 'Stream-X'; however our implementation provides an average of 52.4x better overall execution time (including padding) for applications that utilize varying matrices throughout processing.

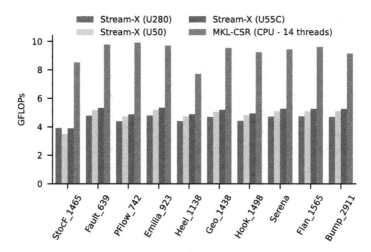

Fig. 7. Performance comparison of the 'Stream-X' implementation on 3 Xilinx Alveo FPGAs and a 14-core CPU running MKL-CSR.

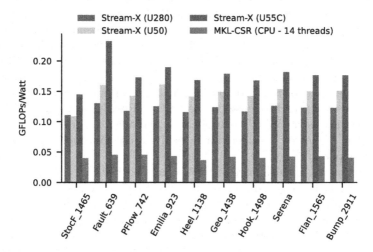

Fig. 8. Energy efficiency comparison of the 'Stream-X' implementation on 3 Xilinx Alveo FPGAs and a 14-core CPU running MKL-CSR.

- VSL requires, through extensive zero padding, for matrices to be increased up to 8x and on average almost 3x compared to their original sizes, leading to excessive utilization of storage/memory resources; on the other hand 'Stream-X' increases original matrices slightly more than 12% compared to their original sizes.
- VSL is currently available only for the U280 FPGA, whereas 'Stream-X' supports U280, U50 and U55C FPGAs.
- 'Stream-X' enables energy-efficient CPU-based deployments, achieving 3.6x (up to 5.1x) better performance-per-Watt ratio compared to a server-class CPU.

Table 3. Supported precision formats for SpMV on HBM-equipped FPGAs

library	fixed point	single precision floating point	double precision floating point
Serpens [17]	✗	✓	✗
HiSparse [3]	✓	✓	✗
VSL [18]	✗	✗	✓
ThunderGP [2]	✓	✗	✗
GraphLily [9]	✓	✗	✗
Our work	✗	✗	✓

5 Related Work

One of the first FPGA designs for SpMV is proposed by Zhuo et al. [20], who design a specialized reduction circuit for CSR SpMV. A similar design [19] adds a custom accumulator, however highlighting the disadvantage of FPGAs when it comes to memory bandwidth. The CVBV format [12] and value compression in CSR [7] attempt to reduce memory bandwidth requirements. The CISR format [4] enables processing of multiple rows in parallel. OpenCL-based CSR SpMV is also evaluated in literature [5,6]. Modifications to the CSR format that allow data streaming, thereby improving memory bandwidth utilization, have also been proposed in [8,15]. In [13,16], matrix reordering on the host side is utilized for better x-vector reuse on the FPGA. Finally, as mentioned [1] supports double-precision SpMV multiplication, however it targets older Virtex5 FPGAs, thus cannot be considered as a ready-to-use solution by today's application developers.

In recent years, with the rise of HBM-equipped FPGAs, several new SpMV accelerators have been introduced, mainly targeting graph-processing workloads, such as ThunderGP [2], GraphLily [9] and Serpens [17]. ThunderGP utilizes DDR memory only and is limited by its low bandwidth. GraphLily introduces a design with a custom representation format and is the first work to implement GraphBLAS kernels for HBM-equipped FPGAs. Serpens splits a matrix in vertical blocks, uses local input and output vector buffers and eliminates off-chip random memory accesses. It applies nonzero coloring, in order to minimize the memory conflicts. HiSparse [3] utilizes input and output vector buffers, and with the help of an arbiter/shuffle unit, ensures that no bank conflicts will occur. However, it only supports fixed-point and single floating-point precision.

Finally, a modular design for an SpMV accelerator, composed of multiple building blocks, is proposed in [11] by Xilinx, but targets non-HBM FPGAs and is designed for single floating-point precision. This is the predecessor to the Vitis SPARSE Library (VSL) [18], which creates a high-throughput computation path by applying a 2D blocking partitioning scheme on the sparse matrix and reusing the x vector through a dedicated Compute Unit. As such, as shown in Table 3, to the best of our knowledge, apart from the VSL, no other implementation on double-precision SpMV has been proposed for HBM-equipped FPGAs.

6 Conclusions

In this work, we explored different approaches for efficient double-precision SpMV multiplication on HBM-supported FPGAs, and proposed 'Stream-X', an architecture that is based on modifications to the Compressed Sparse Row (CSR) format, utilizing common optimizations from prior literature. Based on our evaluation, 'Stream-X' is the best option for applications that facilitate SpMV multiplications with constantly updated input matrices. Compared to other available solutions, to the best of our knowledge, our work and the VSL are the only ones supporting double precision for SpMV multiplication. Results showed that VSL achieves 50% better processing time compared to our work; however 'Stream-X' can reduce on average 52.4x the overall execution time (matrix padding and data processing) compared to VSL. Furthermore, our work increases the original matrix by 12%, whereas VSL requires on average 3x more storage/memory resources to host padded matrices. Finally, 'Stream-X' enables energy-efficient deployments with 3.6x (up to 5.1x) better performance-per-Watt ratio compared to server-class CPUs.

Acknowledgment. This project has received funding from the European High-Performance Computing Joint Undertaking Joint Undertaking (JU) under grant agreement No 955739 (project OPTIMA). The JU receives support from the European Union's Horizon 2020 research and innovation programme and Greece, Germany, Italy, Netherlands, Spain, Switzerland.

Disclosure of Interests. The authors have no competing interests to declare that are relevant to the content of this article.

References

1. Attarde, S., Joshi, S., Deshpande, Y., Puranik, S., Patkar, S.: Double precision sparse matrix vector multiplication accelerator on FPGA. In: International Conference on Pervasive and Embedded Computing and Communication Systems, pp. 476–484. IEEE (2021)
2. Chen, X., Tan, H., Chen, Y., He, B., Wong, W.F., Chen, D.: ThunderGP: HLS-based graph processing framework on FPGAs. In: The 2021 ACM/SIGDA International Symposium on Field-Programmable Gate Arrays, pp. 69–80 (2021)
3. Du, Y., Hu, Y., Zhou, Z., Zhang, Z.: High-performance sparse linear algebra on HBM-equipped FPGAs using HLS: a case study on SPMV. In: Proceedings of the 2022 ACM/SIGDA International Symposium on Field-Programmable Gate Arrays, pp. 54–64 (2022)
4. Fowers, J., Ovtcharov, K., Strauss, K., Chung, E.S., Stitt, G.: A high memory bandwidth FPGA accelerator for sparse matrix-vector multiplication. In: FCCM 2014

5. Gautier, Q., Althoff, A., Meng, P., Kastner, R.: Spector: an OpenCL FPGA benchmark suite. In: FPT 2016
6. Giefers, H., Staar, P., Bekas, C., Hagleitner, C.: Analyzing the energy-efficiency of sparse matrix multiplication on heterogeneous systems: a comparative study of GPU, Xeon Phi and FPGA. In: 2016 IEEE International Symposium on Performance Analysis of Systems and Software (ISPASS), pp. 46–56. IEEE (2016)
7. Grigoras, P., Burovskiy, P., Hung, E., Luk, W.: Accelerating SpMV on FPGAs by compressing nonzero values. In: 2015 IEEE 23rd Annual International Symposium on Field-Programmable Custom Computing Machines, pp. 64–67. IEEE (2015)
8. Hosseinabady, M., Nunez-Yanez, J.L.: A streaming dataflow engine for sparse matrix-vector multiplication using high-level synthesis. IEEE Trans. Comput. Aided Des. Integr. Circuits Syst. **39**(6), 1272–1285 (2019)
9. Hu, Y., Du, Y., Ustun, E., Zhang, Z.: GraphLily: accelerating graph linear algebra on HBM-equipped FPGAs. In: 2021 IEEE/ACM International Conference On Computer Aided Design (ICCAD), pp. 1–9. IEEE (2021)
10. Intel Corporation: Intel math kernel library (2018). https://bit.ly/intel_mkl. Version 2018.1
11. Jain, A.K., Omidian, H., Fraisse, H., Benipal, M., Liu, L., Gaitonde, D.: A domain-specific architecture for accelerating sparse matrix vector multiplication on FPGAs. In: 2020 30th International Conference on Field-programmable Logic and Applications (FPL), pp. 127–132. IEEE (2020)
12. Kestur, S., Davis, J.D., Chung, E.S.: Towards a universal FPGA matrix-vector multiplication architecture. In: 2012 IEEE 20th International Symposium on Field-Programmable Custom Computing Machines, pp. 9–16. IEEE (2012)
13. Li, S., Liu, D., Liu, W.: Optimized data reuse via reordering for sparse matrix-vector multiplication on FPGAs. In: 2021 IEEE/ACM International Conference on Computer Aided Design (ICCAD), pp. 1–9. IEEE (2021)
14. M3E: M3E matrix collection. https://bit.ly/m3e_matrix_collection
15. Mpakos, P., Papadopoulou, N., Alverti, C., Goumas, G., Koziris, N.: On the performance and energy efficiency of sparse matrix-vector multiplication on FPGAs. In: Parallel Computing: Technology Trends, pp. 624–633. IOS Press (2020)
16. Oyarzun, G., Peyrolon, D., Alvarez, C., Martorell, X.: An FPGA cached sparse matrix vector product (SPMV) for unstructured computational fluid dynamics simulations. arXiv preprint arXiv:2107.12371 (2021)
17. Song, L., Chi, Y., Guo, L., Cong, J.: Serpens: a high bandwidth memory based accelerator for general-purpose sparse matrix-vector multiplication. In: Proceedings of the 59th ACM/IEEE Design Automation Conference, pp. 211–216 (2022)
18. Xilinx: Vitis sparse library. https://bit.ly/vitis_sparse_library
19. Zhang, Y., Shalabi, Y.H., Jain, R., Nagar, K.K., Bakos, J.D.: FPGA vs. GPU for sparse matrix vector multiply. In: 2009 International Conference on Field-Programmable Technology, pp. 255–262. IEEE (2009)
20. Zhuo, L., Prasanna, V.K.: Sparse matrix-vector multiplication on FPGAs. In: Proceedings of the 2005 ACM/SIGDA 13th International Symposium on Field-Programmable Gate Arrays, pp. 63–74 (2005)

Deep Quantization of Graph Neural Networks with Run-Time Hardware-Aware Training

Olle Hansson[(✉)] ⓘ, Mahdieh Grailoo ⓘ, Oscar Gustafsson ⓘ,
and Jose Nunez-Yanez ⓘ

Department of Electrical Engineering, Linköping University,
581 83 Linköping, Sweden
`olle.hansson@liu.se`

Abstract. In this paper, we investigate the benefits of hardware-aware quantization in the gFADES hardware accelerator targeting Graph Convolutional Networks (GCNs). GCNs are a type of Graph Neural Networks (GNNs) that combine sparse and dense data compute requirements that are challenging to meet in resource-constrained embedded hardware. The gFADES architecture is optimized to work with the pruned data representations typically present in graph neural networks for the graph structure and features. It is described in High-Level Synthesis (HLS) which enables efficient design-space exploration of mixed precision hardware configurations. In this work, the mixed-precision design is embedded in the forward pass of the PyTorch back-propagation training loop to enable run-time hardware-aware training. It uses different data types to represent adjacency, feature, weight, internal, and output values which allows for a fine-grained optimization at the tensor level. The resulting hardware configuration after training reduces precision to a 4-bit data type for all inputs. It achieves little to no degradation in the classification accuracy, when training on the Planetoid database dataset, compared to the original 32-bit floating-point. The optimized hardware design running on an AMD/Xilinx Zynq Ultrascale+ FPGA device achieves over 600× speedup compared to the optimized PyTorch software implementation running on the multi-core ARM CPU in the processing system.

Keywords: Neural Networks · FPGA · GNN · quantization · low precision

1 Introduction

Artificial Intelligence (AI) and Machine Learning (ML) applications continue to increase in popularity with significant advances done in natural language processing and autonomous driving [7,11]. Within this field, Graph Neural Networks (GNNs) are a type of Neural Networks (NNs) designed to work with graphs or other non-Euclidean data. GNNs can perform tasks such as graph classification,

© The Author(s), under exclusive license to Springer Nature Switzerland AG 2024
I. Skliarova et al. (Eds.): ARC 2024, LNCS 14553, pp. 33–47, 2024.
https://doi.org/10.1007/978-3-031-55673-9_3

node classification, link prediction, and graph clustering, and have been proven very successful in, e.g., anomaly detection, bioinformatics, and cybersecurity. GNN processing uses both dense and sparse data representations and it is thus quite complex in terms of computing and data access requirements [4]. These properties lead to both inference and training of GNNs being more difficult to run on general-purpose computing hardware like CPUs or GPUs than other more regular neural network models like Convolutional Neural Networks (CNNs) and, therefore, is an ideal candidate for specialized hardware acceleration.

This work extends [10] that presented the gFADES (graph Fused Architecture for DEnse and Sparse matrices) graph neural network accelerator based on a deep dataflow architecture for AMD/Xilinx Zynq devices, capable of improving the performance of GNN models developed with PyTorch and PyTorch geometric. The work in [10] focused on half-precision floating-point accuracy (FP16) and the main contributions of this paper are as follows:

- We integrate the hardware accelerator in the forward pass of the backpropagation training loop in PyTorch so the full precision backward pass is aware of the effects of the hardware quantization during gradient computations.
- We investigate the classification accuracy of hardware configurations using a varying number of bits, down to four bits, yielding near to no loss compared to models trained with single-precision floating-point on the CPU.
- We present performance results in terms of execution time for a range of design configurations possible with the architecture and compare these to running directly on the multi-core ARM CPU.

This paper is organized as follows, in Sect. 2 we review related work and discuss the motivation of this work. Section 3 summarizes the computation architecture presented in previous work and highlights some refinements done for this work. In Sect. 4 we discuss the different techniques used to improve the accuracy of the quantized designs. Section 5 presents the results of the different designs analyzing accuracy and performance. Lastly, in Sect. 6 we discuss the findings, and conclusions and propose future work.

2   Related Work and Motivation

The potential of Graph Neural Networks in dealing with unstructured data has resulted in an increasing interest in the acceleration of the computations part of GNN processing such as sparse/dense matrix multiplications, with specialized computing hardware. Sparse matrix multiplications are poorly suited for general processing hardware due to their irregular access patterns and thus can yield great improvement with specialized hardware. These factors have resulted in research of different kinds of hardware accelerators for GNNs such as "FLASH" [6], where they developed an accelerator that they use to extend network switch functionalities to allow for machine learning workloads providing an example of GCN computations. The testing is done using a Xilinx Alveo U280 and shows a speedup advantage of on average 3.4× compared to running a CPU cluster. Another recently developed accelerator for GCNs is "Accel-GCN" [15]. They propose an architecture to address workload imbalance and memory access irregularity in GCNs that aim to run on GPUs. This is done by first a preprocessing stage with sorting and partitioning to improve memory utilization, followed by a kernel-level design to leverage the optimizations done in the preprocessing. Their design outperforms similar solutions by about 1.2 to 2.9× performance. A third recent work investigating GCN acceleration is the work done by the authors of [17]. In the paper they explain how they take a holistic approach to the design, this includes compression formats as well as a generic dataflow design. Additionally, they find their final design by using a genetic algorithm to make a rapid exploration of the design space to find the optimal design. Their design is implemented as a 28 nm ASIC and shows great speedup compared to HyGCN [16], AWB-GCN [3], and GCNAX [9]. Another recent accelerator for GCNs is "PEDAL" [1]. Their work has support for multiple different dataflows and can choose the best best-fit dataflow for the input graph. The design is implemented in a 12 nm ASIC process node and achieves a 2.6× speedup for the tested model.

Regarding quantized execution of machine learning, much work has been done proving that 8-bit integer calculations are sufficient in most cases, but less than 8-bits has not been explored extensively for the graph neural network case. One of the early works proving that running deep learning with less than 32-bit floating-point precision is the work done by the authors of [5]. They developed a GEneral Matrix Multiplication (GEMM) hardware accelerator which uses 16-bit fixed-point and show little to no degradation to the classification accuracy of DNN and CNN models while vastly improving the energy efficiency due to switching from 32-bit floating-point to 16-bit fixed-point. Another work working with low-precision DNNs is [2], where they train Maxout networks for three distinct formats: floating-point, fixed-point, and dynamic fixed-point. Their findings are that it is possible to use down to 10-bit multipliers without losing accuracy, both for inference and for training. A previous work that focuses more on Graph Neural Networks is the work done by the authors of [12]. They explored the viability of training quantized GNNs and developed a stable method, requiring little tuning to obtain good results, to improve the performance of training. They show great results for 8-bit integer representation performing as well as 32-bit floating-point, while 4-bit integer representation falls a bit behind but improves significantly with the proposed method. Another work that focuses on quantized execution of GNNs is "QGTC" [13]. They propose a Tensor Core (TC) based computing framework to support any-bit-width computation for quantized graph neural networks on GPUs. They integrate the framework with PyTorch and can show an on average 2.7× speedup compared to Deep Graph Library (DGL).

Most of the previous work on GNN optimization has focused on server class designs with access to HBM (High Bandwidth memory). In contrast, we target resource-constrained self-contained edge devices such as the Zynq family, and not embedded GPUs nor in conjunction with an HPC device. Embedded GPUs such as the Nvidia Jetson or ARM Mali families do not support sub-byte data types so they will not be able to run the forward pass of the training loop at the reduced bit precisions possible with FPGA logic as done in this work. We also actively aim at integrating the accelerator as part of the PyTorch framework to facilitate ease of use as a drop-in replacement for the sparse/dense computation libraries available in PyTorch. In this work, we focus on energy-efficient solutions focusing on sub-byte data representation, which according to the related work, has received limited attention in the case of graph neural networks.

3   gFADES Computation Architecture

The gFADES design is fully described in C with Xilinx Vitis HLS (High-Level Synthesis) tools, which allows for easy prototyping and simulations which have been widely used during this work. The architecture is designed using a Dataflows of Dataflows (DoD) approach where two separate instances of hardware threads and compute units process combination (features) and aggregation (adjacencies) independently of each other. The feature processing can freely write its output, the intermediate results, to PIPO buffers, whereas the adjacency processing can read from the PIPOs and write the result to the main memory. The design configurations are created according to the following scheme, XtYtZc with X/Y indicating the number of threads in feature and adjacency processing respectively, and Z the number of compute units per thread.

The hardware computes a graph convolutional layer according to Kipf and Welling [8],

$$H^{(l+1)} = \sigma \left(\hat{A} H^{(l)} W^{(l)} \right) \tag{1}$$

in two stages, first feature combination and then adjacency aggregation. The combination engine computes $B = H^{(l)} \cdot W^{(l)}$, where $H^{(l)}$ represents the feature matrix and $W^{(l)}$ the trainable weight matrix, and generates the intermediate output B in chunks (tiles) which are fed into the PIPO buffer. The aggregation engine then reads the chunks of intermediate results and computes $H^{(l+1)} = \hat{A} \cdot B$ to give the results $H^{(l+1)}$. Each stage uses an internal dataflow to read matrices (sparse/dense for features, dense for weights, and sparse for adjacencies) and compute the dot products. The architecture can also be configured to either write the output directly to memory or to take the ReLU of the output before writing to memory. The Compressed Sparse Row (CSR) format is used to store the data for the sparse adjacency and sparse feature matrices.

While the main dataflow of the design remains the same compared to the previous work some additional features and optimizations have been done in this work. The most significant change is the addition of five different datatypes inside the design. The five different datatypes are used for adjacencies, features, weights, intermediate/out, and accumulation. While in the previous work, all data were of the same numerical type and the focus was on analyzing half-precision floating-point, the current design iteration can mix and match between these five types independently. Since the design is written with C++ HLS, we can use the typical datatypes for C++, e.g., float (single precision floating-point), half (half precision floating-point), and int (32-bit integer). Moreover, it also supports arbitrary length integers through Xilinx `ap_int` (signed and unsigned) as well as fixed-point values using Xilinx `ap_fixed` (signed and unsigned). When writing to the PIPOs and the final result the values are saturated from the accumulation buffer ensuring that the sign stays the same. Testing different design configurations is done by changing the format for one of the five types, running a test simulation, and synthesizing a new design (the casting and scaling between the different types is done by HLS seamlessly). In this way, we can investigate mixed precision design and sub-8-bit fixed-point solutions with a much more productive approach than if RTL coding was involved. The pointers data types have also been updated in the version of the design, from 32-bit integer to the smallest possible for the tested dataset. The smaller pointers did not affect the synthesis result a lot but should in theory make it possible to save a significant amount of memory by packing the pointers together. Figure 1 shows the dataflow of a single hardware thread color-coded according to the different data types.

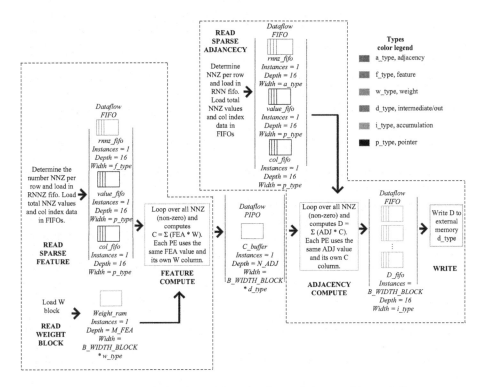

Fig. 1. Dataflow of a single hardware thread color-coded according to different types.

4   Hardware Aware Training

The machine learning models are implemented and trained using PyTorch and PyTorch Geometric which runs on the Processing System (PS) part of the Xilinx Zynq UltraScale+ FPGA used for the testing. To get the PS to work together with our accelerator in the Programmable Logic (PL) we use a PYNQ overlay. The PYNQ overlay enables full control of the accelerator from the Python environment and can specify NumPy arrays as input and output data buffers for the accelerator (adjacencies, features, weights, results). The execution of the graph convolutional layers can then be done by first configuring the accelerator with the addresses to the previously mentioned data buffers, and then starting the execution by setting the `AP_START` signal to 1 and polling the `AP_DONE` to wait for the design to finish. In this work, the outputs obtained in each layer are then converted to a PyTorch tensor to be used during the backward pass which is executed in the processing system in floating-point precision. The integration of the accelerator in the forward pass means that the backward pass is aware of the reduced precision results resulting in a type of quantization-aware training directly in hardware. In previous work, we used 16-bit floating-point to make our tests, this makes the training process rather simple since you can easily cast between the floating-point types. Given that we wanted to investigate how heavily we can quantize the data we decided to use fixed-point arithmetic for the accelerator, and this required a more complicated pre- and post-processing when training on the accelerator. Figure 2 shows on a high-level representation of hardware-aware training and the tight cooperation between the FPGA accelerator and the host CPU.

To convert the values from the floating-point format used in PyTorch to the fixed-point format required for the accelerator, we scale the value and then cast it to an integer. In more detail, the floating-point value is first scaled by multiplying with $2^{(frac\_bits)}$, followed by a rounding operation to not introduce any bias. This, now scaled, value is then clipped/saturated to the minimum and maximum value of the targeted type to avoid any accidental overflow when loaded on the accelerator. Lastly, it is cast to the closest corresponding NumPy data type if, e.g., the accelerator is using all 8-bit data types it can be either cast to `np.int8` or `np.uint8` depending on the sign for the data type. To convert the resulting values from the accelerator the process is done in reverse, excluding clipping. Which means first casting to `np.float32` then scaling by dividing with $2^{(frac\_bits)}$. These conversions are done as closely as possible to the start and the finish of the accelerator, so in case any other pre- or post-processing is done, it is done in the floating-point format on the processor.

This works seamlessly for data types with width supported by NumPy, for other lengths, e.g., 4-bits or 12-bits, we need a slightly altered method. When converting from float-point format to fixed-point format the process is the same except that we always cast to the unsigned type larger than the targeted format, e.g., 4-bits gets cast to `np.uint8` and 12-bit to `np.uint16`. When converting the resulting fixed-point values back to floating-point the method has additional alterations. The resulting fixed-point values are read from a data buffer which

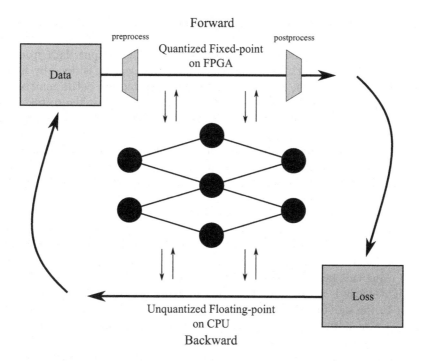

Fig. 2. High-level dataflow of Hardware-Aware Training.

once again has the type of the next larger unsigned NumPy data type, e.g., 6-bits is `np.uint8` and 12-bits is `np.uint16`, this is not to affect any two's complement sign at this stage. The unsigned value is then cast to `np.float32` and every value larger than the maximum value for the signed output type $(2^{(bits-1)})$ is subtracted by $2^{(bits)}$, e.g., for a 6-bit format decimal 63 should be -1. The adjusted value is then, just as before, scaled by dividing with $2^{(frac\_bits)}$.

One of the problems when using a small number of bits in calculations is to balance the precision with the range descriptiveness. In this work, we had to put significant emphasis on having good precision given how machine learning training works with small gradient values. A problem though is how graph convolutional layers use sometimes large matrix multiplications, which must accumulate a lot of values resulting in potential overflows. This was one of the main problems when trying to train the graph convolutional models on the accelerator, accumulating too far thus yielding an overflow and therefore pushing the weights away from the optimum instead of towards it. Other than carefully observing the values during training, two methods were included to improve the training process, scaling input data, and using weight decay.

Regarding scaling, we scale the input features going into the second graph convolutional layer following the approach presented by Wu et al. [14]. We take the resulting values coming out from the first layer which have been passed through a ReLU function thus having values in the interval $[0, d_{max}]$. d_{max} is the maximum value the output type can represent, and mapping them to the input feature type in the interval $[0, f_{\max}]$, $f_{\max}$ being the maximum value of input features. This means that we can compress the output data from one layer to fit the input data from the next layer. The scaling is done by finding the maximum value of the output matrix, then dividing the entire matrix with factor $s = \frac{i_{\max} - i_{\min}}{t_{\max} - t_{\min}}$, here i means input and t is target. After the second layer, the output is then scaled back by multiplying with the same factor restoring the values while being able to use a smaller internal representation. An extended version of this scaling method has been implemented with the final design. This method allows for taking a percentile value of the matrix instead of always taking the maximum value, and then clipping the resulting matrix after scaling. This means that we can decide to clip a specified percentage of values, e.g., top 0.1% or 1%, to better use the available value range, this is to avoid problems of having a few outliers at the top end of the range. This scaling method is only applied in cases where the scaling factor, either the max or a percentile, is larger than $f_{\max}$. We do this because we do not want to increase the input values, since we started using this kind of scaling to avoid overflow.

Weight decay is another method used to avoid overflow. Weight decay adds a factor to the loss function related to the Euclidean (L_2) norm of the weights. This adds a penalty factor to the loss function for overfitting the weights to the data, helping with training versus testing accuracy, but it has also the effect of reducing the magnitude of the outliers, both for the weights themselves and the resulting output. Increasing the weight decay increases the effect, so in this work, we have increased it as far as possible until it shows negative effects on the accuracy. This improves the distribution of weights and outputs fitting better to their corresponding data types.

5   Results

The final optimized design configuration, fxp4, and three other reference fixed-points have the data types as listed in Table 1. The ranges of the types depend on the number of integer bits and the sign bit as follows, for unsigned values $\in [0, 2^{(int)})$ and signed values $\in [-2^{(int-1)}, 2^{(int-1)})$. This design was chosen after carefully stepping one of the data types and training on the different datasets and pushing towards as few bits as possible without significantly lowering the testing accuracy. Three other fixed-point models have been used to compare results. These three models use 8, 16, and 32 bits, with one quarter (2, 4, and 8 bits, respectively) as integer bits. The synthesis results of the tested design are shown in Table 2. The fixed-point designs are limited by BRAM usage, while the floating-point configurations are limited by timing. When going from an 8-bit fixed-point design configuration to the final optimized design it is possible to either double the number of threads or compute units. The datasets used for this work are the Planetoid collection of citation network datasets: Cora, CiteSeer, and PubMed. The model used during the testing is a three-layer model with two graph convolutional layers followed by a fully connected layer. Both GCN layers have 64 hidden features, and the linear layer has according to the number of classes for the corresponding dataset. The models were trained for 64 epochs for Cora and CiteSeer, and 32 for PubMed, this seemed to be a good balance between accuracy convergence and training time.

Table 1. Final design data type configurations. Divided into the different data types during the forward pass; bits is the total number of bits, int is the number of integer bits, and sign is either signed (s) or unsigned (u).

Config	A			F			W			D			I		
	bits	int	sign	bits	int	sign	bits	int	sign	bits	int	sign	bits	int	sign
fxp4	4	−1	u	4	0	u	4	−1	s	6	2	s	16	6	s
fxp8	8	2	s	8	2	s	8	2	s	8	2	s	8	2	s
fxp16	16	4	s	16	4	s	16	4	s	16	4	s	16	4	s
fxp32	32	8	s	32	8	s	32	8	s	32	8	s	32	8	s

Table 2. Synth results for the different design configurations. The first seven designs use the final fxp4 data type configurations.

Design	LUT	FF	BRAM	DSP
1t1t2c	19266	24189	22	9
2t2t2c	28969	37682	52	16
2t2t4c	30965	38813	96	24
4t4t4c	54075	66818	223	48
4t4t8c	60305	71611	431	80
4t4t16c	74911	81132	847	144
8t8t8c	123226	135292	861	162
fxp8_4t4t8c	71095	76742	463	38
fxp16_4t4t4c	63909	75581	591	70
fxp32_2t2t4c	38645	45676	580	85
half_4t4t4c	113810	122896	527	358
float_2t2t4c	107306	127417	372	133

5.1 Training Accuracy

In Figs. 3a to 3c; Cora, CiteSeer, PubMed; we can see how the final design achieves accuracy very near to the one achieved by the more expressive design configurations. The training accuracy for the final design is a bit more unstable and sometimes trains slower, in terms of epochs, but it reaches a comparable level of accuracy. Comparing our results to the results from [12] it is apparent that hardware-aware training can greatly improve the training accuracy when running with 4-bit data representation, where our work can maintain close to 32-bit floating-point accuracy results.

A typical example of what happens when the data types either have too little precision or too small range is seen for fxp8 in the Cora testing. It seems to work correctly during the first few epochs of training but it falls off later on and it never reaches the same accuracy as the more expressive design configurations.

5.2   Performance

In Figs. 4a to 4f, we show the speedup of different design configurations for the "function" layer measurement, speedup compared to running on the CPU. The CPU runs a software implementation optimized given the available hardware platform. Optimized assembly for sparse- and general matrix multiplication kernels uses the capabilities of the available CPU. There is no GPGPU available on the platform so GPU acceleration cannot be used. The function measurement is done when calling the graph convolutional layer in the PyTorch model. This includes some of the pre- and post-processing required to use the accelerator, and the special case for non-power of two like the final design configuration, which is why the final solution is slightly slower than the other fixed-point configurations at the same number of threads and compute units. We also made a "kernel" measurement Figs. 5a and 5b, speedup normalized to the execution time of the smallest design configuration (1t1t2c), not normalized to the CPU since the accelerator is not used during pure CPU execution. These measurements are done on a slightly lower level, as close as possible to the accelerator, right before setting AP_START and right after reading AP_DONE equal to 1. This will remove the pre- and post-processing and thus show even greater speedup, this can be seen as the best-case scenario.

The performance results show a speedup of up to 600× for the first layer of PubMed compared to running on the CPU. The speedup compared to CPU is much higher for the first graph convolutional layer, due to the high degree of sparsity present in the input features, whereas for the second layer, the input is much denser and the speedup is not to the same degree. Something that can be seen with the "kernel" results is that the scaling is even better indicating that the pre- and post-processing overhead is significant yielding less relative improvement for the "function" speedup, important if trying to parallelize even more. If we compare the speedup of the largest optimized final design configuration with the largest half-precision floating-point design from the previous work [10], we see an uplift of around 1.5 to 3×. This is because, in the new optimized design, we can fit more threads and/or compute units on the same FPGA, thus allowing for more parallelism. If we use this speedup factor together with a performance comparison done in the previous work, we see a very competitive performance compared to e.g. HyGCN AWB-GCN, and GCNAX, even though our architecture targets an embedded and simpler application.

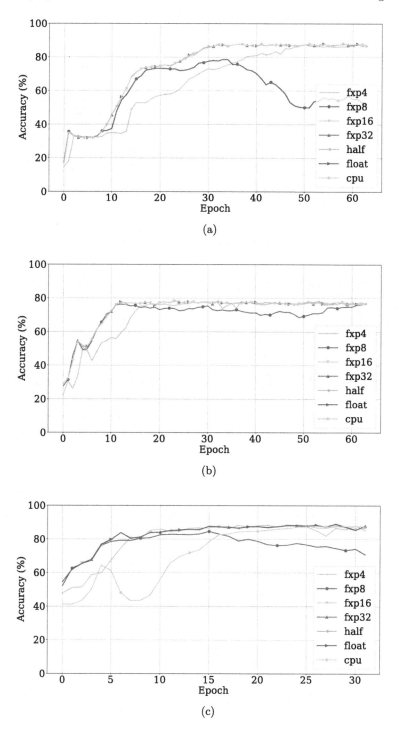

Fig. 3. Training accuracy for: (a) Cora, (b) CiteSeer, and (c) PubMed.

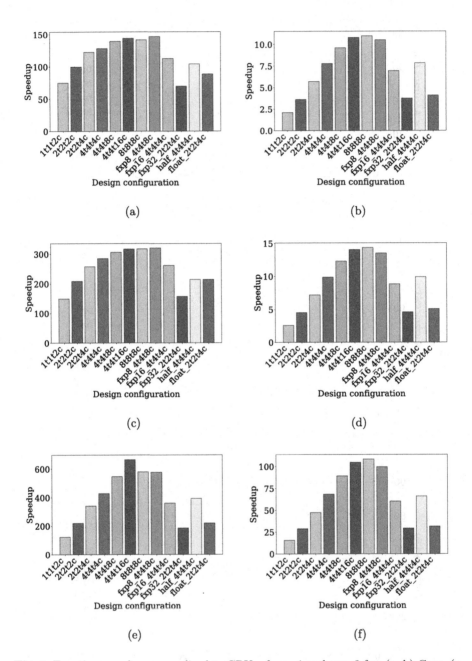

Fig. 4. Function speedup, normalized to CPU, of conv1 and conv2 for: (a, b) Cora, (c, d) CiteSeer, and (e, f) PubMed.

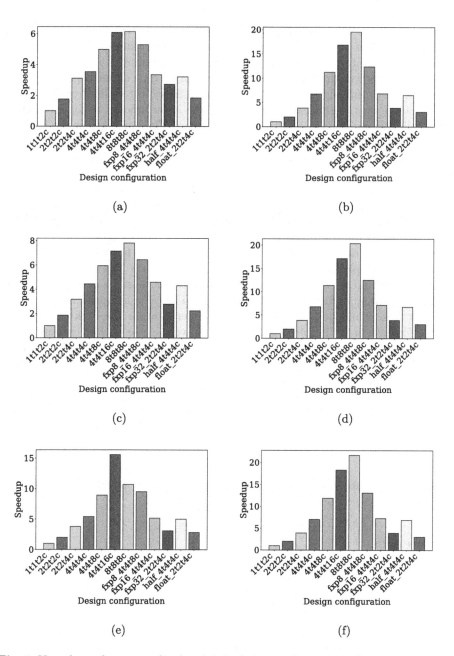

Fig. 5. Kernel speedup, normalized to 1t1t2c design configuration, of conv1 and conv2 for: (a, b) Cora, (c, d) CiteSeer, and (e, f) PubMed.

6   Conclusions and Future Work

In this paper, we have investigated deep quantization strategies and hardware designs using the gFADES dataflow hardware architecture for graph convolutional networks. The results show that the quantization of features, adjacency, weights, and intermediate data improves performance by either being able to fit more hardware threads and compute units to increase throughput or by using a smaller more energy-efficient design due to the lower amount of logic required, while still maintaining close to reference accuracy. The hardware-aware training approach proposed in the paper obtains a 4-bit configuration that is able to keep the classification accuracy comparable to running with 32-bit floating-point. The low-precision design achieves over 600× speed-up compared to using the optimized PyTorch kernel for the multi-core ARM CPU available in the processing system. The improved design works as a drop-in replacement for edge devices, only requiring a small amount of pre- and post-processing and it was tested with three datasets from the Planetoid citation network dataset collection.

In future work, we would like to further test the framework with other datasets and applications. A more general design that supports other GNN models including attention mechanism and datasets most likely requires more advanced techniques to yield satisfying results. The largest improvement in total training time would be to implement the acceleration for the backward as well as the forward pass. Through some analysis, we have seen that currently, the backward pass takes at least 75% of the total training time, which means it would be possible to achieve a minimum of 3 to 4× total training speedup if this was also run on the accelerator.

Acknowledgments. This work was partially supported by the Wallenberg AI, Autonomous Systems and Software Program (WASP) funded by the Knut and Alice Wallenberg Foundation.

Disclosure of Interests. The authors have no competing interests to declare that are relevant to the content of this article.

References

1. Chen, Y., Khadem, A., He, X., Talati, N., Khan, T.A., Mudge, T.: PEDAL: a power efficient GCN accelerator with multiple dataflows. In: Proceedings of Design, Automation & Test in Europe Conference & Exhibition (DATE). IEEE, April 2023. https://doi.org/10.23919/date56975.2023.10137240
2. Courbariaux, M., Bengio, Y., David, J.P.: Training deep neural networks with low precision multiplications (2014). https://doi.org/10.48550/ARXIV.1412.7024
3. Geng, T., et al.: AWB-GCN: a graph convolutional network accelerator with run-time workload rebalancing (2019). https://doi.org/10.48550/ARXIV.1908.10834
4. Grohe, M.: The descriptive complexity of graph neural networks (2023). https://doi.org/10.48550/ARXIV.2303.04613

5. Gupta, S., Agrawal, A., Gopalakrishnan, K., Narayanan, P.: Deep learning with limited numerical precision (2015). https://doi.org/10.48550/ARXIV.1502.02551

6. Haghi, P., et al.: FLASH: FPGA-accelerated smart switches with GCN case study. In: Proceedings of the 37th International Conference on Supercomputing, ICS 2023. ACM, June 2023. https://doi.org/10.1145/3577193.3593739

7. Khurana, D., Koli, A., Khatter, K., Singh, S.: Natural language processing: state of the art, current trends and challenges. Multimedia Tools Appl. **82**(3), 3713–3744 (2022). https://doi.org/10.1007/s11042-022-13428-4

8. Kipf, T.N., Welling, M.: Semi-supervised classification with graph convolutional networks (2016). https://doi.org/10.48550/ARXIV.1609.02907

9. Li, J., Louri, A., Karanth, A., Bunescu, R.: GCNAX: a flexible and energy-efficient accelerator for graph convolutional neural networks, Seoul, Korea (South), pp. 775–788. IEEE (2021). https://doi.org/10.1109/HPCA51647.2021.00070

10. Nunez-Yanez, J.: Accelerating graph neural networks in Pytorch with HLS and deep dataflows. In: Palumbo, F., Keramidas, G., Voros, N., Diniz, P.C. (eds.) ARC 2023. LNCS, vol. 14251, pp. 131–145. Springer, Cham (2023). https://doi.org/10.1007/978-3-031-42921-7_9

11. Padmaja, B., Moorthy, C.V.K.N.S.N., Venkateswarulu, N., Bala, M.M.: Exploration of issues, challenges and latest developments in autonomous cars. J. Big Data **10**(1) (2023). https://doi.org/10.1186/s40537-023-00701-y

12. Tailor, S.A., Fernandez-Marques, J., Lane, N.D.: Degree-quant: quantization-aware training for graph neural networks (2020). https://doi.org/10.48550/ARXIV.2008.05000

13. Wang, Y., Feng, B., Ding, Y.: QGTC: accelerating quantized graph neural networks via GPU tensor core. In: Proceedings of the 27th ACM SIGPLAN Symposium on Principles and Practice of Parallel Programming, PPoPP 2022. ACM, March 2022. https://doi.org/10.1145/3503221.3508408

14. Wu, H., Judd, P., Zhang, X., Isaev, M., Micikevicius, P.: Integer quantization for deep learning inference: principles and empirical evaluation (2020). https://doi.org/10.48550/ARXIV.2004.09602

15. Xie, X., et al.: Accel-GCN: high-performance GPU accelerator design for graph convolution networks (2023). https://doi.org/10.48550/ARXIV.2308.11825

16. Yan, M., et al.: HyGCN: a GCN accelerator with hybrid architecture (2020). https://doi.org/10.48550/ARXIV.2001.02514

17. Yin, L., Wang, J., Zheng, H.: Exploring architecture, dataflow, and sparsity for GCN accelerators: a holistic framework. In: Proceedings of the Great Lakes Symposium on VLSI, GLSVLSI 2023. ACM, June 2023. https://doi.org/10.1145/3583781.3590243

Reconfigurable Edge Hardware
for Intelligent IDS: Systematic Approach

Wadid Foudhaili$^{(\boxtimes)}$ ⓘ, Anouar Nechiⓘ, Celine Thermannⓘ, Mohammad
Al Johmaniⓘ, Rainer Buchtyⓘ, Mladen Berekovicⓘ, and Saleh Mulhemⓘ

Institute of Computer Engineering (ITI), Universität zu Lübeck, Lübeck, Germany
`wadid.foudhaili@uni-luebeck.de`

Abstract. Intrusion detection systems (IDS) are crucial security measures nowadays to enforce network security. Their task is to detect
anomalies in network communication and identify, if not thwart, pos-
sibly malicious behavior. Recently, machine learning has been deployed
to construct intelligent IDS. This approach, however, is quite challenging particularly in distributed, highly dynamic, yet resource-constrained
systems like Edge setups. In this paper, we tackle this issue from multiple angles by analyzing the concept of intelligent IDS (I-IDS) while
addressing the specific requirements of Edge devices with a special focus
on reconfigurability. Then, we introduce a systematic approach to constructing the I-IDS on reconfigurable Edge hardware. For this, we implemented our proposed IDS on state-of-the-art Field Programmable Gate
Arrays (FPGAs) technology as (1) a purely FPGA-based dataflow processor (DFP) and (2) a co-designed approach featuring RISC-V soft-core
as FPGA-based soft-core processor (SCP). We complete our paper with
a comparison of the state of the art (SoA) in this domain. The results
show that DFP and SCP are both suitable for Edge applications from
hardware resource and energy efficiency perspectives. Our proposed DFP
solution clearly outperforms the SoA and demonstrates that required
high performance can be achieved without prohibitively high hardware
costs. This makes our proposed DFP suitable for Edge-based high-speed
applications like modern communication technology.

Keywords: Intrusion detection system · Reconfigurabile Hardware ·
Edge Device · FPGA-based RISC-V Soft-Core

1 Introduction

An Intrusion Detection System (IDS) is crucial in fortifying network security, such as, but not limited to inflicted Distributed Denial-of-Service attacks
(DDoS). Basically, an IDS acts as an additional defense layer, detecting and

This work has been partially funded by the German Ministry of Education and
Research (BMBF) via project RILKOSAN (16KISR010K) and partially via project
SILGENTAS (16KIS1837).

I. Skliarova et al. (Eds.): ARC 2024, LNCS 14553, pp. 48–62, 2024.
https://doi.org/10.1007/978-3-031-55673-9_4

responding to potential threats that may elude preemptive measures. It is also defined [12,32] as a security tool that constantly monitors host or network traffic or both to detect any suspicious behavior that violates the security policy and compromises its confidentiality, integrity, and availability. The typical outcome of the system is to generate alerts about detected malicious behavior to the host or network administrators.

A successful DDoS attack that was reported in 2016 [8] leaves us with the following conclusion *"If there was a distributed intrusion detection system, it might have been able to detect the attack at its early stage and limit the loss caused by the attack."* [29]. This capability of distributed IDS encompasses identifying malware, phishing attacks, and other cyber threats in an interactive manner.

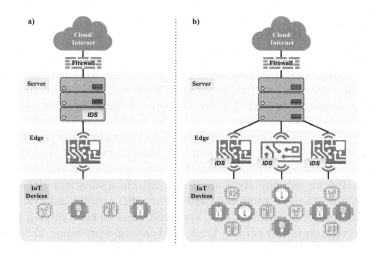

Fig. 1. (a) Conventional IDS vs (b) Distributed IDS on the Edge

Figure 1 shows two deployment scenarios of IDS that we call *conventional* compared to *Distributed Edge-based.* The distributed IDS should satisfy special requirements to meet the hardware and power constraints of the edge level. However, it should be noted that conventional IDS leveraging reconfigurable hardware dramatically improves the detection system's performance [14]. Therefore, reconfigurable hardware such as field-programmable gate arrays (FPGAs) has become one of the foundations for IDS on the Edge as well.

1.1 Machine Learning-Based IDS on the Edge

Machine learning (ML) models, particularly deep neural networks (DNN), have shown a potential to enhance the performance of intrusion detection mechanisms [13]. For instance, support vector machines (SVM) [11] and Hidden Naïve Bayes (HNB) [17] were proposed to enhance the accuracy and speed of the detection capability. The primary goal of ML-based IDS is to increase the number of correct predictions [13], including the not-yet-known attacks (Zero-day attacks), which makes it more efficient than signature-based methods. ML model quality can be evaluated using metrics, notably accuracy and F1 score [13]. Three main technical obstacles stall the building of ML-based IDS on the edge: (1) The considerable size of such a system renders implementations at the edge level a technical challenge, (2) required inference throughput on the resource-limited Edge-node hardware, and (3) update of the ML-based IDS requiring to re-initiate the whole system. Several approaches have been proposed to overcome these challenges, especially for the Edge-based deployment scenario. Therefore, a need exists for a clear methodology and criteria to build an ML-based IDS relying on reconfigurable Edge hardware.

1.2   Paper Contribution

In this paper, we present a systematic selection methodology to construct a machine learning-based intrusion detection system targeting reconfigurable Edge hardware. In particular, we first investigate the pros and cons of the reconfigurable Edge hardware in Sect. 3. Two hardware configurations are selected: an FPGA-based dataflow processor and a RISC-V soft-core as an FPGA-based soft-core processor. Further, we establish hardware/software performance evaluation criteria for ML-based IDS (Intelligent IDS) on the Edge in Sect. 4. Then, we construct several machine-learning models to serve as an Intelligent IDS in Sect. 5. Finally, we validate the established criteria against the detection systems running on the two proposed hardware configurations and evaluate their performance results in Sect. 5.3. Our approach aims at constructing an intelligent IDS relying on reconfigurable Edge hardware and providing high inference throughput to serve in high-performance Edge applications such as the future generation of high-speed communication technology.

To the best of our knowledge, this is the first work that establishes a systematic methodology for selecting a highly accurate ML-based IDS realized on two different configurations of reconfigurable Edge hardware.

2   Related Work

In the following, we highlight the main approaches that leverage the reconfigurable hardware to build an ML-based IDS.

2.1   FPGA-Based Dataflow Processor for ML-Based IDS

While the demand for FPGA-based dataflow processors (FPGA-based DFP) to accelerate ML and DNN algorithms using FPGAs grows, research on IDS designs in this area remains limited. FPGA-based DFP for ML-based IDS has been proposed in a few works, such as [26,31]. For example, a multilayer perceptron

(MLP) was implemented on a Xilinx Virtex-5 FPGA in [26]. The proposed network was trained on a smaller model with only six features from the NSL-KDD dataset [36]. It consists of two hidden layers. This MLP achieved a maximum throughput of 9.86 Gbps with packets containing 1500 bytes featuring a speedup of 11.6× compared to a GPU. In [31], LogicNets *"a methodology that allows trained quantized networks to be directly converted to an equivalent hardware"* [31] was deployed to map a quantized MLP to hardware building blocks. The resulting DFP achieves a highly efficient acceleration rate. In [20], a convolutional neural network (CNN) topology on a PYNQ-Z2 was implemented. A quantization technique to explore 8-, 4-, and 2-bit quantization was employed. Extra pre-processing steps were also applied to reshape the raw data as an image. The experimentation used the CICIDS2017 dataset to detect one of 13 possible attack categories. The demonstrated DFP achieved a throughput of 9635 inferences/s at 100 MHz with 99.4% accuracy for the 2-bit quantized design.

2.2 FPGA-Based Soft-Core Processor for ML-Based IDS

The use of RISC-V in intrusion detection and IoT security is the subject of recent research. A RISC-V SoC was proposed in [9] as a platform to build a test environment for a man-in-the-middle attack simulation. In [21], a new RISC-V SoC was built based on the previous RISC-V SoC [9] to construct a rule-based intrusion detection engine. The system runs Linux and uses Snort [2] to capture network packets. If a match with the rules is found, an alarm will be triggered, and the event will be written into a log file.

Several RISC-V soft cores to be used as a SCP have been proposed for performance-demanding and accelerated applications on the edge [10,16,35]. In [7], an SCP (RISC-V CV32E41P) was synthesized to run at around 65 MHz. The core is coupled to an on-FPGA tracer and arbiter to build a host-based IDS [4]. Moreover, a different IDS implementation [7] traces the hardware performance counters of the processor event values to detect any buffer overflow in the stack or heap in the Long-Range Wide Area Network (LoRaWan) protocol stack.

Following the state-of-the-art, we developed our own approach towards FPGA-based DFP and SCP for use in ML-based IDS targeting reconfigurable edge hardware. We hence will first discuss the advantages of reconfigurable hardware for IDS on the edge in the following section.

3   Reconfigurable Edge Hardware for IDS: Pros and Cons

Besides the relatively lower cost of hardware design deployment on reconfigurable hardware (RHW) compared to other technologies, RHW enables tuning the hardware to current application needs, offering flexible update and extension of an implemented design. This feature also reduces development and re-engineering costs. FPGAs exhibit several advantages, such as low cost in the silicon chip area, high performance, and low power consumption [5,19]. However, there are several limitations of RHW, most notably temporal or operational granularity. In the following, we highlight the pros and cons of FPGA-based DFP and SCP.

FPGA-based DFP feature both a high level of parallelism and a need for reconfigurability. Their design offers high performance and low energy consumption, as highlighted by benchmarking studies [6], particularly in DNN acceleration, making favorable comparisons with CPU and GPU platforms. However, the reconfigurability of FPGAs, while advantageous for computational acceleration, presents challenges due to the time- and power-consuming nature of the reconfiguration process. A trade-off has to be made between the static (running) phase and reconfiguration phases. Despite the long-standing proposal of reconfigurable computing architecture, it has not gained widespread popularity. One reason for this is the requirement to use hardware design languages and dedicated design environments adding complexity and costs for developers [33]. This is, however, mitigated by being able to perform a complete parallelization, hence allowing true parallel execution of operations without sacrificing inference accuracy. Parallelization and reducing an IDS's computational complexity are hence, the most prominent techniques used in an FPGA-based DFP.

FPGA-based SCP being software-programmable by nature, are easier accessible by software programmers. They, however, also come at some cost to be considered when deciding to choose an IDS deployment platform. An FPGA-based SCP implementation offers:

- **Flexibility.** FPGA-based SCP can execute an IDS based on different computation precisions offered by the employed soft-core, such as Float32, INT8, or INT4. Orthogonally, soft-cores can be adjusted, enhanced, and extended, meeting new IDS requirements whenever needed.
- **Execution efficiency (performance).** With the availability of vector extensions to exploit data-parallel workloads [10], very efficient intrusion detection capability can be offered.
- **Portability.** FPGA-based SCP can be implemented using cheaper FPGA resources, reducing overall system cost. Also, the code designed to run on a softcore might take advantage of high-level programming languages and libraries, thus making the developed code easily portable to other platforms.

On the other hand, the development complexity and limited availability are just examples of some disadvantages of FPGA-based SCP.

Table 1. Comparison of FPGA-based DFP and SCP.

Reconfigurable Hardware	Computation Precision	ML Topology Update	ML Parameters Update
FPGA-based DFP	Fixed	Not On fly	Partially
FPGA-based SCP	Flexible	On fly	Flexible

Table 1 shows a comparison between FPGA-based DFP and SCP based on characteristics natively supported by the hardware, namely: computation precision, ML topology, ML parameter update, and required update time, that can deliver the best achievable performance and allow reconfigurability.

FPGA-based DFP can easily accommodate ML hardware designs with floating point (FP), fixed point (FxP), and integer (INT) thanks to their reconfigurability. However, once an ML hardware design is programmed on the FPGA, it cannot be updated easily on the fly. Here, partial-dynamic reconfiguration could be a promising solution that allows a limited, predefined part of ML on an FPGA to be reconfigured while others continue working. Like any other CPU, FPGA-based SCP can easily accept any computation precision and update ML topology. In contrast, FPGA-based DFP requires repeating the process of generating a new hardware design to update ML topology. The same goes for updating trained parameters: FPGA-based DFP require a particular mechanism for external parameter loading. This makes FPGA-based DFP partially able to update trained parameters. In the case of FPGA-based SCP, updating the ML topology or its trained parameters is comparatively less complicated, more straightforward, and less time-consuming.

4 Performance Evaluation Criteria for IDS on the Edge

To evaluate the performance of an IDS on the Edge, specific acceleration criteria must be considered on both levels, i.e. algorithm and reconfigurable hardware. We will detail this in the following two sections.

4.1 IDS Algorithm Evaluation Criteria

The IDS should be accurate from a software perspective, i.e., it should detect an intrusion with high accuracy and negligible false alarms. In the case of *intelligent IDS*, several metrics can be used to evaluate how efficiently the ML model performs; these metrics can be highlighted as follows:

- **Precision (P)**. This metric is fundamental as one goal of an *intelligent IDS* is to minimize false positives. It measures how many of the positive predictions made are correct (true positives) [24].
- **Recall (R)**. It measures how many positive cases the classifier correctly predicted over all the positive cases in the data. This metric is also important because an IDS aims to detect as many attacks as possible [22].
- **F1 Score (F1)** described as the harmonic mean of the metrics *Precision* and *Recall* with both contributing equally to the score [24].

Additionally, it should satisfy the following criterion: Even though there are several types of intrusion with different occurrence frequencies, an IDS should stay accurate when bias toward one attack over the other accrues.

4.2 Reconfigurable Hardware Evaluation Criteria

In addition to meeting algorithmic requirements, also hardware criteria are to be met, which are:

- **Hardware Resource Utilization.** An ideal IDS for edge devices should consume as few as possible resources, especially the DSP components, which are the most power-demanding units. This criteria significantly impacts the other hardware criteria, mainly computational density.
- **Inference Throughput** [25]. This criterion measures how many packets are processed by the intrusion detection system in a given amount of time. The IDS throughput is measured by *Packets/sec*. It should be noted that the network capacity limits this metric.
- **Energy Efficiency** [25]. This criterion can be expressed as the inference throughput over energy consumption. For instance, the energy efficiency of the ML model for an IDS is evaluated by *Packets/sec/Watt*.
- **Computational Density** [25]. Computational density is a metric used in FPGA design, referring to the ratio of computations performed by a particular design over the number of resources utilized. In other words, this criterion indicates whether the hardware design suffers from resource underutilization or not. For instance, when two different accelerators deliver the same inference throughput, the one with the lower DSP usage is considered better regarding computational density. The computational density is expressed as *Throughput/#DSP* or *Throughput/#LUT*.
- **Flexibility** used to measure and compare the complexity of development, maintenance, and new features implementation as well as maintainability and adaptability to new ML models and to new network conditions.

Some of these criteria directly impact the others. For instance, the computational density is directly derived from throughput and resource utilization. Likewise, resource utilization may indirectly decrease energy efficiency if the resources are too power-demanding compared to the achieved throughput.

5   Proposed IDS Design Methodology

The previous discussion is applied to a 4-step approach in order to design, implement, and evaluate FPGA-based DFP and SCP approaches. We 1) construct several IDSs based on state-of-the-art algorithms in the ML domain, then 2) select ML models with high precision (P) and F1 scores and smaller model sizes in terms of byte, before 3) implementing the chosen ML for IDS on FPGA-based DFP and SCP and finally 4) analyzing these implementations regarding the proposed hardware criteria and, following a dedicated edge use-case, choosing the IDS implementation that matches the high-speed requirements of modern communication technology.

5.1   Step 1: Intelligent IDS

In this section, we outline the use and customization of several well-known ML models and MLP, on which our IDS is based. Choosing and adjusting the right model is paramount for both, detection quality and hardware use. As shown in the evaluation section, the resulting *Intelligent IDS* can offer vast performance at minimal hardware cost with NN capability at discerning intricate patterns in extensive datasets.

The BOT-IoT Dataset. Bot-IoT [18] was developed within a testbed environment, employing a constellation of virtual machines featuring diverse operating systems, network firewalls, network taps, the Node-red, and the Argus tools [27,28]. The Bot-IoT dataset is characterized by multiple sets and subsets, each distinguished by file format, size, and feature count variations. Figure 2 shows the dataset balance for each attack category and subcategory, reflecting the whole dataset's general imbalance. The BOT-IoT dataset includes several attack scenarios. From these, we select a subset that covers the following attacks: DoS (TCP, HTTP), reconnaissance (service scan and OS fingerprinting), theft (keylogging and data extraction), and intrusion-free.

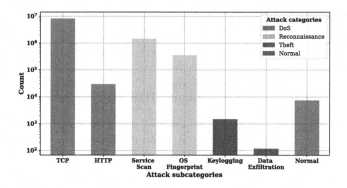

Fig. 2. Attack categories and subcategories distribution of the BOT-IoT dataset

Intelligent IDS Construction. This step involves partitioning the preprocessed data into an 80% training set and a 20% set for testing and evaluation. We first start with training XGBoost (XGB), Support Vector Machine (SVM), Naive Bayes (NB), Random Forest Classifier (RFC), and Decision Tree (DT). Additionally, three Multi-Layer Perceptron (MLP) models are trained, each of them tailored to distinct classification targets: attacks, categories, and subcategories. All of the three MLP models share a nearly identical topology, featuring an input layer with 24 inputs, followed by two hidden layers of sizes 32 and 64, respectively, and Rectified Linear Unit (*ReLU*) activation functions. The sole distinction among the MLP models resides in the configuration of the final layer, i.e., the classification layer. The *Attack* model is designed to discern the presence or absence of an attack; hence, its last layer has a size of 2 followed by a *Softmax* activation. Analogously, the *Category* and *Subcategory* models' classification layers exhibit sizes of 4 and 7, respectively, aligning with their distinct classification objectives.

5.2   Step 2: Intelligent IDS Selection

According to the introduced algorithm evaluation criteria, a performance comparison for each ML model is made. Table 2 compares model detection accuracy and size. NB exhibits a very low F1 Score. Therefore, it will be eliminated and we focus on ML models with a high F1 Score. Overall, XGboost and MLP outperform other models.

Table 2. Evaluation of ML algorithms for IDS: ML Metrics vs Size.

Algorithm	Attack detection				Category classification				Subcategory classification			
	P	R	F_1	size	P	R	F_1	size	P	R	F_1	size
XGB	1.00	1.00	1.00	0.38 MB	1.00	1.00	1.00	1.15 MB	0.99	0.99	0.99	2.15 MB
SVM	0.99	0.99	0.99	164 KB	1.00	0.99	1.00	288 KB	0.97	0.89	0.92	5.7 MB
NB	0.57	0.96	0.62	1.35 KB	0.78	0.94	0.78	2.23 KB	0.78	0.70	0.60	3.62 KB
RFC	1.00	0.97	0.98	123 KB	1.00	0.95	0.97	157 KB	0.70	0.59	0.62	0.2 MB
DT	0.99	0.99	0.99	2.23 KB	1.00	0.99	1.00	3.25 KB	0.83	0.81	0.82	4.35 KB
MLP	1.00	1.00	1.00	15.2 KB	1.00	1.00	1.00	15.8 KB	0.99	0.93	0.96	16.6 KB

5.3   Step 3: FPGA-Based Intelligent IDS Implementation

Here, we describe the experimental setup of the FPGA-based DFP and the RISC-V soft-core as FPGA-based SCP. Both experiments are evaluated using the Xilinx ZCU104 FPGA platform.

Experimental Setup. The experimental setup, illustrated in Fig. 3, includes the FPGA-based RISC-V SCP and the DFP experimental process. Opting for a 64-bit Rocket core [3], configured through the Chipyard framework [1], the Rocket core stands as a 5-stage single-issue in-order processor executing the 64-bit scalar RISC-V ISA [34]. This core can accommodate operating systems and features an optional IEEE 754-2008-compliant FPU for single- and double-precision floating-point operations, including fused multiply-accumulate. MLP models are saved as ONNX models, transformed into C code for seamless porting onto a RISC-V soft-core, and compiled using the appropriate RISC-V GNU toolchain and flags[1] for bare-metal execution.

In contrast, the approach for the FPGA-based DFP involved converting trained models to HLS projects using hls4ml. Notably, hls4ml lacked inherent support for Float32 conversion, prompting manual intervention to adjust data types for different layers and activation functions. The Softmax function

---

[1] $ riscv64-unknown-elf-gcc -std=gnu99 -O2 -Wall -lm -fno-common
   -fno-builtin-printf -specs=htifnano.specs
   $ riscv64-unknown-elf-gcc -static -T riscv64-unknown-elf/lib/htif.ld
   -lm.

is also modified to accommodate Float32 operations, ensuring a fair comparison between the FPGA-based DFP and SCP. Subsequently, IPs for various MLP models are generated and integrated into a corresponding FPGA design, and the resulting Bitstreams are deployed on the FPGA platform for benchmarking.

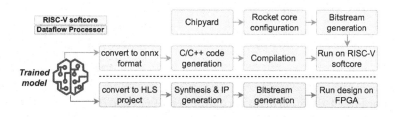

Fig. 3. IDS Experimental Setup RISC-V Soft-core and the FPGA-based DFP.

5.4 Step 4: Systematic Implementation Comparison

Hardware Usage Comparison: Figure 4-(a) shows the required hardware resources to implement FPGA-based DFP as three individual MLP IPs. All the IPs exhibit identical Block RAM (BRAM) utilization ratios for FPGA-based DFP. This uniformity can be attributed to the shared topology among MLP models, except for the last layer. The shared structure comprises two layers, constituting the most memory-intensive part due to their incorporation of most model parameters. However, slight variations in other resources arise from the intentional partitioning of parameters and result arrays in the last Softmax layer, mapped as Look-Up Tables (LUTs) and First-In-First-Out (FIFO) structures. The size of the Softmax layer accounts for the marginal fluctuations in the use of the Digital Signal Processors (DSP).

To compare FPGA-based DFP and RISC-V SCP, we implement them to operate at the same frequency of 100 MHz. Their respective hardware utilization ratios are illustrated in Fig. 4-(b). The high parallelization of the FPGA-based DFPs requires more resources than the FPGA-based RISC-V SCP, except for the BRAM units, which seem to be used more by the softcore for the caches. In contrast, FPGA-based DFPs require more LUTs, FIFOs, and DSPs for parallelized processing.

Comparison of Throughput, Energy Efficiency and Logic Density. We analyze and compare the two designs based on the earlier-defined criteria. The FPGA-based DFP is configured so that every compute unit executes only four multiply-accumulate operations sequentially, resulting in a higher parallelism. A design parameter, namely *Reuse factor*, controls such a parallelism mechanism. Additionally, the last Softmax layer was fully unrolled to compensate for the extra latency overhead caused by using Float32 arithmetic. As a result, FPGA-based DFP exhibits ≈ 6× higher throughput than the FPGA-based RISC-V SCP, as shown in Table 3. FPGA-based RISC-V SCP, in the term, draws only

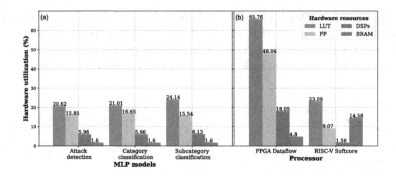

Fig. 4. Hardware Utilization of (a) our 3 MLPs on FPGA and (b) FPGA-based RISC-V SCP vs. Overall MLPs as FPGA-based DFP.

2.34 W, almost half the power of the FPGA-based DFP. However, its throughput superiority makes the latter ≈ 3× more energy efficient than FPGA-based RISC-V SCP. Also, this is why it exhibits between 5 and 6x higher logic density. These measures can undoubtedly be even higher with low-precision arithmetic such as fixed-point and integer, especially for FPGA-based DFP.

Table 3. FPGA-based DFP vs RISC-V SCP with Float32 Precision

MLP Model	Throughput *Packets/sec*	Energy Efficiency *Packets/sec/W*	Logic Density *Packets/sec/LUT*
FPGA-based DFP			
Attack	1166861 (1.16 M)	265799 (265 K)	24.55
Category	1135073 (1.13 M)	255589 (255 K)	23.44
Subcategory	1118568 (1.11 M)	249346 (249 K)	20.11
RISC-V SCP - Optimized Baremetal			
Attack	202849 (202 K)	86650 (86 K)	4.157
Category	197500 (197 K)	84365 (84 K)	4.047
Subcategory	197342 (197 K)	84298 (84 K)	4.44

Flexibility Comparison. Both processing systems have been evaluated based on their flexibility as detailed in Table 4. The flexibility comparison is dedicated to the implemented processors and is based on the above-mentioned aspects: precision, topology, and parameter updates. Additionally, we investigate the

Table 4. Flexibility Comparison of FPGA-based DFP and RISC-V SCP.

Processor	Precision			Topology	Parameters	Update
	FP	FxP	INT	update	update	time
FPGA-based DFP	yes	yes	yes	no	no[1]	longer
FPGA-based RISC-V SCP	yes	no	yes[2]	yes	yes	shorter

1 Only possible if the design includes an external weights loading mechanism.
2 Supports only a subset of integers, such as INT8/16/32.

required time to update. The proposed FPGA-based DFP is very flexible regarding computation precision, such as floating point (FP), fixed point (FxP), and integer (INT) due to FPGA reconfigurability. The chosen FPGA-based RISC-V SCP, in term, has a fixed data-path, which limits its precision capability to FP and a specific set of integers, such as INT8, 16, and 32. Consequently, it offers fewer options to optimize the ML-based IDS through quantization. However, updating the ML topology or its trained parameters is significantly less complicated and, therefore, more straightforward in the case of FPGA-based RISC-V SCP; it only requires a new source-code compilation.

Table 5. State of the Art FPGA-based DFP for ML-based IDS.

References	[20]	[31]	[26]	[15]	This work		
FPGA	xc7Z020	xc7Z020	xc5vtx	xc7Z020	xczu7ev		
Frequency (MHz)	100	471	104	76	100		
Dataset	CICIDS2017 [30]	UNSW-NB15 [23]	NSL-KDD [36]	NSL-KDD	BOT-IoT [18]		
ML topology	CNN	MLP	MLP	MLP	MLP		
Number of layers	4×Conv + 2×FC	5×FC	2×FC	3×FC	3×FC		
Intrusion Classes	13	2	2	2	2	4	7
Accuracy (%)	99.4	91.3	87.3	80.52	99.9	99.9	99.9
Throughput (Packets/sec)	9635	754292	821667	217074	1.16 M	1.13 M	1.11 M
LUT usage	24635	15494	117082	26463	47514	48413	55627
Usage ratio (%)	46.3	29.12	78.2	50	20.6	21	24.1

Proposed FPGA-Based DFP Compared to the State of the Art.
Table 5 compares our proposed FPGA-based DFP for ML-based IDS and the state of the art in this domain. The results show our proposed intelligent IDS detects 13 different intrusion classes, and its implementation as FPGA-based DFP exhibits very high throughput, yet low hardware resources. This makes it suitable for application at the edge level and clearly demonstrates that such a high-performance solution does not necessarily come at prohibitively high hardware costs.

6 Conclusion

Current modern approaches to intrusion detection systems (IDS) feature the use of machine learning (ML). However, ML-based IDSs still face technical obstacles such as their considerable size, and their update requires re-initiating the whole IDS. In this paper, we investigate ML-based IDS targeting the edge level, featuring reconfigurable edge nodes. Here, typically high throughput is required in order to keep up with the real-time data transmissions, yet node resource use is constrained. Orthogonally, intrusion detection in a reconfigurable system also demands an equally flexible adaptability with respect to detection itself. We hence construct a systematic approach to ML-based intrusion detection on the edge, leading to the proposed Intelligent IDS. We discuss two possible FPGA-based implementation scenarios, one plain hardware implementation (FPGA-based dataflow processor, DFP) and one featuring a RISC-V softcore. Both implementations are evaluated and compared to each other and the state of the art. The results clearly demonstrate that the high performance of a hardware implementation does not necessarily come at prohibitively high hardware cost, with our solution exhibiting higher throughput, better energy efficiency, and better logic density in addition to an overall better configurability. Our proposed DFP hence can be employed in high-performance Edge-based applications like modern communication technology.

Disclosure of Interests. The authors have no competing interests to declare that are relevant to the content of this article.

References

1. Amid, A., et al.: Chipyard: integrated design, simulation, and implementation framework for custom SoCS. IEEE Micro **40**(4), 10–21 (2020). https://doi.org/10.1109/MM.2020.2996616
2. Amon, C., Shinder, T.W., Carasik-Henmi, A.: Introducing snort. In: The Best Damn Firewall Book Period, pp. 1183–1208. Syngress, Burlington (2003). https://doi.org/10.1016/B978-193183690-6/50070-4
3. Asanović, K., et al.: The rocket chip generator. Technical report, UCB/EECS-2016-17, EECS Department, University of California, Berkeley, April 2016
4. Azad, T.B.: Locking down your XenApp server. In: Azad, T.B. (ed.) Securing Citrix Presentation Server in the Enterprise, pp. 487–555. Syngress, Burlington (2008). https://doi.org/10.1016/B978-1-59749-281-2.00007-X
5. Babu, P., Parthasarathy, E.: Reconfigurable FPGA architectures: a survey and applications. J. Inst. Eng. Ser. B **102**, 143–156 (2021)
6. Blott, M., et al.: Evaluation of optimized CNNs on FPGA and Non-FPGA based accelerators using a novel benchmarking approach. In: Proceedings of the 2020 ACM/SIGDA International Symposium on Field-Programmable Gate Arrays, FPGA 2020, p. 317. Association for Computing Machinery, New York, NY, USA (2020). https://doi.org/10.1145/3373087.3375348

7. Bouazzati, M.E., Tessier, R., Tanguy, P., Gogniat, G.: A lightweight intrusion detection system against IoT memory corruption attacks. In: 2023 26th International Symposium on Design and Diagnostics of Electronic Circuits and Systems (DDECS), pp. 118–123 (2023). https://doi.org/10.1109/DDECS57882.2023. 10139718

8. Brewster, T.: How hacked cameras are helping launch the biggest attacks the internet has ever seen. Forbes (2016). https://www.forbes.com/sites/thomasbrewster/ 2016/09/25/brian-krebs-overwatch-ovh-smashed-by-largest-ddos-attacks-ever/

9. Cai, B., Xie, S., Liang, Q., Lu, W.: Research on penetration testing of IoT gateway based on RISC-V. In: 2022 International Symposium on Advances in Informatics, Electronics and Education (ISAIEE), pp. 422–425 (2022). https://doi.org/10.1109/ ISAIEE57420.2022.00093

10. Chander, V.N., Varghese, K.: A soft RISC-V vector processor for edge-AI. In: 2022 35th International Conference on VLSI Design and 2022 21st International Conference on Embedded Systems (VLSID), pp. 263–268 (2022). https://doi.org/ 10.1109/VLSID2022.2022.00058

11. Chen, W.H., Hsu, S.H., Shen, H.P.: Application of SVM and ANN for intrusion detection. Comput. Oper. Res. **32**(10), 2617–2634 (2005)

12. Denning, D.E.: An intrusion-detection model. IEEE Trans. Softw. Eng. **SE-13**(2), 222–232 (1987)

13. Disha, R.A., Waheed, S.: Performance analysis of machine learning models for intrusion detection system using Gini impurity-based weighted random forest (GIWRF) feature selection technique. Cybersecurity **5**(1), 1 (2022)

14. Hutchings, B., Franklin, R., Carver, D.: Assisting network intrusion detection with reconfigurable hardware. In: Proceedings. 10th Annual IEEE Symposium on Field-Programmable Custom Computing Machines, pp. 111–120 (2002). https://doi.org/ 10.1109/FPGA.2002.1106666

15. Ioannou, L., Fahmy, S.A.: Network intrusion detection using neural networks on FPGA SoCS. In: 2019 29th International Conference on Field Programmable Logic and Applications (FPL), pp. 232–238. IEEE (2019)

16. Kimura, Y., Ootsu, K., Tsuchiya, T., Yokota, T.: Development of RISC-V based soft-core processor with scalable vector extension for embedded system. In: Proceedings of the the 8th International Virtual Conference on Applied Computing & Information Technology, ACIT 2021, pp. 13–18. Association for Computing Machinery, New York, NY, USA (2021). https://doi.org/10.1145/3468081.3471061

17. Koc, L., Mazzuchi, T.A., Sarkani, S.: A network intrusion detection system based on a hidden Naïve Bayes multiclass classifier. Expert Syst. Appl. **39**(18), 13492–13500 (2012)

18. Koroniotis, N., Moustafa, N., Sitnikova, E., Turnbull, B.: Towards the development of realistic botnet dataset in the internet of things for network forensic analytics: Bot-IoT dataset. Futur. Gener. Comput. Syst. **100**, 779–796 (2019)

19. Kuon, I., Rose, J.: Measuring the gap between FPGAs and ASICs. In: Proceedings of the 2006 ACM/SIGDA 14th International Symposium on Field Programmable Gate Arrays, pp. 21–30 (2006)

20. Le Jeune, L., Goedemé, T., Mentens, N.: Towards real-time deep learning-based network intrusion detection on FPGA. In: Zhou, J., et al. (eds.) ACNS 2021. LNCS, vol. 12809, pp. 133–150. Springer, Cham (2021). https://doi.org/10.1007/978-3-030-81645-2_9

21. Liang, Q., Xie, S., Cai, B.: Intelligent home IoT intrusion detection system based on RISC-V. In: 2023 IEEE 3rd International Conference on Power, Electronics and

Computer Applications (ICPECA), pp. 296–300 (2023). https://doi.org/10.1109/ICPECA56706.2023.10076248

22. Mishra, A.: Evaluating machine learning models, pp. 115–132. John Wiley and Sons, Ltd. (2019). https://doi.org/10.1002/9781119556749.ch5

23. Moustafa, N., Slay, J.: UNSW-NB15: a comprehensive data set for network intrusion detection systems (UNSW-NB15 network data set). In: 2015 Military Communications and Information Systems Conference (MilCIS), pp. 1–6 (2015). https://doi.org/10.1109/MilCIS.2015.7348942

24. Müller, A.C., Guido, S.: Introduction to Machine Learning with Python: A Guide for Data Scientists. O'Reilly Media, Inc. (2016)

25. Nechi, A., Groth, L., Mulhem, S., Merchant, F., Buchty, R., Berekovic, M.: FPGA-based deep learning inference accelerators: where are we standing? ACM Trans. Reconfigurable Technol. Syst. **16**(4) (2023). https://doi.org/10.1145/3613963

26. Ngo, D.-M., Tran-Thanh, B., Dang, T., Tran, T., Thinh, T.N., Pham-Quoc, C.: High-throughput machine learning approaches for network attacks detection on FPGA. In: Vinh, P.C., Rakib, A. (eds.) ICCASA/ICTCC -2019. LNICST, vol. 298, pp. 47–60. Springer, Cham (2019). https://doi.org/10.1007/978-3-030-34365-1_5

27. Node-RED: Low-code programming for event-driven applications (2021). https://nodered.org/

28. QOSIENT, LLC: Argus (2023). https://openargus.org/

29. Sha, K., Yang, T.A., Wei, W., Davari, S.: A survey of edge computing-based designs for IoT security. Digit. Commun. Netw. **6**(2), 195–202 (2020)

30. Sharafaldin, I., Lashkari, A.H., Ghorbani, A.A.: Toward generating a new intrusion detection dataset and intrusion traffic characterization. In: 4th International Conference on Information Systems Security and Privacy (ICISSP), Portugal (2018)

31. Umuroglu, Y., Akhauri, Y., Fraser, N.J., Blott, M.: LogicNets: co-designed neural networks and circuits for extreme-throughput applications. In: 2020 30th International Conference on Field-Programmable Logic and Applications (FPL), pp. 291–297 (2020). https://doi.org/10.1109/FPL50879.2020.00055

32. Vasilomanolakis, E., Karuppayah, S., Mühlhäuser, M., Fischer, M.: Taxonomy and survey of collaborative intrusion detection. ACM Comput. Surv. (CSUR) **47**(4), 1–33 (2015)

33. Wang, T., Wang, C., Zhou, X., Chen, H.: An overview of FPGA based deep learning accelerators: challenges and opportunities. In: 2019 IEEE 21st International Conference on High Performance Computing and Communications; IEEE 17th International Conference on Smart City; IEEE 5th International Conference on Data Science and Systems (HPCC/SmartCity/DSS), pp. 1674–1681 (2019). https://doi.org/10.1109/HPCC/SmartCity/DSS.2019.00229

34. Waterman, A.: Design of the RISC-V instruction set architecture. Ph.D. thesis, EECS Department, University of California, Berkeley, January 2016. https://www2.eecs.berkeley.edu/Pubs/TechRpts/2016/EECS-2016-1.html

35. Yiannacouras, P., Steffan, J.G., Rose, J.: VESPA: portable, scalable, and flexible FPGA-based vector processors. In: Proceedings of the 2008 International Conference on Compilers, Architectures and Synthesis for Embedded Systems, CASES 2008, pp. 61–70. Association for Computing Machinery, New York, NY, USA (2008). https://doi.org/10.1145/1450095.1450107

36. Zhao, R.: NSL-KDD (2022). https://doi.org/10.21227/8rpg-qt98

Bridging the Gap in ECG Classification: Integrating Self-supervised Learning with Human-in-the-Loop Amid Medical Equipment Hardware Constraints

Guilherme Silva[ID], Pedro Silva[ID], Gladston Moreira[ID], and Eduardo Luz[✉][ID]

Federal University of Ouro Preto, Ouro Preto, MG 35.400-000, Brazil
guilherme.lopes@aluno.ufop.edu.br, eduluz@ufop.edu.br
https://csilab.ufop.br/

Abstract. Arrhythmia, a cardiac condition, is frequently diagnosed by classifying heartbeats using electrocardiograms (ECG). This classification is a crucial step in medical diagnosis and can be significantly improved by employing computational methods to analyze the ECG data. Despite the extensive literature on this subject, the high inter-patient variability and noise in ECG signals pose challenges in the development of computational methods. Deep learning methods represent state-of-the-art solutions to diverse problems in computer vision, signal processing, and pattern recognition, mainly due to advancements enabled by self-supervised learning. In this work, we propose a self-supervised approach for ECG beat classification and a specific pretext task for ECG, termed ECGPuzzle. This approach allows for fine-tuning a deep learning model to an individual, improving the model's generalization. Given the low computational power of medical equipment and the need for on-site training, hardware acceleration is indispensable. Thus, we investigate the feasibility of this proposal on three distinct computational systems and discuss potential manners to train a model on an embedded system.

Keywords: Self-supervised Learning · Hardware-acceleration · Arrhythmia Detection · ECG

1 Introduction

Arrhythmia classification in ECG signals is complex and error-prone, especially in real-time monitoring [12]. Computational methods can improve detection accuracy and diagnostic assertiveness. Adhering to medical standards, like those from the Association for the Advancement of Medical Instrumentation (AAMI) [2], is crucial for building accurate systems. This includes using certified databases like the MIT-BIH and following recommendations for data division, such as the patient-wise heartbeat division suggested by de Chazal *et al.* [6]. However, algorithms face a significant performance drop under these standards, reflecting the challenges of real-life scenarios [11].

© The Author(s), under exclusive license to Springer Nature Switzerland AG 2024
I. Skliarova et al. (Eds.): ARC 2024, LNCS 14553, pp. 63–74, 2024.
https://doi.org/10.1007/978-3-031-55673-9_5

The main challenge regarding arrhythmia detection is the intra-patient variation due to the nature of the ECG signal and its susceptibility to all sorts of noise. Thus, applying a general machine learning model in practice is a difficult task to solve. A simple solution is to make the model learn the specificities of the ECG signal for each individual through a self-supervised learning (SSL) strategy. The use of SSL may allow a customized adjustment of the machine-learning models with humans in the loop.

By leveraging unlabeled data, the SSL strategy offers an alternative to specializing in a pre-trained model for a specific user, potentially overcoming the intra-class variability and noise inherent in ECG signals. Adopting these advanced methods has costs, particularly regarding computational resources, but specializing in a model without labeling new data for a specific individual is a feasible alternative.

Empirical research has underscored the efficacy of SSL in the realm of ECG analysis. For instance, one study implemented SSL to anticipate the occurrence of the QRS complex and leveraged the features learned during this process to enhance the accuracy of ECG classification [17]. Additionally, another study corroborated the superiority of representations derived from SSL over conventional features in the context of arrhythmia detection [3].

Several studies have utilized FPGAs to accelerate CNNs. For instance, Liu et al. [10] developed an FPGA-based AI accelerator for ECG analysis using a 1-D CNN and heart rate estimator on an Intel Cyclone V FPGA. This system achieved speeds 43.08 times faster than an ARM-Cortex A53 and 8.38× faster than an Intel Core i7-8700 CPU, with remarkable energy efficiency (63.48 GOPS/W) and low power consumption (67.74 mW), making it suitable for wearable ECG devices. Similarly, Bie et al. [4] created a scalable, high-performance CNN accelerator optimized for depthwise separable convolution. Tested with MobileNetV2 on an Arria 10 SoC FPGA, it processed ImageNet pictures in 3.75 ms (266.6 fps), achieving a 20x speedup over CPU performance.

Boutros et al. [5] evaluated three computational architectures - ASU-like, Intel-DLA-like, and Chain-NN-like - for CNN inference acceleration on an Intel Arria 10 FPGA and compared them with 28 nm ASICs. Tested across VGG-16, AlexNet, and ResNet-50 models, the study found that FPGAs had an 8.7x larger area ratio and were 2.8x to 6.3x slower than ASICs, with the Intel-DLA-like architecture having the smallest performance discrepancy. This suggests a need for further investigation into the most effective algorithm for CNN acceleration, comparing FPGAs and ASICs.

Considering the substantial computational requirements of self-supervised learning (SSL) and deep learning, particularly in the context of Convolutional Neural Networks (CNNs), the feasibility of implementing SSL-based methods on medical devices with limited hardware capabilities becomes a crucial consideration. Despite these advancements, none of these studies have investigated the acceleration of CNNs using a self-supervised approach. This highlights a gap in the current research and underscores the importance of exploring SSL in the context of CNN acceleration on modest hardware platforms.

Upon this fact, we aim to answer the research question of whether an SSL strategy could be integrated into an embedded system similar to medical equipment (such as a Raspberry Pi) and enhance the accuracy without making its use unfeasible. The investigation is within the context of the proposed ECG-WavePuzzle pretext task, aimed at refining and adapting deep learning models for individual patients to improve generalization in clinical settings. We aim to facilitate timely and accurate diagnostics for heart diseases.

To properly answer the research question, three distinct computational systems were investigated: two hardware-accelerated systems (a desktop with an NVIDIA 3090 GPU and an NVIDIA Jetson for embedded systems) and a non-accelerated system (Raspberry Pi with only an ARM CPU). The results emphasize the urgent need for efficient computational strategies and hardware acceleration to ensure the practical deployment of SSL models in medical diagnostics, a central theme pursued in the ongoing research [15]. Experimental data showed SSL improved global accuracy by 10.77% and reduced VEB class false negatives. A smaller batch size correlated with faster processing. However, SSL's high processing time on Raspberry Pi suggests a need for hardware acceleration.

2   Methodology

This section introduces a self-supervised learning approach for arrhythmia classification. We use an Autoencoder algorithm to filter out anomalous beats, optimizing the self-supervised learning process designed primarily for normal beats. The method involves segmenting the ECG signal into beats, removing abnormal heartbeats with an Autoencoder, and then applying a pretext task as the initial step in self-supervised learning.

2.1   Segmentation

The proposed method requires a sequence of heartbeats from a patient's cardiac signal. The process involves normalizing the signal to a range of $[-1, 1]$, identifying ECG R-peaks, segmenting the signal into heartbeats based on R-peak locations and labeling them per the associated disease, and resizing each ECG heartbeat to 300 samples. Notably, this preprocessing excludes filtering or noise removal.

2.2   Anomaly Detection with Autoencoders

An Autoencoder (AE) is a neural network for unsupervised learning, aiming to represent data in a lower dimension [18]. It has an encoder, a bottleneck, and a decoder to minimize reconstruction error - the difference between input and output. AEs identify anomalies by comparing this error against a threshold, trained on normal data, with higher errors indicating anomalies [19]. In the study, the AE was trained on normal ECG beats with the exclusion of minority classes, and the inputs were scaled between 0 and 1 to achieve optimal performance and facilitate the interpretation of results. The output range of the AE, which is governed by the activation function, was aligned with the input range by employing a sigmoid function in the output layer, thereby enhancing the classification of anomalies.

An ECG is deemed anomalous if its reconstruction error exceeds one standard deviation from the normal training examples, referred to as the threshold. This threshold is computed using the following Eq. 1:

$$Th = mean(TL) + std(TL),\tag{1}$$

where Th is the threshold, TL is the train loss, $mean()$ is the mean function and $std()$ is the standard deviation function.

2.3   Self-supervised Learning for ECG

In SSL applied to ECG analysis, the training model engages in a preliminary task (pretext task) that leverages the inherent structure of ECG signals. This process aims to derive meaningful representations beneficial for subsequent tasks, such as detecting and classifying arrhythmias. For instance, the model may undergo training to anticipate the sequence of fiducial points-namely the P wave, QRS complex, and T wave-within a single heartbeat. Through this exercise, the model acquires an understanding of critical ECG characteristics instrumental in identifying cardiac irregularities.

Pretext task: *ECGWavePuzzle.* The ECGWavePuzzle is a pretext function designed for a machine learning model to passively recognize the fiducial points of an ECG waveform: the P, QRS, and T waves. The segmented heartbeat is divided into three fiducial points based on the QRS complex demarcation. The beginning of each segment is employed by a proportion of the QRS complex (P_{QRS}), as defined in the following equation:

$$B_{QRS} = trunc\left(\frac{BS}{2}\right) - trunc\left(\frac{BS \cdot P_{QRS}}{2}\right),\tag{2}$$

where $trunc$ is a truncate function and BS indicates the beat size. The end of a segment is defined:

$$E_{QRS} = B_{QRS} + trunc\left(BS \cdot P_{QRS}\right),\tag{3}$$

where the parameter P_{QRS} was ascertained via a grid search strategy. The segmentation of the ECG signal is depicted in Fig. 1.

With the segmented beats and fiducial points delimited (B_{QRS} and E_{QRS}), a synthetic database is developed. The arrhythmia problem is then reformulated as a jigsaw problem through the permutation of fiducial points into six distinct classes, as visually represented in Fig. 2.

A neural network is employed in the ECGWavePuzzle task to solve the jigsaw puzzle and reconstruct the original sequence. Through this process, the trained model is expected to passively learn the shape of the fiducial points.

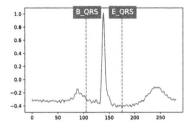

Fig. 1. Signal partition based on the P, QRS, and T waves.

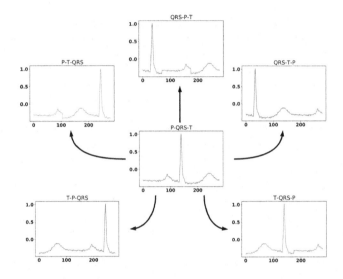

Fig. 2. The original beat in the center (P-QRS-T) with variations created by the pretext task.

Proposed Approach. Within the framework of our study, a model was initially trained using a self-supervised learning (SSL) technique on an expansive database without labels, employing a specifically designed pretext task. This training phase was followed by fine-tuning the model for a targeted supervised task supported by a comparatively small set of labeled data. The novel approach adopted in this research successfully addresses the challenge of architectural conformity traditionally required for both SSL and supervised tasks. It achieves this by excluding the final layer, tailored to the pretext task, thereby refining the model's architecture for enhanced classification of arrhythmias.

The schematic representation of the framework is illustrated in Fig. 3.

The methodology employed in this study encompasses two distinct phases: the offline and online stages. The offline stage is characterized by the analysis of ECG data conducted in a laboratory setting, separate from clinical

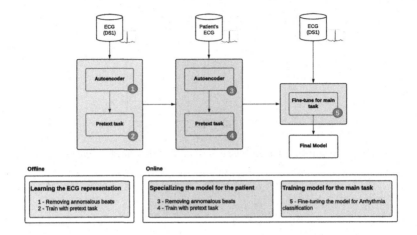

Fig. 3. Proposed Self-Supervised Learning with human-in-the-loop approach.

environments. Conversely, the online stage is implemented within a clinical context, emphasizing the training of models on patient-specific heartbeat data.

This approach is structured around five principal steps:

1. **Step 1:** Segment and select normal heartbeats from the training database and use an autoencoder to remove abnormal ones.
2. **Step 2:** Train the model on the pretext task with the filtered data to learn ECG morphology, using a final layer with six output neurons for ECG permutation prediction.
3. **Step 3:** Use the autoencoder to filter out arrhythmic heartbeats from a patient's five-minute ECG, keeping only normal class beats.
4. **Step 4:** Customize the model for each patient using the pretext task on the filtered data, applying a human-in-the-loop approach.
5. **Step 5:** Remove the pretext task's final layer from the patient-specific model and introduce a new layer with three neurons for classifying arrhythmias into three categories. Train this model on the DS1 database heartbeats and evaluate it on the patient's remaining heartbeats.

CNN Model. The network used for training and testing is referred to as ECGnet, specifically developed for this evaluation. The ECGnet model is shown in Fig. 4. The first layer is a 1D convolutional layer with 64 filters, a kernel size of 3, and ReLU activation function followed by a max pooling. The next layer is another 1D convolutional layer with 128 filters and a kernel size of 3, followed by a max pooling layer. The next three layers are similar to 1D convolutional layers with increasing filter sizes and max pooling layers. The last layer before the output layer is a flatten layer, which flattens the output from the previous layers into a 1D array. The output layer consists of two dense layers, each with ReLU activation and a dropout layer with a dropout rate of 0.5 in between. The first dense layer has 512 units, and the second has 256 units.

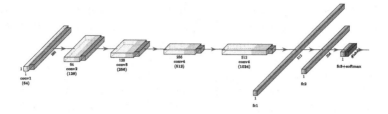

Fig. 4. ECGNet, the CNN model employed in our approach

3   Experiments and Preliminary Results

How feasible is it to integrate a Self-Supervised Learning (SSL)-based ECG classification method into a modest computational system, similar to standard hospital medical equipment? - we have conducted experiments, which are detailed in the subsequent section.

3.1   Database

In this study, the MIT-BIH Arrhythmia Database was utilized, featuring records with two ECG leads to account for variations in electrode placement: a modified lead II for beat detection and another lead, often V1 but sometimes V2, V5, or V4, for specific arrhythmia classification like SVEB and EBV [8]. The research methodology was aligned with clinical realities by adhering to the ANSI/AAMI EC57:1998/(R)2008 standard [2], which provides guidelines for reporting arrhythmia classification algorithm results. Additionally, a patient-based division approach, as outlined in [6], was employed to ensure no patient beat overlap between training and testing, mirroring real-world hospital scenarios.

3.2   Embedded System Viability: With/Without Acceleration Approach

SSL Efficacy in Enhancing Generalization of Classification. The study was conducted on a computing system with an AMD Ryzen Threadripper 3960X (24-core, 2.2 GHz), 128 GB DDR4 RAM, and a GeForce RTX 3090 GPU. It expands the work in [15] on the ECGWavePuzzle task and Self-Supervised Learning (SSL) technique for arrhythmia detection, using a Human-in-the-loop approach and a network adjusted for a 0.40 QRS complex proportion. The research evaluated the efficacy of SSL in Arrhythmia Classification under two conditions, with and without the pretext task. The findings demonstrated that SSL increased the average global accuracy by 10.77% and lowered the average false negative rate for the Ventricular Ectopic Beat (VEB) class. Additionally, the method uniquely identified arrhythmic patterns, particularly in the Supraventricular Ectopic Beat (SVEB) class, across several recordings (e.g., 100, 103, 219, 222, 228, 234), highlighting SSL's potential to uncover subtle arrhythmic patterns that might be overlooked in conventional supervised methods.

Embeddeding Self-supervised Leaning. Our approach to replicating real-world clinical scenarios involves an initial offline stage (described in Sect. 2.3) on a desktop GPU, followed by model specialization to each patient's heartbeat patterns on an embedded system. We focused on heartbeats from five patients in the DS2 set for concentrated analysis. The study aimed to assess the computational cost of deploying our approach across various hardware platforms in hospital settings. This involved comparing the model's performance in three different hardware environments:

1. NVIDIA Jetson Nano Development Kit: Ideal for machine learning with its Quad-core ARM Cortex-A57 CPU, 128-core Maxwell GPU, and 4 GB LPDDR4 memory, offering 472 GFLOPs of performance. It's a balanced option for computational power and energy efficiency in hospitals.
2. Raspberry Pi 4 (4 GB Model): Lacks a GPU but is similar to hardware employed in healthcare (RISC CPU). Equipped with a Broadcom BCM2711 and Quad-core Cortex-A72 SoC, it's suitable for testing in less resource-intensive environments and is the most common setup in hospital equipment.
3. NVIDIA 3090 GPU: A high-end server setup with an AMD Ryzen Threadripper 3960X CPU, 128 GB DDR4 RAM, and a GeForce RTX 3090 GPU. This setup benchmarks maximum performance, contrasting the capabilities of the Jetson Nano and Raspberry Pi.

The model was deployed in each of these hardware environments, and critical performance metrics, including processing speed, memory usage, and power consumption, were measured. These metrics offer valuable insights into the computational requirements of the model and its aptness for real-time applications within a hospital context. The comparative analysis across the three platforms is intended to underscore the trade-offs between computational prowess and resource limitations, thereby informing the decision-making process for selecting the most suitable hardware in healthcare settings.

3.3   Experimental Results

The study reveals distinct performance variations across the three different hardware platforms. This underscores a pivotal challenge in balancing resources, efficient processing, and hardware constraints, particularly in settings with limited space and energy resources. Figure 5 illustrates each batch size's average processing time. The decision to cap the batch size at 35 was largely influenced by the Jetson Nano's maximum capacity for batch sizes. Exceeding this threshold causes a malfunction in Jetson Nano which established 35 as the upper boundary for the analysis.

Based on Fig. 5, it is immediately apparent that there is an inverse correlation between batch size and average processing time on all platforms, illustrating the efficacy of batch processing in data-intensive operations. Notably, the desktop GPU exhibits markedly lower processing times, underscoring its superior computational power over the Jetson Nano and Raspberry Pi. However, the feasibility

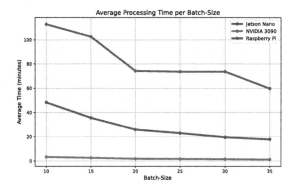

Fig. 5. Comparison of Average Processing Time for ECG Classification between Jetson Nano, Desktop with NVIDIA 3090, and Raspberry Pi with Adjusted Time Scale

of deploying such computational resources in embedded systems is questioned, as Raspberry Pi's processing times are prohibitively long, indicating the necessity for hardware acceleration to enable practical application.

In the forthcoming phase of our investigation, we intend to incorporate FPGA implementation for the classification of arrhythmias using the ecgWavePuzzle methodology. This decision emerges from experiments carried out across three distinct computational platforms, designed to elucidate the performance disparities inherent to machines typically deployed in ECG research. A significant portion of extant literature in this domain has predominantly utilized processing capabilities comparable to the NVIDIA 3090 GPU. However, approaches often neglect consideration of real-world applicabilities, where hardware constraints are more closely representative of those found in devices such as the Raspberry Pi. Our study endeavors to bridge this gap by evaluating performance in a more diverse range of computational environments, especially the use of reconfigurable hardware.

Benefits are particularly noteworthy in terms of customization, energy efficiency, and processing capacity [7,16]. In contrast to the more generalist CPU and GPU-based solutions, FPGAs and ASICs enable the creation of circuits specifically designed for certain tasks, such as the convolution operation. This specialization results in augmented efficiency and processing speed, which are crucial for real-time medical applications like bedside monitors. Integrating our ECGPuzzle methodology with FPGA and ASIC technologies could markedly enhance ECG classification latency. Promising avenues include the development of algorithms optimized for FPGAs and ASICs, aimed at performing tasks such as data quantization, dimensionality reduction, and the execution of efficient convolutional operations [13] and feedforward phases [1], all while maintaining the high precision required for clinical diagnostics [9]. These approaches have the potential to facilitate rapid parameter adjustments for mini-batches of data, thereby accelerating online learning in a manner that aligns with the requirements of medical equipment [14,20].

Furthermore, we aim to explore the effectiveness of FPGA-based implementations for ECG classification, with a particular focus on Temporal Convolutional Networks (TCNs). This emphasis is inspired by the promising results demonstrated in [1], which highlights the potential of TCNs in efficiently processing temporal data, a critical aspect of ECG wave analysis. Their approach to a hardware inference accelerator for TCNs underscores the feasibility and advantages of using FPGA in this context, which we believe could significantly advance the field of ECG classification alongside self-supervised learning.

4   Conclusion

The presented study outlines an innovative approach for ECG heartbeat classification, employing self-supervised learning methods, such as the ECGPuzzle, to effectively address challenges like significant inter-patient variability and intrinsic noise in ECG signals. Our approach enhances the capacity of deep learning models to adapt to individual characteristics, significantly improving their generalization capability in medical contexts. This research underscores the importance of integrating hardware accelerators, particularly FPGAs and ASICs, in both the training and deployment of these models within embedded systems. Such integration is vital due to the computational limitations of standard medical devices and the need for human-in-the-loop model training. The utilization of FPGA and ASIC hardware acceleration is paramount for the practical application of our ECGPuzzle methodology. These reconfigurable technologies present an optimal blend of performance, efficiency, and adaptability, thereby making them exceptionally suitable for refining ECG signal classification in various clinical scenarios, enhancing patient care, and advancing medical technology.

Acknowledgments.. The authors would also like to thank the *Coordenação de Aperfeiçoamento de Pessoal de Nível Superior* - Brazil (CAPES) - Finance Code 001, *Fundação de Amparo á Pesquisa do Estado de Minas Gerais* (FAPEMIG, grants APQ-01518-21, PQ-01647-22), *Conselho Nacional de Desenvolvimento Científico e Tecnológico* (CNPq, grants 308400/2022-4, 307151/2022-0) and Universidade Federal de Ouro Preto (PROPPI/UFOP) for supporting the development of this study.

Disclosure of Interests. The authors declare that they have no known competing financial interests or personal relationships that could have appeared to influence the work reported in this paper.

References

1. Ali, R., et al.: A hardware inference accelerator for temporal convolutional networks. In: 2019 IEEE Nordic Circuits and Systems Conference (NORCAS): NORCHIP and International Symposium of System-on-Chip (SoC), pp. 1–7. IEEE (2019)
2. ANSI/AAMI: Testing and reporting performance results of cardiac rhythm and ST segment measurement algorithms. American National Standards Institute, Inc. (ANSI), Association for the Advancement of Medical Instrumentation (AAMI), ANSI/AAMI/ISO EC57, 1998-(R)2008 (2008)
3. Antczak, J., Pyskir, D., Czajka, A., Leszczuk, M.: Self-supervised representation learning for electrocardiogram analysis. arXiv preprint arXiv:2007.15653 (2020)
4. Bai, L., Zhao, Y., Huang, X.: A CNN accelerator on FPGA using depthwise separable convolution. IEEE Trans. Circuits Syst. II Express Briefs **65**(10), 1415–1419 (2018)
5. Boutros, A., Yazdanshenas, S., Betz, V.: You cannot improve what you do not measure: FPGA vs. ASIC efficiency gaps for convolutional neural network inference. ACM Trans. Reconfigurable Technol. Syst. (TRETS) **11**(3), 1–23 (2018)
6. De Chazal, P., O'Dwyer, M., Reilly, R.B.: Automatic classification of heartbeats using ECG morphology and heartbeat interval features. IEEE Trans. Biomed. Eng. **51**(7), 1196–1206 (2004)
7. Desai, M.P., Caffarena, G., Jevtic, R., Márquez, D.G., Otero, A.: A low-latency, low-power FPGA implementation of ECG signal characterization using hermite polynomials. Electronics **10**(19), 2324 (2021)
8. Goldberger, A.L., et al.: PhysioBank, PhysioToolkit, and PhysioNet: components of a new research resource for complex physiologic signals. Circulation **101**(23), e215–e220 (2000)
9. Karataş, F., Koyuncu, I., Tuna, M., Alçın, M., Avcioglu, E., Akgul, A.: Design and implementation of arrhythmic ECG signals for biomedical engineering applications on FPGA. Eur. Phys. J. Spec. Top. **231**(5), 869–884 (2022)
10. Liu, W., et al.: A fully-mapped and energy-efficient FPGA accelerator for dual-function AI-based analysis of ECG. Front. Physiol. **14**, 1079503 (2023)
11. Luz, E., Menotti, D.: How the choice of samples for building arrhythmia classifiers impact their performances. In: 2011 Annual International Conference of the IEEE Engineering in Medicine and Biology Society, pp. 4988–4991. IEEE (1 2011)
12. Luz, E.J.D.S., Schwartz, W.R., Cámara-Chávez, G., Menotti, D.: ECG-based heartbeat classification for arrhythmia detection: a survey. Comput. Methods Programs Biomed. **127**, 144–164 (2016)
13. Maji, P., Bates, D., Chadwick, A., Mullins, R.: Adapt: optimizing CNN inference on IoT and mobile devices using approximately separable 1-D kernels. In: Proceedings of the 1st International Conference on Internet of Things and Machine Learning, pp. 1–12 (2017)
14. Park, S.S., Chung, K.S.: CONNA: configurable matrix multiplication engine for neural network acceleration. Electronics **11**(15) (2022). https://doi.org/10.3390/electronics11152373. http://www.mdpi.com/2079-9292/11/15/2373
15. Silva, G.A.L.: Self-supervised learning for arrhythmia classification. Thesis, Master in Computer Science, Federal University of Ouro Preto, Ouro Preto (2023), http://www.repositorio.ufop.br/jspui/handle/123456789/17740
16. Tefai, H.T., Saleh, H., Tekeste, T., Alqutayri, M., Mohammad, B.: ASIC implementation of a pre-trained neural network for ECG feature extraction. In: 2020

IEEE International Symposium on Circuits and Systems (ISCAS), pp. 1–5. IEEE (2020)

17. Tian, Y., Li, Y., Yang, S., Wang, L.: Self-supervised electrocardiogram representation learning for abnormality detection. IEEE J. Biomed. Health Inf. (2021)
18. Zhang, A., Lipton, Z.C., Li, M., Smola, A.J.: Dive into Deep Learning. Cambridge University Press (2023)
19. Zhou, C., Paffenroth, R.C.: Anomaly detection with robust deep autoencoders. In: Proceedings of the 23rd ACM SIGKDD International Conference on Knowledge Discovery and Data Mining, pp. 665–674 (2017)
20. Zhu, L., Liu, D., Li, X., Lu, J., Wei, L., Cheng, X.: An efficient hardware architecture for epileptic seizure detection using EEG signals based on 1D-CNN. In: 2021 IEEE 14th International Conference on ASIC (ASICON), pp. 1–4 (2021). https://doi.org/10.1109/ASICON52560.2021.9620467

Enabling FPGA and AI Engine Tasks in the HPX Programming Framework for Heterogeneous High-Performance Computing

Torben Kalkhof$^{(\boxtimes)}$ ⓘ, Carsten Heinz ⓘ, and Andreas Koch ⓘ

Embedded Systems and Applications Group, TU Darmstadt, Darmstadt, Germany
{kalkhof,heinz,koch}@esa.tu-darmstadt.de

Abstract. The increasing complexity of modern exascale computers, with a growing number of cores per node, poses a challenge to traditional programming models. To address this challenge, Asynchronous Many-Task (AMT) runtimes such as the C++-based HPX, divide computational problems into smaller tasks that are executed asynchronously by the runtime. By unifying the syntax and semantics of local and remote task execution, the scalability for distributed execution is enhanced. The asynchronous execution model conceals communication latency in distributed systems and eliminates global synchronization barriers, which improves the overall utilization of computation resources.

While HPX and other AMT runtimes often support GPUs, there is still a lack of support for other accelerators, such as FPGAs, or more coarse-grained AI processing elements such as AMD's AI Engines (AIE).

In this work, we extend the TaPaSCo framework so that TaPaSCo FPGA and AIE tasks can be transparently integrated into HPX applications. We show results for both microbenchmarks as well as the complete LULESH proxy HPC application to demonstrate this concept and evaluate the overheads. Both applications show that the combination of TaPaSCo and HPX can be efficiently used for cooperative computing between CPU software and FPGA/AIE hardware. Compared to CPU-only execution, we achieve a speedup of up to 2.4x in our stencil microbenchmark and a wall-clock speedup of 1.37x for the entire LULESH application, with 2.12x in the accelerated kernels itself. Our TaPaSCo/HPX integration is released as open-source.

Keywords: FPGA · task-based programming · HPC · AI engines

1 Introduction

The demand for computation power of modern applications is higher than ever, and we have arrived in the era of exascale computing [15]. On the one hand, such huge computation power is achieved by a steadily growing number of compute nodes. On the other hand, there is also a trend to increase the number

© The Author(s), under exclusive license to Springer Nature Switzerland AG 2024
I. Skliarova et al. (Eds.): ARC 2024, LNCS 14553, pp. 75–89, 2024.
https://doi.org/10.1007/978-3-031-55673-9_6

of *CPU cores per node*. This results in a significant challenge for traditional parallel programming models in High-Performance Computing (HPC), such as OpenMP and MPI, due to the increase in inter- and intra-node parallelism and concurrency.

In these models, computational problems are divided and statically scheduled to different cores and nodes, respectively. Synchronization barriers are primarily used to synchronize threads within a single node, e.g., at the end of parallel loops. Communication and data exchange between nodes is usually done by message passing, which may introduce implicit global synchronization barriers as well.

Load imbalance between threads and processes as well as communication latency may cause node starvation, as threads or processes block while waiting for messages or other threads to reach a barrier. This degrades the overall resource utilization. Hence, new programming models are desirable to use exascale supercomputers efficiently [14].

A promising approach are Asynchronous Many-Task (AMT) runtimes. In this programming model, the programmer divides the computational problem into small tasks and defines dependencies between these tasks, resulting in a dataflow graph.

The AMT runtime then asynchronously executes these tasks. By expressing data dependencies on a per task level, local as well as global synchronization barriers are reduced. Although AMT systems cannot *eliminate* communication latency, they can hide some or all of the latency. If a task is blocked due to waiting for a message, the runtime will suspend the current task and execute other tasks that are ready to compute.

Many AMT frameworks will have abstraction layers which unify local and remote execution of tasks to provide good scalability, improve load-balancing and, in turn, resource utilization on the intra- and inter-node level of distributed systems.

Besides the increase of cores and nodes, heterogeneity is another important trend in HPC. Due to their versatility, GPUs are most commonly applied in supercomputers and used for hardware acceleration in many applications. Hence, AMT runtimes often provide support for GPU kernels. However, other domain-specific accelerators continue gain in popularity, including more energy-efficient FPGAs or specialized AI hardware such as AMD Versal AI Engines (AIE). Unfortunately, AMT runtimes often lack support for these more specialized architectures.

In this work, we combine HPX [11], a C++-based AMT runtime targeting HPC and scientific applications, with TaPaSCo [9], a framework enabling the easy use of FPGA and AIE for task processing. By extending TaPaSCo, we enable a seamless integration of tasks running on FPGA- or AIE-based accelerators into HPX applications.

In our evaluation, we do not aim to show the highest possible accelerations by using FPGAs or AIEs. Instead, we examine whether HPX makes a suitable framework for the low-overhead integration of these computing elements in heterogeneous HPC applications.

To this end, we first use a stencil-based microbenchmark which allows us to easily measure the impact of different numbers of tasks and task sizes offloaded to an FPGA, including a comparison to an implementation solely based on the C++ standard library.

Then, we move on to a full application, namely the LULESH proxy HPC application [1], which we port to HPX and offload parts of the computation to an AIE-based accelerator. The performance results show that our TaPaSCo/HPX integration can achieve speedups in real-world applications, and that HPX enables this at *lower overheads* than the traditional approaches of the C++ library.

The paper is structured as follows. In Sect. 2, we provide an overview of HPX and TaPaSCo before discussing related work in Sect. 3. Afterward, we describe our implementation of the TaPaSCo integration with HPX in Sect. 4. Our benchmarks are introduced in Sect. 5 followed by presenting the evaluation results in Sect. 6. Section 7 then concludes the paper.

2   Background

In the following sections, we introduce both of the frameworks this work is based on, namely HPX and TaPaSCo.

2.1   HPX

HPX [11] is an AMT C++ library, and provides an API conforming to the C++ standard API for asynchronous execution.

HPX utilizes the concept of *futures* to execute asynchronous tasks. When we create an asynchronous task, e.g. using `hpx::async()`, the task is not executed immediately, and hence we cannot obtain the task's return value instantly. Instead, a future object is generated as a wrapper around the actual return value, and the current thread continues to execute. We can create an entire task graph using so-called *continuations* on these futures. Continuations define tasks that are executed after the preceding future becomes ready.

Finally, when we need to access the value of a future, the current thread is suspended until the corresponding task is executed and the value is computed.

HPX launches tasks as *lightweight* threads that are executed on a fixed number of operating system (OS) threads. Generally, one worker is assigned per CPU core. The HPX runtime completely manages the lightweight threads, leading to faster context switches when compared to multi-threading on the OS level. The task scheduler ensures good load balancing between the worker threads by applying techniques such as work stealing and sharing.

Further features of HPX include templates for parallel algorithms, remote task execution with a uniform API, and already support for GPUs using CUDA or HIP.

2.2   TaPaSCo

TaPaSCo [9] is a task-based framework providing simple and platform-independent integration of FPGAs into heterogeneous systems. It is made up of two parts: a toolflow that generates bitstreams for the FPGA and a runtime that interfaces with the accelerators. The framework supports various platforms ranging from Zynq SoCs (e.g. Ultra96) to PCIe-based data center cards (e.g. Alveo U280).

Hardware designs in TaPaSCo are built using Processing Elements (PEs), which are supplied by the user as HLS kernel or HDL-written IP with standard AXI4 interfaces. The infrastructure components, such as interrupt controllers and DMA engines, are automatically generated. Additionally, the TaPaSCo toolflow offers a design space exploration to optimize a hardware design for frequency or utilized area.

The TaPaSCo runtime consists of a device driver and a Rust user-space runtime. Also, a clear and platform-independent C++ API is provided for easy integration of the hardware accelerator into a host application. Users can pass their PE arguments to the `launch` call, and TaPaSCo handles requested data transfers to device-local memories automatically, as well as forwarding the arguments and launching the PE. By calling the returned `job_future`, the PE is released after it has finished and TaPaSCo performs data transfers back to host memory if necessary. Users can also manage device memory explicitly by using manual allocations and data transfers.

Furthermore, TaPaSCo provides a plugin system offering additional extensions such as 100G networking or shared virtual memory. Recently, the support for AMD Versal boards has been added, providing access to the AI engines. Moreover, a DMA streaming mode has been introduced, which avoids copies to device-local memory by streaming data directly into PEs.

3   Related Work

There are several other frameworks for AMT computation apart from HPX. The most common approach is to provide a library. While HPX uses the syntax of asynchronous function calls from the C++ standard API, other frameworks use different methods to define tasks. For instance, Charm++ [12] has special objects and interfaces, or StarPU [2] uses custom data structures called *codelets*.

In contrast, Chapel [4] and X10 [5] are domain specific task-based programming languages. Legion [3] provides both, a C++ API as well as the custom language Regent [16], following a more data-centric approach than HPX. In Regent, tasks operate on defined data regions, resulting in a well-defined data flow and execution graph.

OmpSs uses OpenMP-like pragmas and also supports FPGA tasks [6]. In contrast to this work, FPGA task compilation using HLS is completely integrated into the custom compiler, so non-HLS accelerators are not supported.

The stencil microbenchmark we employ below is also used by Grubel et al. [8] to evaluate the impact of different task sizes on the performance of HPX. Karlin et al. [13] use LULESH to explore and compare different programming models excluding HPX, while Jin et al. [10] implement LULESH kernels using OpenCL HLS on an FPGA. However, Jin et al. only present the execution times of single kernels, without taking into account data movements between host and device. Additionally, it is unclear to us which program arguments they used in particular, preventing a direct comparison.

4   Implementation

In this section, we describe the required changes in TaPaSCo to enable an efficient integration into HPX.

TaPaSCo uses blocking calls to implement launching and releasing of PEs. This means that if currently no PE of the requested type is available to service a task, the calling thread is halted until a PE has finished the previous task and can be re-launched. The executing OS thread is suspended, and in a multi-threaded application, other threads can take over and be executed. The same happens when a PE should be released but has not finished executing yet.

In HPX, this would mean that the current worker thread is suspended and cannot execute other tasks, which goes against the underlying concept of HPX. Thus, non-blocking calls need to be added to TaPaSCo for launching and releasing PEs, that *always* return immediately, whether the PE could be launched or released or not.

These non-blocking calls are then used inside a wrapper that just suspends the current HPX lightweight thread, instead of the underlying OS thread, allowing the HPX scheduler to assign other tasks to this worker thread. The TaPaSCo task will be rescheduled until the PE is ready.

All the user has to do is call this wrapper function inside the HPX task, and pass the PE and required arguments to the wrapper function call.

In the launch call, TaPaSCo first allocates space in off-chip memory for input and output data, and then tries to acquire a PE for this job. During testing, we realized that this can lead to oversubscription of memory, since many tasks are created long in advance of their actual launches when using HPX. Hence, we change the order and first acquire a PE, *before* moving data to off-chip memory. In certain applications, it can be beneficial to coordinate the transfer of data in separate tasks. This allows for increased parallelism by overlapping data transfers and PE jobs. Additionally, HPX offers an `io_pool_executor` specially designed for I/O intensive tasks that may be utilized for these transfers.

5   Benchmarks

In this section, we introduce our stencil microbenchmark and LULESH case study which we use to evaluate our work. We describe the design of our accelerators, and discuss challenges we encountered while using FPGA and AIE tasks in HPX.

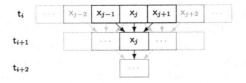

Fig. 1. Computation flow of the 1D-stencil microbenchmark.

5.1   Microbenchmark: 1D-Stencil

The stencil microbenchmark iteratively simulates heat diffusion in a ring over time given by the following formula

$$x_i(t_{j+1}) = x_i(t_j) + k\frac{dt}{dx^2}(x_{i-1}(t_j) - 2x_i(t_j) + x_{i+1}(t_j)) \tag{1}$$

where x_i denotes the i-th element in the array representing the ring, and t_j the current iteration. k, dt and dx are constants denoting the heat transfer coefficient, time step, and grid spacing. Figure 1 visualizes the computation flow. The array is then divided into equally sized partitions and one task is created to calculate one timestep for one partition each.

We implement an HLS kernel using Vitis HLS to offload tasks to the FPGA. It is fully pipelined and computes eight values in parallel. In total, we put 16 of these PEs onto the Alveo U280 and connect them to the 16 ports of the left HBM stack available on this UltraScale+ device. The PEs run at 450 MHz so that frequency and datawidth match with the HBM ports. At the beginning of the benchmark, we offload a given number of partitions to the on-device HBM where they stay for the entire benchmark. All tasks working on the offloaded partitions are then executed by the PEs, avoiding costly data transfers in between iterations. Only values on the partition boundaries must be exchanged as the neighboring partitions require them in the next iteration.

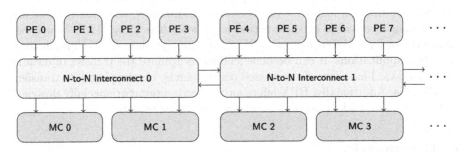

Fig. 2. Structure of the built-in crossbar between user PEs and HBM memory controllers (MC).

To exploit the high bandwidth of HBM, it is crucial to allow as many parallel memory accesses as possible. The left stack of the HBM on the Alveo

U280 has eight memory controllers with 2 pseudo-channels each, with one AXI port per pseudo-channel. Although we do not use the entire 4 GB of the HBM stack, we distribute the partitions equally over the stack to improve parallelism. Located between the AXI ports and pseudo-channels of the memory controller, there is a built-in crossbar to allow access from each AXI port to the entire stack, as depicted in Fig. 2. However, the crossbar only provides direct n-to-n-interconnects for *four* ports and pseudo-channels each, which we call a *group*. Inter-group accesses become expensive, since they may congest the single connection crossing group boundaries. Thus, we schedule tasks on the PEs in a way that avoids interference on the inter-group interconnects.

Since launching a PE has potentially much higher overhead, due to the PCIe latency, than scheduling a lightweight thread on the CPU, we implement two strategies for partitioning tasks on the FPGA. In the first variant, we have *equally sized* partitions on CPU and FPGA and vary the number of partitions that are offloaded to the PEs. Secondly, we also vary the total amount of data offloaded to the FPGA, but always split it into 16 partitions *independent of the partition size* on the host. In this approach, there is always exactly one task per PE in every iteration.

To evaluate the benefits of using TaPaSCo with light-weight threads in HPX compared to OS multi-threading, we implement a non-HPX baseline, only using the asynchronous functions provided by the C++ standard library and original blocking TaPaSCo calls. Here, an OS thread is created for each task.

5.2   Case Study: LULESH

The Livermore Unstructured Lagrangian Explicit Shock Hydrodynamics (LULESH) proxy application models hydrodynamics codes by solving the Sedov blast wave problem. As a proxy application, LULESH is highly simplified while maintaining the typical structure of similar scientific applications allowing benchmarking of a real-world problem without physical background.

In LULESH, the physical problem space is divided into a hexahedral mesh on which the computation is performed. The underlying algorithm is a Lagrange leapfrog algorithm, consisting of three phases. During the first phase, the force on each node of the mesh at the current timestep is calculated. Based on this, acceleration, velocity, and position of the nodes are updated.

In contrast to the nodal-based first phase, the second part of the algorithm updates the properties of each mesh element, i.e. each hexahedron in the mesh. Mainly, pressure, internal energy, and relative volume of the elements are calculated as well as the sound speed in each element. To simulate different materials, the mesh is split into multiple regions. Although the material properties are the same in LULESH, each region must be handled in a separate loop. Additionally, the computational intensity of the regions is varied, which is simulated by simply repeating the computation of the element quantities for some of the regions.

The last phase calculates the timestep of the next iteration. However, its runtime is negligible compared to the other two phases.

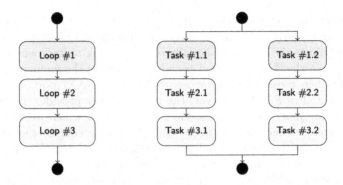

Fig. 3. Comparison of loop structure (left) to our task structure (right). Loops impose a synchronization barrier, while tasks only depend on their respective predecessors and require a single synchronization barrier at the end.

The OpenMP reference implementation consists of 45 parallel-for loops performing the different computation steps after each other. An existing HPX implementation of LULESH takes the approach of simply converting all OpenMP loops to HPX-provided parallel for-loops [17].

However, the performance of that implementation is shown to be *worse* than the OpenMP reference implementation in our measurements. This non-optimal HPX implementation does not remove any synchronization barriers, and due to its "too static" scheduling, there is no load imbalance to be expected between OpenMP threads, which in turn could be exploited using the AMT mechanisms of code better matching the HPX paradigm.

To obtain a higher-quality baseline, we thus carefully created our own, better optimized software-only LULESH implementation using HPX. To this end, we decided to manually decompose the computation into tasks and try to remove barriers as far as possible.

We maintain the partitioning in kernels from the reference implementation in large parts, but heavily use continuations to chain the tasks performing computations on the same subset of data in consecutive kernels, as illustrated in Fig. 3.

Furthermore, we launch tasks of completely independent kernels in parallel. This way we can reduce the number of synchronization barriers to six per iteration. After all optimizations, our CPU-based application is even slightly faster than the original OpenMP reference implementation of LULESH.

Due to expensive data movements to and from FPGA off-chip memory in every iteration of the leapfrog algorithm, we need to offload kernels in which we do multiple calculations on the same input data. At the same time, the offloaded part should be *independent* of other tasks, so that we can still run calculations on the CPU in parallel.

Based on this, we choose the update of the element properties in the most expensive region during phase two. Since this computation is floating point intensive, we use the AMD Versal AI Engines (AIE) on the VCK5000.

The AIE consists of 400 tiles with VLIW architecture and SIMD vector processors including single-precision floating point pipelines. All tiles are connected via a streaming interconnect, and neighboring tiles can also use buffers in local memory to exchange data.

We design specialized hardware on the Programmable Logic (PL) part of the Versal device to efficiently feed the AIE with data. To this end, we implement a custom PE streaming input data from off-chip memory into the AIE and output data vice versa. The entire computation is repeated as many times as it would been executed on the host.

One challenge in implementing the computation graph for the AIE is that the structure of the LULESH computation does not perfectly match the streaming-based architecture of the AIE, e.g., many input and intermediate variables are reused in multiple steps of the calculation. This means they have to be buffered in between.

Input variables are buffered in FIFOs in the PL and streamed into the AIE *again* at a later stage using an additional port. However, intermediate variables are buffered in the AIE by dummy kernels, which just forward the data from one buffer to another.

6   Evaluation

As described in the Introduction, we begin our evaluation with the more focused 1D-stencil microbenchmark, before moving on to a full HPC code, namely the LULESH hydrodynamics proxy application.

All tests were run on an AMD Epyc 7443 24-core processor equipped with 256 GB RAM. The stencil benchmark is run on an Alveo U280 clocked at 450 MHz and connected with PCIe 3.0×16 to the host. Our LULESH accelerator runs on a VCK5000 connected via PCIe 4.0×8. While the AIE run at 1.25 GHz, the custom data streaming engine we implemented in the Versal PL part is clocked with 200 MHz, which is sufficient to completely saturate the AIE bandwidth by using multiple streaming ports in parallel.

We use HPX v1.9.0 with jemalloc. All benchmarks are compiled with GCC 11.2.1 and -DCMAKE_BUILD_TYPE=Release.

6.1   Microbenchmark: 1D-Stencil

The presented numbers of our stencil microbenchmark are averaged over 100 runs. For the two smallest partition sizes of the non-HPX version, we reduced the number of runs to 50 due to long execution times. Each run calculates 300 timesteps of the heat distribution on an array with $256 \cdot 2^{20}$ single-precision floating point numbers (1 GB). The absolute execution times are shown in Fig. 4, depending on the partition size and ratio of offloaded partitions to the FPGA.

We achieve faster computation times through collaborative computing using CPU and FPGA in all our measurement series. The shortest execution time of 3 s is achieved using HPX with a partition size of 4 MB on the host and 16 hardware

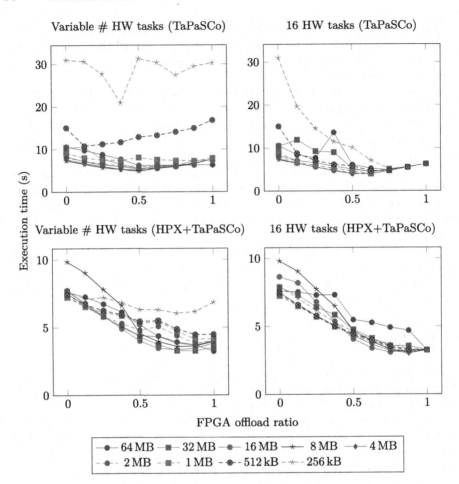

Fig. 4. Absolute execution times of the stencil microbenchmark dependent on partition size and offload ratio of partitions to the FPGA. The upper two graphs show results for the non-HPX variant using the standard C++ library, the lower graphs contain the results of the TaPaSCo/HPX integration. In the left two graphs, partition sizes on FPGA and host are equal, thus the number of offloaded tasks is variable. On the right, the offloaded calculations are always split into 16 partitions.

tasks that account for 87.5 % of the calculations. This results in a speedup of 2.4x compared to the fastest software-only computation using HPX with 1024 partitions of 1 MB each, which takes 7.22 s.

When comparing the upper and lower plots in Fig. 4 to each other, you can see that the implementation using HPX, shown in the lower plots, is faster for all run configurations. Scheduling, suspending, and switching threads is much more efficient in HPX's lightweight threading model compared to OS threads. This is especially true when dealing with hundreds or thousands of concurrent threads, as in this benchmark. Due to this increased management overhead, the implementation without HPX cannot benefit from more offloaded tasks and reaches minimal runtimes around an offload ratio of 0.5. In contrast, the HPX implementation performs best if between 75 % to 87.5 % of the calculation is offloaded to the FPGA.

The performance of parallel computing on CPUs benefits from fine-grained parallelism due to smaller partitions to a certain degree. However, for FPGA tasks, it is better to keep the number of tasks low to improve execution times. The right plots in Fig. 4 show that the overall execution time is shortened by setting the number of tasks running on hardware to 16 for each iteration and resizing the partition size accordingly to the offload ratio. This is particularly true for the measurement series with partition sizes smaller than 16 MB.

Each PE launch involves PCIe latency during writing control registers and handling the PE interrupt. Additionally, the threads managing the TaPaSCo tasks on the host side must be scheduled, which introduces overhead, although no actual computation is performed on the CPU.

6.2 Case Study: LULESH

We evaluate our LULESH implementation with three different problem sizes and three different numbers of regions each. The problem size specifies the number of elements in each mesh dimension. In addition to the default size of 45, we evaluate with 60 and 75 elements. We use the standard configuration for the region costs: half of the regions are computed once or twice respectively, but on one region the calculation is repeated 20 times. The presented numbers are the mean over 100 runs with 200 iterations of the Lagrange leapfrog algorithm each.

Note that we have very carefully optimized our HPX software-only baseline, making it even faster than the OpenMP reference code. The respective speedup factors are shown in Fig. 5 while Table 1 lists the corresponding absolute numbers. Compared to that reference code, the wall-clock speedups of our AIE-accelerated version would be even higher than reported below. However, as our focus was on examining the overheads of the HPX/TaPaSCo integration, instead of examining absolute performance gains, we use our optimized HPX software code as baseline for our measurements.

Figure 6 illustrates how the cooperative execution of TaPaSCo and HPX has improved the total execution time and the execution time of the AIE-accelerated part compared to our software-only implementation. The corresponding absolute numbers can be found in Table 2.

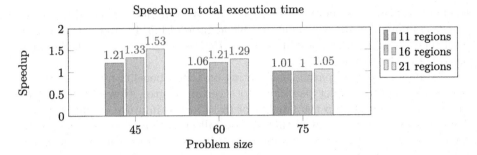

Fig. 5. Speedup of our software-only LULESH implementation using HPX compared to the OpenMP reference implementation.

Table 1. Absolute runtimes of our software-only LULESH implementation using HPX and the reference OpenMP implementation.

Problem size	45		60		75	
Runtime	HPX	OpenMP	HPX	OpenMP	HPX	OpenMP
11 regions	1.663 s	2.018 s	3.074 s	3.246 s	4.748 s	4.785 s
16 regions	1.574 s	2.092 s	2.765 s	3.341 s	4.882 s	4.904 s
21 regions	1.422 s	2.180 s	2.697 s	3.476 s	4.816 s	5.062 s

For some instances, we use different task sizes for the software-only and AIE-accelerated versions and report the optimal runtimes for each. The chosen task size can affect other parts of the application, not just the part accelerated by AIE, as evidenced by the numbers for software-only execution and a problem size of 75. Despite the differences in the lower table, the total runtimes are very similar. To indicate the limited comparability in the lower table, we have underlined the respective numbers.

The smallest problem size of 45 provides the best speedups for all three numbers of regions in our AIE-accelerated HPX implementation when compared to the HPX baseline. The highest speedup achieved is 1.37x on the total execution time and 2.12x on the accelerated part with 16 regions. As the problem size increases, the speedups decrease for 11 and 16 regions. For 21 regions, the speedup for a problem size of 60 is lower than for 45, but rises to 1.25x on the total execution time and 1.9x on the accelerated part for the largest problem size.

To understand the speedup, it is important to examine the absolute numbers of the accelerated part of the application. These numbers are listed in the lower table in Table 2. In the AIE-accelerated implementation, the runtime of this part is mainly influenced by the calculation of the most expensive region, which is repeated 20 times. The computation of this region on the AIE takes longer than processing all other regions on the CPU in parallel. However, as the number of

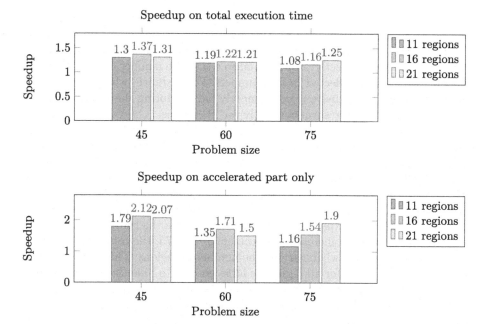

Fig. 6. Speedup of the HPX LULESH implementation running cooperatively on CPU and AIE compared to running in software only. The speedup is given on the total execution time as well as the execution time of the accelerated part only.

Table 2. Absolute execution times of the HPX LULESH implementation running cooperatively on CPU and AIE compared to running in software only. Numbers are given for the total execution time and the time of the accelerated part only. Underlined numbers indicate that different task sizes are used for the software-only and AIE-accelerated variants.

Total execution time						
Problem size	45		60		75	
Runtime	HPX	HPX+AIE	HPX	HPX+AIE	HPX	HPX+AIE
11 regions	1.663 s	1.277 s	3.074 s	2.575 s	4.749 s	4.414 s
16 regions	1.574 s	1.149 s	2.765 s	2.262 s	4.882 s	4.196 s
21 regions	1.422 s	1.088 s	2.697 s	2.225 s	4.816 s	3.860 s
Execution time of accelerated part only						
Problem size	45		60		75	
Runtime	HPX	HPX+AIE	HPX	HPX+AIE	HPX	HPX+AIE
11 regions	0.910 s	0.510 s	1.393 s	1.028 s	1.887 s	1.623 s
16 regions	0.819 s	0.387 s	1.228 s	0.718 s	2.138 s	1.383 s
21 regions	0.667 s	0.322 s	1.016 s	0.675 s	2.070 s	1.092 s

regions increases, the most time-consuming region becomes smaller, resulting in reduced computation time for both the specific region and the total runtime.

The heuristic determining the sizes of the regions includes some randomness, though, and it is not directly proportional to either the number of regions or the problem size. This is reflected in the numbers. For instance, when the problem size is 60, the most expensive region is nearly halved during the step from 11 to 16 regions, but then only shrinks slightly for 21 regions.

In the software-only implementation, the runtime depends mainly on how parallelizable the AIE-accelerated part is. When the problem size is 45, the most expensive region dominates the runtime and is split into very few tasks. This limited parallelizability actually allows for the highest speedups by our AIE accelerator. However, if we increase the problem size to 60, all regions become larger, which allows for more tasks per region and improves parallelism. Nonetheless, the most expensive region still dominates the runtime.

Conversely, when we increase the problem size to 75, the total runtime does not change significantly when varying the number of regions. This is because the overall number of tasks for all regions is large enough to hide the higher computation cost of the expensive region. However, the runtime of the AIE-accelerated variant decreases with the increasing number of regions in this scenario as well, enabling higher speedups with a larger number of regions.

7   Conclusion

This work enables the transparent integration of TaPaSCo tasks executed on FPGA and AIE accelerators in HPX. The main benefit of this integration is that applications can leverage the asynchronous and lightweight execution model on the CPU, while being able to include custom hardware accelerators on FPGA or AIE at the same time.

We are able to achieve up to 2.4x speedup in our stencil-based microbenchmark by offloading tasks to an FPGA, as compared to executing all tasks on a CPU. Our comparison to an implementation using the C++ standard library for concurrency, demonstrates that the lightweight HPX tasks, based on lightweight threads in turn, significantly reduce overhead compared to multi-threading using OS-level threads, especially when launching thousands of tasks in parallel.

Furthermore, we implement the LULESH proxy HPC application in HPX and use the AMD Versal AIE to accelerate key parts. Our results showed that we were able to achieve speedups of up to 1.37x on the total wall-clock time, which serves as a proof of the usability of the HPX + TaPaSCo approach for real-world applications.

TaPaSCo is already available as open-source on GitHub, where we will also provide our HPX integration [7].

Acknowledgments. This research was funded by the German Federal Ministry for Education and Research (BMBF) with the funding ID 01 IS 21007 B.

Disclosure of Interests. The authors have no competing interests to declare that are relevant to the content of this article.

References

1. Hydrodynamics Challenge Problem, Lawrence Livermore National Laboratory. Technical report. LLNL-TR-490254
2. Augonnet, C., Thibault, S., Namyst, R., Wacrenier, P.A.: StarPU: A Unified Platform for Task Scheduling on Heterogeneous Multicore Architectures. CCPE - Concurrency and Computation: Practice and Experience, Euro-Par 2009, February 2011
3. Bauer, M., Treichler, S., Slaughter, E., Aiken, A.: Legion: expressing locality and independence with logical regions. In: 2012 International Conference for High Performance Computing, Networking, Storage and Analysis, pp. 1–11, November 2012
4. Chamberlain, B., Callahan, D., Zima, H.: Parallel programmability and the chapel language. Int. J. High Perform. Comput. App. **21**(3), 291–312 (2007)
5. Charles, P., Grothoff, C., Saraswat, V., Donawa, C., Kielstra, A., Ebcioglu, K., Von Praun, C., Sarkar, V.: X10: an object-oriented approach to non-uniform cluster computing. ACM SIGPLAN Notices **40**(10), 519–538 (2005)
6. Deharo, J.M., et al.: OmpSs@FPGA framework for high performance FPGA computing. IEEE Trans. Comput. 1–1 (2021)
7. Embedded Systems and Applications Group, TU Darmstadt: ESA group on Github. https://github.com/esa-tu-darmstadt
8. Grubel, P., Kaiser, H., Cook, J., Serio, A.: The performance implication of task size for applications on the HPX runtime system. In: 2015 IEEE International Conference on Cluster Computing (2015)
9. Heinz, C., Hofmann, J., Korinth, J., Sommer, L., Weber, L., Koch, A.: The TaPaSco open-source ToolFlow. J. Signal Process. Syst. (2021)
10. Jin, Z., Finkel, H.: Evaluating LULESH kernels on OpenCL FPGA. In: Hochberger, C., Nelson, B., Koch, A., Woods, R., Diniz, P. (eds.) ARC 2019. LNCS, vol. 11444, pp. 199–213. Springer, Cham (2019). https://doi.org/10.1007/978-3-030-17227-5_15
11. Kaiser, H., et al.: HPX - the c++ standard library for parallelism and concurrency. J. Open Source Softw. **5**(53), 2352 (2020)
12. Kale, L., Krishnan, S.: Charm++: a portable concurrent object oriented system based on c++. In: Proceedings of the Conference on Object-Oriented Programming Systems, Languages, and Applications, OOPSLA, pp. 91–108, October 1993
13. Karlin, I., et al.: Exploring traditional and emerging parallel programming models using a proxy application. In: IEEE 27th International Symposium on Parallel and Distributed Processing (2013)
14. Kogge, P., et al.: Exascale computing study: Technology challenges in achieving exascale systems. DARPA IPTO, Technical Representative 15, January 2008
15. RIKEN: Japan's fugaku gains title as world's fastest supercomputer. https://www.riken.jp/en/news_pubs/news/2020/20200623_1/
16. Slaughter, E., Lee, W., Treichler, S., Bauer, M., Aiken, A.: Regent: a high-productivity programming language for HPC with logical regions. In: Proceedings of the International Conference for High Performance Computing, Networking, Storage and Analysis, pp. 1–12. SC 2015, November 2015
17. Wei, W.: LULESH-HPX on Github. https://github.com/weilewei/lulesh-hpx

LiDAR 3D Object Detection in FPGA with Low Bitwidth Quantization

Henrique Brum[1(✉)], Mário Véstias[2], and Horácio Neto[1]

[1] INESC-ID/IST/UL, Lisboa, Portugal
henriquebrum@tecnico.ulisboa.pt, hcn@inesc-id.pt
[2] INESC-ID/ISEL/IPL, Lisboa, Portugal
mario.vestias@inesc-id.pt

Abstract. Detection of objects from LiDAR point clouds is an important task for several applications, like autonomous driving. Deep neural network models for LiDAR processing require a large processing computing capacity and storage. So, real-time execution of these models requires a high-performance computing platform on-board. To reduce the stress over the onboard computer, some proposals consider lite models at the cost of some accuracy. Instead of model reengineering, an integrated model/architecture optimization can reduce the computing requirements without compromising accuracy. This work optimizes a 3D object detection CNN model (PointPillars) and proposes an FPGA-based accelerator for efficient model inference. Fixed point quantization was performed for both weights and activations, with a vast exploration of the quantization possibilities for the selected model. This allowed us to improve the hardware accelerator while maintaining good detection accuracy. The proposed accelerator was implemented with a hybrid quantization with 8 and 2 bits for weights and 8 bits for activations. The final architecture achieved a throughput of 15.6 frames per second using 85K LUTS, 149 DSPs and 200 BRAM.

Keywords: Convolutional Neural Network · PointPillars · LiDAR Processing · Quantization · FPGA

1 Introduction

Autonomous vehicles and general autonomous robots depend on several machine learning algorithms, like object detection, classification, segmentation, among others [1]. Data from the surrounding environment can be sensed by radars, RGB cameras, thermal cameras, ultrasonic or LiDAR sensors. Initial solutions consider cameras or radars. LiDAR sensors are a more recent technology with some disadvantages like beam scattering in certain weather conditions, sparsity of data as the distance increases and higher cost. However, LiDAR sensors have low sensitivity to illumination conditions and offer a 3D mapping of the environment, which is quite attractive. LiDAR sensors produce a point cloud representation of the environment. Points are associated with a polar coordinate system and a reflection intensity.

© The Author(s), under exclusive license to Springer Nature Switzerland AG 2024
I. Skliarova et al. (Eds.): ARC 2024, LNCS 14553, pp. 90–105, 2024.
https://doi.org/10.1007/978-3-031-55673-9_7

Point clouds must be processed to extract important information about the detected objects. Classical machine learning algorithms, like support vector machines, apply some preprocessing tasks to extract feature vectors followed by classification. Better results are achieved with deep learning models at the cost of computational and memory complexity. The natural direction when running point cloud processing in onboard computers should be the reduction of computation and storage at the cost of accuracy. However, accuracy is a very important aspect in autonomous systems and it must be maintained as high as possible.

Graphics Processing Units (GPUs) are generally used to deploy CNNs due to their high-performance computing power. However, GPUs are power hungry and cannot be deployed in edge devices with reduced energy [2]. Dedicated computing solutions are therefore important for the successful deployment of LiDAR object detectors on edge devices. Field Programmable Gate Arrays (FPGAs) offer high computing power with high energy efficiency. Also, the hardware flexibility allows custom design for particular constraints of the system target.

In this paper, we propose a hardware/software embedded system for Lidar 3D object detection using a CNN model based on PointPillars in a SoC-FPGA platform. The quantization of the CNN model is explored to find an efficient solution in terms of area and performance with low accuracy reduction.

The accelerator was integrated into a full System-on-Chip (SoC) and prototyped in a Zynq Ultrascale+ XCZU7EV FPGA. The accelerator with an hybrid low bitwidth quantization achieves a throughput of 15.6 frames per second with an average 3D detection mAP of 61.27 and an average BEV detection mAP of 68.31 (in all cases, mAP_{50} for pedestrians and bicycles and mAP_{70} for cars).

The paper is organized as follows. Section 2 describes related work on models and architectures for LiDAR processing. Section 3 describes the quantization process of the model. Section 4 describes the architecture of the hardware accelerator and how the CNN model is mapped on the architecture. Section 5 presents the results of the solution and compares the proposed system with other computing platforms and other FPGA-based works. Finally, Sect. 6 concludes the paper.

2   Models and Architectures for 3D Object Detection

There are various models for 3D Object Detection with CNNs for different types of input, from images captured with a camera, a point cloud based on LIDAR, to mixed sensor models with image and point cloud data and sometimes even more sensors, like ultrasonic and radar. The models all have the same goal, 3D Object Detection, but can achieve it with different methods depending on the available data for the model. Cameras usually acquire RGB or monochromatic data as an image. A LIDAR captures a point cloud which is a series of points with a reflectance value distributed in 3D space where each point of the point cloud has four dimensions: spatial dimensions, X, Y, Z, and reflectance (R).

Camera based models typically suffer from poor depth perception specially for medium to long range classification, this occurs even in non-monocular models due to the loss of the 3D depth effect at long range. Another factor is the reduced image resolution as the objects get further away. Point cloud based models have very precise depth information even tough the density of points in the point cloud reduces. This means that, as long as the model can classify correctly the object with a relatively small amount of points, its location is likely more precise and accurate compared to a camera based model. Mixed sensor models try to use both types of data inputs to maximize precision and accuracy. However, these models usually take more resources to process and need extra complexity to preprocess and merge the two different data inputs into a single useful data format.

The first approaches to LiDAR data processing with neural networks considered as input a projection of the point cloud into one or more 2D planes [3]. This mapping onto 2D images allows the direct application of known convolutional neural networks (CNN). The disadvantage of this approach is that some information is lost. To avoid loosing important information from the point cloud, 3D-based methods consider the entire space. In [4] the entire point cloud is treated as an object and considered for semantic segmentation and classification. To reduce the complexity of the model, cell based methods divide the space into cells of fixed size, extract features from them and then apply 2D or 3D CNNs. Known examples are PointPillars [5] and VoxelNet [6]. Hybrid methods integrate both cell based CNNs and PointNet-based representations to learn more discriminative point cloud features [7].

Most cell-based methods apply 3D convolutions, which are computationally more demanding than 2D convolutions. An exception is PointPillars, a cell-based method that uses 2D convolutions. Compared to recent works, precision drops of 6% in Bird's Eye View (BEV) and 11% in 3D view are observed when compared to more accurate models [8]. However, PointPillars only use 2D convolutions, which reduces the complexity of the solution, more appropriate for embedded devices. Therefore, PointPillars was chosen in this work.

Only a few works have designed accelerators of deep neural networks for LiDAR processing. In [9], the authors propose an FPGA design of VoxelNet. A few quantizations (from 12 to 32 bits) are tested, but there are no details about the hardware architecture. In [10] the authors consider 8 and 16 bit quantizations with PointNet model to run classification and segmentation. The throughput doubles with 8 bit quantization but the detection accuracy is not reported. The Vitis AI framework from Xilinx includes an implementation of a small version of PointPillars [17] that runs at around 19 frames per second with an accuracy drop. In [11] the authors also consider a few network simplifications before designing a hardware implementation with the FINN tool with an AP loss of 19% in 3D and 8% in BEV and a throughput close to 4 frames per second. Quantization of the model is a very important aspect when the target is an embedded device. The work in [12] explores different quantizations for different parts of the PointPillars and conclude with an hybrid quantization that could be further optimized with pruning. The study does not consider the hardware design and therefore the hardware tradeoffs implementing hybrid quantization and prunning are not analyzed.

In this work the tradeoff between quantization and hardware complexity is explored for the PointPillars neural model. A hardware accelerator is then proposed to run the inference of the most efficient quantization solution. The architecture was designed with high level synthesis (HLS) and tested in a Zynq Ultrascale+ ZU7EV. The results show that it is possible to design a very efficient accelerator for PointPillars without model reduction using an aggressive quantization with a small accuracy reduction.

3   Model Analysis and Quantization Methodology

3.1   PointPillars Network Model

PointPillars [13] is a 3D Object Detection model for point clouds, where the point cloud data is extracted into a 2D pseudo image, before applying the backbone and the detection layer. Following the taxonomy proposed in [14], this model has a Pillar based data representation, with a 2D CNN-backbone and a single stage detector with no refinement stage.

This first step creates a 2D pseudo image from the point cloud, designated Pillar Feature Net (PFN), using a series of sub-steps. The points in the point cloud are associated with the pillar in space. These pillars are defined in the implementation and can change in length and width in order to change the resolution of the final pseudo-image. Then, more data is extracted from each point. From the four original dimensions of the points, five additional dimensions are added: X_c, Y_c, Z_c, X_p and Y_p. These dimensions encode the distance to the mean of the points positions in the pillar for X, Y and Z dimensions and also the offset to the center of the pillar in X and Y dimensions.

Even though some pillars will have a big number of points, most of the pillars will be empty. Empty pillars are disregarded because they do not add useful data. After the association of points to pillars, the number of points per pillar and the total amount of pillars selected are limited to N and P, respectively. Following that, points and pillars are chosen randomly to fill a (D,N,P) seized tensor, keeping points of the same pillar in the same position of P and all data that goes beyond the N and P dimensions is discarded. Where no data exists in the tensor, either due to not having N or more points in a pillar or not having P pillars in the point cloud with points, zero padding is applied. While this tensor is being built, a vector that store the X,Y position on the pillar grid is also being generated in order to know where each pillar is in the 2D top down view of the point cloud representation. Then, a PointNet followed by BatchNorm and ReLU activation function sequence is used to generate a (C,P,N) tensor, where C is the number of features extracted from the nine dimensions of the points. Then max pooling is used in the N dimension to reduce the data to a (C,P) tensor.

Finally, to end the Pillar Feature Net, the (C,P) tensor data is mapped using the vector created in step two, into a pseudo-image of the size and dimension equal to the pillars defined at the start. The back-end of PointPillars has a simple design based on sequential sections of 2D convolutions, Batch Normalization and ReLUs. The first section has four blocks of 2D convolutions, Batch Normalization and ReLU, and the second and third section have six of those same blocks. The features increase to double in each section, starting with C, and the other two dimensions half in each section, starting with H/2 and W/2. The output of each section is the input of the next section. Then the Neck is designed has the 2D deconvolution with 2D transpose convolutions of the outputs of each of the sections, and the concatenation of all of them, before being sent to the Detection Head.

Table 1. PointPillars model layers

	layers	filters	size	stride	input	output
PFN	Voxelization					
	conv1d | Bn	64	1	1	$12000 \times 100 \times 9$	$12000 \times 100 \times 64$
Backbone Sequence 1	conv2d | Bn | ReLU	64	3×3	2	$432 \times 496 \times 64$	$216 \times 248 \times 64$
	conv2d | Bn | ReLU	64	3×3	1	$216 \times 248 \times 64$	$216 \times 248 \times 64$
	conv2d | Bn | ReLU	64	3×3	1	$216 \times 248 \times 64$	$216 \times 248 \times 64$
	conv2d | Bn | ReLU	64	3×3	1	$216 \times 248 \times 64$	$216 \times 248 \times 64$
Backbone Sequence 2	conv2d | Bn | ReLU	128	3×3	2	$216 \times 248 \times 64$	$108 \times 124 \times 128$
	conv2d | Bn | ReLU	128	3×3	1	$108 \times 124 \times 128$	$108 \times 124 \times 128$
	conv2d | Bn | ReLU	128	3×3	1	$108 \times 124 \times 128$	$108 \times 124 \times 128$
	conv2d | Bn | ReLU	128	3×3	1	$108 \times 124 \times 128$	$108 \times 124 \times 128$
	conv2d | Bn | ReLU	128	3×3	1	$108 \times 124 \times 128$	$108 \times 124 \times 128$
	conv2d | Bn | ReLU	128	3×3	1	$108 \times 124 \times 128$	$108 \times 124 \times 128$
Backbone Sequence 3	conv2d | Bn | ReLU	256	3×3	2	$108 \times 124 \times 128$	$54 \times 62 \times 256$
	conv2d | Bn | ReLU	256	3×3	1	$54 \times 62 \times 256$	$54 \times 62 \times 256$
	conv2d | Bn | ReLU	256	3×3	1	$54 \times 62 \times 256$	$54 \times 62 \times 256$
	conv2d | Bn | ReLU	256	3×3	1	$54 \times 62 \times 256$	$54 \times 62 \times 256$
	conv2d | Bn | ReLU	256	3×3	1	$54 \times 62 \times 256$	$54 \times 62 \times 256$
	conv2d | Bn | ReLU	256	3×3	1	$54 \times 62 \times 256$	$54 \times 62 \times 256$
Neck	convT2d | Bn | ReLU	128	1×1	1	$216 \times 248 \times 64$	$216 \times 248 \times 128$
	convT2d | Bn | ReLU	128	2×2	2	$108 \times 124 \times 128$	$216 \times 248 \times 128$
	convT2d | Bn | ReLU	128	4×4	4	$54 \times 62 \times 256$	$216 \times 248 \times 128$
Head	conv2d	18	1×1	1	$216 \times 248 \times 384$	$216 \times 248 \times 18$
	conv2d	42	1×1	1	$216 \times 248 \times 384$	$216 \times 248 \times 42$
	conv2d	12	1×1	1	$216 \times 248 \times 384$	$216 \times 248 \times 12$

The Detection Head used is a Single Stage Detector or SSD [15], that, in this case, is used to predict in 2D space the position of each of the bounding boxes. The vertical prediction is not being used, as it is common in this kind of algorithms, due to the KITTI dataset low variance in vertical positioning of objects. The z dimension and position are preset values defined in the model.

In Table 1 we can see how the PointPillars layers are configured and their sizes. The input for each of the three layers of the Neck are the outputs of each of the Backbone sequences, and at the end of the Neck all the three outputs are put in sequence to make the input of the detection Head.

All convolutions of the backbone consider kernels of size 3×3 followed by ReLU activation function. Convolutions in the PFN (Pillar Feature Net) and in the Head use 1×1 kernels. The Neck section applies transposed convolutions to decode the input maps to the same output size.

3.2 KITTY Dataset

The KITTI dataset was created by the Karlsruhe Institute of Technology (KIT) and Toyota Technological Institute at Chicago (TTI-C). This creation was done in order to have a good extensive and diverse dataset of vehicle sensor data, to later develop computer vision systems and establish a benchmark of the capabilities of this computer vision systems.

The raw data is composed of thousands of data frames, each with a pair of stereo gray scale 0.5 Megapixel images in png format; a pair of stereo color 0.5 Megapixel images in png format; a 3D Velodyne (LiDAR) point cloud, with 100k points per frame, stored as a binary float matrix; 3D GPS and IMU data with location, speed, acceleration and meta information in a text file; Calibration data for all the sensors as a text file; and finally the labels of the objects that are present in the frame, cars, trucks, trams, pedestrians and cyclists were stored as a xml file.

3.3 Methodology for Model Quantization

The number of operations to run a single inference of the model determines the processing and memory requirements of the embedded computing platform for real-time performance. A detailed analysis of the PointPillars model reveals that most of the computation and memory usage is in the Backbone and Neck, meaning that it should be the focus of the optimization efforts, as we can see in Table 2.

Quantization is a hardware-oriented optimization that reduces the hardware complexity of the arithmetic operations. While the number of operations is kept the same, quantization maps floating-point representations of weights and activations into low bitwidth fixed-point quantization. Smaller bit widths have a smaller memory footprint and the operators require less hardware resources to be implemented. A tradeoff exists between reducing the model size and the quantization bitwidth. Most previous works reduce the model complexity to improve the system throughput at the cost of some accuracy. The work in [12] explores bitwidth quantization and accuracy of PointPillars with model reduction.

The methodology proposed in this work explores the tradeoff between bitwidth quantization, hardware resources and accuracy without reducing the model. The original model is trained with data represented with floating-point and then a quantization aware training is applied with data represented with homogeneous fixed-point representation. Considering the pair 'activation $\times$ weight', the quantizations considered were: 8×8, 8×4, 4×4, 4×2, 2×2, where ternary quantization was considered with narrow range ({-1, 0, 1}) and without narrow range ({-2, -1, 0, 1}). For a particular quantization, different layers may have different scales.

Table 2. PointPillars MAC operations and Memory usage of weights

	Layers	MAC (Mop)	Weights MEM (KiB)
PFN	Voxelization		
	conv1d | Bn	691	1
Backbone Sequence 1	conv2d | Bn | ReLU	1975	36
	conv2d | Bn | ReLU	1975	36
	conv2d | Bn | ReLU	1975	36
	conv2d | Bn | ReLU	1975	36
Backbone Sequence 2	conv2d | Bn | ReLU	987	72
	conv2d | Bn | ReLU	1975	144
	conv2d | Bn | ReLU	1975	144
	conv2d | Bn | ReLU	1975	144
	conv2d | Bn | ReLU	1975	144
	conv2d | Bn | ReLU	1975	144
Backbone Sequence 3	conv2d | Bn | ReLU	987	288
	conv2d | Bn | ReLU	1975	576
	conv2d | Bn | ReLU	1975	576
	conv2d | Bn | ReLU	1975	576
	conv2d | Bn | ReLU	1975	576
	conv2d | Bn | ReLU	1975	576
Neck	convT2d | Bn | ReLU	439	8
	convT2d | Bn | ReLU	3511	64
	convT2d | Bn | ReLU	28085	512
Head	conv2d	370	7
	conv2d	864	16
	conv2d	247	5

To compare the hardware complexity of different model quantizations, the size of the arithmetic units is considered. A complexity factor is proposed to compare the relative complexity of hardware implementations with different quantizations. This factor considers the occupied resources to implement the dot product between vectors with 16 elements. Hardware implementations for the several configurations of quantization were developed and the number of occupied LUTs in an FPGA device was obtained (see Table 3).

For example, the dot product with a quantization of 8×2 utilizes about one quarter of the resources used to implement the same unit with a quantization of

Table 3. Resource consumption in LUTs of a dot-product between vectors of 16 elements for different operand bitwidths)

Quantization	8×8	8×4	8×2	$8 \times 2*$	4×4	4×2	$4 \times 2*$
LUTs	1423	687	335	284	431	181	150
Complexity factor	1	0.48	0.24	0.20	0.30	0.13	0.11

* - narrow range

8×8. Considering that most of the resources of a CNN accelerator are consumed by the dot products, the ratio of occupied resources between each implementation is a close approximation of the reduction in complexity achieved when a smaller quantization is used.

4   Architecture of the Hardware Accelerator

A typical architecture of CNN accelerators considers a single configurable hardware module that supports the execution of different types of layers and runs them one at a time. The module is initially configured to run a particular layer. Then, it reads the input maps and weights, executes the convolutions, and sends the output map back to external memory for the next layer.

Other type of architecture considers multiple dedicated processing modules, one for each layer of the network [16]. The modules are organized in a dataflow like a coarse pipeline. This approach reduces the accesses to external memory to store and retrieve intermediate maps but requires more memory to locally store weights and intermediate maps. The single core architecture consumes more energy since intermediate maps are moved between on-chip and external memories.

Knowing that the PointPillars model has close to 40 MParameters, the dataflow architecture would require a large on-chip memory, not available in FPGAs for embedded computing. Therefore, in this work, the single configurable core was chosen (see Fig. 1).

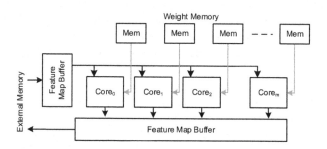

Fig. 1. Configurable CNN accelerator

The number of cores is statically configurable and multiple modules can be used in parallel. The cores can execute 2D convolutions with kernels of size 3×3 and 1×1, stride of 1 or 2, as well as transposed convolutions. The activation function is ReLU. Each core of the architecture can run one convolution with multiple multiplications in parallel (see Fig. 2).

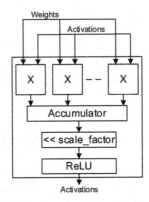

Fig. 2. Architecture of each identical core of CNN accelerator

The activation function is applied right after the convolution of the whole filter. There is a specific way the data of the input and output is encoded, to be sent to the accelerator, and it is also received encoded in that specific way. For the input and output map, this codification, is done in the Z axis and for filter and bias data this is done with input kernel first.

To better understand the input and output map codification by the z axis, we can give the following example. If a input map is composed by 20 images that are 10 by 10 pixels, first the pixel (0,0) of the 20 images will be sent; then the pixels (0,1) of the 20 images and so on. This is done first in the X dimension then in the Y dimension.

The processing in the cores is designed through nested loops of the sizes of the input and output data, with the outer most loop being the input Y, then input X, output Z, kernel Y, kernel X and the last loop being kernel/input Z as seen in the pseudo code in Figure 3. On each of the compute cycles the compute core, defined as a PE, is responsible for the compute of one Z output data point.

```
OutYLOOP:for(int y = 0; y < inputMapYSize ; y++)
    OutXLOOP:for(int x = 0; x < inputMapXSize; x++)
        FilterLOOP:for(int f=0; f < inputMapZSize; f++){
            KernelYLOOP:for(int ky = 0; ky < kernelSize; ky++){
                KernelXLOOP: for(int kx = 0; kx < kernelSize; kx++){
                    ChannelLOOP:for(int kn=0; kn < outputMapZSize; kn++){
```

Fig. 3. Main processing loops pseudo code

Considering the processing in the Z axis, the convolution with different kernel sizes and strides reduces to the address manipulation when accessing the activation memory, while the filters are always read in sequence.

The 2D transpose convolution, works by multiplying each of the input pixels by the weights and offsetting the output by the stride, this means there will be some overlay where it is summed.

However, the 2D transposed convolutions can be done as a sequence of 2D convolutions stitched together in a specific way. This was achieved because the stride and kernel size of the 2D Transpose convolution were the same in all these layers of the model.

As we can see, because there is no overlay of the results of the multiplication of the kernel by the input matrix, the computation can be done as a collection of regular 2D convolutions with kernel 1 by 1 and stride 1, where each of the kernel's is one of the original kernel's position. The results can be assembled by building the output as shown in the Fig. 4.

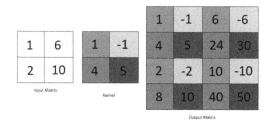

Fig. 4. Explanation of the transpose convolution optimization

As can be seen, the input kernel is applied completely to each entry of the input matrix. Therefore, each entry of the input kernel is applied to the input matrix and the results store in the output memory with a stride of two. This change in the way the computation is done, in this particular case, reduced the total amount of MAC operations by 90%.

5   Experimental Results

This section describes the results obtained with the quantization exploration flow and the hardware accelerator.

5.1   Model Quantization Results

The quantization exploration considered quantization-aware training. All quantized model instances were trained using the KITTY dataset.

This model used the LiDAR (Velodyne) point cloud information from the dataset to produce its results. The dataset was segmented in two parts for the neural network training process, with a training set to train the network and a testing set to test the training of the network. The official training set was split into 3712 training samples and 3769 validation samples, as in [5]. The loss function is optimized using the Adam optimizer with an initial learning rate of 2×2^{-4} and the 1cycle learning rate policy. All experiments were executed in a desktop computer with an Intel i7-11700F processor with 64 GB of DDR4 RAM and a GPU NVIDIA GeForce RTX 3090 with 24 GB GDDR5 video memory.

The results achieved after training were 69.41%, 63.42% and 70.75% of accuracy for AOS AP, BBox 3D and BBox BEV respectively. The original model was then quantized and trained for 160 epochs (see Table 4)

Table 4. PointPillars Quantization testing accuracy

Model Section	A	W	Max accuracy medium difficulty				
			BBox_2D	AOS	BBox_bev	BBox_3D	Complx
baseline	-	-	76,00	69,76	70,75	63,42	
Full	8	8	73,89	67,55	69,45	62,34	1
	8	4	73,68	67,11	69,08	60,77	0.48
	8	2	69,42	62,55	65,19	57,21	0.24
Backbone	8	4	74,95	68,06	70,93	62,83	0.48
	4	4	72,18	64,04	67,63	59,54	0,30
	8	2	74,09	67,32	69,99	61,95	0,24
	4	2	64,13	54,62	60,13	49,11	0,13
	8	2*	73,15	65,84	69,27	61,07	0,20
Backbone/Neck	8	2*	71,92	65,10	68,54	61,18	0,20
Backbone/Neck/Head	8	2	69,14	61,04	63,95	54,96	0,24
	8	2*	67,28	59,21	56,87	46,32	0,20
	8	2*/8	71,84	65,35	68,31	59,27	—

* - Narrow range: {-1, 0, 1}

The last column indicates the relative hardware complexity compared to a 8×8 quantization.

From the results, it is possible to conclude that the model is mostly sensitive to activation precision, meaning that reducing the precision of the activations has a higher impact over the accuracy of the model, compared to reducing the weights precision. For example, the model accuracy reduces by about 5% with activations at 8 bits and reducing the weights from 8 to 2 bits. In the other direction, reducing the activations to 4 or 2 bits with the weights at 2 bits, reduces the model precision much more, which can not be attributed to a margin of error or variance.

Another observation is that going from 2 bits weights to 2 bits weights with narrow range, mostly does not change the results. This implies that going from a 4 possible value multiplication {-2, -1, 0 and 1} to only three value multiplication by {-1, 0 or 1}, the accumulation is either a sum (+1), a subtraction (−1) or 0.

For -2 it would add a shift left to the subtraction that in the narrow range case becomes unnecessary.

Considering the accuracy and complexity, it can be concluded that the 8×2 is the most efficient for the backbone and neck parts. The accuracy is within 1% lower than that achieved with the 8×8 quantization. The most aggressive quantizations, 4×2 and 2×2 have a reduction in accuracy higher than 10%, in spite of the very high reduction in the relative complexity. However, when the quantization 8×2 applied to the Head part, it is evident that there is a relative drop in accuracy. Therefore, an 8×8 quantization was considered for the Head.

5.2   Area and Performance Results

The hardware accelerator was developed using Vitis HLS 2022.2 from Xilinx. The PointPillars model was mapped on both the programmable logic (PL) and processing system (PS) of the Zynq ZCU7EV FPGA of a ZCU104 development board. The PL runs the backbone, head and neck sections, while the voxelization and postprocessing tasks are left to be executed in the PS.

The accelerator consists of two modules: one for the convolutions with 8×2 quantization and another for the 8×8 quantization. For the first module, different designs were synthesized with a different number of cores: 8, 16, 32, and 64 with 64 parallel multipliers each. This permits to verify the scalability of the accelerator and that it can be applied to devices with a different number of resources (see Table 5). All solutions consider a target frequency of 150 MHz.

Table 5. Occupation of resources of the module with 8×2 quantization for different number of cores

		DSP	LUT	BRAM
Quantization	Number of cores	1,728	230 K	310
8×2	8	15	12,096	160
8×2	16	15	20,792	160
8×2	32	15	38,184	160
8×2	64	15	72,968	160

As we can see from Table 5 the increase in resources is almost linear with the number of cores, showing the scalability of the solution. In spite of the large number of multiplications, the number of resources is relatively low since the multipliers have size 8×2. The architecture implements the multiplications with LUT. The DSPs are only used for the address generators.

The number of BRAMs is determined by the number of cores and the size of the reading buses. All memories are simple dual port. The bus size of the memory to store input and output maps is 512 bits and the buses of the weights memories are 128 bits.

For the second module, a relative parallelism proportional to the number of operations executed by each one of the two modules was considered, namely, 1, 2 and 4 cores with 64 parallel multipliers each. In this case, the number of resources is given in Table 6.

Table 6. Occupation of resources of the module with 8 × 8 with 1, 2 and 4 cores

		DSP	LUT	BRAM
Quantization	Number of cores	1,728	230 K	310
8 × 8	1	36	3,198	16
8 × 8	2	71	6,217	24
8 × 8	4	134	12,310	40

The accelerator was integrated with the PS of Zynq FPGA. The external memory access is through the HP ports and using Direct Memory Access (DMA) blocks. The PS is programmed to configure the DMAs to send the input feature maps and weights to the IP accelerator and to receive the respective output map, one layer at a time. The delay (ms) and the throughput (FPS - Frames per Second) for each configuration of the accelerator are given in Table 7.

Table 7. Performance of the hardware/software system running the PointPillars CNN for different configurations of the IP accelerator.

Cores	Delay (ms)	Throughput (FPS)
8	393	2.5
16	201	5.0
32	112	8.9
64	64	15.6

We can see that the processing of the CNN on the 64 cores version of the accelerator achieved a throughput of 15.6 FPS. From Table 7 we can also see that the improvement by doubling the number of cores gets reduced as the nominal number of cores increase. This can be explained by the setup time of the IP, that becomes more and more meaningful for the total processing time, as it does not improve as the number of cores increases.

All solutions are computation limited since the available memory bandwidth to access external memory is enough to guarantee communication/computation overlap of parameters and maps transfer, which only requires around 1.2 GBytes/s of memory bandwidth.

Following the software implementation in [8] for the voxelization and postprocessing tasks, the software tasks are within the execution time of the PointPillars model executed by the accelerator. This allows a coarse pipeline execution of the full PointPillars model.

The proposed accelerator was compared to previous works in terms of accuracy and performance (see Table 8).

Table 8. Comparison of the proposed accelerator against previous accelerators for PointPillars

Work	DSP	LUT	BRAM	All 3D (%)	All BEV (%)	Car 3D	Car BEV	FPS
[8]	88	189,074	159	—	—	57.1	79.3	3.8
[17]	562	53,540	257	—	—	69.1	79.7	19
This work	149	85,278	200	59.3	68.3	72.56	84.68	15.6

The proposed work managed to achieve the lowest accuracy reduction since it implements the original PointPillars Network. The throughput is 15% lower than that of Vitis AI, but works at a frequency of 150 MHz against 325/650 MHz of Vitis AI. This has a great impact in the consumption of energy when dealing with embedded computing. In terms of resources, the proposed solution consumes less DSP and BRAM and more LUTs. This was expected since most of the multipliers of the accelerator do not use DSPs.

6   Conclusion and Future Work

This work succeeded in developing a hardware IP capable of massively acceleration of a 3D Object detection model, PointPillars, on FPGA, keeping most of the accuracy of the original model, while improving the area and performance efficiency. This work also succeeded in understanding and demonstrating the possibility of performing 2D transpose convolutions were stride is equal to the kernel size, with a sequence of 2D convolutions, achieving massive reduction in total MAC operations. The hardware accelerator was developed and implemented in the Xilinx ZynqZCU7EV FPGA achieving 15.6 FPS throughput. Compared to previous works, it shows that it is possible to keep an accuracy close to the original floating-point model with a good throughput.

Acknowledgments. This work was supported by national funds through Fundação para a Ciência e a Tecnologia (FCT) with reference UIDB/50021/2020.

Disclosure of Interests. The authors have no competing interests to declare that are relevant to the content of this article.

References

1. Li, Y., et al.: Deep learning for lidar point clouds in autonomous driving: a review. IEEE Trans. Neural Netw. Learn. Syst. **32**(8), 3412–3432 (2021)
2. Véstias, M.P., Duarte, R.P., de Sousa, J.T., Neto, H.C.: Moving deep learning to the edge. Algorithms **13**(5), 125 (2020). https://www.mdpi.com/1999-4893/13/5/125
3. X. Chen, H. Ma, J. Wan, B. Li, T. Xia, "Multi-view 3d object detection network for autonomous driving," in 2017 IEEE Conference on Computer Vision and Pattern Recognition (CVPR). Los Alamitos, CA, USA: IEEE Computer Society, Jul 2017, pp. 6526–6534. [Online]. Available: https://doi.ieeecomputersociety.org/10.1109/CVPR.2017.691
4. Charles, R., Su, H., Kaichun, M., Guibas, L.J.: Pointnet: deep learning on point sets for 3d classification and segmentation. In: 2017 IEEE Conference on Computer Vision and Pattern Recognition (CVPR). Los Alamitos, CA, USA, Jul 2017, pp. 77–85. IEEE Computer Society. https://doi.ieeecomputersociety.org/10.1109/CVPR.2017.16
5. Lang, A.H., Vora, S., Caesar, H., Zhou, L., Yang, J., Beijbom, O.: PointPillars: Fast encoders for object detection from point clouds. In: 2019 IEEE/CVF Conference on Computer Vision and Pattern Recognition (CVPR), pp. 12 689–12 697 (2019)
6. Zhou, Y., Tuzel, O.: Voxelnet: end-to-end learning for point cloud based 3d object detection. In: 2018 IEEE/CVF Conference on Computer Vision and Pattern Recognition (CVPR). Los Alamitos, CA, USA, pp. 4490–4499. IEEE Computer Society, June 2018. https://doi.ieeecomputersociety.org/10.1109/CVPR.2018.00472
7. Shi, S., et al.: PV-RCNN: point-voxel feature set abstraction for 3d object detection. In: 2020 IEEE/CVF Conference on Computer Vision and Pattern Recognition (CVPR), Los Alamitos, CA, USA, June 2020, pp. 10 526–10 535. IEEE Computer Society. https://doi.ieeecomputersociety.org/10.1109/CVPR42600.2020.01054
8. Stanisz, J., Lis, K., Gorgon, M.: Implementation of the PointPillars network for 3d object detection in reprogrammable heterogeneous devices using FINN. J. Signal Process. Syst. **94**(7), 659–674 (2022). https://doi.org/10.1007/s11265-021-01733-4
9. López, J.G., Agudo, A., Moreno-Noguer, F.: 3d vehicle detection on an FPGA from lidar point clouds. In: Proceedings of the 2019 2nd International Conference on Watermarking and Image Processing, ser. ICWIP 2019. New York, NY, USA: Association for Computing Machinery, pp. 21–26 (2020). https://doi.org/10.1145/3369973.3369984
10. Bai, L., Lyu, Y., Huang, X.: Pointnet on FPGA for real-time lidar point cloud processing. In: 2020 IEEE International Symposium on Circuits and Systems (ISCAS), pp. 1–5 (2020)
11. Stanisz, J., Lis, K., Gorgon, M.: Implementation of the PointPillars network for 3d object detection in reprogrammable heterogeneous devices using FINN. J. Signal Process. Syst. **94**, 07 (2022)
12. Stanisz, J., Lis, K., Kryjak, T., Gorgon, M.: Optimisation of the PointPillars network for 3d object detection in point clouds. In: 2020 Signal Processing: Algorithms, Architectures, Arrangements, and Applications (SPA), pp. 122–127 (2020)
13. Lang, A.H., Vora, S., Caesar, H., Zhou, L., Yang, J., Beijbom, O.: PointPillars: fast encoders for object detection from point clouds. CoRR, vol. abs/1812.05784, 2018. https://openaccess.thecvf.com/content_CVPR_2019/papers/Lang_PointPillars_Fast_Encoders_for_Object_Detection_From_Point_Clouds_CVPR_2019_paper.pdf

14. Fernandes, D., et al.: Point-cloud based 3d object detection and classification methods for self-driving applications: a survey and taxonomy. Inf. Fusion. **68**, 161–191 (2021). https://www.sciencedirect.com/science/article/pii/S1566253520304097
15. Liu, W., Anguelov, D., Erhan, D., Szegedy, C., Reed, S., Fu, C.-Y., Berg, A.C.: SSD: single shot multibox detector. In: Leibe, B., Matas, J., Sebe, N., Welling, M. (eds.) ECCV 2016. LNCS, vol. 9905, pp. 21–37. Springer, Cham (2016). https://doi.org/10.1007/978-3-319-46448-0_2
16. Blott, M., et al.: FINN-R: an end-to-end deep-learning framework for fast exploration of quantized neural networks. ACM Trans. Reconfig. Technol. Syst. (TRETS). **11**(3), 1–23 (2018)
17. PointPillars implementation in vitisai. https://github.com/Xilinx/Vitis-AI/blob/master/model_zoo/model-list/pt_pointpillars_3.5/model_info.md

Cryptographic Security Through a Hardware Root of Trust

Luis F. Rojas-Muñoz[1](✉) [iD], Santiago Sánchez-Solano[1] [iD],
Macarena C. Martínez-Rodríguez[1] [iD], Eros Camacho-Ruiz[1] [iD],
Pablo Navarro-Torrero[1] [iD], Apurba Karmakar[1] [iD], Carlos Fernández-García[1] [iD],
Erica Tena-Sánchez[1,2] [iD], Francisco E. Potestad-Ordóñez[1,2] [iD],
Alejandro Casado-Galán[1] [iD], Pau Ortega-Castro[1] [iD],
Antonio J. Acosta-Jiménez[1,3] [iD], Carlos J. Jiménez-Fernández[1,2] [iD],
and Piedad Brox[1] [iD]

[1] Instituto de Microelectrónica de Sevilla, IMSE-CNM, CSIC,
Universidad de Sevilla, 41092 Sevilla, Spain
rojas@imse-cnm.csic.es
[2] Escuela Politécnica Superior, Universidad de Sevilla, 41011 Sevilla, Spain
[3] Facultad de Física, Universidad de Sevilla, 41012 Sevilla, Spain

Abstract. This work presents a novel approach to a Hardware Root-of-Trust that leverages System-on-Chip technology for the implementation of hardware cryptographic functions. Taking advantage of the processing power of a System-on-Chip, the solution established promotes hardware-based security solutions over software-only solutions. The proposed Root-of-Trust, developed around a Xilinx Zynq-7000 SoC device, integrates components based on cryptographic algorithms and physical phenomena. This innovative Root-of-Trust is tailored to support a spectrum of security tasks within cryptographic systems, including device-specific identifiers and keys, encryption and decryption, hashing, and signature generation and verification. The study adopts a unified design methodology, capitalizing on collaborative efforts to efficiently develop hardware primitives that significantly contribute to enhancing security in computing environments. Aligned with the advantages of reconfigurable hardware, this Hardware Root-of-Trust addresses the critical need for robust hardware-level security and introduces a set of countermeasures to fortify the design against potential threats.

Keywords: AES · Elliptic Curves · FPGA · PUF · Root-of-Trust · SHA · SoC · TRNG

This research was supported in part by the SPIRS Project with Grant Agreement No. 952622 under the EU H2020 research and innovation programme. The authors want to thank the ARES Project PID2020-116664RB-100 funded by MCIN/AEI/10.13039/501100011033 and the EU NextGeneration EU/PRTR, and the Programa Operativo FEDER 2014-2020 and Consejería de Economía, Conocimiento, Empresas y Universidad de la Junta de Andalucía under Project US-1380823. M.C.M.R. holds a postdoc fellowship from the Andalusia Government with support from PO FSE of EU.

I. Skliarova et al. (Eds.): ARC 2024, LNCS 14553, pp. 106–119, 2024.
https://doi.org/10.1007/978-3-031-55673-9_8

1   Introduction

Reconfigurable devices, such as Field-Programmable Gate Arrays (FPGAs), have become important in the dynamic field of computing systems. Their notable flexibility and adaptability make them suitable to fulfill specific application requirements, providing advantages in performance, energy efficiency, and rapid prototyping. Furthermore, FPGA-based Systems-on-Chip (SoCs) combine processing power and flexibility into a single chip, allowing for an exciting potential to further exploit FPGA capabilities by bridging the gap between software and hardware [12,19].

SoC technology is an important element for creating and developing cryptographic hardware solutions in the field of secure computing. By utilizing its built-in processing power and related benefits, this technology provides a versatile scenario to design and achieve complex security requirements. In this regard, security protocols have been grounded in hardware to achieve true effectiveness, and to avoid reliance only on software-based solutions [16].

To establish a secure starting point for a chain of trust within a computing system, and to ensure the integrity and authenticity of data across critical processes while protecting against various forms of attacks and unauthorized access, a hardware Root-of-Trust (RoT) emerges as an essential element that supports booting process, authentications, and encryptions. The RoT is commonly composed of primitives that are designed based on cryptographic algorithms or different physical phenomena that enable functions exploited by higher-level software components [10].

As modern systems become more interconnected and the digital domain continues to expand, vulnerabilities at the hardware level represent significant risks. The implementation of a Hardware RoT in an SoC not only aligns with the advantages of reconfigurable hardware but also addresses the critical need for robust security measures in facing evolving threats. In addition, the anchoring of security in silicon manufacturing processes establishes a hardened layer of protection, providing confidence in electronic systems.

This work introduces a new RoT approach to secure cryptographic systems by leveraging the inherent capabilities and benefits of Xilinx SoCs technology through the design and hardware implementation of a set of security primitives, highlighting its potential and contribution to the evolving landscape of trusted computing environments.

To guide the readers through this paper, Sect. 2 presents the used methodology. Sections 3 and 4 detail the development and performance evaluation of the RoT primitives. Finally, Sect. 5 summarizes the results and the main conclusions.

2   Design Methodology

In the context of the SPIRS project [1], a comprehensive exploration of components was carried out to facilitate a secure implementation of hardware and cryptographic functions for establishing the necessary elements of a RoT approach.

The combination of these diverse components must ensure the authenticity and uniqueness of each device while providing confidentiality, integrity, and reliability. As a result, the selected components cover a range of essential functions, including a Physically Unclonable Function (PUF) for device identification and generation of cryptographic keys and random numbers, Advanced Encryption Standard (AES) for secure data encryption and decryption, Secure Hash Algorithms (SHAs) to efficiently ensure data integrity, and an Edwards-curve Digital Signature Algorithm (EdDSA) for generating and verifying digital signatures.

The hardware design of this set of primitives provides an excellent opportunity for collaborative efforts, aiming to optimize the time required to achieve a functional RoT implementation. Collaborative work of a high number of authors, while advantageous, brings notable challenges in integration, such as design software version compatibility, communication interfaces, resource consumption, and debugging. Consequently, a unified design methodology was developed, allowing for the development of each hardware primitive and ensuring a smooth integration process for the RoT.

A key decision in the design process was to develop an easily updatable and configurable RoT, leading to the adoption of a modular hierarchy. The initial step in this methodology involves identifying innovative areas where the development of each primitive over SoCs contributes to the state-of-the-art. This identification process sets the stage for a Hardware/Software (HW/SW) co-design, where computationally intensive operations are strategically migrated from full software execution to hardware, achieving a balance between performance and resource utilization.

Each primitive design has been parameterized to ensure reusability, scalability, and flexibility, facilitating rapid adaptation to different requirements and scenarios. The development board chosen for this goal is the Pynq Z2, which features a dual-core ARM Cortex-A9 processor integrated with Xilinx Zynq-7000 SoC. The hardware primitives are encapsulated as Intellectual Property (IP) modules through Vivado software, equipped with AXI4 Lite interfaces to optimize resource utilization and establish smooth connectivity between Programmable Logic (PL) and the processing system (PS) (see Fig. 1).

The Pynq Z2 board is well-suited for running an Ubuntu-based operating system, and this feature is leveraged for the integration of IP primitives into the hybrid system. A C-API is employed to simplify interaction with software components, ensuring efficient communication between software and hardware. This strategic use of the Ubuntu-based operating system optimizes the development and execution of on-site applications for each RoT component.

The design methodology finishes with the creation of software components tailored for in-depth characterization, validation, and operation of the selected cryptographic functions. This comprehensive approach ensures a robust and adaptable framework for the design and implementation of the Hardware RoT system.

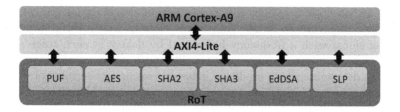

Fig. 1. RoT block diagram

Taking advantage of SoCs features through the described methodology allows for the generation of ad-hoc RoTs by adding or removing specific components, ensuring efficient implementations for particular applications. Additionally, this level of flexibility allows the RoT to be conceived as an evolving element capable of updating over time, enabling the continuous exploration of new vulnerabilities that are constantly discovered and must be addressed.

3   RoT Components

3.1   Physically Unclonable Function

A PUF maps an input, known as challenge, to an output, known as response, while meeting specific features: First, different PUF instances must generate distinct responses for the same challenge to be **unique**; second, a PUF instance should produce a response as unchanged as possible with repeated application of the same challenge to be **reliable**; finally, the PUF response should have a balanced distribution of 0 s and 1 s to be **uniform**. These three requirements facilitate the use of PUF responses for the reconstruction of a device-specific digital identifier on demand.

Silicon-based PUFs exploit the slight variations that occur during the manufacturing process of an integrated circuit to generate unique identifiers extracted from the physical characteristics of the underlying hardware. This approach avoids the use of memory for key storage, reducing vulnerabilities to physical attacks and manufacturing costs.

Silicon-based PUFs have been widely researched and employed in various security applications. Among the different categories, delay-based PUFs that use the relative time-delay differences between two theoretically identical circuits have demonstrated their effectiveness and reliability. Delay-based PUF implementations on FPGA-based SoCs have mainly focused on Ring Oscillators (ROs) since they have proven to provide a good trade-off between integration complexity and efficiency, along with low hardware overhead. Despite identical layouts and the same number of stages for each RO, manufacturing process variability leads to unique characteristic frequencies, differentiating one RO from another. Additionally, this inherent variability across each instance of the PUF allows for the identification of individual hardware devices. The operation of an

RO-PUF is based on frequency differences within closed chains (rings) with an odd number of inverters. When the ring is closed, each inverter produces an oscillating signal with a frequency influenced by delays at each stage and connection paths. The RO-PUF compares oscillation frequencies of RO-pairs using counters to determine which oscillator is faster, capturing the value of the slower one. The output is a bit-stream formed by concatenating bits selected from the values captured after a sequence of RO-pairs comparisons.

As a resource optimization option, True Random Number Generators (TRNGs) can be built using circuit architectures that make use of ring oscillators (ROs) since random manufacturing variations and intrinsic noise sources causing small changes in oscillation frequencies, known as jitter, have been validated and widely investigated as a source of entropy.

Implementation Design: The implemented PUF is based on a reconfigurable architecture shaped by 3 inverting stages and an enabling stage. The inverting stages contain 4 NOT gates in parallel, whose outputs are the inputs of a 4:1 multiplexer controlled by a 2-bit select signal. A 6:1 LUT is required for each inverting stage. The enabling stage includes 2 AND gates of 3 inputs in parallel. The outputs of these AND gates are connected to a 2:1 multiplexer, which requires a 1-bit select signal. A 5:1 LUT is required for this stage (see Fig. 2-left). Given the logic resources that constitute each CLB in the Series-7 family, it is possible to implement 2 configurable 4-stage ROs per CLB, and this fact translates into the striking ability to implement 256 different ROs.

The core components of the PUF are a matrix of ROs (*RO_bank*), which requires only 4×4 CLBs, and two blocks to perform simultaneous RO-pair comparisons (*cmp1* & *cmp2*) using binary or Gray-code counters. It also includes a challenge generation block (*chll_gen*) that limits to two the number of comparisons where each RO is involved in the challenge sequence and allows discarding the most unfavorable ones (*chll_mem*) to enhance PUF response reliability by applying a challenge selection mechanisms, as well as blocks to store and retrieve the output (*out_mem*) and to control system operation (*ctrl*) (see Fig. 2-right).

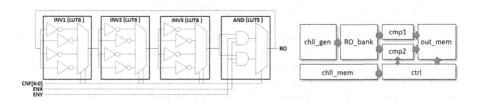

Fig. 2. Configurable 4-stage RO (left), and PUF block diagram (right)

To ease the use of the PUF/TRNG from high-level programming languages, as well as to speed up the characterization and quality assessment processes, the design has been encapsulated as a configurable IP module equipped with an AXI4

Lite interface. The PUF IP parameters allow users to set the operating mode by choosing the main function (PUF/TRNG) and different configuration options: RO-pair comparison strategy (Close/Remote); counter coding (Gray/Binary); and selected bits (Low/High) [14]. Additionally, a Software Development Kit (SDK) has been generated including drivers, functions, utilities, and applications necessary to control the operation of the IP module [15].

Characterization and Quality Assessment: In PUF operation mode, the response quality is assessed by means of the SDK to determine the values of the conventional metrics. **Reliability** is quantified through the Hamming Distance (HD) among multiple responses of the same PUF ($HDintra$), **uniqueness** is quantified through the HD among responses of multiple instances of the same PUF ($HDinter$), and **uniformity** is quantified through the Hamming weight of its output for a single PUF response. The ideal values of these metrics are 0%, 50%, and 50%, respectively. In the TRNG operation mode, the SDK is used in conjunction with the NIST 800-22 standard tests to assess the randomness of the response. Similarly, SDK is used in conjunction with the NIST 900-80b recommendation tests to validate the entropy source.

The statistical results show an $HDintra$ falling within the range of (0%–3%) across all PUF configurations, except for the two involving Binary and High parameters, where the range was narrowed to (0%–1%). The $HDinter$ results fall within a range of (47.5%–48.5%), and the output has shown a high *uniformity* level, falling within the range of (48%–51.5%). This closeness to the ideal values of those metrics demonstrates its strong reliability, uniqueness, and uniformity.

As a result, the PUF presents an ultra-compact design optimizing both resource utilization and output bit-stream length, capable of providing a key length of up to 1024 bits with an Error Correction Code algorithm that uses a Repetition Code value of 15. Furthermore, the implemented comparison sequence provides the design with a high-security level since it minimizes vulnerabilities to electromagnetic Side Channel Attacks by avoiding the possibility of determining the RO frequencies and ensuring non-correlation. Furthermore, the evaluation of the TRNG operation mode successfully met the aforementioned NIST criteria.

3.2   Advanced Encryption Standard

AES was chosen as the symmetric cryptography algorithm for its widespread adoption since becoming a NIST standard in 2001 [6]. Operating on the principle of a substitution-permutation network, AES processes 128-bit data blocks, with key lengths of 128, 192, or 256 bits, depending on the desired security level. The algorithm employs several rounds, each consisting of four basic operations: *AddRoundKey*, *SubBytes*, *ShiftRows*, and *MixColumns*. The number of rounds varies: 10 for 128-bit keys, 12 for 192-bit keys, and 14 for 256-bit keys. The *KeyExpansion* operation, part of the AES key schedule, derives round keys from the cipher key.

In the context of IoT devices and sensor networks, AES finds application through diverse integration methods, including hardware implementations. Numerous designs have been tailored to optimize aspects of the AES architecture or specific operations on FPGA, focusing on factors such as speed, power consumption, hardware resources, and security levels, thereby proving the effectiveness of the algorithm.

Implementation Design: The AES included in the RoT has been designed to perform encryption and decryption operations for both 128-bit and 256-bit key sizes. The basic operations of the cipher were covered using VHDL descriptions from an open repository [5]. Subsequently, these operations were integrated with a control module and the data path to complete the AES design.

The designed architecture performs each of the AES rounds in one clock cycle. Due to the different operation requirements for encryption and decryption, four blocks handle basic encryption operations, while another four blocks handle basic decryption operations. Thus, the AES design contains the functional blocks depicted in Fig. 3. These include the *Key Schedule*, responsible for generating the subkey used in each round; *Key Addition*, which performs the XOR operation between the subkey and the status register; and the *Datapath*, including the state register and all the combinational operations occurring in each round. The *Datapath* is further divided into two segments. If an encryption process (ENC) is performed, the signals IN_TEXT and OUT_TEXT would represent the plaintext and the ciphertext, respectively, using the output corresponding to the ENCRYPTION DATAPATH logic. In the decryption process, the signals IN_TEXT and OUT_TEXT would correspond to the ciphertext and the plaintext, respectively, using the output corresponding to the DECRYPTION DATAPATH logic. Additionally, the *Controller* block plays a crucial role by providing the necessary control signals for the other blocks in the design and generating the constants required by the Key Schedule block.

In terms of security, the AES design has been provided with two countermeasures: a signature generator for Fault Injection Attacks (FIA) and a Low-Entropy Masking Scheme (LEMS) for Side-Channel Attacks (SCA). These complementary countermeasures are compatible to be integrated into a unified AES implementation.

Characterization and Validation: The AES design functionality was successfully validated utilizing the tests within the Advanced Encryption Standard Algorithm Validation Suite (AESAVS) provided by NIST [8] following the FIPS 197 standard, which is available in [7].

3.3   Secure Hash Algorithms

The implementation of SHA-2 and SHA-3 algorithms will ensure data integrity, supporting various software applications such as secure booting, remote attestation protocols, or privacy-preserving protocols. While SHA-2 is widely

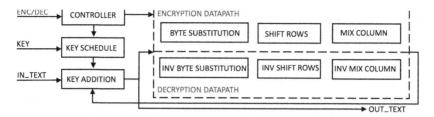

Fig. 3. Simplified AES cipher block diagram

implemented in security applications and protocols, SHA-3 is gradually incorporated into cryptography libraries and is currently recognized as a Post-Quantum Cryptography (PQC) primitive, being used internally by PQC algorithms (e.g., CRYSTALS-Kyber). Thus, the RoT will deliver efficient hashing through full hardware implementations, ensuring both security and efficiency in terms of area and throughput.

SHA-256: This hardware implementation, requiring minimal logical resources, presents a scheme that uses a reduced number of cycles in the hash operation and improves the operational frequency. This leads to a substantial enhancement in both throughput and efficiency for the module. To ensure comprehensive coverage, implementations for all versions of the SHA-2 standard (FIPS 180-4 [17]) have been included and encapsulated in a single parametrizable IP core following the scheme presented in Fig. 4. Additionally, for HW/SW integration, drivers and communication protocols have been developed and tailored to achieve compatibility across the standards. To handle all SHA-2 standard versions, a C-coded test suite has been created to encompass all NIST tests, accounting for both byte and bit inputs for each version, as detailed in [3] and [2] respectively. This aims to reinforce testing capabilities and ensure the robust evaluation of the implemented standards.

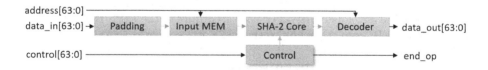

Fig. 4. SHA-2 block diagram

SHA3-512: This implementation focuses on developing a novel architecture for the Keccak function, a key component of the SHA-3 hash function standard as presented in [11]. The design strategy for the Keccak core aligns with the architectural framework initially introduced in [9], which has gained widespread acceptance in the literature. Building upon this foundational approach, two optimized versions of the operation have been developed to enhance the performance of the original Keccak core.

One proposed scheme aims to directly reduce the initial number of cycles (24) by concatenating the Keccak function STG times. For example, when $STG = 2$, the completion time is reduced to 12 cycles, and when $STG = 24$, the completion time is reduced to a single cycle. However, this strategy comes with trade-offs, including increased resource utilization and decreased operational frequency as the value of STG rises.

The second strategy aims to enhance the efficiency. This approach provides more design flexibility compared to prior methods by enabling the insertion of intermediate registers between Keccak function blocks through a parameter labeled as STG_REG. Unlike the first strategy, this does not reduce the cycles per block but boosts the number of blocks processed per cycle, maintaining a constant operating frequency without a significant resource increase.

The SHA-3 function design presented here has been encapsulated into a parameterized IP module as depicted in Fig. 5, including the Keccak core along with its own Keccak control logic. This IP module offers all versions of SHA-3: SHA3-224, SHA3-256, SHA3-386, or SHA3-512. Additionally, users have the flexibility to choose one of the two types of optimized versions, as well as the number of stages to implement.

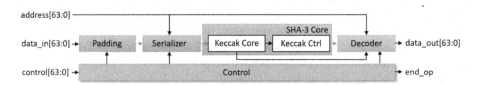

Fig. 5. SHA-3 block diagram

Characterization and Validation: The functionalities of SHA-2 and SHA-3 have been verified using the Cryptographic Algorithm Validation Program (CAVP) provided by NIST [18]. The tests included in CAVP facilitated the validation of the developed SHA-2 IP core according to the FIPS 180-4 standard and the SHA-3 IP core according to the FIPS 202 standard.

3.4   Edwards-Curve Digital Signature Algorithm

EdDSA is well-suited for embedded devices, offering efficiency and robust security. Its efficiency comes from optimized elliptic curve parameters, minimizing computational overhead for faster signature generation and verification. EdDSA employs deterministic nonce generation, ensuring consistent signatures for identical message and private key pairs, simplifying security auditing. In terms of security, EdDSA excels in resisting side-channel attacks due to hardened cryptographic techniques and curve operations designed to thwart timing attacks and power analysis.

Implementation Design: The curve that has been chosen for implementation is a specific instantiation of EdDSA that utilizes Edwards25519 curve as it is known for its efficiency, simplicity, and security, which make it suitable for embedded systems. Since point addition and point multiplication, which involve modular multiplication, represent the highest computational overhead within finite field operations, a dedicated hardware accelerator has been developed for them, while other tasks like hashing, encoding, and decoding are handled by software.

The proposed hybrid architecture is based on a 4-level recursive Karatsuba multiplier and a modular reduction using fast arithmetic techniques since the Karatsuba algorithm offers better performance in terms of time and resource consumption. The design performs a recursive Karatsuba multiplication process, decomposing a 255-bit integer multiplication into 81 operations of 16-bit at four levels. A DSP block facilitates efficient computation. The modular multiplication block, including a reduction component, addresses modular reduction concerning the prime number $p = 2^{255} - 19$ in Ed25519. The high-level EdDSA accelerator block integrates a controller for automating point operations, modular exponentiation, and multiplication. The scheme of the encapsulated IP module is presented in Fig. 6.

The architecture has been validated for signature processes, with control circuitry modified for memory-mapped interfaces. While the main focus is on digital signatures, the design is versatile and applicable to modular operations as well.

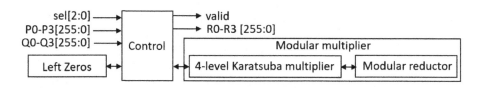

Fig. 6. EdDSA block diagram

Characterization and Validation: By guaranteeing that the implementation fulfills to the protocols and security considerations specified in RFC 8032 [13], the EdDSA proves compliance. Furthermore, following the guidelines of FIPS 186-5 standard [4] improves the reliability of the implementation.

3.5 System Level Protection

In order to protect all RoT components against Fault Injection Attacks (FIAs), a System-Level Protection (SLP) block has been integrated into the system. This block, depicted in Fig. 7, continuously monitors crucial parameters like clock signals, control signals, supply voltages, and temperature. On the one hand, to detect changes in the environment and working conditions such as temperature and voltage, the Xilinx-specific analog-to-digital conversion module, called

XADC, has been used. This module allows the detection of changes outside normal operating ranges and activates different alarms to alert the system. On the other hand, two glitch detectors have been added, one for possible manipulations of the clock signal, and another for the control signals. These potentially vulnerable signals are monitored and in case of manipulation trigger an alarm. The XADC is a pre-existing resource for monitoring and alarms, while the glitch detector is a purpose-designed module. This approach boosts system resistance against unanticipated challenges, contributing to a secure computing environment.

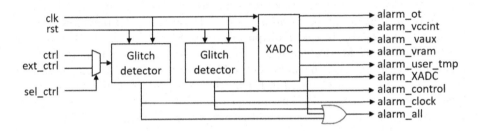

Fig. 7. SLP block diagram

4   Root-of-Trust Integration

The integration of the RoT on the Pynq-Z2 board, establishing consistent connectivity through the utilization of the AXI4 Memory Mapped interface between the RoT components and the Zynq PS, is depicted through a block diagram in Fig. 8. This diagram illustrates the inclusion of the modules presented in the previous section, specifying the incorporation of a double instance of the PUF IP to ensure the retrieval of the $HDinter$ metric if it is involved in any required process, along with the specific versions implemented for the hashing algorithms. The resource consumption is detailed in Table 1, showing that LUTS and Slices represent the most demanded resources surpassing 60% and 90%, respectively.

To showcase the robust capabilities of the RoT, a demonstrator has been developed highlighting the resulting synergy from the combination of both software and hardware components. The demonstrator utilizes bash files to automate the invocation of IPs, employing their respective C-coded software for efficient utilization. Each associated software for the IPs includes functions dedicated to the validation and utilization of the functionalities provided through the RoT. Intensive testing of the demonstrator was conducted, and it confirmed the effectiveness of the RoT integration. This approach highlights the robustness of the IPs in a real-world context, particularly on the Pynq-Z2 SoC device.

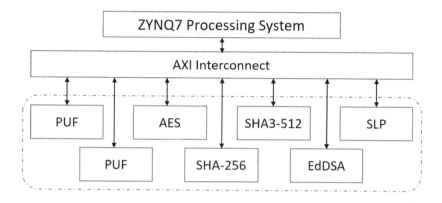

Fig. 8. Block diagram of the RoT integration with Zynq PS

Table 1. RoT resource utilization on ZYNQ XC7Z020-1CLG400C SoC.

Component	LUTs (%)		Registers (%)		Slices (%)		BRAMs (%)	
PUF/TRNG 1	496	(0.93%)	615	(0.58%)	280	(2.11%)	1	(0,71%)
PUF/TRNG 2	495	(0.93%)	615	(0.58%)	262	(1.97%)	1	(0,71%)
AES	10 474	(19.69%)	1183	(1.11%)	2823	(21.23%)	0	(0,00%)
SHA-256	1571	(2.95%)	1196	(1.12%)	499	(3.75%)	0,5	(0,36%)
SHA3-512	3615	(6.80%)	2532	(2.38%)	1134	(8.53%)	0	(0,00%)
EdDSA	17 776	(33.41%)	17 048	(16.02%)	6701	(50.38%)	0	(0.00%)
SLP	141	(0.27%)	276	(0.26%)	101	(0.76%)	0	(0,00%)
AXI Inter	691	(1.30%)	689	(0.65%)	353	(2.65%)	0	(0,00%)
PS Reset	17	(0.03%)	33	(0.03%)	11	(0.08%)	0	(0,00%)
Total	**35276**	**(66.31%)**	**24187**	**(22.73%)**	**12164**	**(91.46%)**	**2.5**	**(1.78%)**

5   Conclusions

This work introduces an innovative approach to a hardware RoT centered around a Xilinx Zynq-7000 SoC device. It capitalizes on its processing power by adopting a unified design methodology and leveraging collaborative efforts to efficiently develop the hardware primitives. This approach achieves a significant contribution to the field of cryptographic security in computing environments.

The hardware implementation of the presented RoT on the Pynq-Z2 board showcases its capability to validate the correct operation of all hardware and cryptographic components. This ensures the authenticity and uniqueness of the target device while providing confidentiality, integrity, and reliability according to established standards. Additionally, strategic system and individual counter-measures have been implemented to fortify the design against potential physical attacks, introducing an additional layer of security. Consequently, the presented hardware RoT addresses critical needs for robust hardware-level security.

The adaptability and scalability of the RoT components are highlighted through IP encapsulation with AXI4 Lite interfaces for both hardware and cryptographic functions. This positions the RoT as a versatile solution capable of effectively addressing evolving security threats. Moreover, the successful collaboration of diverse designers and the efficacy of the chosen design methodology underscore the importance of optimizing hardware development by exploiting SoC capabilities. In this case, the result is a secure, adaptable, and reliable RoT.

Disclosure of Interests. The authors have no competing interests to declare that are relevant to the content of this article.

References

1. Secure Platform for ICT Systems Rooted at the Silicon Manufacturing Process. https://cordis.europa.eu/project/id/952622/es. Accessed 15 Dec 2023
2. SHA-2 Hash Function Test Vectors for Hashing Bit-Oriented Messages. https:// csrc.nist.gov/CSRC/media/Projects/Cryptographic-Algorithm-Validation-Program/documents/shs/shabittestvectors.zip. Accessed 4 Sept 2023
3. SHA-2 Hash Function Test Vectors for Hashing Byte-Oriented Messages. https:// csrc.nist.gov/CSRC/media/Projects/Cryptographic-Algorithm-Validation-Program/documents/shs/shabytetestvectors.zip. Accessed 4 Sept 2023
4. Digital signature standard (DSS). Technical report (2023). https://doi.org/10.6028/nist.fips.186-5
5. Hadipourh AES Repository (2001). https://github.com/hadipourh/AES-VHDL
6. Advanced Encryption Standard (AES) (2001). https://nvlpubs.nist.gov/nistpubs/fips/nist.fips.197.pdf
7. Advanced Encryption Standard (AES), FIPS Publication 197, National Institute of Standards and Technology (2001). https://nvlpubs.nist.gov/nistpubs/fips/nist.fips.197.pdf
8. The Advanced Encryption Standard Algorithm Validation Suite (AESAVS) (2015). https://csrc.nist.gov/CSRC/media/Projects/Cryptographic-Algorithm-Validation-Program
9. Arshad, A., Kundi, D.e.S., Aziz, A.: Compact implementation of SHA3-512 on FPGA. In: Conference on Information Assurance and Cyber Security (CIACS), pp. 29–33 (2014). https://doi.org/10.1109/CIACS.2014.6861327
10. Bhasin, S., et al.: Secure your SOC: building system-an-chip designs for security. In: 2020 IEEE 33rd International System-on-Chip Conference (SOCC), pp. 248–253 (2020). https://doi.org/10.1109/SOCC49529.2020.9524760
11. Camacho-Ruiz, E., Sánchez-Solano, S., Martínez-Rodríguez, M.C., Brox, P.: A complete SHA-3 hardware library based on a high efficiency Keccak design. In: IEEE Nordic Circuits and Systems Conference 2023 (2023, accepted)
12. Goksoy, A.A., Hassan, S., Krishnakumar, A., Marculescu, R., Akoglu, A., Ogras, U.Y.: Theoretical validation and hardware implementation of dynamic adaptive scheduling for heterogeneous systems on chip. J. Low Power Electron. Appl. **13**(4) (2023). https://doi.org/10.3390/jlpea13040056. https://www.mdpi.com/2079-9268/13/4/56
13. Josefsson, S., Liusvaara, I.: Edwards-Curve Digital Signature Algorithm (EdDSA). RFC 8032 (2017). https://doi.org/10.17487/RFC8032

14. Martínez-Rodríguez, M.C., Rojas-Muñoz, L.F., Camacho-Ruiz, E., Sánchez-Solano, S., Brox, P.: Efficient RO-PUF for generation of identifiers and keys in resource-constrained embedded systems. Cryptography **6**(4) (2022). https://doi.org/10.3390/cryptography6040051. https://www.mdpi.com/2410-387X/6/4/51
15. Rojas-Muñoz, L.F., Sánchez-Solano, S., Martínez-Rodríguez, M.C., Brox, P.: Online evaluation and monitoring of security features of an RO-based PUF/TRNG for IoT devices. Sensors **23**(8) (2023). https://doi.org/10.3390/s23084070. https://www.mdpi.com/1424-8220/23/8/4070
16. Rosero-Montalvo, P.D., István, Z., Hernandez, W.: A survey of trusted computing solutions using FPGAS. IEEE Access **11**, 31583–31593 (2023). https://doi.org/10.1109/ACCESS.2023.3261802
17. The Secure Hash Algorithm Validation System (SHAVS) (2014). https://csrc.nist.gov/CSRC/media/Projects/Cryptographic-Algorithm-Validation-Program/documents/shs/SHAVS.pdf
18. Cryptographic Algorithm Validation Program (CAVP) (2016). https://csrc.nist.gov/Projects/Cryptographic-Algorithm-Validation-Program/Secure-Hashing#shavs
19. Zhang, Z., et al.: High-efficiency parallel cryptographic accelerator for real-time guaranteeing dynamic data security in embedded systems. Micromachines **12**(5) (2021). https://doi.org/10.3390/mi12050560. https://www.mdpi.com/2072-666X/12/5/560

Analysis of Clock Tree Buffer Degradation Caused by Radiation

Minoru Watanabe[✉]

Faculty of Environmental, Life, Natural Science and Technology,
Okayama University, Okayama, Japan
minoru-watanabe@okayama-u.ac.jp

Abstract. Current commercial field programmable gate arrays (FPGAs) take serial configuration architecture to realize their programmability. However, the serial configuration circuit is very weak for radiation in terms of both total-ionizing-dose and soft-error tolerances. If radiation permanently breaks even only a few transistors inside an FPGA, the serial configuration circuit is easily down at an extremely high probability. Always, the total-ionizing-dose tolerance of radiation-hardened FPGAs is limited to up to 2 Mrad. In order to increase the total-ionizing-dose, a radiation-hardened FPGA with a triple-modular-redundant configuration circuit that can achieve 730 Mrad total-ionizing-dose tolerance has been developed. The radiation-hardened FPGA can allow a number of transistors to be broken by radiation and can have a large clock skew margin. This paper presents the analysis result of the clock tree buffer degradation caused by radiation based on the experimental result of the degradation of look-up tables and clarify the suitable clock skew margin of the radiation-hardened FPGA.

1 Introduction

Up to now, various radiation-hardened semiconductor devices have become available: processors [1,2], FLASH memories [3,4], static random access memories (SRAMs) [5], field programmable gate arrays (FPGAs) [6], and so on. The radiation-hardened semiconductor devices are used mainly for space embedded systems. Such devices can achieve 300 krad – 2 Mrad total-ionizing-dose tolerance necessary for space embedded systems.

However, nuclear power plants and their decommissioning operations require over 100 Mrad total-ionizing-dose tolerant devices for remotely controlled robots [7]. In particular, a decommissioning operation to remove reactors and melted nuclear fuel at the Fukushima Daiichi nuclear power plant requires 1 Grad total-ionizing-dose tolerant devices used on-site because decommissioning robots to remove melted nuclear fuel and broken reactors must work under a 1000 Sv/h strong radiation environment. To achieve higher total-ionizing-dose tolerance than that of current very large scale integrated circuits (VLSIs), microelectromechanical systems (MEMS) [8,9] and SiC technologies [11–13] are being investigated intensively. Although their radiation tolerance is sufficiently higher than

© The Author(s), under exclusive license to Springer Nature Switzerland AG 2024
I. Skliarova et al. (Eds.): ARC 2024, LNCS 14553, pp. 120–133, 2024.
https://doi.org/10.1007/978-3-031-55673-9_9

that of current radiation-hardened VLSIs, current VLSIs cannot be replaced with either MEMS or SiC since numerous elements cannot be implemented onto a single chip and their operating clock frequency is much lower than that of current VLSIs. Therefore, a complementary metal oxide semiconductor (CMOS) process technology must still be used to realize processors, memories, and other VLSIs.

In order to increase the total-ionizing-dose tolerance of VLSIs using a current CMOS process technology, optically reconfigurable gate arrays (ORGAs) that can support a repairable VLSI concept based on programmable architecture have been proposed [14]. In the repairable VLSI concept, a partly broken VLSI is used continuously by avoiding faulty gate array regions and by using remaining non-damaged gate array regions so that the total-ionizing-dose tolerance of the programmable gate array VLSI can be increased drastically. However, in order to realize the repairable VLSI concept, one necessary condition is that the configuration circuit must be robust for radiation. ORGAs have realized a robust configuration circuit by introducing optical techniques [15–17]. As a result, ORGAs have achieved over 1.15 Grad total-ionizing-dose tolerance which is about 1,000 times higher total-ionizing-dose tolerance than current radiation-hardened VLSIs. However, ORGAs have one important disadvantage point that ORGAs require optical components. ORGAs' package size is larger than current VLSIs and the fabrication process is complicated.

On the other hand, programmable devices such as FPGAs and complex programmable logic devices (CPLDs) might be seen as useful to realize the repairable VLSI concept. However, it is difficult to realize a repairable VLSI concept using such a current FPGA or a current CPLD. According to previous radiation experiments conducted for MAX3000A CPLDs and Cyclone II FPGAs [18,19], the configuration function on the FPGAs and the CPLDs is the first to malfunction although their gate arrays continue to function correctly. Therefore, the repairable VLSI concept cannot be applied for FPGAs and CPLDs with a serial configuration circuit.

In order to increase the total-ionizing-dose, a radiation-hardened FPGA with a triple-modular-redundant configuration circuit that can achieve 730 Mrad total-ionizing-dose tolerance has been developed [20]. The radiation-hardened FPGA can allow a large clock skew caused by radiation-degradation. This paper presents the analysis result of the clock tree buffer degradation caused by radiation based on the experimental result of the degradation of look-up tables and clarify the suitable clock skew margin of the radiation-hardened FPGA.

2 Triple-Modular-Redundant System

A triple-modular-redundant system consists of three same units and three majority voting circuits with three inputs as shown in Fig. 1. The operation result of each unit is distributed to an input of three majority voting circuits. Each majority voting circuit executes its majority voting operation individually based on the

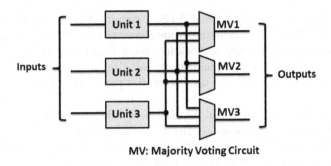

Fig. 1. Triple-modular-redundant system.

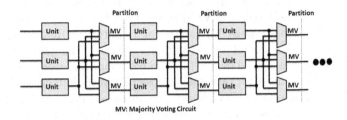

Fig. 2. A system including a lot of triple-modular-redundant units.

outputs from the three units. Even if a radiation is incident to a unit, three identical correct outputs can be generated through the majority voting operations. Even if a radiation is incident to a majority voting circuit, although the output of the majority voting circuit to which the radiation is incident might be incorrect, two identical correct outputs can be generated by the rest majority voting circuits. In triple-modular-redundant systems, three outputs must be treated as taking a majority voting operation. Based on this consideration, anytime, a correct result can be gotten from the triple-modular-redundant system. Therefore, it can be assumed that only one radiation incidence to a triple-modular-redundant system at once never causes any soft-error while the triple-modular-redundant system cannot block soft-error when two or more units or two or more majority voting circuits receive radiation simultaneously. In addition, if a lot of partitions are applied to a triple-modular-redundant system as shown in Fig. 2, the soft-error tolerance can be increased.

However, current triple-modular-redundant systems have a weak point related to clock distribution. Conventional triple-modular-redundant systems always use a single clock distribution and the single clock is used for three modules. Therefore, if radiation is incident to a buffer constructing the single clock tree on a triple-modular-redundant system, a soft-error inevitably happens on the system. If three different clock distributions can be used for three modules

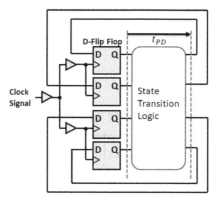

Fig. 3. Sequential circuit example.

in a triple-modular-redundant system, the soft-error tolerance can be increased drastically. The reason that three clock distributions are not applied and a single clock distribution is used in a lot of conventional triple-modular-redundant systems is the issue of clock skew margin.

3   Clock Skew Issue Under Radiation Environments

3.1   Clock Skew

A sequential circuit in a digital system usually consists of many delay flip-flops (D flip-flops) and a state transition logic that creates the next state from a current state as shown in Fig. 3. The output Q from each D flip-flop is validated with a delay of t_{co} from the rising clock edge. Subsequently, the next state is fed back to the terminal D of the D-flip-flops with state transition logic delay t_{PD}. The clock signal is generally supplied by a clock tree, as shown in Fig. 4, in which buffers are connected in a tree shape. A clock skew means a clock signal arrives at the clock terminal of D flip-flops at different times. The clock skew is always caused by the different number of buffer stages, different wiring length, different load capacitance of a clock tree. Also, the clock skew depends on the voltage and temperature of VLSIs. Letting t_{su} be the D-flip-flop setup time, then the maximum operating clock frequency including the factor of this clock skew t_{skew} can be evaluated using the following equation.

$$f = \frac{1}{t_{co} + t_{PD(max)} + t_{skew} + t_{su}} .$$
(1)

In that equation, $t_{PD(max)}$ represents the maximum delay of the critical path among multiple input-output paths in the state transition logic. In addition, the following condition is necessary for the sequential circuit to operate correctly.

$$t_{co(min)} + t_{PD(min)} > t_{skew} .$$
(2)

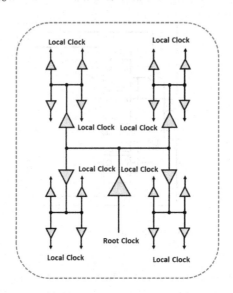

Fig. 4. Clock distribution.

In that expression, $t_{PD(min)}$ represents the minimum time not to change the outputs of the state transition logic even after the inputs of the state transition logic are changed. Also, $t_{co(min)}$ represents time from the rising clock edge to be able to keep the previous state when the flip-flops respond most rapidly. A smaller clock skew can increase the maximum operating clock frequency and make it easier to satisfy the Eq. (2). Therefore, in current digital system designs, the clock tree is designed to be the smallest clock skew. Of course, several methods of reducing clock skew have been proposed. For example, clock skew can be reduced using a mesh clock distribution instead of the clock tree [21, 22]. In addition, a correction methods using hot electron injection has been proposed [23]. However, even so, the clock skew cannot be zero. As another well-known method, there is a buffer insertion technique [24]. In the technique, a number of buffers are inserted for paths with the minimum delay on a state transition logic to increase the $t_{PD(min)}$. As a result, clock skew margin (Eq. 2) can be increased. However, since the additional delays by inserting buffers are generally small, to address a large clock skew, numerous buffers must be inserted. As a result, a large additional implementation area is required. Particularly, shift register circuits used in FPGA's configuration circuits have the smallest clock skew margin because the output Q from a D flip-flop in the previous stage is directly connected to the input D of another D flip-flop in the next stage without any state transition logic. Therefore, since $t_{pd(min)}$ is zero, shift register circuits have the smallest clock skew margin. Of course, although buffers can be inserted between the output Q of previous D flip-flop and the terminal D of the next flip-flops, this is not a good choice because of the heavy penalty of increased implementation area. Existing FPGAs must use shift register circuits in their

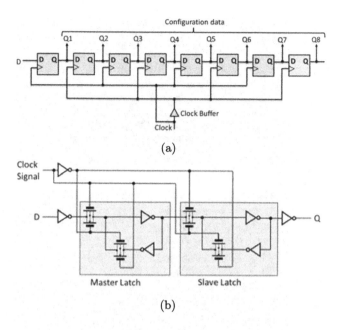

Fig. 5. Example of an 8-bit shift-register circuit.

configuration circuit. Therefore, in FPGAs, the configuration circuit becomes the weakest point in terms of the clock skew margin.

3.2 Clock Skew Margin of an 8-Bit Shift-Register

In order to measure the clock skew margin of shift-register circuits, as an example, an 8-bit shift register circuit was designed by using a 0.18 μm CMOS process technology. The 8-bit shift-register circuit is shown in Figs. 5(a) and (b). HSPICE simulation results are also shown in Fig. 6. It has been confirmed that the 8-bit shift-register can work correctly when using a clock signal distribution with a 242 ps clock skew as shown in upper panel. On the other hand, a wrong shift-register operation has also been confirmed when using a clock signal distribution with a 250 ps clock skew as shown in lower panel. So, the clock skew margin of the shift-register circuits is very small or less than 242 ps.

3.3 Clock Skew Margin of Triple-Modular-Redundant Systems

In the case of a triple modular redundant system, in order to increase soft-error tolerance, the clock distribution should be separated to three clock signals individually used for three modules. However, in this case, all the three clock signals

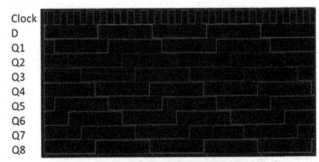

(a) Correct operation of when the clock skew margin is set to 242 ps

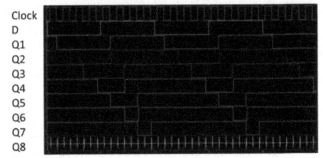

(b) Defect operation of when the clock skew margin is set to 250 ps

Fig. 6. HSPICE simulation result of the 8-bit shift-register circuit.

must satisfy with a clock skew margin. Since it is difficult to distribute three separate clock signals for three modules within a small clock skew margin, conventional triple-modular-redundant system always used a single clock distribution. However, if radiation is incident to the clock tree, soft-error happens inevitably. In conventional triple-modular-redundant systems, this clock distribution was a weak point for radiation in terms of soft-error.

3.4   Clock Skew Increase Under Radiation Environments

An FPGA placed under a radiation environment is constantly deteriorated. Inside the FPGA, clock buffers are constantly degraded under a radiation environment. However, its degraded speed of each clock buffer is much different from each other. So, as increasing the total-ionizing-dose exposed to the FPGA, the clock skew is also increased. Therefore, degraded FPGA cannot work always even if the operating clock frequency is decreased drastically. In order to increase the total-ionizing-dose tolerance of FPGAs, a clock skew free circuit must be used.

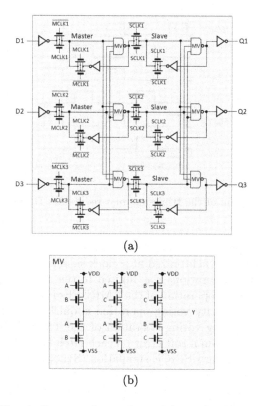

(a)

(b)

Fig. 7. Circuit diagram of a triple-modular-redundant D-flip-flop.

4 Radiation-Hardened Triple Modular Redundant Configuration Circuit

4.1 Triple Modular Redundant D-Flip-Flop Design

The circuit diagram of a triple-modular-redundant flip-flop (TMRDFF) is shown in Fig. 7(a). The TMRDFF consists of three master latches with a majority voting operation and three slave latches with a majority voting operation. Each latch consists of an inverter, a majority voting circuit, and two transmission gates. The majority voting circuit consists of 12 transistors as shown in Fig. 7(b). Since the output of the majority voting circuit is inverted, the majority voting circuit can be replaced with one of two inverters in a typical latch. As a result, in each latch, majority voting circuit and an inverter are cascaded through a transmission gate. Each latch can keep a result voted by own latch output and other two latch outputs. If radiation is incident to a single master or slave latch, soft-error happen on the latch. However, soft-error situation is quickly removed by votes of other two latches.

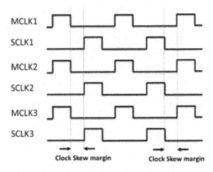

Fig. 8. Timing diagram of the triple-modular-redundant D-flip-flop (TMRDFF).

Conventional majority voting operations using D-flip-flops and majority voting circuits were always synchronized at a clock signal. Therefore, the frequency of the majority voting operations was limited to the clock frequency. However, since the majority voting operation of the TMRDFFs is an unsynchronized operation, anytime, the majority voting operation is quickly executed. In addition, the period of the majority voting operation of the TMRDFF is very short. In fact, the recovery time from a soft error on each latch has been evaluated as less than 200 picoseconds using HSPICE simulation (Synopsys, Inc.). The frequency of TMRDFF corresponds to 5 GHz synchronized operation.

In conventional D-flip-flops, the inverted gate signal of the master latch and the gate signal of the slave latch are connected to a single clock signal. Therefore, the clock skew margin must be considered when using any D-flip-flops. However, in the TMRDFF, the master latch and slave latch are separately controlled not using a single clock signal. The master latches and slave latches of TMRDFFs are controlled respectively by three master clock signals (MCLK1, MCLK2, and MCLK3) and three slave clock signals (SCLK1, SCLK2, and SCLK3) as shown in Fig. 8. As shown in Fig. 8, depending on the necessary clock skew margin, control signals with an arbitrary clock skew can be made. As a result, the TMRDFF is a clock skew free D-flip-flop. By controlling the phase between three master clock signals (MCLK1, MCLK2, and MCLK3) and three slave clock signals (SCLK1, SCLK2, and SCLK3) as shown in Fig. 8, the clock skew margin can be adjusted to suitable value without any limitation. Even if radiation increase the clock skew of the three clock trees used in TMRDFFs on an FPGA, by increasing the timing space between three master clock signals (MCLK1, MCLK2, and MCLK3) and three slave clock signals (SCLK1, SCLK2, and SCLK3), the FPGA can be used continuously (Fig. 9).

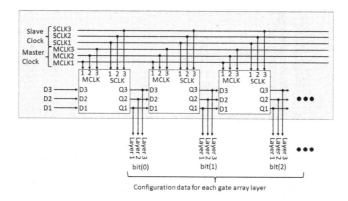

Fig. 9. Circuit diagram of a triple-modular-redundant configuration circuit.

4.2 Radiation-Hardened Triple Modular Redundant Configuration Circuit Design

A new radiation-hardened triple-modular-redundant configuration circuit was designed using a 0.18-μm 5-metal standard CMOS process technology. The triple-modular-redundant configuration circuit consists of triple-modular-redundant D flip-flops (TMRDFFs). Since the new radiation-hardened triple-modular-redundant configuration circuit can realize full triple-modular redundancy including the clock distribution, it has no weak point in terms of soft error.

4.3 FPGA Design

An FPGA was designed using 0.18 μm CMOS process technology. The basic construction and function of the FPGA resemble those of currently available FPGAs. The chip size is 5 mm × 5 mm. The FPGA takes an island-style gate array as well as commercial FPGAs. However, to increase the soft-error tolerance, the FPGA has three identical island-style programmable gate array layers as triple-modular redundancy. Each programmable gate array layer comprises 70 logic blocks, 77 switching matrices, and 7 I/O blocks, as shown in Figs. 11 and 12. The total gate count of each programmable gate array layer is 2,380 gates.

5 Experiment Results

For this experiment, a radiation-hardened FPGA chip were exposed to Cobalt 60 gamma rays up to TID of 2.9 MGy and 7.3 MGy at 6.6–6.7 kGy/h. In order to confirm the clock skew increase by radiation, 15 ring oscillators with a single stage were implemented onto 15 look-up tables. The frequencies of the 15 ring oscillators were measured at 0 MGy, 2.9 MGy, and 7.3 MGy total-ionizing-dose. Firstly, the average propagation delay increase of 15 look-up tables versus

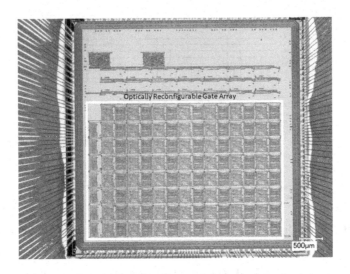

Fig. 10. New radiation-hardened FPGA chip.

total-ionizing-dose (TID) was measured. The periods of 15 ring oscillators at 0 MGy, 2.9 MGy, and 7.3 MGy total-ionizing-dose were 16.170 ns, 20.467 ns, and 24.195 ns, respectively. Then, the period disperse of 15 ring oscillators at 0 MGy, 2.9 MGy, and 7.3 MGy total-ionizing-dose were 0.7934 ns, 1.3056 ns, and 2.0137 ns, respectively. The ratios of the period disperse to the propagation delay at 0 MGy, 2.9 MGy, and 7.3 MGy total-ionizing-dose were 4.91%, 6.38%, and 8.32%, respectively. The average propagation delays of 15 ring oscillators is linear to the total-ionizing-dose. Also, it is important that the period disperse is also increased as increasing the total-ionizing-dose. Although this experimental result is based on 15 ring oscillators on look-up tables, the experimental result can be considered as similar to buffers' degradation for clock distribution. Firstly, in a triple modular redundant system with three clock distributions, the clock skew is increased compared with a single clock distribution. Moreover, under a radiation environment, as increasing the total-ionizing-dose of VLSIs, the clock skew is increased from the initial condition. Therefore, radiation-hardened VLSI must have large clock skew margin. The proposed radiation-hardened FPGA has a clock skew free architecture. From this experiment, the ratio of the clock skew margin to the clock tree propagation delay at 7.3 MGy total-ionizing-dose should be designed as larger than 8.3%. In this case, a sufficient clock skew margin can be realized even for the radiation-hardened FPGA with 7.3 MGy total-ionizing-dose. When clock skew margin was set to 10 ns, even after the radiation-hardened FPGA was exposed to 7.3 MGy total-ionizing-dose, the radiation-hardened FPGA could work correctly (Fig. 10).

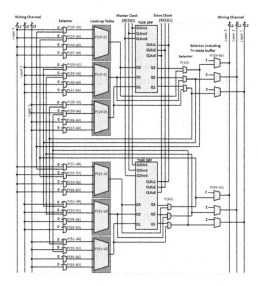

Fig. 11. Block diagram of a configurable logic block (CLB).

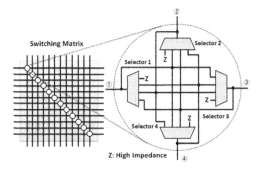

Fig. 12. Block diagram of a configurable switching matrix (CSM).

6 Conclusion

Current commercial field programmable gate arrays (FPGAs) takes a serial configuration architecture to realize their programmability. However, the serial configuration circuit was very weak for radiation in terms of both total-ionizing-dose and soft-error tolerances. In order to increase the total-ionizing-dose and soft-error tolerances of FPGAs, a triple modular redundant design with three separate clocks was introduced to FPGA design. This paper has presented ring-oscillator experimental results on a radiation-hardened FPGA with a triple-modular-redundant configuration circuit. Based on the analysis result, when clock skew margin was set to 10 ns, even after the radiation-hardened FPGA was exposed to 7.3 MGy total-ionizing-dose, the radiation-hardened FPGA could work correctly.

Acknowledgements. This research was partly supported by the Initiatives for Atomic Energy Basic and Generic Strategic Research No. JPJA22F22683756, the Ministry of Education, Science, Sports and Culture, Grant-in-Aid for Scientific Research(B), No. 21H03407, and the Ministry of Education, Science, Sports and Culture, Grant-in-Aid for Challenging Research (Pioneering), No. 22K18415. The VLSI chip in this study was fabricated in the chip fabrication program of VLSI Design and Education Center (VDEC), the University of Tokyo in collaboration with Rohm Co. Ltd. and Toppan Printing Co. Ltd.

References

1. Haddad, N.F., et al.: Second generation (200MHz) RAD750 microprocessor radiation evaluation. In: European Conference on Radiation and Its Effects on Components and Systems, pp. 877–880 (2011)
2. Karakozov, A.B., Korneev, O.V., Nekrasov, P.V., Sokolov, M.N., Zagryadsky, D.A.: Bias conditions and functional test procedure influence on PowerPC7448 microprocessor TID tolerance. In: European Conference on Radiation and Its Effects on Components and Systems, pp. 1–2 (2013)
3. Oldham, T.R., et al.: TID and SEE response of an advanced Samsung 4Gb NAND flash memory. In: IEEE Radiation Effects Data Workshop (2007)
4. Schmidt, H., Grurmann, K., Nickson, B., Gliem, F., Sorensen, R.H.: TID test of an 8-Gbit NAND flash memory. IEEE Trans. Nucl. Sci. **56**(4), 1937–1940 (2009)
5. Zheng, Q., et al.: Read static noise margin decrease of 65-nm 6-T SRAM cell induced by total ionizing dose. IEEE Trans. Nucl. Sci. **65**(2), 691–697 (2018)
6. Benfica, J., et al.: Analysis of SRAM-based FPGA SEU sensitivity to combined EMI and TID-imprinted effects. IEEE Trans. Nucl. Sci. **63**(2), 1294–1300 (2016)
7. Leray, J.L., et al.: CMOS/SOI hardening at 100 Mrad (SiO/sub 2/). IEEE Trans. Nucl. Sci. **37**(6), 2013–2019 (1990)
8. Proie, R.M., et al.: Total ionizing dose effects in piezoelectric MEMS relays. IEEE Trans. Nucl. Sci. **60**(6), 4505–4511 (2013)
9. Augustyniak, I., Dziuban, J., Knapkiewicz, P., Matusiak, M., Olszacki, M., Pons, P.: MEMS high-doses radiation sensor. In: The 17th International Conference on Solid-State Sensors, Actuators and Microsystems (2013)
10. Qin, T., Bleiker, S.J., Rana, S., Niklaus, F., Pamunuwa, D.: Performance analysis of nanoelectromechanical relay-based field-programmable gate arrays. IEEE Access **6**, 15997–16009 (2018)
11. Masunaga, M., Sato, S., Shima, A., Kuwana, R.: The performance of operational amplifiers consisting of 4H-SiC CMOS after gamma irradiation. IEEE Trans. Electron Devices **66**(1), 343–348 (2019)
12. Dong, P., et al.: Electron radiation effects on the 4H-SiC PiN diodes characteristics: an insight from point defects to electrical degradation. IEEE Access **7**, 170385–170391 (2019)
13. Li, D., Zhang, Y., Tang, X., He, Y., Song, Q., Zhang, Y.: Effects of 5 MeV proton irradiation on 1200 V 4H-SiC VDMOSFETs ON-state characteristics. IEEE Access **8**, 104503–104510 (2020)

14. Fujimori, T., Watanabe, M.: Parallel light configuration that increases the radiation tolerance of integrated circuits. Opt. Express **25**(23), 28136–28145 (2017)
15. Fujimori, T., Watanabe, M.: Optically reconfigurable gate array using a colored configuration. Appl. Opt. **57**(29), 8625–8631 (2018)
16. Seto, D., Watanabe, M.: Radiation-hardened optically reconfigurable gate array exploiting holographic memory characteristics. Jpn. J. Appl. Phys. **54**(9S), 09MA06-1–09MA06-5 (2015)
17. Fujimori, T., Watanabe, M.: A 1.15 Grad total-ionizing-dose tolerance parallel operation oriented optically reconfigurable gate array VLSI. In: IEEE International Workshop on Metrology for AeroSpace, Torino (2019)
18. Ito, H., Watanabe, M.: Total-ionizing dose tolerance of the serial configuration on cyclone II FPGA. In: IEEE International Conference on Space Optical Systems and Applications, pp. 1–4 (2015)
19. Fujimori, T., Watanabe, M.: Total-Ionizing-Dose Tolerance of the configuration function of MAX3000A CPLDs. In: Data Workshop (2018)
20. Watanabe, M.: Radiation-hardened triple-modular redundant field programmable gate array with a two-phase clock. In: IEEE International Symposium on Circuits and Systems (ISCAS), 1–6 May 2023
21. Tam, S., Rusu, S., Desai, U.N., Kim, R., Zhang, J., Young, I.: Clock generation and distribution for the first IA-64 microprocessor. IEEE J. Solid-State Circuits **35**, 1545–1552 (2000)
22. Rajaram, A., Pan, D.Z.: MeshWorks: a comprehensive framework for optimized clock mesh network synthesis. IEEE T. Comput. Aid. D. **29**, 1945–1958 (2010)
23. Pu, Y., et al.: Post-silicon clock Deskew employing hot-carrier injection trimming with on-chip skew monitoring and auto-stressing scheme for sub/near threshold digital circuits. IEEE Trans. Circ. Syst. II Express Br. **58**, 294–298 (2011)
24. Neves, J.L., Friedman, E.G.: Optimal clock skew scheduling tolerant to process variations. In: 33rd Design Automation Conference Proceedings, pp. 623–628 (1996)

NEUROSEC: FPGA-Based Neuromorphic Audio Security

Murat Isik[1]([✉]), Hiruna Vishwamith[2], Yusuf Sur[3], Kayode Inadagbo[4],
and I. Can Dikmen[5]

[1] Drexel University, Philadelphia, PA, USA
mci38@drexel.edu
[2] University of Moratuwa, Moratuwa, Sri Lanka
vishwamithpgh.20@uom.lk
[3] Abdullah Gul University, Kayseri, Turkey
yusuf.sur@agu.edu.tr
[4] Prairie View A&M University, Prairie View, TX, USA
[5] Temsa R&D Center, Adana, Turkey
can.dikmen@temsa.com

Abstract. Neuromorphic systems, inspired by the complexity and functionality of the human brain, have gained interest in academic and industrial attention due to their unparalleled potential across a wide range of applications. While their capabilities herald innovation, it is imperative to underscore that these computational paradigms, analogous to their traditional counterparts, are not impervious to security threats. Although the exploration of neuromorphic methodologies for image and video processing has been rigorously pursued, the realm of neuromorphic audio processing remains in its early stages. Our results highlight the robustness and precision of our FPGA-based neuromorphic system. Specifically, our system showcases a commendable balance between desired signal and background noise, efficient spike rate encoding, and unparalleled resilience against adversarial attacks such as FGSM and PGD. A standout feature of our framework is its detection rate of 94%, which, when compared to other methodologies, underscores its greater capability in identifying and mitigating threats within 5.39 dB, a commendable SNR ratio. Furthermore, neuromorphic computing and hardware security serve many sensor domains in mission-critical and privacy-preserving applications.

Keywords: neuromorphic computing · FPGA · hardware security ·
audio processing

1 Introduction

Computer hardware that emulates the intricate functions of the human brain has been termed neuromorphic hardware. Drawing inspiration from biological

I. Skliarova et al. (Eds.): ARC 2024, LNCS 14553, pp. 134–147, 2024.
https://doi.org/10.1007/978-3-031-55673-9_10

neural systems, neuromorphic hardware aims to replicate the way these systems process information, bridging the gap between biological cognition and artificial computation. Neuromorphic computing represents a paradigm shift from traditional computing methodologies. At its core, it seeks to emulate the brain's neural structures and functionalities, offering a more natural and efficient way to process information. The significance of neuromorphic computing lies in its potential to revolutionize various domains, from artificial intelligence to robotics, by providing systems that can learn, adapt, and evolve in real-time [6,7,16]. Field-Programmable Gate Arrays (FPGAs) have emerged as a pivotal component in the neuromorphic computing landscape. Their inherent reconfigurability and parallel processing capabilities align seamlessly with the demands of neuromorphic systems. FPGAs offer the flexibility to design and customize neuromorphic architectures, enabling researchers and engineers to experiment with and optimize neural network designs, thereby pushing the boundaries of what neuromorphic systems can achieve. As with any computing system, security remains paramount in neuromorphic systems. Given their potential applications in sensitive areas such as defense, healthcare, and finance, ensuring the integrity, confidentiality, and availability of data processed by neuromorphic systems is crucial. Furthermore, the unique architecture and operation of neuromorphic systems present both challenges and opportunities in the realm of security, requiring specialized approaches to safeguard them against threats [2,9,10,15,17,20]. Neuromorphic hardware, inspired by the intricate functions of the human brain, seeks to bridge the gap between biological cognition and artificial computation. This approach represents a paradigm shift, offering a more natural and efficient way to process information. FPGAs, with their inherent reconfigurability and parallel processing capabilities, have emerged as a pivotal component in this landscape, enabling the design and customization of neuromorphic architectures. Given the potential applications of neuromorphic systems in sensitive areas such as defense and healthcare, ensuring their security is paramount. The unique architecture of these systems presents both challenges and opportunities in the realm of security.

In this paper, we present the following contributions:

- We explore SNN-based neuromorphic audio processing, a niche compared to image/video processing.
- We analyze security threats in neuromorphic audio, emphasizing adversarial attacks like FGSM and PGD that introduce audio artifacts.
- Our FPGA-integrated system boasts a 94% detection rate, efficient spike encoding, and a balanced signal-to-noise ratio.
- We compare our framework with existing methods, highlighting its superior threat detection and mitigation within a favorable SNR.

2 Neuromorphic Hardware: Evolution, Applications, and Security

Neuromorphic hardware has transitioned from basic silicon neurons to sophisticated neuromorphic chips, offering benefits, especially in security. FPGAs enhance these systems with their flexibility in design and parallel processing capabilities. Several studies have explored the integration of neuromorphic systems with FPGAs, touching upon design methodologies, applications, and security implications. The journey of neuromorphic computing began with the vision of replicating the brain's neural structures in silicon. Early endeavors focused on creating silicon neurons, aiming to capture the parallel processing capabilities of the brain. Over time, advancements in technology and research led to the development of advanced neuromorphic chips, which are now at the forefront of many cutting-edge applications. FPGAs offer flexibility in design, allowing for the customization of neuromorphic architectures. Their reconfigurability and parallel processing capabilities align well with the inherent characteristics of neuromorphic systems. Several studies and research endeavors have delved into the integration of neuromorphic systems with FPGAs. These works have explored various aspects, from design methodologies to applications, and have also touched upon the security implications of such integrations. Neuromorphic hardware offers a range of benefits, especially in the context of security. Neuromorphic hardware, with its unique architecture and capabilities, holds immense promise in the realm of security. Its integration with FPGAs further amplifies its potential, paving the way for adaptive security solutions [5,8,18,26]. Researchers explored the use of temporal dependency in audio data to mitigate the impact of adversarial examples, particularly in automatic speech recognition (ASR) systems. The study shows that input transformations, often used in image adversarial defense, provide limited robustness improvement in audio data and are susceptible to advanced attacks. Conversely, exploiting temporal dependencies in audio can effectively discriminate against adversarial examples and resist adaptive attacks on Recurrent Neural Network (RNN) [25]. It was showed the vulnerability of Deep Neural Networks (DNNs) to adversarial examples, particularly in the audio field. Adversarial examples are crafted by adding subtle noise to original samples, which can deceive machines while remaining imperceptible to humans. The paper proposes a defense method that introduces low-level distortion via audio modification to detect these adversarial examples. The idea is that while the classification of the original sample remains stable under this distortion, the adversarial example's classification changes significantly. This method was tested using the Mozilla Common Voice dataset and the DeepSpeech model, showing a significant drop in the accuracy of adversarial examples, thereby effectively detecting them [12]. U-Net based attention model were introduced for enhancing adversarial speech signals. The proposed self-attention speech U-Net is designed to improve the robustness against adversarial examples in speech recognition systems. The model uses attention mechanisms in its upsampling blocks to better process adversarial noise in speech signals. The study demonstrates that while traditional methods of speech enhancement can increase signal-to-noise ratio (SNR) scores, they often fail to improve other key metrics such as PESQ, STI, and STOI. The authors also found that adversarial training can further enhance the performance of the Convolutional Neural Network (CNN), making it more robust against adversarial attacks in speech recognition [24] (Table 1).

Table 1. Features of Neuromorphic Systems.

Feature	Description
Speed	Emulates brain for fast parallel processing
Power Efficiency	Energy-efficient chips for continuous monitoring
Adaptive Learning	Evolves algorithms for new threats
Anomaly Detection	Flags deviations as threats
Hardware Security	Robust protection via FPGA integration
Parallel Processing	Processes multiple data streams
Scalability	Supports expansion for security needs
Resilience	Resists conventional system attacks
Real-time Response	Instant threat response
Integration	FPGA versatility offers comprehensive security

2.1 Spiking Neural Networks (SNNs)

SNNs are designed to computationally emulate the behavior of biological neurons. As the intricacies of these networks grow, so do the computational demands associated with SNN inference. This growth has intensified the trade-off between hardware resources, power consumption, and acceleration performance, making it a focal point of contemporary research. Consequently, there's a burgeoning need for specialized hardware accelerators that can optimize computing-to-power efficiency ratios, especially in embedded and lightweight applications. One of the salient features of SNNs, from a hardware implementation perspective, is their communication mechanism. Neurons in SNNs communicate using spikes, which, in terms of logic resources, can be equated to a single bit, thereby reducing logic occupation. Recent studies have highlighted the potential of SNNs in enhancing security. For instance, researchers have shown that noise filters for Dynamic Vision Sensors (DVS) can act as defense mechanisms against adversarial attacks. They conducted experiments with various attacks, specifically in the setting of two different noise filters tailored for DVS cameras [16]. In another notable study, a novel attack method tailored for rate coding SNNs was introduced, named the Rate Gradient Approximation Attack (RGA). This method was employed to detect abnormal traffic patterns, indicative of attacks, in Networks-on-Chip data using SNNs [1,14]. Figure 1 illustrates a generic framework for implementing hardware security in neuromorphic audio systems.

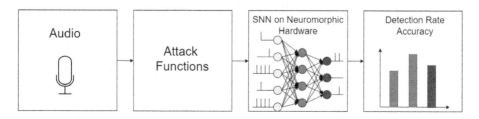

Fig. 1. Hardware Security Framework for Neuromorphic Audio Systems.

2.2   Event-Based Applications in Audio Processing

Event-based audio processing is an emerging paradigm that draws inspiration from the asynchronous nature of the human auditory system which is depicted schematic representation of the audio processing workflow in Fig. 2. Unlike traditional audio processing techniques that operate on uniformly sampled data, event-based methods focus on capturing and processing significant audio events as they occur. Researchers provide a comprehensive review of event-based sensing and signal processing across various sensory domains, including the auditory system [23]. Their work explains the advantages of event-based approaches, especially in mimicking biological sensory systems, and offers insights into the potential applications and challenges of this paradigm. The authors delve into the post-processing of audio event detectors, employing reinforcement learning to enhance their performance [4]. Their approach underscores the potential of combining advanced machine-learning techniques with event-based audio processing to achieve superior detection accuracy and efficiency. Furthermore, the significance of neuromorphic auditory computing in the context of robotics is highlighted in [3]. The author emphasizes the potential of a digital, event-based implementation of the hearing sense, paving the way for more responsive and adaptive robotic systems that can interact seamlessly with their environment.

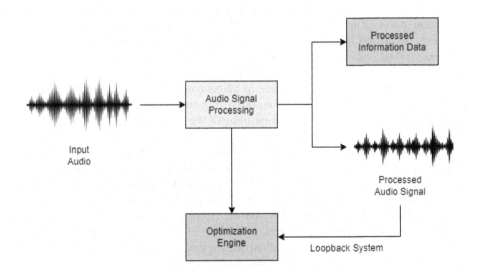

Fig. 2. Audio Processing Diagram.

2.3   Security Challenges

Neuromorphic systems have garnered significant attention due to their potential in various applications, from robotics to artificial intelligence. However, like all computing systems, they are not immune to security threats. This section delves into the unique security challenges posed by FPGA-based neuromorphic systems, drawing from existing literature and current research findings. The integration of neuromorphic computing with FPGA technology presents a novel set of vulnerabilities. FPGA platforms, while offering flexibility and performance advantages, have been shown to be susceptible to a range of security threats. FPGA provides the capability to process vast amounts of data in parallel, mimicking the human brain's neural networks. On the other hand, this complexity can introduce multiple points of vulnerability. These vulnerabilities can be exploited by adversaries to compromise the integrity, confidentiality, or availability of the system. Specific attacks on FPGA-based neuromorphic systems include:

- **Side-channel attacks:** These attacks exploit information leaked during the physical operation of the system, such as power consumption or electromagnetic radiation. Given the unique architecture of neuromorphic systems, they may exhibit distinct side-channel signatures that can be exploited by attackers.
- **Hardware Trojans:** Malicious alterations to the hardware can be introduced during the design or manufacturing process. These Trojans can lie dormant until triggered, leading to unexpected and potentially harmful behaviors.
- **Model Vulnerability Analysis:** The security of neuromorphic systems depends on identifying and counteracting vulnerabilities in neural network models, a key step in preventing adversarial attacks. These attacks, often imperceptible to human observers, manipulate model inputs to provoke incorrect responses or reveal confidential information. Therefore, a comprehensive vulnerability analysis is vital to develop effective defenses, ensuring the integrity and dependability of these advanced systems in adversarial scenarios which are focused on this work.

Addressing the security challenges of FPGA-based neuromorphic systems requires a multi-faceted approach. The solutions must be tailored to the unique architecture and operation of these systems. Dedicated hardware modules can be integrated into the FPGA to monitor and detect malicious activities. For instance, hardware performance counters can be used to detect anomalies in system operation, indicative of an ongoing attack. To safeguard data integrity and confidentiality, advanced encryption techniques can be employed. Homomorphic encryption, for instance, allows for computations on encrypted data, making it particularly suitable for neuromorphic systems where data privacy is paramount. Additionally, the design and implementation of FPGA-based neuromorphic systems should adhere to secure coding practices. This includes regular code reviews, vulnerability assessments, and the use of trusted libraries and tools. Ensuring that the software aspect of the system is secure can mitigate potential exploitation of hardware vulnerabilities [1, 13, 21, 22].

3   Proposed Design Methodology

We describe a specific neuromorphic hardware system, detailing its architecture and relevant features. In response to these identified threats, we put forth a suite of tailored security measures and methodologies, all grounded in a well-articulated theoretical framework. A salient challenge that emerges in this domain is the susceptibility of audio-denoising systems to adversarial attacks. The core intent behind these attacks is to induce the denoising system to yield inaccurate or suboptimal outputs. Two primary modalities of these attacks can be discerned: Gradient-based Attacks, PGD (Projected Gradient Descent) and FGSM (Fast Gradient Sign Method), which exploit a comprehensive understanding of the model's architecture and its gradient information, and Black-box Attacks, which function in the absence of intimate knowledge of the model's internals, instead relying on surrogate models or alternative methodologies. The effects of such adversarial endeavors are significant. For instance, within a security paradigm that leverages surveillance audio, an adversary employing adversarial samples might manipulate the system to exclude or modify critical audio data. Analogously, within the consumer electronics sector, such attacks present the risk of degrading user experience or spreading false information. The strategic emphasis on audio input-based adversarial attacks, particularly in computational tasks extending beyond mere classification, underscores the inherent vulnerabilities extant in contemporary deep learning paradigms. This focus reiterates the pressing imperative for supported robustness across the spectrum of machine learning endeavors, extending beyond the purview of classification alone.

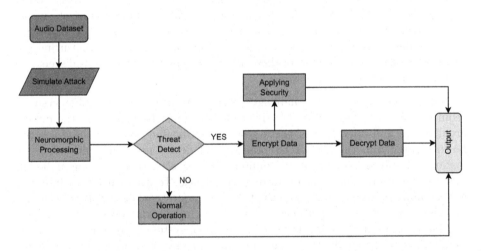

Fig. 3. Overview of the steps involved in this work.

The proposed algorithm highlights the key aspects of the security protocol for a neuromorphic system, emphasizing the detection and mitigation of potential threats. As illustrated in Fig. 3, the algorithm begins with the initialization phase, where the dataset and the attack model are loaded, ensuring all necessary data is available for processing and potential attack simulation. Subsequently, the model is integrated into the attack mechanism, setting the stage for potential threat simulations and evaluations. To optimize computational efficiency, the system processes the dataset in batches, handling 32 batches at a time. Each audio batch, which comprises both noisy and clean data, undergoes a splitting process where it's divided into its absolute value and argument components using the Short-Time Fourier Transform (STFT). To simulate real-world processing latencies, the absolute values and arguments of both the noisy and clean audio are delayed, with the clean audio undergoing a similar delay. The core of the algorithm lies in the attack generation phase. Here, an attack is synthesized by comparing the absolute values of the noisy and clean audio. If an attack is to be simulated, it targets the noisy audio's absolute value. This synthesized attack, when combined with the argument of the noisy audio using the SFT mixer, produces a composite signal. The Signal-to-Noise Ratio (SNR) of this composite signal is then computed. A significant deviation of the SNR from a predefined threshold indicates the detection of an attack. In response to a detected threat, the Advanced Encryption Standard (AES) is employed to encrypt the data, ensuring its confidentiality. If required, the encrypted data can be decrypted to restore its original form. However, in the absence of any detected threats, the model outputs the denoised absolute value. This denoised value, when combined with the noisy audio's argument using the SFT mixer, represents the output under standard operation. The algorithm concludes its operation, marking the end of the processing cycle. This comprehensive framework ensures the security of neuromorphic systems, addressing potential threats through a combination of proactive and reactive measures.

3.1   CPU/GPU Implementation

We utilized Python to execute implementations on the CPU and GPU. The study leveraged the computational prowess of NVIDIA's GeForce RTX 3060 GPU and Intel's Core i9 12900H CPU, both of which are optimized for different tasks, ensuring an efficient execution of our implementations.

3.2   FPGA Implementation

The presented implementation delineates the operational flow and interconnections of a neuromorphic system integrated with an FPGA. The schematic representation captures the core components and their interactions, providing a comprehensive overview of the system's architecture and functionality. Figure 4 showcases the implementation of the framework within the FPGA architecture.

The following elucidates the individual components and their roles:

1. **Memory (Weights, Patterns):** Essential data, such as synaptic weights, neural patterns, and bias values, are stored in this module. These are crucial for neuromorphic processing. We utilized DDR4 SDRAM for reading the audio dataset and writing feedback from the design. The data, initialized in the MIF file type, is stored in RAM and is fed into the neuromorphic processor for further processing.

2. **STFT (Short-Time Fourier Transform):** This section processes the audio input, converting it into the frequency domain, making it suitable for neuromorphic processing and aiding in the detection of adversarial attacks with Xilinx FFT core.
3. **Security Attack Module:** This module plays a pivotal role in identifying and mitigating security threats, specifically targeting FGSM and PGD adversarial attacks on incoming audio inputs. It operates under a defined attacker model, where such attacks are anticipated during the inference phase, necessitating robust pre-processing security measures, including encrypted data handling. To address concerns of potential security breaches, the system is designed to process encrypted data, maintaining security integrity while effectively detecting adversarial manipulations.
4. **Neuromorphic Processor:** This module performs advanced neuromorphic computations, leveraging the distinct capabilities of the SNN detector. While it receives the processed data and checks for potential FGSM and PGD attacks using the Perturbation Detector, the SNN detector plays a complementary role. It is instrumental in initial attack identification and feature extraction, providing a secondary layer of analysis that works in tandem with SNR computations. The system processes the input through its layers to produce the output, and if an attack is detected, it enters a hard reset state with error flags for FGSM and PGD set. The layers and neurons in this processor are designed parametrically, allowing for easy configurability across various application areas and enhancing the system's capability to identify and respond to complex security threats. Upon detection of an attack, the

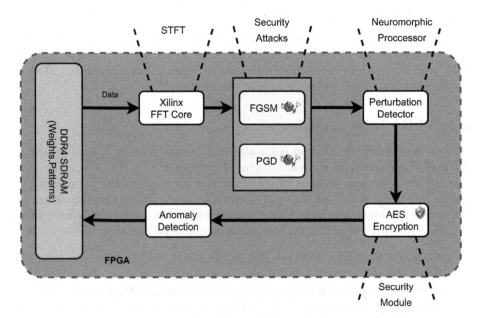

Fig. 4. Implementation of the Neuromorphic Audio Processing Framework on FPGA Architecture.

module signals the neuromorphic processor to initiate a hard reset and set appropriate error flags, thereby preserving the system's integrity and responsiveness in the face of sophisticated cyber threats.

5. **Security Module:** Given the sensitivity of neuromorphic computations and the potential threats they face, a dedicated security module is integrated. This module encrypts the data using AES encryption before it's processed, ensuring data confidentiality.

6. **Anomaly Detection:** Operating in tandem with the security module, the anomaly detection unit continuously monitors the system's operations. It identifies and reports any detected threats or anomalies to the security module, ensuring the system's integrity. Our rigorous testing regime, which includes a variety of attack scenarios, ensures a high threat detection accuracy, mitigating risks of overfitting.

Our threat model, specifically targeting Gradient-based, PGD, FGSM, and Black-box Attacks in audio denoising, addresses the nuanced vulnerabilities inherent in neuromorphic systems. We chose AES encryption for its proven robustness and security, ensuring data integrity against sophisticated cyber threats, a priority given the sensitivity of audio data in our application. The positioning of the anomaly detection module post-encryption strategically aligns with our security protocol, enabling efficient threat detection without compromising encrypted data integrity, a critical factor in maintaining system-wide security and operational efficiency. Our FPGA architecture underscores the importance of a holistic approach, integrating advanced neuromorphic processing with robust security measures. By ensuring seamless interactions between the modules and prioritizing data integrity and security, the system is poised to deliver efficient and secure neuromorphic computations.

4 Evaluation

Table 2. Our Framework characteristics.

Metric	Value
Sampling Rate	16000 kHz
Resolution	16 bits
Frequency Response	8000 Hz
Signal-to-Noise Ratio (SNR)	5.395 dB
Total Harmonic Distortion (THD)	39.50%
Spike Rate	7994.8 spikes/s
Neural Network Topology	SNN
Detection Rate	94%
False Positive Rate	6%
Type of Attacks Tested	FGSM, PGD
Encryption Standards	AES

Table 2 delineates the salient features and metrics of proposed framework underscoring its robustness and precision in neuromorphic audio processing. Operating at a high sampling rate of 16000 kHz and a resolution of 16 bits, the framework ensures fine-grained audio capture and processing. Its frequency response, capped at 8000 Hz, is aptly tailored for human auditory perception. A noteworthy metric is the SNR of 5.395 dB, indicating a commendable balance between the desired signal and background noise. While the Total Harmonic Distortion (THD) at 39.50% suggests the presence of harmonics, the spike rate of 7994.8 spikes/s accentuates the framework's efficiency in encoding information. The adoption of SNNs as the neural network topology further emphasizes the biological fidelity and energy efficiency of the system. With a detection rate of 94% and a 6% false positive rate, the framework's reliability in adversarial scenarios, especially against FGSM and PGD attacks, is evident. Moreover, the incorporation of the AES encryption standard signifies a commitment to data security and integrity, ensuring the secure transmission and storage of audio data. While AES encryption itself does not directly counteract adversarial signals affecting the audio-processing neural network, it plays a crucial role in safeguarding the data against unauthorized access or tampering. Once securely transmitted and decrypted, our neuromorphic system, equipped with its robust detection capabilities, efficiently handles the adversarial attacks, thus providing a comprehensive security solution.

Table 3. Evaluation results on CPU, GPU, and our processor.

	i9 12900H (CPU)	RTX 3060 (GPU)	VU37P (FPGA)
Technology [nm]	10	8	16
Frequency [MHz]	3700	1320	100
# of MAC [GOP]	4.306	4.306	4.306
Latency [ms]	395.91	16.99	72.81
Throughput [GOP/s]	11.01	256.622	59.16
Power [Watt]	20.03	69	14.53
Power Efficiency [GOP/s/W]	0.54	3.71	4.07

Table 3 provides a comprehensive evaluation of three distinct computing platforms: an i9 12900H CPU, an RTX 3060 GPU, and a VU37P FPGA. The table encompasses several pivotal metrics, ranging from manufacturing technology and operating frequency to performance indicators such as latency, throughput, and power efficiency. GPU stands out with a remarkable 256.622 GOP/s, dwarfing the CPU's 11.01 GOP/s and the FPGA's 59.16 GOP/s. This underscores the GPU's prowess in parallel processing capabilities, making it well-suited for tasks that can exploit such parallelism. The GPU, with its high throughput, consumes a substantial 69 W, whereas the CPU and FPGA consume 20.03 W and 14.53 W, respectively. However, when evaluating power efficiency, which measures the performance per unit of power, the FPGA emerges as the most efficient with 4.07 GOP/s/W, slightly surpassing the GPU's 3.71 GOP/s/W and significantly outperforming the CPU's 0.54 GOP/s/W, underlining the suitability of FPGA devices for tasks where power efficiency is critical. This comparison reveals the distinctive characteristics and advantages of each technology, and their appropriateness would largely depend on the specifics of the application at hand.

Table 4. Comparison of neuromorphic hardware security for audio processing.

	[25]	[12]	[24]	**Our Framework**
Neural Network Type	RNN	DNN	CNN	**SNN**
Task	Detecting	Defense	Detecting	**Defense**
Adversarial Example	FGSM	Carlini and Wagner Attacks	FGSM	**FGSM, PGD**
SNR (dB)	12	12	5.40	**5.39**
Latency [ms]	-	-	-	**72.81**
Detection Rate (%)	93.7	93.79	93	**94**

Table 4 shows a detailed comparative analysis of neuromorphic hardware methodologies for audio processing, focusing on their resilience to adversarial attacks. Different neural network architectures, from RNNs, DNNs, and CNNs, have been explored, but our introduction of SNNs marks a significant advancement, given their biological inspiration and energy efficiency. While various methodologies aim at either detecting or defending against adversarial inputs, our framework emphasizes a proactive defense, showcasing robustness against both FGSM and PGD attacks. This robustness is further highlighted by the SNR values, indicating maintained signal quality amidst adversarial noise. Additionally, the latency metric in our framework underscores its suitability for real-time applications. Overall, our methodology, with its integration of SNNs and comprehensive defense mechanisms, sets a benchmark for adversarial robustness in neuromorphic audio processing.

5   Conclusions

We offer a comprehensive overview of the salient points discussed, underscoring the paramount importance of security within FPGA-based neuromorphic systems and delineating potential mitigation strategies. The integration of SNNs in our framework marks a significant advancement in neuromorphic audio processing. With its biological inspiration, energy efficiency, and flawless detection rate, our system sets a benchmark in adversarial robustness. The inclusion of the AES encryption standard further emphasizes our commitment to ensuring data security and integrity. Event-driven audio processing, as discussed, emerges as a promising paradigm, offering both enhanced security and efficiency. We envision architecting solutions that ensure efficiency and security by leveraging the advantages of event-centric systems and neuromorphic architectures. It has been shown that the VCK190 board employed offers a robust implementation of AI-Engine (AIE) cores, capable of achieving notable throughput [11,19]. As a next step of this research, we intend to further explore and evaluate the proposed framework within a real-time environment, specifically leveraging the capabilities of the AIE cores. We anticipate validating these outcomes in an industrial setting, in collaboration with our funding partners and affiliated enterprises.

Acknowledgment. We acknowledge the Temsa Research R&D Center for their generous financial support and the reviewers for their invaluable insights and suggestions that significantly contributed to the enhancement of our paper.

Disclosure of Interests. The authors have no competing interests to declare that are relevant to the content of this article.

References

1. Bu, T., Ding, J., Hao, Z., Yu, Z.: Rate gradient approximation attack threats deep spiking neural networks. In: Proceedings of the IEEE/CVF Conference on Computer Vision and Pattern Recognition, pp. 7896–7906 (2023)
2. Chen, X., Li, S., Huang, H.: Adversarial attack and defense on deep neural network-based voice processing systems: an overview. Appl. Sci. **11**(18), 8450 (2021)
3. Galán, D.G.: Neuromorphic auditory computing: towards a digital, event-based implementation of the hearing sense for robotics. Ph.D. thesis, Universidad de Sevilla (2022)
4. Giannakopoulos, P., Pikrakis, A., Cotronis, Y.: Improving post-processing of audio event detectors using reinforcement learning. IEEE Access **10**, 84398–84404 (2022)
5. Gongye, C., Luo, Y., Xu, X., Fei, Y.: HammerDodger: a lightweight defense framework against RowHammer attack on DNNs. In: 2023 60th ACM/IEEE Design Automation Conference (DAC), pp. 1–6. IEEE (2023)
6. Huynh, P.K., Varshika, M.L., Paul, A., Isik, M., Balaji, A., Das, A.: Implementing spiking neural networks on neuromorphic architectures: a review. arXiv preprint arXiv:2202.08897 (2022)
7. Inadagbo, K., Arig, B., Alici, N., Isik, M.: Exploiting FPGA capabilities for accelerated biomedical computing. In: 2023 Signal Processing: Algorithms, Architectures, Arrangements, and Applications (SPA), pp. 48–53. IEEE (2023)
8. Isik, M.: A survey of spiking neural network accelerator on FPGA. arXiv preprint arXiv:2307.03910 (2023)
9. Isik, M., Inadagbo, K.: Astrocyte-integrated dynamic function exchange in spiking neural networks. In: Kofroň, J., Margaria, T., Seceleanu, C. (eds.) International Conference on Engineering of Computer-Based Systems, pp. 263–273. Springer, Cham (2023). https://doi.org/10.1007/978-3-031-49252-5_24
10. Isik, M., Paul, A., Varshika, M.L., Das, A.: A design methodology for fault-tolerant computing using astrocyte neural networks. In: Proceedings of the 19th ACM International Conference on Computing Frontiers, pp. 169–172 (2022)
11. Jia, X., et al.: XVDPU: a high performance CNN accelerator on the Versal platform powered by the AI engine. In: 2022 32nd International Conference on Field-Programmable Logic and Applications (FPL), pp. 01–09. IEEE (2022)

12. Kwon, H., Yoon, H., Park, K.W.: Poster: detecting audio adversarial example through audio modification. In: Proceedings of the 2019 ACM SIGSAC Conference on Computer and Communications Security, pp. 2521–2523 (2019)
13. Liu, B., Yang, C., Li, H., Chen, Y., Wu, Q., Barnell, M.: Security of neuromorphic systems: challenges and solutions. In: 2016 IEEE International Symposium on Circuits and Systems (ISCAS), pp. 1326–1329. IEEE (2016)
14. Madden, K., Harkin, J., McDaid, L., Nugent, C.: Adding security to networks-on-chip using neural networks. In: 2018 IEEE Symposium Series on Computational Intelligence (SSCI), pp. 1299–1306. IEEE (2018)
15. Maji, S., Lee, K., Gongye, C., Fei, Y., Chandrakasan, A.P.: An energy-efficient neural network accelerator with improved protections against fault-attacks. In: ESSCIRC 2023- IEEE 49th European Solid State Circuits Conference (ESSCIRC). pp. 233–236 (2023). https://doi.org/10.1109/ESSCIRC59616.2023.10268746
16. Marchisio, A., Pira, G., Martina, M., Masera, G., Shafique, M.: DVS-attacks: adversarial attacks on dynamic vision sensors for spiking neural networks. In: 2021 International Joint Conference on Neural Networks (IJCNN), pp. 1–9. IEEE (2021)
17. Merchant, F.: Security as an important ingredient in neuromorphic engineering. In: 2022 IEEE Computer Society Annual Symposium on VLSI (ISVLSI), pp. 314–319. IEEE (2022)
18. Peng, H., et al.: PASNet: polynomial architecture search framework for two-party computation-based secure neural network deployment. In: 2023 60th ACM/IEEE Design Automation Conference (DAC), pp. 1–6. IEEE (2023)
19. Perryman, N., Wilson, C., George, A.: Evaluation of Xilinx Versal architecture for next-gen edge computing in space. In: 2023 IEEE Aerospace Conference, pp. 1–11. IEEE (2023)
20. Salehi, S., et al.: Neuromorphic-enabled security for IoT. In: 2022 20th IEEE Interregional NEWCAS Conference (NEWCAS), pp. 153–157. IEEE (2022)
21. Sepulveda, J., Reinbrecht, C., Diguet, J.P.: Security aspects of neuromorphic MPSoCs. In: 2018 IEEE/ACM International Conference on Computer-Aided Design (ICCAD), pp. 1–6. IEEE (2018)
22. Staudigl, F., et al.: Fault injection in native logic-in-memory computation on neuromorphic hardware. arXiv preprint arXiv:2302.07655 (2023)
23. Tayarani-Najaran, M.H., Schmuker, M.: Event-based sensing and signal processing in the visual, auditory, and olfactory domain: a review. Front. Neural Circuits **15**, 610446 (2021)
24. Yang, C.H., Qi, J., Chen, P.Y., Ma, X., Lee, C.H.: Characterizing speech adversarial examples using self-attention U-Net enhancement. In: ICASSP 2020–2020 IEEE International Conference on Acoustics, Speech and Signal Processing (ICASSP), pp. 3107–3111. IEEE (2020)
25. Yang, Z., Li, B., Chen, P.Y., Song, D.: Characterizing audio adversarial examples using temporal dependency. arXiv preprint arXiv:1809.10875 (2018)
26. Zhou, T., Luo, Y., Ren, S., Xu, X.: NNSplitter: an active defense solution to DNN model via automated weight obfuscation. arXiv preprint arXiv:2305.00097 (2023)

Design Methods and Tools

Secure eFPGA Configuration: A System-Level Approach

Allen Boston[✉], Roman Gauchi, and Pierre-Emmanuel Gaillardon

University of Utah, Salt Lake City, UT 84112, USA
{allen.boston,roman.gauchi,pierre-emmanuel.gaillardon}@utah.edu
https://www.ece.utah.edu

Abstract. Field Programmable Gate Arrays (FPGAs) have repeatedly proven their importance in modern computing, delivering high flexibility while minimizing performance trade-offs and engineering costs compared to Application-Specific Integrated Circuits (ASICs). However, to achieve this level of flexibility, FPGAs require configuration, presenting a non-trivial initialization procedure accompanied by the inherent hardware security challenge focused on protecting the confidentiality of the user's sensitive configuration data. This paper presents the Programming Management Unit (PMU) as an open-source core to address embedded FPGA (eFPGA) configuration and bitstream protection with a co-design implementation approach. The PMU hardware is meant to be adaptable for easy integration into open-source projects, providing a nexus for standardized communication protocols, cryptographic cores, and eFPGA configuration memory architectures. Moreover, this project aims to support the entire end-to-end configuration procedure, spanning from bitstream generation to eFPGA configuration memory, necessitating a software-based frond-end for encipherment, encoding, and delivery to PMU hardware. Showcasing the PMU within a practical context, this paper details an application where the PMU interfaces with JTAG, AES, SHA, and OpenFPGA eFPGA fabric carried out in the Skywater130 technology node. This demonstration highlights the PMU's efficiency by illustrating the system-level trade-offs between area, power consumption, configuration time, and security protocols.

Keywords: FPGA Configuration · Bitstream · Hardware Security

1 Introduction

Field Programmable Gate Arrays (FPGAs) have played a key role in modern computing, and, in parallel, the continued advancement in performance, design techniques, and usability has further leveraged the viability of this architecture within industrial and academic applications. For this reason, FPGAs and embedded FPGAs have become an appealing hardware solution and rapid system prototyping mechanism, often operating in security-sensitive hardware environments, i.e., medical, aerospace, and defense [12,18,23,24]. Since nearly all

I. Skliarova et al. (Eds.): ARC 2024, LNCS 14553, pp. 151–165, 2024.
https://doi.org/10.1007/978-3-031-55673-9_11

hardware systems experience vulnerability to device counterfeiting, intellectual property (IP), sensitive data confiscation, etc., they necessitate robust security protocols at both the hardware and software levels [13,25]. Consequently, substantial effort is dedicated to the implementation and verification of co-designed security systems with a dynamic focus on attacks and countermeasures.

In the matter of re-configurable hardware, the security paradigm undergoes a distinctive shift where the configuration data uploaded to programmable hardware becomes the primary target of malicious activity, generating opportunities for new exploitable weaknesses and security techniques [31]. In addition to a complex security environment, eFPGA bitstream configuration is a non-trivial task, often requiring some external circuitry near the eFPGA to handle the configuration procedure [7]. To address these challenges, state-of-the-art implementations have proposed the following solutions [2,3,15,21], presented in Sect. 3.

Advanced open-source design tools now offer a method for the rapid design of cutting-edge domain-specific eFPGA architectures at a low engineering cost, expanding the practicality of open-source toolchains for eFPGA integration yet lacking available circuitry specific to secure eFPGA bitstream configuration. With that, an open-source solution would provide bitstream configuration that accurately targets available eFPGA configuration protocols and supports security features to protect user IPs from malicious attacks.

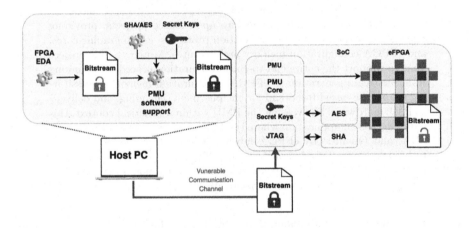

Fig. 1. Overview of proposed system: PMU provides intermediate support between eFPGA EDA tools and eFPGA core configuration.

In this paper, we propose the Programming Management Unit (PMU) as an open-source core, designed to enable secure bitstream configuration whilst remaining adaptable to varying communication protocols, cryptographic implementations, key storage methods, and eFPGA configuration architectures. The proposed architecture will act as a prototype configuration circuit, giving more insight to the designer within the open-source environment for the secure integration of eFPGAs into a larger system. To demonstrate the integration of the

PMU within an applied system, we implement the proposed hardware using Joint Action Test Group (JTAG), targeting an OpenFPGA [27] shift-register-based 'configuration chain' protocol, and interfacing highly standardized cryptographic cores: Advanced Encryption Standard (AES) and Secure Hash Algorithm (SHA). The PMU hardware is supported by Python-based code which generates an enciphered and encoded bitstream based on the plaintext bitstream, user-defined cipher keys, and user-defined instructions. This bitstream is then presented to the PMU hardware where it is decrypted, on-the-fly, following the applied security protocol during bitstream upload. To the best of our knowledge, this is the first open-source end-to-end security-aware eFPGA configuration system readily adaptable for deployment in real-world applications. The proposed end-to-end system is presented in Fig. 1.

To evaluate the design trade-off related to the PMU's operation and observe the open-source practicality, a physical system was implemented in Skywater130 nm technology, integrating the PMU core with existing open-source Hardware Definition Language (HDL) blocks; JTAG, AES, SHA, and OpenFPGA eFPGA, using an entirely open-source tool-chain. The implemented system, through Register Transfer Level (RTL) verification, has been demonstrated to configure OpenFPGA configuration memory accurately and implement features protecting the plaintext bitstream.

The remainder of this paper is organized as follows: Section 2 introduces relevant concepts related to FPGA configuration, Sect. 3 outlines related proposed and existing works, Sect. 4 details the intended security objectives of the system, Sect. 5 presents the proposed architecture, Sect. 6 provides an overview of integration within a practical system and observations related to cost of securing bitstream configuration protocol, and finally, Sect. 7 concludes the paper.

2   Background

2.1   Joint Action Test Group

Joint Test Action Group (JTAG) is a standardized interface [14], widely used in the electronics industry for testing and debugging integrated circuits. Initially developed for testing Printed Circuit Boards (PCBs) during manufacturing, JTAG has become a versatile tool for a range of system-level tasks, for example, testing individual Integrated Circuit (IC) components, debugging embedded systems, and programming devices in-circuit. The JTAG interface, like other popular communication protocols, provides a standardized way to communicate with and control multiple devices on a circuit board, enabling efficient and reliable testing and development processes. The widespread adoption of JTAG has led to its utilization by many system designers to adopt it for FPGA/eFPGA bitstream configuration, testing, and verification.

2.2   Bitstream and FPGA Configuration Protocols

Given that eFPGAs are programmable hardware, they require external information at the time of configuration to carry out the desired functions of the user.
Configuration information, represented in a string of bits, is often referred to
as a bitstream and ranges in size from a few hundred to several thousand bits.
Look-up Tables (LUTs) and Flip Flops (FF) represent the most basic elements
of a eFPGA fabric, and interact directly with configuration memory to emulate
a user design. Bitstreams are fabric-dependent user designs that are generated
by EDA tools to be uploaded to an eFPGA based on a "configuration protocol".
The configuration protocol determines the way an eFPGA architecture or fabric will interpret a bitstream when provided to the configuration hardware. A
variety of configuration methods exist; however, across all eFPGA architectures,
memory elements are required to store the configuration bits. With that, volatile
storage techniques are often utilized due to their size and speed, requiring most
eFPGAs to be configured at each power-up sequence.

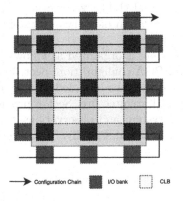

Fig. 2. Configuration chain: A flip-flop based configuration protocol

Several state-of-the-art techniques for configuration storage employ Static
Random Access Memory (SRAM) cells or flash memory to hold the configuration data, necessitating advanced design and verification techniques that are not
easily accomplished within the open-source toolchain [2,3,15,21]. A "configuration chain", shown in Fig. 2, is an alternatively used protocol that is comprised
of a shift register inside the FPGA core that contains enough D flip-flops to
hold the entire bitstream. At the time of configuration, the binary bitstream
is serially loaded into the shift register chain at a rate of 1 bit per clock cycle
until the entire bitstream is stored in the configuration chain. The configuration
chain, depicted in Fig. 2, is an attractive protocol for those in the open-source
environment since it can be realized using only standard cells.

3   Related Works

Industry and academic efforts are aimed at designing circuits and systems for eFPGA bitstream configuration in a secure environment, although commonly, these implementations target highly specific commercial applications or are outlined with abstract documentation, leaving the open-source hardware designer to develop custom configuration and security circuits. Academic works proposed solutions for high-speed JTAG configuration [11], microprocessor configuration [6], and bitstream compression [8], providing a means of configuration. Above that, security-aware implementations propose varying alternative security schemes, for example, [17] proposes, from a high level, a secure bitstream configuration method. [28] demonstrates an encryption-based protocol for JTAG. [4] proposes a security scheme consisting of AES encryption in conjunction with Cipher-based message authentication code (CMAC) to prevent downgrade attacks and integrates the system on a commercial FPGA. [30] outlines a security protocol for encrypting and verifying bitstreams for cloud-based systems.

State-of-the-art hardware implementations consist of advanced cores containing an array of cryptographic cores, tamper sensors, decompression cores, non-volatile bitstream storage interfaces, and several user-defined configuration options. For example, a variety of Intel implementations utilize a Secure Device Manager (SDM), which manages bitstream configuration with JTAG interface and contains blocks such as AES 256-bit, SHA256/384-bit, and ECDSA 256/384 cores, decompression module, tamper sensing circuitry, a key vault containing a Physically Unclonable Function (PUF) generator for cryptographic keys, as well as Battery-Backed RAM (BBRAM) and Fuse memory for writable keys [15]. Other commercial solutions, for example, Microsemi and AMD, have similar implementations containing slightly different and unique cryptographic algorithm collections, key management solutions, security protocols, and other proprietary design features [2,3,21]. As a result of SRAM utilization in the configuration memory of state-of-the-art implementations, in general, most of the proposed systems target SRAM-based configuration circuitry. To improve the level of security provided to a customer, proprietary solutions have limited public documentation surrounding the operation and organization of the configuration control circuitry.

Often, proposed implementations attempt to strike a balance between configuration complexity and security despite extensive efforts to implement robust security mechanisms for bitstream configuration. Ultimately, this work aims to carry out an end-to-end bitstream configuration system that implements features comparable to contemporary works and is easily available and, therefore, more suitable to the open-source environment.

4   PMU Security Analysis

4.1   Cryptographic Algorithms

Cryptographic algorithms protect sensitive data by encipherment or providing authenticity and integrity verification such that data can be exchanged securely. The basic idea is to take plaintext data and use a mathematical algorithm to transform it into ciphertext, where only intended users can retrieve the plaintext data from the ciphertext. Properties such as achieved confidentially of plaintext, data integrity, and hardware implementation complexity become design trade-offs when organizing a cryptographic system [20]. Furthermore, the significance of keys in cryptography must be balanced. Careful consideration of cryptographic key properties becomes crucial in determining the effectiveness and suitability of cryptographic algorithms for a given application. Accordingly, some algorithms are more suitable for a given application, requiring careful consideration of design trade-offs when creating a cryptographic system.

The cryptographic algorithms used for this project were chosen based on the following criteria. First, the chosen algorithms must be highly standardized and be applicable to the intended countermeasure or system. Second, they must be fully available to the open-source ecosystem with complete source code and abundant documentation. For that reason, we selected AES and SHA, as together, they provide a robust security solution for the PMU application to ensure the confidentially and integrity of the bitstream data, as well as the restriction of unauthorized users during the eFPGA configuration procedure.

AES has been extensively used and tested in academia and industry as well as adopted by many organizations for secure communication; due to its robustness and widespread trust, AES is a symmetric block cipher algorithm that provides strong data confidentially via encryption using a fixed-length key and plaintext "blocks" of data (128-bit, 192-bit, or 256-bit) [26]. SHA is a hash function that generates a unique fixed-length (224-bit, 256-bit, or 384-bit, 512-bit) digital certificate of a message called a digest, which ensures the plaintext integrity and verifies the authenticity of the plaintext source [19]. Again, due to substantial use and testing in academia and industry, SHA, specifically its subsequent versions SHA-2 and SHA-3, are widely trusted dual-purpose algorithms for data integrity and authentication. SHA relies on a private key and generates a digest. At the time of decryption, SHA is again computed using the private key and plaintext; the result is then compared to the original digest obtained at the encryption stage to verify plaintext data.

4.2   PMU Threat Model

The hardware security landscape is expansive and continually evolving, encompassing a broad spectrum of attacks and corresponding countermeasures. Therefore, the scope of PMU hardware security application is deliberately constrained to protecting the bitstream throughout the eFPGA configuration sequence. To better define the scope of the vulnerabilities expected from the PMU, we adopt two terms, 'at rest' and 'loading,' to describe stages in the bitstream life-cycle [9]. The bitstream life cycle describes stages between a bitstream being generated by an EDA tool to the point of obsoletion known as 'end-of-life.' 'At rest', the bitstream is held somewhere in memory, post EDA generation, for example, the configuration memory inside the eFPGA core or external non-volatile memory that later supplies the configuration memory. At this stage, configuration data is susceptible to confiscation via memory exploitation attacks and reverse engineering IP theft. The 'loading' stage describes the transfer of configuration data between the host, usually a PC, and the memories of the configuration circuitry through a vulnerable communication channel. A plaintext bitstream in the loading phase is at risk of confiscation via side-channel and replay attacks. The PMU security protocol will focus only on protecting the bitstream during states of 'at-rest' and bitstream 'loading.' It will not consider, for example, protecting the bitstream at the time of generation by EDA tools or when the FPGA uses bitstream information during run time and not related to the configuration sequence.

Since the effectiveness of cryptographic algorithms relies, for the most part, on the confidentiality and sharing methodology of keys, as discussed in Sects. 4.1, key storage, generation, and management techniques quickly become critical when considering an extensive security system [5,10,16]. However, given the nature of this new entrant open-source design, achieving advanced key storage is beyond the reach of the objectives; therefore, straightforward techniques for cryptographic key storage, like hard coding and register storage, were employed.

4.3   Proposed Security System

For the proposed security system, we combine AES at the interior level to encrypt the configuration data with SHA on the exterior to check the data and user integrity on the encrypted AES output. With AES, the proposed system achieves plaintext confidentiality by AES encipherment in the 'at-rest' stage and during 'loading' over a non-secure communication channel. Authentication and data integrity checks are achieved with an SHA algorithm, ensuring the user carrying out instructions with the PMU has permission via a private key and that the data received is indeed the data sent by a known user. SHA check also prevents random bit sequences from being uploaded to detect possible attacks that utilize random bit sequences to expose FSM deadlock and vulnerable registers.

With the proposed countermeasures, the PMU will prevent the bitstream data from being exposed through memory exploitation attacks, bitstream reverse engineering, side-channel attacks, and replay attacks. Partial upload attacks, described in Sect. 3, could be prevented by performing several authentication checks in user-defined intervals, thus more often checking that the bitstream has not been tampered with the trade-off of increased eFPGA configuration time.

5   Architecture

5.1   Bitstream Encoding

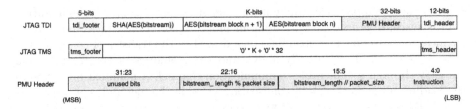

Fig. 3. PMU Encoding Scheme: JTAG compatible 'tdi' and 'tms' signals and serially encoded PMU header.

JTAG and configuration chain circuits have serial ports; consequentially, the PMU uses a serial encoding scheme to interpret information, including PMU instruction and the bitstream length, necessitating an encoding scheme. Since the bitstream ultimately passes through the JTAG interface, PMU, and cryptographic cores before arriving at the configuration memory, two additional encoding layers are on top of the cryptographic encipherment. The first encoding layer consists of a 12-bit JTAG header and five-bit JTAG footer, consisting of two signals: "tms" to configure the JTAG TAP controller to the correct instruction and "tdi" to deliver the bitstream data. Next is the PMU header, which contains a five-bit PMU instruction, the number of 128-bit AES packets, and the excess bitstream bits that exceed the 128-bit block size. Figure 3 outlines the entire encoding scheme used by the PMU architecture. The project includes Python-based software support to automate the encipherment and encoding of the PMU-compatible bitstream according to the following description.

5.2   Top Level Organization

Designed to lie on the periphery of an eFPGA, the PMU is a hardware solution for bitstream configuration; for that reason, the implementation of the device requires coordination with the surrounding functional blocks. Shown in Fig. 1, the PMU lies between and organizes the data movement between an eFPGA and cryptography cores. To support the PMU, the open-source JTAG project was customized with an additional instruction register and control signal for the PMU, enabling it to supply serial data from the Host PC to the PMU data-in port.

The PMU must pass the bitstream data through the cryptographic cores according to the PMU security scheme, requiring special attention concerning the data flow of the bitstream information. Since the sourced AES and SHA hardware implementations have different computation times and input lengths, 128-bit and 256-bits respectively, custom memory interfaces facilitate accurate

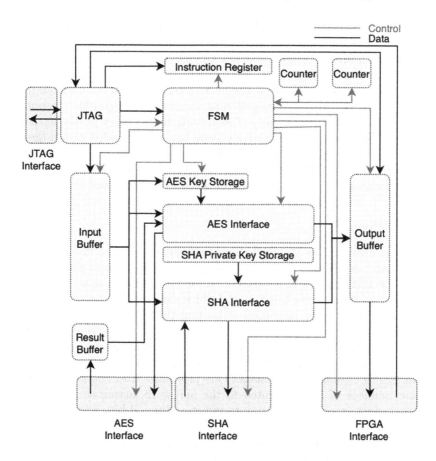

Fig. 4. PMU Core Architecture.

data movement to the cryptographic cores. Including handling data dependencies and reducing the total number of I/O ports between the PMU, AES, and SHA. A system designer could start with this implementation as a template and adapt it to specific needs, for example, replacing JTAG for SPI or AES for another encipherment algorithm.

In this section, we provide an overview of the PMU architecture, which principally consists of a 13-stage Finite State Machine (FSM) responsible for all control signals, data movement, and sequence management between cores during the configuration sequence. The instruction bits within the serially encoded PMU header dictate the core's specific configuration sequence or operation and get loaded into a dedicated instruction register with each PMU deployment. Two counters aid the FSM in keeping track of and correctly managing the duration of the configuration sequence. To support on-the-fly description during the bitstream configuration sequence, the computation latency of the cryptographic cores and block style inputs are addressed with serialization and deserialization.

Double buffering of the bitstream data is made feasible with three buffers to minimize data storage time in unsecured memories, further preventing memory exploitation attacks. Figure 4 shows a block diagram of the proposed PMU architecture.

For simplicity, the PMU uses a 128-bit register such that the user can upload a unique secret AES key and demonstrate accurate cryptographic computation of the bitstream with the flexibility of modifying the AES key post-silicon. Similarly, for the SHA core, the respective private key is hard-coded within the HDL and is not modifiable post-silicon. While these key storage methods are not secure, they emulate the behavior of more advanced key management methodologies and ultimately allow the demonstration of the proposed system.

5.3   Functionality

This section outlines how the PMU hardware carries out a secure configuration procedure and describes some additional operations capable of the core. When enabled, the PMU moves to a "decode" state to interpret the serially encoded instruction and then moves to the next FSM state in the sequence based on the instruction. The primary operation is loading the eFPGA configuration data with AES and SHA protection according to the protocol described in Sect. 4.3. This is done by buffering serial data from JTAG, providing appropriately sized blocks to cipher cores, buffering the cipher output data, and serially loading into the eFPGA configuration chain. This procedure uses counters to monitor the exact number of bits presented to the hardware, acting as a preventative measure against attacks attempting to inject additional bits into the bitstream during configuration.

PMU aims to balance bitstream upload time and cryptographic effectiveness; therefore, the FSM double buffers bitstream data while being modified by the cryptographic cores, minimizing the configuration latency overhead associated with implemented security measures. Buffers are cleared between instruction and intermediate steps of the upload sequence to minimize the overall time plaintext data is held outside of eFPGA configuration memory. If the SHA check fails during bitstream upload, PMU operation terminates, the configuration chain is cleared, and PMU is locked until the system reset occurs.

In addition to the functionality detailed above, the architecture is capable of five other institutions designed for testing intermediate functions. Specifically, it can load an AES secret key with and without SHA authentication, load bitstreams with AES and SHA decryption as options, and load a bitstream without cryptographic support altogether. The hardware also carries out a bitstream read function such that the user can read out the contents of the configuration memory. Furthermore, status registers and spy pads were included in the physical design to observe the current FSM state, configuration sequence status, internal signals, and intermediate computation results.

6   PMU Integration and System Evaluation

To comprehensively evaluate the integration effort and the effectiveness of the proposed PMU design, the architecture was physically implemented using the conventional tape-out flow, beginning with the Hardware Description Language (HDL) code, written and functionally verified using Icarus Verilog [29]. Register Transfer Level (RTL) representation of the PMU was verified using a robust simulation platform design to test both intended and random bit sequences. Resilience to random bit sequence further improves the level of security achieved by preventing unintentional behavior of the PMU hardware. To further ensure the robustness of the security system, Common Weakness Analysis (CWA) techniques performed on the proposed design show security flaws such as FSM deadlock, vulnerable registers, and locked registers were not present in RTL level design [1]. Therefore, the resulting hardware demonstrates robustness to common weakness while performing the functions described in Sects. 4 and 5.

To leverage the benefits of the open-source environment, we use SiliconCompiler [22], a framework for automated RTL to GDSII generation for synthesis, floorplanning, place and route, and clock tree synthesis. Using this methodology, we implemented a hardened PMU design alongside a basic eFPGA architecture utilizing 6, 4-input luts per logic element, an AES core, and a SHA core, with SkyWater130 nm technology. This design was contained within the caravel project design space and submitted to the Efabless multi-project wafer program 7. Table 1 outlines the achievements of the proposed design. Since the PMU is compatible with any sized FPGA we present the area and power values of the PMU, AES, and SHA, along with the area of one 4-input lut. From our findings we determine that the PMU is approximately the size of 625 LUTs, resulting in a minimal overhead that is less than 1% for typical FPGA sizes containing more than 100K LUTs.

Table 1. Power and area breakdown evaluated at 100 MHz with Skywater130 nm.

Block	4-Input LUT	PMU	AES	SHA
Total Power (W)	2.79e−10 W	4.14e−03 W	4.66e−02 W	2.76e−02 W
Area (μm^2)	230 μm²	143,635 μm²	519,890 μm²	311,805 μm²

With the advantage of a fully realized system, it is possible to make observations about the design trade-offs experienced during the creation of the PMU. To examine the cost of implementing a secure configuration system alongside an eFPGA, we present a comparative analysis of several security protocol configurations with varying levels of security as well the associated energy and cycle time cost. Since the outlined security protocol configurations have the same hardware, they will experience the same area and power overheads presented in Table 2; therefore, they are distinguished by comparing the required cycles to complete the bitstream configuration procedure.

The first row of Table 2 lists the standalone eFPGA having zero overhead where n represents the number of bits in the plaintext bitstream. The second row outlines the systems consisting only of eFGPA and the PMU, representing configuration support without any security measures. Adding the PMU necessitates a 32-bit encoding overhead compared to the plaintext bitstream. The following two protocols use AES or SHA alone, respectively. From Table 2, these protocols assume the same PMU encoding overhead of 32 bits plus the cycles needed to accommodate computation latency of 51 for AES and 65 for SHA. The use of SHA also requires a 256-bit digest, which is included in the encoding overhead for systems containing the cipher. The fifth configuration contains the PMU operation with AES implemented on the entire plaintext bitstream with an SHA check at the end of the bitstream sequence. The number of required cycles was extracted by taking the total bit length of the encoded bitstream. To extract values for energy, the maximum period based on the 100 MHz operation frequency is multiplied by the total average power consumption of the system, based on Table 1. Our analysis shows that the configuration time and energy consumption linked to a security protocol become negligible for FPGA fabrics of significant size, where bitstreams are more than 100K bits in length.

Table 2. Energy per Cycle Overhead for Varying Security Protocols. Evaluated at 100 MHz.

Cycle Time Breakdown (n = bitstream length, i = SHA Evaluations)		
System	Cycles	Energy/Cycle Overhead
eFPGA	n	-
eFPGA+PMU	n+32	41.4pJ
eFPGA+PMU+ AES	n+32+51	500pJ
eFPGA+PMU+SHA	n+32+65+i(256)	310pJ
eFPGA+PMU+AES+SHA	n+32+51+65+i(256)	783pJ

7   Conclusion

In this paper, we introduced the PMU, an open-source core that enables hardware designers in the open-source environment to implement bitstream configuration circuitry along with the appropriate hardware security features through a readily adaptable hardware and software framework. We proposed an application using the following standardized components JTAG, AES, SHA, with an eFPGA from OpenFPGA framework, where on-the-fly decryption and accurate bitstream configuration was achieved while implementing features to protect the bitstream from plaintext confiscation and unauthorized usage based on the proposed security objectives. Accurate comparisons of power, performance, area, and cycle to commercial solutions were not possible due to the overall complexity of commercial solutions compared to the bare-bones PMU. Instead we demonstrate the readily adaptable framework of the open-source core by implementing a physical system using Skywater130 nm technology and a completely open-source toolchain. Through the exhibition of the proposed system containing the PMU, we identify trade-offs between area, power consumption, configuration time, and security metrics, while illustrating the negligible area and power footprint of the configuration system. The PMU, including source codes, documentation, and physical implementation flow scripts, is publicly available at https://github.com/lnis-uofu/FPGA_Secured_Bitstream.

Acknowledgments. This work was supported by the NSF PPoSS Award No. 2217154.

Disclosure of Interests. P.-E. Gaillardon has financial interests in the company RapidSilicon, Inc.

References

1. Ahmad, B., et al.: Don't CWEAT it: toward CWE analysis techniques in early stages of hardware design. In: Proceedings of the 41st IEEE/ACM International Conference on Computer-Aided Design, pp. 1–9 (2022)
2. AMD: 7 Series FPGAs Configuration, User Guide, December 2023. https://docs.xilinx.com/v/u/en-US/ug470_7Series_Config
3. AMD: Virtex-5 FPGAs Configuration User Guide, February 2023. https://docs.xilinx.com/v/u/en-US/ug191
4. Badrignans, B., Elbaz, R., Torres, L.: Secure FPGA configuration architecture preventing system downgrade. In: 2008 International Conference on Field Programmable Logic and Applications, pp. 317–322 (2008). https://doi.org/10.1109/FPL.2008.4629951
5. Barker, E.: Recommendation for key management: Part 1 - general. NIST Special Publication 800-57 Part 1 4 (2020)
6. Blodget, B., McMillan, S., Lysaght, P.: A lightweight approach for embedded reconfiguration of FPGAs. In: 2003 Design, Automation and Test in Europe Conference and Exhibition, pp. 399–400 (2003). https://doi.org/10.1109/DATE.2003.1253642
7. Boutros, A., Betz, V.: FPGA architecture: principles and progression. IEEE Circuits Syst. Mag. **21**(2), 4–29 (2021). https://doi.org/10.1109/MCAS.2021.3071607
8. Daoud, L., Hussein, F., Rafla, N.: Real-time bitstream decompression scheme for FPGAs reconfiguration. In: 2018 IEEE 61st International Midwest Symposium on Circuits and Systems (MWSCAS), pp. 1082–1085 (2018). https://doi.org/10.1109/MWSCAS.2018.8624003
9. Duncan, A., Rahman, F., Lukefahr, A., Farahmandi, F., Tehranipoor, M.: FPGA bitstream security: a day in the life. In: 2019 IEEE International Test Conference (ITC), pp. 1–10 (2019). https://doi.org/10.1109/ITC44170.2019.9000145
10. Barker, E., Roginsk, A.: Recommendation for key generation. NIST Special Publication 800-113 (2012)
11. Gruwell, A., Zabriskie, P., Wirthlin, M.: High-speed FPGA configuration and testing through JTAG. In: 2016 IEEE AUTOTESTCON, pp. 1–8 (2016). https://doi.org/10.1109/AUTEST.2016.7589601
12. Hill, B., et al.: Precision medicine and FPGA technology: challenges and opportunities (2017). https://doi.org/10.1109/MWSCAS.2017.8053008

13. Hu, W., Chang, C.H., Sengupta, A., Bhunia, S., Kastner, R., Li, H.: An overview of hardware security and trust: threats, countermeasures, and design tools. IEEE Trans. Comput. Aided Des. Integr. Circuits Syst. **40**(6), 1010–1038 (2021). https://doi.org/10.1109/TCAD.2020.3047976

14. Institute of Electrical and Electronics Engineers: IEEE Std. 1149.1 - Standard Test Access Port and Boundary-Scan Architecture. Technical report, 1149.1-2013. IEEE (2013)

15. Intel: Executing SDM Commands via JTAG Interface, March 2021. https://www.intel.com/content/www/us/en/docs/programmable/683313/current/overview.html

16. Joshi, S., Mohanty, S.P., Kougianos, E.: Everything you wanted to know about PUFs. IEEE Potentials **36**(6), 38–46 (2017). https://doi.org/10.1109/MPOT.2015.2490261

17. Kean, T.: Secure configuration of a field programmable gate array. In: The 9th Annual IEEE Symposium on Field-Programmable Custom Computing Machines (FCCM 2001), pp. 259–260 (2001). https://doi.org/10.1007/3-540-44687-7_15

18. Leong, P.H.W.: Recent trends in FPGA architectures and applications. In: 4th IEEE International Symposium on Electronic Design, Test and Applications (delta 2008), pp. 137–141 (2008). https://doi.org/10.1109/DELTA.2008.14

19. Lin, C.H., Yeh, Y.S., Chien, S.P., Lee, C.Y., Chien, H.S.: Generalized secure hash algorithm: SHA-X. In: 2011 IEEE EUROCON - International Conference on Computer as a Tool, pp. 1–4 (2011). https://doi.org/10.1109/EUROCON.2011.5929187

20. Maqsood, F., Ahmed, M., Ali, M.M., Shah, M.A.: Cryptography: a comparative analysis for modern techniques. Int. J. Adv. Comput. Sci. Appl. **8**(6) (2017)

21. Microsemi: IGLOO PLUS FPGA Fabric User's Guide, August 2012. https://ww1.microchip.com/downloads/aemDocuments/documents/FPGA/ProductDocuments/UserGuides/iglooplus_ug.pdf

22. Olofsson, A., Ransohoff, W., Moroze, N.: A distributed approach to silicon compilation: Invited. In: Proceedings of the 59th ACM/IEEE Design Automation Conference, DAC 2022, pp. 1343–1346. Association for Computing Machinery, New York, NY, USA (2022). https://doi.org/10.1145/3489517.3530673

23. Research, G.V.: Field programmable gate array (FPGA) market size, share trends analysis report. https://www.grandviewresearch.com/industry-analysis/fpga-market

24. Saday, A.: A review of FPGA-based applications and FPGA usage in the industrial area. In: Innovations and Technologies in Engineering, p. 171 (2022)

25. Sklavos, N., Chaves, R., Di Natale, G., Regazzoni, F.: Hardware Security and Trust Design and Deployment of Integrated Circuits in a Threatened Environment. 1st edn. Springer, Cham (2017). https://doi.org/10.1007/978-3-319-44318-8. http://lib.ugent.be/catalog/ebk01:3710000001022125

26. National Institute and Technology of Standards: Advanced encryption standard. NIST FIPS PUB 197 (2001)

27. Tang, X., Giacomin, E., Alacchi, A., Chauviere, B., Gaillardon, P.E.: OpenFPGA: an opensource framework enabling rapid prototyping of customizable FPGAs. In: 2019 29th International Conference on Field Programmable Logic and Applications (FPL), pp. 367–374 (2019). https://doi.org/10.1109/FPL.2019.00065

28. Valea, E., Silva, M.D., Flottes, M.L., Natale, G.D., Rouzeyre, B.: Encryption-based secure JTAG. In: 2019 IEEE 22nd International Symposium on Design and Diagnostics of Electronic Circuits Systems (DDECS), pp. 1–6 (2019). https://doi.org/10.1109/DDECS.2019.8724654

29. Williams, S., Baxter, M.: Icarus verilog: open-source verilog more than a year later. Linux J. **3** (2002)
30. Zeitouni, S., Vliegen, J., Frassetto, T., Koch, D., Sadeghi, A.R., Mentens, N.: Trusted configuration in cloud FPGAs. In: 2021 IEEE 29th Annual International Symposium on Field-Programmable Custom Computing Machines (FCCM), pp. 233–241 (2021). https://doi.org/10.1109/FCCM51124.2021.00036
31. Zhang, J., Qu, G.: Recent attacks and defenses on FPGA-based systems. ACM Trans. Reconfigurable Technol. Syst. **12**(3) (2019). https://doi.org/10.1145/3340557

Graphtoy: Fast Software Simulation of Applications for AMD's AI Engines

Jonathan Strobl[ID], Leonardo Solis-Vasquez[(✉)][ID], Yannick Lavan[ID],
and Andreas Koch[ID]

Embedded Systems and Applications, Technical University of Darmstadt, Darmstadt,
Germany
Jonathan.Strobl@gmx.de, {solis,lavan,koch}@esa.tu-darmstadt.de

Abstract. This work presents Graphtoy, a coroutine-based compute
graph simulator built in C++20, which can be embedded into a target application for rapid step-by-step prototyping of graphs targeting
AMD's AI Engines, as used in Versal FPGAs and Ryzen 7040 CPUs.
By using a molecular docking application as a case study, we demonstrate: 1) how compute graphs developed using Graphtoy can be ported
to the AI Engines with no modifications to the graph structure, and
2) that C++20 coroutines are well suited for simulating many-core systems with complex inter-core communication schemes. Furthermore, our
set of molecular docking graphs ported to Graphtoy achieves an order-of-
magnitude increase in simulation speed compared to AMD's AI Engine
graph simulators. The corresponding code is released as open source
under: https://github.com/esa-tu-darmstadt/graphtoy.

Keywords: Versal FPGA · AI-Engines · C++20 coroutines ·
prototyping · simulation · compute graphs · molecular docking

1 Introduction

AI Engines (AIEs) are a new kind of compute element AMD has introduced
in its Versal series of FPGAs [6] and recently added to mobile CPUs, such as
its Ryzen AI 7040 processors. For the discussion here, we will focus on the
use of AIEs on the Versal platform. However, the discussed techniques are also
applicable to the processor-integrated units.

The AIEs consist of a parallel set of tiled Very Long Instruction Word (VLIW)
vector processors, providing a truly Multiple Instruction Multiple Data (MIMD)
processing model. These processors are connected through a configurable routing
fabric that enables stream-based communication between them, which makes the
architecture well suited for executing compute graphs or pipelines. These graphs
consist of 1) compute kernels (i.e., the graph's vertices) performing computations
on incoming data, and 2) stream connections between those kernels (i.e., the
graph's edges) moving data from one kernel to the next one. Each kernel can
execute different code, hence implements the MIMD programming model.

© The Author(s), under exclusive license to Springer Nature Switzerland AG 2024
I. Skliarova et al. (Eds.): ARC 2024, LNCS 14553, pp. 166–180, 2024.
https://doi.org/10.1007/978-3-031-55673-9_12

The AIE toolchain provided by AMD imposes a rigid development methodology when porting an application to AIE graphs. In particular, graphs must be separated from the application's host code, running on the conventional processor(s), while the entire application must be ported to the Versal SoC framework (i.e., Vitis [4]) for testing the functional correctness across the conventional and AIE portions of the code [7,13]. This means that there is a large up-front porting effort required before it is even possible to execute an AIE graph design in conjunction with the host code for a particular application. Furthermore, AIE compile and simulation times are often lengthy when compared to traditional software, and debugging is as well complicated due to the separation of host and AIE graph code.

To tackle this, we propose an alternative approach to AIE graph prototyping: instead of porting an application to the compute graph framework, a graph simulator can be *embedded* into the application. For development and debugging purposes, this allows the use of a traditional software-only compile and debug flow, which will also be much faster and easier to use than the actual AIE tools. Our solution is called *Graphtoy* and provides a fast architecture-independent compute graph simulator that heavily exploits C++20 coroutines in its internal architecture. While Graphtoy was developed primarily for AIE graph simulation, it can also be applied to other architectures and problems outside of AIE development.

Our contributions are summarized as follows:

- We present Graphtoy, our embeddable coroutine-based compute graph simulator built in C++20, and discuss its design, usage, and overall porting methodology.
- We compare the structure of graphs implemented in Graphtoy and the AIE framework.
- We benchmark Graphtoy's performance against that of AMD's AIE simulators. For this purpose, we use a molecular docking application as a case study.

The remainder of this paper is structured as follows: Section 2 compares our work, Graphtoy, to previous studies. Section 3 describes in detail the architecture of the Graphtoy compute graph simulator, while Sect. 4 shows how we use Graphtoy to port a molecular docking application: first, to generic compute graphs; and thereafter, to the actual AIEs. Finally, Sect. 5 concludes this paper with a summary and outlook to future work.

2   Related Work

Other efforts to make AIEs easier to use exist. For instance, PyAIE [13] is a Python-based programming framework that performs the following: 1) it enables users to implement algorithms in Python instead of C/C++, and 2) it maps these user-written functions into host code as well as to Versal compute units (Programmable Logic (PL), AIEs) by automatically translating Python into

C/C++ code. In contrast to PyAIE, which is a high-level abstraction, Graphtoy does not perform automatic code-generation but rather enables users to iterate more quickly on low-level AIE kernel and graph designs, *without* having to rely on the vendor-provided AIE toolchains and simulators. Moreover, Graphtoy is explicitly designed as a library to be integrated into pre-existing C++ codebases, and not as a framework to write applications in from scratch.

Versal SoCs are currently examined with great interest for High Performance Computing (HPC) applications, e.g., [7] leverages AIEs and AMD's Vitis framework for accelerating atmospheric advection computations. In comparison, Graphtoy aims to speed up and simplify the development of compute graphs by decoupling graph design from vendor-provided frameworks and boosting the simulation speed. Similarly to the above work, we attempt to port an HPC application (namely, molecular docking) to the AIEs, but with a focus on easy-to-use, rapid turnaround simulation, instead of optimizing the performance of executing on actual hardware AIEs.

3   The Graphtoy Library

3.1   Design

Graphtoy uses C++20 coroutines [8] and a simple task scheduler to implement cooperative multitasking, which enables the high-throughput simulation of a multi-core system on a single host CPU thread *without* the overhead of actual thread context switches. Listing 1.1 shows an example of a compute kernel implemented in Graphtoy. Each kernel in a compute graph is represented by a potentially infinitely-running coroutine, which can receive and emit data via an arbitrary number of typed input and output streams. The rate at which data is transferred via these streams is also arbitrary: a kernel coroutine can read from and write to any of its connected streams at any point during its execution.

```
1  struct ExampleKernel: GtKernelBase {
2      ExampleKernel(GtContext *ctx): GtKernelBase(ctx) {}
3
4      GtKernelIoStream<int> *m_input1 = addIoStream<int>();
5      GtKernelIoStream<int> *m_input2 = addIoStream<int>();
6      GtKernelIoStream<int> *m_output = addIoStream<int>();
7
8      GtKernelCoro kernelMain() override {
9          while (true) {
10             int a = co_await m_input1->read();
11             int b = co_await m_input2->read();
12             co_await m_output->write(a + b);
13         }
14     }
15 }
```

Listing 1.1. Complete source code of a compute kernel implemented in Graphtoy. This kernel reads integers from two input streams and writes their sums to an output stream.

Internally, these streams are backed by multi-producer multi-consumer FIFOs with per-stream configurable sizes. When a stream read or write can not be fulfilled immediately (because the FIFO is empty or full, respectively), the calling kernel coroutine is suspended by saving its execution state to a pre-allocated memory arena (the *coroutine frame*). Graphtoy's scheduler can then resume another coroutine from its *ready list*. Once the condition that caused a kernel coroutine to suspend is alleviated, the coroutine is placed on the scheduler's ready list for eventual resumption. The order in which pending coroutines are resumed is unspecified, as Graphtoy does not implement any kind of scheduling priority system.

Figure 1 indicates that Graphtoy stores the kernels of a graph and their connections in a context object. This object must be reconstructed for each invocation of a particular graph, as it also contains management information. Examples of management information includes the kernel coroutine instances, the scheduler's ready list, and the input/output connections that push data into and drain data out of the graph, respectively. As (re)construction of the context can be performed very quickly, this requirement does not hamper the speed of Graphtoy-based development flows.

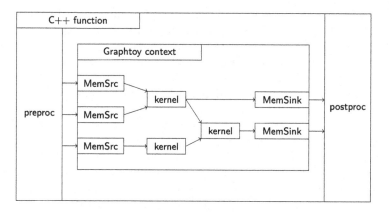

Fig. 1. Scheme of a simulated compute graph embedded into a plain C++ function using Graphtoy.

One particularity of Graphtoy is the way that graph execution is terminated: there is no explicit termination condition, and the graph execution cannot be terminated early. Instead, the scheduler continuously resumes coroutines until its ready list is empty, at which point the simulation ends[1]. As a result, Graphtoy executes a graph until all of its coroutines are halted and the graph can therefore no longer make forward progress. This happens when either a) all input data has been fully processed (i.e., all kernels are idle and blocked waiting for data), or b) the graph encounters a deadlock (i.e., cyclic wait).

---

[1] C++20 coroutines can be destroyed cleanly whenever they are suspended, which makes this graph termination scheme possible. Any local variables that are alive within the coroutine at its point of destruction will be destroyed and deallocated as well.

```
1  WARNING: Graphtoy detected data stuck in one or more I/O buffers of kernel 4 (an
        instance of 31Kernel_InterE_InterpolateEnergy).
2  => Input stream 2 (of type d) contains unprocessed data: 1 of 1 FIFO entries in use.
3  => Currently active coroutine frames in this kernel (frame trace), deepest last:
4     #1 in virtual graphtoy::GtKernelCoro Kernel_InterE_InterpolateEnergy::kernelMain()
         (./processligand_graphtoy.cpp, line 611, col 60)
5  => Note: This kernel is likely the cause of the deadlock because none of its output
        streams are blocked.
```

Listing 1.2. Example of Graphtoy's deadlock detection trace (truncated). We encountered this deadlock while implementing the Inter_E compute graph of the molecular docking algorithms (detailed in Sect. 4 and Fig. 4).

We considered but ultimately rejected adding an explicit termination call for the following reason: if a graph is terminated when it can still make forward progress, it has not fully processed all input data yet and the graph's output will be incorrect[2]. Conversely, once a graph has processed all input data, it can no longer make forward progress and will terminate automatically anyway. However, this does mean that Graphtoy cannot currently simulate infinitely-running compute graphs.

To ease debugging of graph deadlocks caused by buffer back-pressure, Graphtoy checks whether any FIFOs still contain unprocessed data once the graph has terminated. While this method of detecting deadlocks is not fully reliable due to false positives (e.g., when a graph intentionally does not consume all input data), it can still be helpful in many situations, especially when the graph in question is acyclic. Once a potential deadlock has been found, Graphtoy prints the state of all involved FIFOs and kernels and then resumes normal operation.

For this purpose, we implement a tracer that maintains a call stack for each kernel coroutine as it suspends, resumes, and recurses into sub-coroutines. This is necessary because the call stack of a C++20 coroutine is lost between suspension and resumption, as only the coroutine's immediate execution state is saved. By using this information, Graphtoy can print the source location at which each involved kernel is suspended, even if it is in a deeply nested stack of sub-coroutines. Listing 1.2 shows an example of such a trace. Furthremore, other debugging tasks, such as single-stepping and placing breakpoints, can be performed using a standard C++ debugger such as *gdb* (the GNU debugger).

Besides connections between kernels, Graphtoy also supports simulated stream-based DMA, which can read data from a linear memory region (MemSrc) and stream it into the compute graph, or take a stream of data from the graph and write it out to memory (MemSink). This functionality is implemented as a pair of helper kernels and emulates the AI Engines' GMIO. Additionally, Graphtoy supports basic packet routing (stream splitting, merging, and broadcasting), as well as input overlap windows, which are also implemented using helper kernels and coroutines.

---

[2] Due to the unspecified kernel scheduling order, the output might also be unpredictable as some pending kernel iterations may or may not have been run yet at the time of early graph termination.

3.2   Usage

In order to use Graphtoy, there are two prerequisites: 1) a C++ compiler supporting coroutines, and 2) the addition of Graphtoy's source files into the target application project (i.e., an HPC program). Once this is done, the user can *incrementally* add compute kernels and graphs to the traditional application, as depicted in Fig. 1, and does not have to perform a "big bang" port to a new tool flow and execution environment.

Graphtoy represents kernels as heap-allocated objects. As indicated in Listing 1.1, to create a new kernel, the user creates a class that derives publicly from `GtKernelBase`. This class must provide a constructor taking a `GtContext *` as its first argument, which in turn must be forwarded to the constructor of `GtKernelBase`. The "contents" of the kernel are specified by overriding the `GtKernelBase::`**`kernelMain`** `()` function, which is actual the kernel coroutine. I/O streams are instantiated as needed within the kernel by using the `GtKernelBase::`**`addIoStream`** function template. The three main characteristics of Graphtoy's kernels are the following: 1) kernel classes can be instantiated and added to graphs as often as desired. 2) Kernels can be parameterized (analogously to runtime parameters in the AIE framework) as well as preloaded with look-up tables, both by adding further arguments to the kernel's constructor. 3) As kernels are just regular C++ classes, they can be templated if desired.

Once the kernel(s) have been defined, the actual *compute graph* can be constructed. On each invocation of the graph, a new `GtContext` object has to be created, which can then be populated with its constituent kernels as well as memory sources and sinks (including the definition of memory regions read by the sources). Once incorporated into the context, all of these components can be connected to each other via graph edges. Finally, the graph can be executed and the results can be read from the memory sinks.

Listing 1.3 shows the source code of such a function, which contains and simulates a simple one-kernel graph that adds two arrays of integers. It is important to note that the `GtContext` object cannot be reused once the graph has been run. Instead, it is necessary to re-create the graph on every invocation, as implemented in the example.

As graphs formulated using Graphtoy are completely encapsulated within regular C++ functions, it is possible to easily replace pre-existing functions of the target application – one at a time – with graph versions, without having to change the application's overall software architecture. This means that the user retains a running application at *all times* during their graph prototyping effort. Additionally, since Graphtoy kernels are regular C++ code, which is compiled and linked together with the rest of the user application, it is possible to call pre-existing library and helper functions from within those kernels.

```
1   auto addIntsWithGraph(
2       std::span<const int> a,
3       std::span<const int> b)
4   {
5       GtContext ctx{};
6
7       auto& srcA  = ctx.addKernel<GtMemStreamSource<int>>(a);
8       auto& srcB  = ctx.addKernel<GtMemStreamSource<int>>(b);
9       auto& adder = ctx.addKernel<ExampleKernel>();
10      auto& sink  = ctx.addKernel<GtMemStreamSink<int>>();
11
12      ctx.connect(srcA.output(), adder.m_input1);
13      ctx.connect(srcB.output(), adder.m_input2);
14      ctx.connect(adder.m_output, sink.input());
15
16      ctx.runToCompletion();
17
18      return sink.data();
19  }
```

Listing 1.3. Complete source code of a compute graph instantiation and simulation using Graphtoy. This compute graph is based on the compute kernel from Listing 1.1.

3.3   Porting Graphs from Graphtoy to the AI Engines

Up to this step, compute graphs written in Graphtoy are generic (target-independent). While this level of description already is very helpful when incrementally moving over an application into a graph-parallel form, it is necessary to perform an additional porting step in order to run them on physical hardware.

Therefore, once the user is satisfied with the functionality of the Graphtoy-simulated compute graph, the user must modify these graphs to address two key differences between Graphtoy and the actual AIEs. First, in Graphtoy, kernels do not have to explicitly terminate. Instead, the execution of a graph stops when all of its kernels are blocked. For the actual AIEs, kernels are terminated explicitly. Second, Graphtoy does not distinguish between different types of streams between kernels, while the AIEs do (e.g., AXI4 streams, cascade accumulator connections, and direct inter-tile local memory accesses). Hence, when targeting actual AIE hardware, the nature of the streams must be specified.

In general, this refinement process starts with: 1) copying the kernel source code (`kernelMain` function) into the AIE project, and naming it appropriately. 2) The kernel's I/O streams and runtime parameters must be added to its function signature, choosing an appropriate I/O mechanism for each one. 3) All I/O operations in the kernel, which use `co_await` in Graphtoy, must be replaced with the corresponding AIE intrinsics, i.e., `readincr`, `writeincr`, and asynchronous window or buffer lock/unlock[3]. 4) For the explicit kernel termination used by the AIEs, a termination condition must be added to the kernel's main loop. E.g., a sentinel value to be pushed through the entire graph after all data has been processed.

---

[3] It is important to note that the I/O windows or buffers must be asynchronous to allow the kernel *itself* to acquire and release them when desired, which is not possible with their synchronous versions, as those are managed automatically between kernel invocations by the AIE framework.

5) The kernels must be connected appropriately in a graph class, with the AIE window and buffer I/O ports being marked as asynchronous at connection time.
6) The entire graph can be started, generally with an iteration count of one for a single execution.

The addition of manual looping and termination to the kernels is necessary because the AIE framework only supports running a graph either indefinitely, or for a fixed number of iterations that is predetermined (and ideally equal) for all of its kernels [3]. Graphtoy does not impose such a restriction and allows kernel repetition counts to be determined *dynamically* at runtime. In fact, with Graphtoy, it is possible to write kernels with arbitrary control flow, including non-repeating kernels, dynamic dispatch, and kernels with multiple main loops. By manually implementing kernel repetition and termination for the AIEs and setting an iteration count of one, it is possible to replicate Graphtoy's more generic behavior on the actual platform. To some extent, some of these transformations could be automated, either by suitable C++ abstractions or external tooling. However, we believe that even in its current form, Graphtoy is an extremely useful tool due to the significantly improved development productivity we have observed, compared to using the AIE tools directly.

4   Case Study: Molecular Docking

As a sample use-case of Graphtoy, we discuss some of the steps required when porting a full-scale HPC scientific computing code to the AIE platform. Note that this use-case is *not* intended for benchmarking AIE hardware performance, as we have observed a number of issues with the AMD AIE toolchain that currently lead to the binaries being non-functional in AIE native mode. However, all of the graphs we discuss below *do* run correctly when executed in the AMD toolchain's x86 simulation mode.

Our use-case is AutoDock, a widely used molecular docking application that can employ, among others, a genetic algorithm to predict a chemical ligand's orientation and conformation as it docks to a biological receptor [9]. A real world application for AutoDock is drug discovery, where the interactions of many chemical compounds, e.g., with a bacterial or viral surface, is examined.

The core algorithms in AutoDock have been previously ported to run on GPUs [10], FPGAs [12], and even vector processors [11]. This part of our work explores the process of porting a mini-version of AutoDock to the AIE architecture, using Graphtoy as a rapid-turnaround prototyping tool.

4.1   Algorithm Overview

The mini-version of AutoDock that we employ for our porting efforts implements only the genetic algorithm variant. Based on that, genotypes produced by the genetic algorithm encode the ligand's bond rotation angles, as well as its absolute position and orientation in space. The fitness function is the ligand conformation's energy, which must be minimized for a high quality docking (ligand and receptor molecules "fit" well together in the computed conformation).

Figure 2 shows the phases of the core docking algorithm. First, new genotypes (solution representations) are created via the genetic algorithm and a local search heuristic. Then, the genotype is interpreted to derive the conformation of the ligand in space, which in turn, is used to compute the intramolecular (atom interactions *within* the ligand) and intermolecular (*between* ligand and receptor atoms) energies. During these computations, the ligand is represented as a list of atoms (each with type, coordinates, and charge). On the other hand, the receptor is modeled as a spatial grid with smoothing via trilinear interpolation.

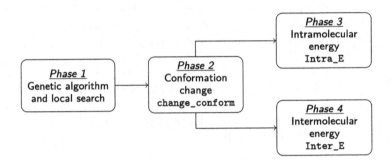

Fig. 2. Pipeline processing in our molecular docking case study.

4.2   Porting Methodology

To port this mini-version of AutoDock to the AIE array, we first include the Graphtoy library into the AutoDock source code. Then, by using Graphtoy, we develop compute graphs for three out of the four core docking algorithms: the conformation change, as well as the two energy calculation functions. In particular, we do not attempt to port the genetic algorithm nor the local search portions to the AIE array, as their code is branch intensive, rather than compute focused, making them more suitable for execution on a CPU core than on a graph processing array.

The **conformation change** algorithm (change_conform) needs to rotate each of the ligand atoms around a varying number of rotational bonds to determine their final positions. For each ligand atom, the order of rotations must remain the same, while all of these atoms are also streamed into and out of the AIE array in order. To keep the design of the compute graph simple, we use a *dynamic pipelining* approach.

Figure 3 illustrates the corresponding graph including its dynamic pipeline, which is based on a management kernel (Build rotate input) that determines the number of rotation operations that each one of a chain of downstream compute kernels (Partial rotation) should perform on atoms as they pass through the pipeline. Atom data is passed from one pipeline kernel to the next using asynchronous window I/O (win).

In order to evenly distribute workload in `change_conform`, the above number of rotations performed by each pipeline kernel varies for each processed atom. The genotype data is uploaded via global memory I/O (GMIO) and broadcast to all pipeline kernels once the graph is invoked, which requires only a single DMA channel, as the broadcast operation happens *within* the AIE array. Each pipeline kernel stores a copy of the genotype in local SRAM for fast lookup of the required bond rotation angles as atoms subsequently pass through.

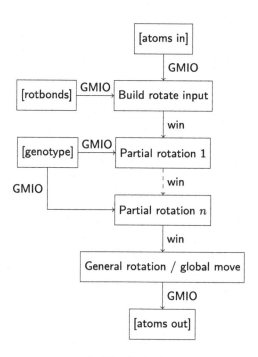

Fig. 3. `change_conform` compute graph. The dashed edge represents a chain of n identical *partial rotation* kernels.

The **intramolecular energy calculation** function (`Intra_E`) computes the distance-dependent energy contribution of pairs of atoms within the ligand. To speed this up, the algorithm uses a precomputed table that indicates which atom pairs must be processed and which can be skipped in the calculations. Transforming this algorithm into a compute graph was relatively straightforward, as it is suitable for *static* pipelining. The graph takes the precomputed atom pair table as input, and returns the final energy values via a runtime parameter (RTP) after they have been accumulated at the end of the pipeline. Additionally, the ligand-atoms' data is uploaded into one of the kernels' local SRAM using another input stream.

The main challenge of porting Intra_E was the large number of look-up tables that must be kept within the graph. To address this, we partition the algorithm into multiple kernels, so that none of these kernels requires more memory to hold look-up tables than the maximum available on an AIE tile (i.e., 32 KiB, including stack and management data).

Finally, the **intermolecular energy calculation** function (Inter_E) computes the energy contribution of the interactions between the ligand atoms and the receptor. The resulting energy value is again returned to the host system via a runtime parameter. Since the receptor is represented as a spatial grid, the algorithm has to perform lookups in the grid (based on the atoms' positions), leading to a random memory access pattern.

This pattern is problematic because the AIE array lacks the ability to autonomously perform random accesses on system DRAM [2], which means that Inter_E cannot be fully implemented on the AIE array alone. To actually perform such DRAM accesses, we will use a separate HLS kernel executing on the Programmable Logic (PL) of the Versal device, which we simulate by using a host-side helper in the AIE port of the graph. In the hardware implementation, this kernel will be connected to the rest of the graph using the programmable logic I/O (PLIO) interfaces of the SoC. Figure 4 illustrates this host-side helper as the DRAM reader (PL) kernel. In Graphtoy, modelling this HLS kernel does not need any special handling, as indicated in Listing 1.4. By transferring only DRAM addresses into and grid elements out of the PL fabric, we avoid the need to instantiate floating-point ALUs in the PL and can instead use the AIEs' floating-point vector units for energy interpolation. We also avoid transferring atom data across the AIE/PL boundary and can instead transfer a homogeneous stream of linear 32-bit addresses.

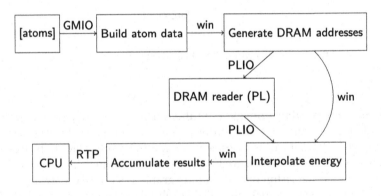

Fig. 4. Inter_E compute graph.

During development of these three AIE graphs, we are able to verify their correctness by comparing their intermediate results and final output to the pre-existing software version of the docking algorithm, which we compile into the

```
1   template<typename T>
2   struct DramReader: GtKernelBase {
3       DramReader(GtContext *ctx, std::span<const T> mem):
4           GtKernelBase(ctx), m_memoryRegion(mem) {}
5
6       std::span<const T> m_memoryRegion;
7
8       GtKernelIoStream<uint32_t> * m_addrIn  = addIoStream<uint32_t>();
9       GtKernelIoStream<T>        * m_dataOut = addIoStream<T>();
10
11      GtKernelCoro kernelMain() override {
12          while (true) {
13              uint32_t addr = co_await m_addrIn->read();
14              co_await m_dataOut->write(m_memoryRegion[addr]);
15          }
16      }
17  }
```

Listing 1.4. A DRAM reader kernel, as used in the Inter_E compute graph, modelled for Graphtoy simulation. An HLS implementation of this kernel will be later used on the actual Versal hardware.

same binary and run side-by-side. Their results were bit-for-bit identical when the full docking simulation was run on an example ligand. Once the graphs are implemented and tested using Graphtoy, we are able to port them to the AIEs with no changes to their overall architecture. In addition, no large-scale debugging is required using the more complex AIE development flows, as the architecture has already been shown to be functionally correct using Graphtoy. Moreover, a minor change that does need to be made is switching the algorithms from double-precision floats to a mix of single-precision and fixed-point arithmetic on the AIEs. The latter is needed since trigonometric functions are only available as fixed-point variants on the AIE hardware [1]. A comparison between a Graphtoy kernel and its corresponding AIE version is shown in Listing 1.5.

4.3   Benchmarking Simulation Speed

As Graphtoy is designed to simplify compute graph prototyping as well as to speed-up simulation, we benchmark the simulation runtimes achieved by Graphtoy against those by AMD's AIE graph simulators (*x86sim* and *aiesim*) [5]. For this purpose, we employ the AutoDock molecular docking mini-version already discussed configured with a precomputed set of 10^4 ligand genotypes as input data for all experiments. Moreover, all evaluations are performed on an Intel Xeon W-3265 CPU, using Vitis 2022.2 for the *x86sim* and *aiesim* versions, and GCC 12 with the -O2 optimization setting for the native (the original non-graph AutoDock code) and Graphtoy versions[4].

---

[4] We also tried -O3, which led to a slight performance degradation for Graphtoy, and no change for the non-graph version.

Table 1 shows the corresponding simulation runtimes. As AMD's *aiesim* needed about 45 min to complete a *single* iteration of Intra_E, we canceled the simulation run after two iterations and extrapolated from the above baseline runtime. Hence, the estimated value for *aiesim* (i.e., 10+ months of simulation time) is only a *lower* bound. The actual time required to complete the simulation on *aiesim* is likely higher due to the additional time that would be required for simulating change_conform and Inter_E.

```
1    // Graphtoy version.
2
3    // Runtime parameters, set in kernel constructor
4    double m_genrot_unitvec[3] = {};
5    double m_genrot_angle;
6    double m_globalmove_xyz[3] = {};
7
8    GtKernelCoro kernelMain() override {
9        while (true) {
10           auto data = co_await m_inputStream->read();
11           double *atom_xyz = &data.m_atomdata.m_atom_idxyzq[1];
12
13           const double genrot_movvec[3] = {0, 0, 0};
14           rotate(atom_xyz, genrot_movvec, m_genrot_unitvec, &m_genrot_angle, 0);
15           vec3_accum(atom_xyz, m_globalmove_xyz);
16
17           co_await m_outputStream->write(data.m_atomdata);
18       }
19   }
20
21   // AIE version.
22   // Uses float because double is unsupported on AIE.
23
24   void changeConform_GeneralRotation_GlobalMove(
25           input_window<uint8> *atomData_in,
26
27           // Runtime parameters, set via graph API
28           const float (&genrotUnitvec)[3],
29           const float genrotAngle,
30           const float (&globalMoveXyz)[3],
31
32           output_stream<float> *idxyzq_out)
33   {
34       while (true) {
35           auto data = readTypedWindowData<ChangeConform_AtomData>(atomData_in);
36           if (data.m_isTerminationSentinel) break;
37
38           float * const atom_xyz = &data.m_atom_idxyzq[1];
39
40           static constexpr float genrotMovvec[3] = {0, 0, 0};
41           rotate(atom_xyz, genrotMovvec, genrotUnitvec, genrotAngle);
42           vec3_accum(atom_xyz, globalMoveXyz);
43
44           for (uint32 i = 0; i < 5; ++i) {
45               writeincr(idxyzq_out, data.m_atom_idxyzq[i]);
46           }
47       }
48   }
```

Listing 1.5. Comparison of the Graphtoy and AIE versions of the General rotation / global move kernel, as used in the change_conform compute graph.

The overall results can be interpreted as follows: the Graphtoy simulator introduces significant overhead over the native (non-graph) version of AutoDock, due to the additional simulation of kernel-to-kernel communication. This was determined via profiling with `perf`. However, Graphtoy is around an order of magnitude faster than AMD's *x86sim*.

Graphtoy and *x86sim* are directly comparable, since they both compile compute graphs natively for the x86 host architecture and do not emulate microarchitectural details of the AIEs. AMD's *aiesim* is the slowest among all tested simulators. This is because *aiesim* does simulate AIEs on a micro-architectural level, unlike the others.

Table 1. Graph simulation runtime benchmarks.

AMD x86sim	AMD aiesim	Native (non-graph)	Graphtoy
299 s	10+ months	0.311 s	27.5 s

5   Conclusions and Future Work

In this work, we have used C++20 coroutines as a building block for Graphtoy, which is a new compute graph simulator optimized for ease of development and low simulation overhead. For our case study consisting of compute graphs for a mini-AutoDock, Graphtoy achieves simulation times *at least an order of magnitude faster* compared to AMD's AI Engine simulators (*x86sim* and *aiesim*).

Our Graphtoy-based port of molecular docking algorithms into compute graphs showed that the kernel and graph constructs provided by Graphtoy map well to the real AIEs. As we have also shown, Graphtoy easily enables a straightforward prototyping of algorithms requiring co-processing between the AIEs and the FPGA PL, e.g., for custom memory accesses. For instance, in cases where random accesses to large memory blocks were needed, we were able to prototype such PL interfaces by simply adding a Graphtoy kernel, without the need to fully develop an HLS or RTL hardware kernel for the PL in advance.

As mentioned above, we will consider to extend Graphtoy to further simplify/automate the Graphtoy-to-AIE porting process in a future refinement of the system. We expect the main hurdles for automation of this process to be a) achieving direct source-compatibility between Graphtoy and AIE kernels, and b) generating the AIE graph definition (kernel instantiation and graph edges) from the Graphtoy version.

Acknowledgments. We would like to thank AMD/Xilinx for donations of AIE hardware and design tools.

Disclosure of Interests. The authors have no competing interests to declare that are relevant to the content of this article.

References

1. AMD: AI Engine Intrinsics: Elementary Functions (2021). https://www.xilinx.com/htmldocs/xilinx2021_2/aiengine_intrinsics/intrinsics/group__intr__elem.html
2. AMD: AI Engine Kernel and Graph Programming Guide (UG1079): Graph Programming Model (2023). https://docs.xilinx.com/r/en-US/ug1079-ai-engine-kernel-coding/Graph-Programming-Model
3. AMD: AI Engine Kernel and Graph Programming Guide (UG1079): Run-Time Graph Control API (2023). https://docs.xilinx.com/r/en-US/ug1079-ai-engine-kernel-coding/Run-Time-Graph-Control-API
4. AMD: AMD AI Engine Technology: AI Engine Development Flows (2023). https://www.xilinx.com/products/technology/ai-engine.html#developers
5. AMD: Versal Adaptive SoC Design Guide (UG1273): Design Flows (2023). https://docs.xilinx.com/r/en-US/ug1273-versal-acap-design/Design-Flows
6. AMD: Versal Adaptive SoC Design Guide (UG1273): System Architecture (2023). https://docs.xilinx.com/r/en-US/ug1273-versal-acap-design/System-Architecture
7. Brown, N.: Exploring the Versal AI engines for accelerating stencil-based atmospheric advection simulation. In: ACM/SIGDA International Symposium on Field Programmable Gate Arrays (FPGA), pp. 91–97. ACM (2023). https://doi.org/10.1145/3543622.3573047
8. cppreference.com: Coroutines (C++20) (2023). https://en.cppreference.com/w/cpp/language/coroutines
9. Morris, G.M., et al.: AutoDock User's Guide, Version 3.0.5 (2001). https://autodock.scripps.edu/wp-content/uploads/sites/56/2022/04/AutoDock3.0.5_UserGuide.pdf
10. Santos-Martins, D., Solis-Vasquez, L., Tillack, A.F., Sanner, M.F., Koch, A., Forli, S.: Accelerating AutoDock4 with GPUs and gradient-based local search. J. Chem. Theory Comput. (JCTC) **17**(2), 1060–1073 (2021). https://doi.org/10.1021/acs.jctc.0c01006
11. Solis-Vasquez, L., Focht, E., Koch, A.: Mapping irregular computations for molecular docking to the SX-Aurora TSUBASA vector engine. In: 11th Workshop on Irregular Applications: Architectures and Algorithms (IA3), pp. 1–10. IEEE (2021). https://doi.org/10.1109/IA354616.2021.00008
12. Solis-Vasquez, L., Koch, A.: A case study in using OpenCL on FPGAs: creating an open-source accelerator of the AutoDock molecular docking software. In: 5th International Workshop on FPGAs for Software Programmers (FSP), pp. 1–10. VDE Verlag (2018). https://ieeexplore.ieee.org/document/8470463
13. Tian, H., Yang, S., Cha, Y., Huang, S.: Late breaking results: PyAIE: a Python-based programming framework for Versal ACAP platforms. In: 60th ACM/IEEE Design Automation Conference (DAC), pp. 1–2. IEEE (2023). https://doi.org/10.1109/DAC56929.2023.10247843

A DSL and MLIR Dialect for Streaming and Vectorisation

Manuel Cerqueira da Silva[1]([⊠]), Luís Sousa[1,2] [iD], Nuno Paulino[1,2] [iD],
and João Bispo[1,2] [iD]

[1] Faculty of Engineering, University of Porto, Porto, Portugal
up201806391@edu.fe.up.pt, {lm.sousa,jbispo}@fe.up.pt
[2] INESC TEC, Porto, Portugal
nuno.m.paulino@inesctec.pt

Abstract. This work addresses the contemporary challenges in computing, caused by the stagnation of Moore's Law and Dennard scaling. The shift towards heterogeneous architectures necessitates innovative compilation strategies, prompting initiatives like the Multi-Level Intermediate Representation (MLIR) project, where progressive code lowering can be achieved through the use of *dialects*. Our work focuses on developing an MLIR dialect capable of representing streaming data accesses to memory, and Single Instruction Multiple Data (SIMD) vector operations. We also propose our own Structured Representation Language (SRL), a Design Specific Language (DSL) to serve as a precursor into the MLIR layer and subsequent inter-operation between new and existing dialects. The SRL exposes the streaming and vector computational concepts to a higher-level, and serves as intermediate step to supporting code generation containing our proposed dialect from arbitrary input code, which we leave as future work. This paper presents the syntaxes of the SRL DSL and of the dialect, and illustrates how we aim to employ them to target both General-Purpose Processors (GPPs) with SIMD co-processors and custom hardware options such as Field-Programmable Gate Arrayss (FPGAs) and Coarse-Grained Re-configurable Arrays (CGRAs).

Keywords: DSL · MLIR · Compilation · Streaming · Vectorisation · SIMD · Heterogeneous Systems

1 Introduction

In the past decade, there has been a noteworthy transformation in the field of computing, marked by the stagnation of Moore's Law and Dennard scaling [13]. This shift has introduced a period where the conventional methods of achieving performance improvements confront unprecedented challenges. The spotlight has turned towards heterogeneous architectures, which encompass diverse processing

This work was supported by national funds through Fundação para a Ciência e a Tecnologia (FCT), under project 2022.06780.PTDC (DOI:10.54499/2022.06780.PTDC). We also acknowledge the contributions from FCT grant SFRH/BD/10002/2022.

units and have the potential to leverage hardware specialisation [13]. However, the compilation of applications for such systems, or for application-specific computing engines, poses difficulties when relying on traditional high-level source code. In response, initiatives such as the MLIR project have emerged [6]. Nested within the LLVM ecosystem, MLIR introduces a unified Intermediate Representation (IR), utilising the concept of dialects. These dialects can represent different functionalities or paradigms of data manipulation. The intention is to facilitate generation of code for targets (i.e., hardware platforms or processors) containing heterogeneous components.

This work contributes to this by introducing a streaming DSL and an equivalent MLIR dialect as an intermediary layer for code generation tailored to heterogeneous architectures. In this context, streaming refers to a sequence of data flowing between the memory and the processor. Specifically, we will focus on designing a dialect capable of representing data stream accesses and operations on vector data types (i.e., SIMD-like). To validate the new dialects' abstractions, the compilation targets will include an existing instruction set extension named the Unlimited Vector Extension (UVE) for RISC-V dedicated for streaming and vector operations. Additionally, our validation process will encompass the generation of hardware for supporting these operations [2].

The paper is organised as follows: Section 2 summarises the related work, including existing efforts in introducing into the MLIR ecosystem dialects for hardware generation, and other DSLs for streaming computation; Sect. 3 presents our proposed DSL and respective MLIR dialect for streaming and vectorisation, and Sect. 4 concludes the paper.

2   Related Work

Existing approaches for streaming, and other computation paradigms such as vectorisation or fully custom compute, exist at different abstraction levels. Some designs chose to present the unconventional hardware capabilities to the programmer explicitly via DSLs, while in contrast, compiler level approaches delegate the task of identifying streaming opportunities during code generation. We briefly summarise both cases in the following sections.

2.1   DSLs for Streaming Computation

Existing DSLs for streaming (also referred to as dataflow), propose adding specific syntax to high-level languages to expose the computing paradigm. This serves as a wrapper to functionalities implemented by a middle-layer, which may still require the use of dedicated compilers to fully realise.

The *StreamIt* methodology [3] involves the utilisation of various techniques aimed at representing and manipulating abstractions that serve as representations of data streams and operations. This design choice provides the programmer with a notable degree of control over the configuration of the dataflow, enabling the exploration of diverse design variations. The implementation of

StreamIt is carried out in Java, capitalising on the language's mature features. However, it is worth noting, as acknowledged by the authors, that there exists an opportunity for improvement in terms of enhancing the clarity of the syntax employed in the language.

In the MaxCompiler [7] flow for generating FPGA bitstreams, the developer is required to provide a host application in C/C++, and kernels and a manager encapsulating those kernels in MaxJ, a Java-based high-level DSL with operator overloading. Kernels delineate the computations chosen for hardware acceleration, while the manager configures their interfaces for interaction with the host application. The *FAST* language [4] serves as an imperative language for dataflow models. It utilizes the MaxComplier as a back-end, but provides support for C/C++ by introducing a transformation step which generates MaxJ code. The code is transformed based on user supplied source annotations in the form of pragmas. This approach does not require modifying the target C/C++ code with custom DSL syntax, but is only suitable for targeting FPGAs.

The SARA [16] approach generates code for the Plasticine [12] CGRA by using Spatial [5], a DSL for hardware accelerator specification, as a front-end, whereas SARA proper is the proposed back-end compiler. The use of Spatial as a means of representing compute kernels mandates that developers articulate the kernel code within the confines of the DSL, potentially impacting code portability. Therefore, the approach offers a structured flow for optimisation exploration, albeit with the trade-off of language-specific algorithm expression, and only specifically for CGRAs.

2.2 Compiler Support for Streaming Computation

While previously presented approaches made use of some compiler support, these were custom compilers tailored for the respective DSLs or hardware targets. It was also up to the developer to exploit the features exposed by the DSLs. In contrast, approaches presented in this section identify streaming opportunities during code generation by relying on existing compilation front-ends which produce LLVM-IR code (or MLIR dialects).

The *OXiGen* [11] flow is based on extracting dataflow graphs from LLVM-IR code generated from any front-end language compilable to this representation. The targeted LLVM-IR code is restricted to a user-specified function name. OXiGen then infers streams, albeit with access pattern limitations, from memory accesses performed through any iteration variable in the outermost loop dimension. Vectorization is inserted by modifying input and output data types of the inferred streams. Graphs are finally translated into MaxJ code for use with the MaxCompiler [7], i.e., only FPGAs are targeted.

SODA-OPT and Bambu [1] emerge as a possible option in the domain of high-level compilation and hardware synthesis. These tools harness MLIR to contribute to the generation of hardware accelerators. SODA-OPT utilises MLIR to generate finely-tuned LLVM-IR code optimised for High-Level-Synthesis (HLS) enhancements. Its architecture extracts essential kernels from high-level applications, facilitating the creation of specialised accelerators tailored for specific

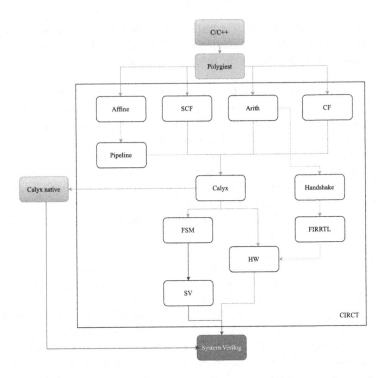

Fig. 1. Subset of current CIRCT ecosystem, focusing on dialects and transformation paths which take C/C++ as input (complete figure in [14])

tasks. The Bambu HLS tool complements SODA-OPT by consuming the LLVM-IR and producing hardware descriptions for ASICs and FPGAs.

Most similar to our approach is work the Circuit IR Compilers and Tools (CIRCT) project, and the streaming dialect proposed in [15]. The CIRCT project is part of the LLVM ecosystem and extends MLIR's capabilities into the realm of hardware design [14]. Figure 1 shows a C/C++ focused subset view of CIRCT's work-in-progress for the integration of several representations for hardware generation in the MLIR ecosystem. As a domain-specific compiler infrastructure, CIRCT focuses on optimising and transforming code from various high-level languages into Hardware Description Languages (HDLs) such as SystemVerilog [14]. It exploits the modular and extensible features of MLIR, enabling it to gain advantages in expressing hardware designs in a structured and compos-able fashion, by resorting dialects specifically designed for hardware description. These dialects encapsulate the semantics of hardware constructs and facilitate the transformation of high-level designs into code suitable for synthesis.

In the recent work presented in [15], the authors implemented a streaming abstraction as an MLIR dialect. While the dialect expresses dataflow patterns (e.g., mapping of input streams into output streams), the computation performed over stream items is expressed in existing dialects like *arith*. By defining a generic transformation of a data stream into CIRCT's *handshake* dialect, the flow reutilises other existing core dialects to generate HDL. Specifically, each operation applied over a stream item is mapped to a *handshake* operation, which facilitates the incorporation of transformations to generate scheduled pipelines exploiting data parallelism and iteration overlapping. The approach was validated by generating circuits for a small set of synthetic cases, for a setup consisting of a host CPU and PCIe-based FPGA.

3   DSL and MLIR Dialect for Streaming and Vectorization

Our work aims to develop components in the MLIR ecosystem to achieve support towards architectures capable of exploiting fast memory access, via streaming, and data parallelism, via vectorization. To achieve this, we propose defining a syntax and parser for a text-based Intermediate Representation (IR), capable of representing structural data-flow information, and to use this DSL as an easily mappable entry point into a new MLIR dialect. We believe that this will be a viable path for emission of code onto different streaming-capable architectures. Namely, onto GPPs with streaming extensions, and onto reconfigurable hardware, such as FPGAs or CGRAs, as shown in the compilation flow in Fig. 2.

Relative to the state-of-the-art, existing CIRCT dialects focus on custom HDL generation from high-level languages (e.g., generating function accelerators), and no layer exists to represent this kind of computing model prior to committing to a particular architecture. Instead, our approach is most similar to [15], where a stream dialect is proposed. However, we aim to also include vectorisation over both primitive and structured data types, as well as demonstrating support for multiple targets beyond FPGAs. The novel components are the SRL DSL (*SRL Native*), the mapping of this input into the SRL dialect, and the lowering steps onto compatible targets.

We propose the SRL DSL in order to easily expose the features of the SRL dialect to a higher-level, suitable to be written by a human developer, similar to

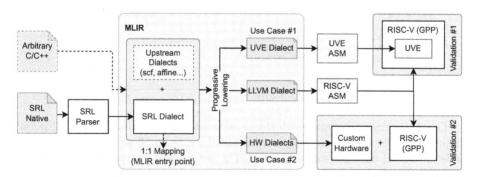

Fig. 2. Compilation flow from SRL Native (i.e., the SRL DSL) to two hardware targets. Support for SRL Dialect generation from standard source code is planned future work.

existing approaches. Simultaneously, the DSL is a first entry point into the MLIR eco-system to allow easy generation of the SRL at this stage. The entry point from C/C++ will be done via Polygeist, or from LLVM-IR produced by Clang. Further transformation work will then be required to derive the same information the native SRL DSL expressiveness allows. Alternatively, some minor *pragma* based annotations in the C/C++ could be used as hints.

The SRL Dialect is then lowered to a compatible target. In our work, we will first consider targeting the UVE RISC-V extension [2,9]. This will also require defining a UVE Dialect. In this case, the streaming and vector features are integrated into a single processor, but we will also consider targeting architectures where the specialised computing is exploited by a co-processor managed by an baseline RISC-V. Depending on the input SRL, this co-processor will be realised by either exploiting the viable paths identified in the CIRCT ecosystem to generate HDL (e.g., generating SystemVerilog via the *HW* dialect, or the Calyx IR [10]. See Fig. 1 below). This co-processor HDL, coupled to a soft-core RISC-V, can then be deployed to FPGA targets. Alternatively, CGRA overlays coupled to the same RISC-V can be targeted by modifying the lowering process as required.

3.1   SRL DSL

The SRL DSL allows for expression of computational loops where the operands are data streams, and where the data types can be vector types. To illustrate the application of the proposed DSL, consider an example of the *Single precision A X plus Y (SAXPY)* kernel, represented by the equation:

$$\text{dest}[i] = \text{src2}[i] + \text{src1}[i] \times \text{value}, \quad \text{for } i = 0 \text{ to size} - 1$$

The provided code snippet, representing this equation, delineates the structure of the SRL, highlighting how it captures streaming-specific optimisations:

```
1  func saxpy(src1, src2, dest, size, stride, value) {
2      u1 = Stream<f16>(src1, stride, size);   // Stream declarations
3      u10 = Stream<f16>(src2, stride, size);  // (with f16 vector data type)
4      u3 = Stream<f16>(dest, stride, size);
5      float u4 = value;
6      // Computation
7      for (int i = 0, i < size; i++) {
8          f16 u5 = u1.load(i) * u4;
9          u3.store(i, u10.load(i) + u5);
10      }
11 }
```

Listing 1.1. Proposed SRL DSL syntax for saxpy function

This SRL example starts with the declaration of three 16 bits floating-point streams, namely *u1*, *u3*, and *u10*. Additionally, a scalar floating-point variable *u4* is initialised with the value of *value*. The subsequent computation involves a loop iterating over the range of *size*. Within each iteration, *u5* is calculated as the product of the element at index *i* in *u1* and the scalar *u4*. This result is then utilised to update the element at index *i* in *u3* by adding it to the corresponding element fetched from *u10*.

3.2 SRL Dialect

We intend to lower the SRL dialect into two types of targets, so we needed to determine the required computational features, at which abstraction level the dialect should be placed, and determine what existing lowering paths that can be re-utilised given this placement.

Since UVE assembly is the most concrete architectural target, the currently proposed dialect semantics and constructs are designed to facilitate this lowering. To support this target, RISC-V assembly with UVE instructions has to be generated, so the dialect must be placed at an abstraction level near, or above, the standard upstream dialects (as shown in Fig. 2), in order to still allow for generation of LLVM-IR dialect using conventional compilation.

To find a path from this layer onto HDL for the second validation path, we tested possible paths between hardware related dialects in CIRCT, which is the subset previously shown in Fig. 1. We limit our scope to C/C++, so we tested transformation paths starting from the Polygeist compiler [8], the current C/C++ entry point into MLIR. Paths shown in green represent successful transformations, dotted paths are reported as possible, but no examples were available for testing, while the path between *FSM* and *SV* (dialect for the SystemVerilog syntax) failed, even for the provided example cases. We determined that the Calyx dialect supports processing of code containing the established dialects *affine*, *sfc*, *arith*, and *cf*. Thus if we place SRL dialect above this level, and transform it into code relying on these dialects, there is a viable path to generate HDL code implementing the streaming and vector operations, fulfilling our requirement.

The following code snippet exemplifies our proposal for the SRL dialect, given the features we must represent, and the abstraction layer we have chosen.

```
1  func @saxpy(%src1: memref<? x f16>, %src2: memref<? x f16>,
2     %dest: memref<? x f16>, %size: index, %stride: index, %value: f16) {
3     ; Stream declaration
4     %u1 = srl.create_float_stream %src1, %stride, %size:
5        memref<? x f16>, index, index -> stream<? x f16>
6     %u3 = srl.create_float_stream %dest, %stride, %size:
7        memref<? x f16>, index, index -> float16_stream
8     %u10 = srl.create_float_stream %src2, %stride, %size:
9        memref<? x f16>, index, index -> float16_stream
10    %u4 = srl.constant %value : f16
11    ; Computation
12    %zero = srl.constant 0 : index
13    %one = srl.constant 1 : index
14    ; Define the loop
15    srl.for %i = %zero to %size step %one {
16       %u5 = srl.load %u1 index: %i
17       %u5 = srl.mul %u5, %u4 : f16
18       %u10_i = srl.load %u10 index: %i
19       %u5 = srl.add %u5, %u10_i : f16
20       srl.store %u3, %u5 index: %i
21    }
22    return
23 }
```

Listing 1.2. MLIR Level implementation of the SAXPY function including SRL dialect statements

This dialect functions as a near 1:1 representation of our DSL, serving as a means to integrate our DSL into the MLIR environment. This creates a pathway for diverse lowering pathways for our streaming and vectorisation DSL by leveraging MLIR.

Regarding the stream declaration, the statement `"u1 = stream<f16>(src1, stride, size);"` transitions smoothly into the MLIR representation: `%u1 = srl.create_float_stream %src1, %stride, %size: memref<?xf16>, index, index -> stream<?xf16>`. Operations like load or multiplication are straightforwardly integrated into the MLIR representation. This code exemplifies the intrinsic streaming computation pattern within the SRL dialect, mirroring the characteristics of SRL itself. This characteristic positions it as a potential future target for integration with other sources focused on optimising code execution through streaming and vectorisation operations.

3.3 Lowering Example into UVE Assembly

The particular streaming engine we will target in this work implements the RISC-V UVE instruction set extension as its interface [2]. This framework emerges as an innovative solution tailored to address challenges inherent in SIMD extensions, specifically those optimised for fixed-size registers, such as ARM Scalable Vector Extension (SVE) and RISC-V Vector (RVV). Within the streaming paradigm employed by UVE, a direct streaming mechanism facilitates the seamless flow of input directly into the register file, eliminating explicit memory accesses and their overhead.

While work exists on a compiler based approach to generate UVE code [9], it relies on analysing LLVM-IR to determine streaming opportunities (e.g., identifying iterators and bounds), and then regenerating a modified executable with UVE assembly. We posit that at LLVM-IR level the information loss complicates the analysis, thus under-utilising UVE's support for complex access patterns. We aim to use SRL (both DSL and dialect) to retain this contextual and structural (e.g., loop structure) information at a higher-level. Consider the example of the following translation of the code in Listing 1.2 into UVE assembly:

```
 1  ss.ld.d u1, %[src1], %[size], %[stride] #Loads stream data to register
 2  ss.cfg.vec u1 #Configure vector registers as a vector dimension
 3  ss.ld.d u10, %[src2], %[size], %[stride] #Same as u1
 4  ss.cfg.vec u10
 5  ss.st.d u3, %[dest], %[size], %[stride]
 6  ss.cfg.vec u3 #Same as u1
 7  so.v.dp.d u4, %[value], p0 #loads to u4 the 'value'
 8 .L1%=: #Perform a vector addition between u10 and u5, store the result in u3
 9  so.a.mul.fp u5, u1, u4, p0
10  so.a.add.fp u3, u10, u5, p0
11  so.b.nc u1, .L1%= #Branch to L1 if stream not complete
```

Listing 1.3. UVE assembly implementarion of SAXPY function

In the SRL dialect, as in the UVE assembly, the code follows the same sequence: it loads data from the source (u1 and u10), configures vectors, stores data to the destination (u3), and executes the dot product operations, multiplication, and addition in a loop. The 'create_float_stream' operation was replaced with the stream load (ss.ld.d) and configuration (ss.cfg.vec) operations. The computation operations were substituted with equivalent UVE instructions, eliminating the need for implicit loads and stores present in the MLIR dialect. It is important to note that these passes or conversions from SRL dialect to UVE are proposals and are yet to be implemented.

4   Conclusions and Future Work

In the landscape of contemporary computing, characterised by the shifts in Moore's Law and Dennard scaling, this work proposes addressing post-Moore's Law challenges, by investing in novel compilation approaches for custom computing systems. It focuses on the MLIR project as a crucial element for compilation onto our currently planned targets, i.e., custom hardware generation, and the Unlimited Vector Extension (UVE) for the RISC-V.

To achieve our objectives, we presented an approach based on defining a syntax and parser for a Structured Representation Language (SRL), mapping it to the MLIR framework, and exploring pathways for efficient integration into existing dialects. In the future, we plan to employ the SRL dialect as an interface for high-level languages like `C/C++` and Python, as well as Machine Learning frameworks. This aims to eliminate the necessity for users to be familiar with the native SRL. Lastly, we intended to implement optimisations specifically for streaming within the SRL dialect, and broaden the applicability of the SRL dialect to target other SIMD architectures beyond UVE.

In summary, this work tackles contemporary compilation challenges, aiming to provide contributions to the state-of-the-art regarding support for heterogeneous architectures.

Disclosure of Interests. The authors have no competing interests to declare that are relevant to the content of this article.

References

1. Agostini, N.B., et al.: An MLIR-based compiler flow for system-level design and hardware acceleration. In: Proceedings of the 41st IEEE/ACM International Conference on Computer-Aided Design, pp. 1–9 (2022)
2. Domingos, J.M., Neves, N., Roma, N., Tomás, P.: Unlimited vector extension with data streaming support. In: Proceedings of the 48th Annual ACM/IEEE International Symposium on Computer Architecture (ISCA), pp. 209–222 (2021). https://doi.org/10.1109/ISCA52012.2021.00025
3. Gordon, M.I., et al.: A stream compiler for communication-exposed architectures. In: Proceedings of the 10th International Conference on Architectural Support for Programming Languages and Operating Systems, pp. 291–303. Association for Computing Machinery (2002). https://doi.org/10.1145/605397.605428

4. Grigoras, P., Niu, X., Coutinho, J.G.F., Luk, W., Bower, J., Pell, O.: Aspect driven compilation for dataflow designs. In: Proceedings of the 24th IEEE International Conference on Application-Specific Systems, Architectures and Processors (ASAP), pp. 18–25. IEEE, June 2013. https://doi.org/10.1109/ASAP.2013.6567545. http://ieeexplore.ieee.org/document/6567545/

5. Koeplinger, D., et al.: Spatial: a language and compiler for application accelerators. In: Proceedings of the 39th ACM SIGPLAN Conference on Programming Language Design and Implementation, pp. 296–311 (2018)

6. Lattner, C., et al.: MLIR: scaling compiler infrastructure for domain specific computation. In: Proceedings of the IEEE/ACM International Symposium on Code Generation and Optimization (CGO), pp. 2–14 (2021). https://doi.org/10.1109/CGO51591.2021.9370308

7. Maxeler Technologies: MaxCompiler White Paper (2011). https://www.maxeler.com/media/documents/MaxelerWhitePaperMaxCompiler.pdf. Accessed 16 Feb 2024

8. Moses, W.S., Chelini, L., Zhao, R., Zinenko, O.: Polygeist: raising C to Polyhedral MLIR. In: 30th International Conference on Parallel Architectures and Compilation Techniques (PACT), pp. 45–59 (2021). https://doi.org/10.1109/PACT52795.2021.00011

9. Neves, N., Domingos, J.M., Roma, N., Tomás, P., Falcao, G.: Compiling for vector extensions with stream-based specialization. IEEE Micro **42**(5), 49–58 (2022). https://doi.org/10.1109/MM.2022.3173405

10. Nigam, R., Thomas, S., Li, Z., Sampson, A.: A compiler infrastructure for accelerator generators. In: Proceedings of the 26th ACM International Conference on Architectural Support for Programming Languages and Operating Systems, pp. 804–817 (2021). https://doi.org/10.1145/3445814.3446712

11. Peverelli, F., Rabozzi, M., Del Sozzo, E., Santambrogio, M.D.: OXiGen: a tool for automatic acceleration of C functions into dataflow FPGA-based kernels. In: Proceedings of the 32nd IEEE International Parallel and Distributed Processing Symposium Workshops (IPDPSW), pp. 91–98. Institute of Electrical and Electronics Engineers Inc., August 2018. https://doi.org/10.1109/IPDPSW.2018.00023

12. Prabhakar, R., et al.: Plasticine: a reconfigurable architecture for parallel patterns. In: Proceedings of the 44th Annual ACM/IEEE International Symposium on Computer Architecture (ISCA), pp. 389–402 (2017). https://doi.org/10.1145/3079856.3080256

13. Shalf, J.: The future of computing beyond Moore's law. Phil. Trans. R. Soc. A **378**(2166), 20190061 (2020)

14. The LLVM Project: CIRCT - Circuit IR Compilers and Tools (2020). https://circt.llvm.org/. Accessed 16 Feb 2024

15. Ulmann, C.: Multi-level rewriting for stream processing to RTL compilation. Master thesis, ETH Zurich, Zurich (2022). https://doi.org/10.3929/ethz-b-000578713

16. Zhang, Y., Zhang, N., Zhao, T., Vilim, M., Shahbaz, M., Olukotun, K.: SARA: scaling a reconfigurable dataflow accelerator. In: Proceedings of the 48th ACM/IEEE Annual International Symposium on Computer Architecture (ISCA), pp. 1041–1054 (2021). https://doi.org/10.1109/ISCA52012.2021.00085

Applications and Architectures

Analysis of Process Variation Within Clock Regions of AMD-Xilinx UltraScale+ Devices

Bardia Babaei[1]([✉])[iD] and Dirk Koch[1,2][iD]

[1] The University of Manchester, Manchester, UK
barida.babaei@postgrad.manchester.ac.uk, dirk.koch@manchester.ac.uk
[2] Heidelberg University, Heidelberg, Germany

Abstract. As semiconductor technology advances and transistor feature sizes shrink, the increasing significance of process variation poses critical challenges to the reliability of semiconductor devices. This paper thoroughly explores the impact of process variation within the Clock Regions (CRs) of AMD-Xilinx UltraScale+ devices. We employ a novel method to characterize process variation with significantly higher precision than conventional ring oscillator (RO)-based sensors. Our experimental findings on ZYNQ XCZU9EG reveal that the latency of resources during rising and falling transitions may differ. Additionally, the proximity of Interconnect (INT) tiles to various tile types can influence the latency of resources within a column in a given CR. Moreover, we demonstrate that specific segments within CRs consistently exhibit faster performance compared to other areas within the same CR.

Keywords: AMD · UltraScale+ · Process Variation · Clock Region

1 Introduction

Process variation is the deviation in the electrical properties of transistors, such as threshold voltage and effective gate length of transistors, leading to variation in speed and power performance of nominally identical circuits. Not only does it decrease the yield, but also results in the poor performance of electronic circuits. Process variation stems from both random (intrinsic) and systematic (extrinsic) sources. Random variation, which is uncorrelated and unpredictable, occurs due to factors like gate-metal Work function variability [10], random-dopant fluctuation [1], line-edge roughness [4], gate oxide thickness variation [5], etc. In comparison, systematic variation results from layout-dependent effects and operation shifts of the fabrication equipment, such as photoresist development, rapid thermal annealing, etching, etc. Both random and systematic variations can occur within a die or among supposedly identical dies [7,8,12]. The former is referred to as intra-die (within-die) variation, and the latter is called inter-die (die-to-die) variation.

I. Skliarova et al. (Eds.): ARC 2024, LNCS 14553, pp. 193–209, 2024.
https://doi.org/10.1007/978-3-031-55673-9_14

Having knowledge about the exact speed of functional blocks on the FPGA and the routing as well as the variation of these is important for several applications and characteristics including security (e.g., detecting deliberate chip manipulations), reliability (e.g., detecting anomalies), and performance tuning (e.g., through save overclocking). Moreover, studying process variation can be used for tuning process parameters during production or for post-fabrication measures at runtime. For instance, CAD tools can be tuned to implement user designs in high-performance areas of the chip or consider scaling factors for doing timing analysis [13]. Knowing the accurate values of process variation of different resources, users can also develop variation-aware designs [7]. However, obtaining an accurate model requires a detailed and comprehensive characterization which, in turn, requires a rigorous process variation analysis.

In this paper, we present a detailed analysis of process variation within CRs of an AMD-Xilinx UltraScale+ device. The structure of the paper is organized as follows: Sect. 2 provides a detailed review of relevant literature. In Sect. 3, we briefly discuss the architecture of UltraScale+ devices with a focus on the clock architecture and routing resources of this family. This is followed by Sect. 4, where we describe the characterization method employed in our experiments and introduce the segmented architecture of our characterization system. Section 5 is dedicated to discussing the necessary experimental parameters that need to be taken into consideration. We also present the results of our findings, drawing a connection with the architecture of UltraScale+ devices. Finally, the paper concludes in Sect. 6, where we summarize the key points of our work.

2   Related Work

Authors in [12] investigated the intra-die variation in a set of 90 nm Cyclone II devices. They implemented a network of RO-based sensors in 34 rows and 26 columns in each FPGA. Each RO was fitted into a single logic block and used the same local routing. This implementation guarantees the identity of ROs' nominal delays. To avoid the self-heating effect of ROs, only one RO was activated at a time. The experiment was conducted on 18 devices at room temperature, and the results showed that the systematic intra-die variation ranges from 3.13% to 4.47% with an average of 3.54%.

In [13], a comprehensive intra-die variation characterization in 65 nm Virtex 5 FPGAs was presented. The authors used an array of 120×54 RO-based sensors, which could measure the variation in rising and falling transitions independently. The experiment results showed 22% intra-die variation in total. Deploying the Down Sampled Moving Average (DSMA) method with a 5 × 5 window, they decomposed the variation into random and systematic components. Accordingly, the peak-to-peak random intra-die variation reached 5.8% while the systematic intra-die variation was calculated as large as 15%, where the center of the chip was recognized faster than the corners.

The intra-chip and inter-chip variability in eight 28 nm AMD-Xilinx ZYNQ 7000 devices was measured in [8]. The sensors were based on a three-stage RO along with four pass-through latches to add extra delay to the RO loop so that the RO delay was measurable with an up-counter. Deploying 408 ROs at the ambient temperature of 26 °C, the authors measured the intra-chip variation between 5.2% and 7.7%. In contrast, the inter-chip variation measured as 7.4%, which increased up to 17% for a specific chip.

Authors in [7] provided a detailed inter-die and intra-die process variation analysis in AMD-Xilinx ZYNQ 7000 devices. Deploying RO-based sensors, they measured the inter-die and intra-die variations as large as 30% and 13%, respectively. Their experiment proved that supply voltage downscaling has a relatively negative inverse effect on intra-die variation.

The performance variation in a 16 nm AMD-Xilinx UltraScale+ ZYNQ devices studied in [9]. That work assessed the variability of logic and interconnects independently under various ranges of voltage and temperature conditions. Decoupling the total variation into random and systematic components using DSMA and regression methods, the authors showed that variability increases with the decrease of operating voltage in both cases. In contrast, they proved that the variation increases with escalating the temperature in this process node. The highest measured intra-die and inter-die variations reached 9.9% and 12% under certain operating conditions and specific types of sensors.

In contrast to prior publications that have primarily explored process variation in FPGAs at a broader level, this study aims to delve more profoundly into the variability of nominally identical resources within individual CRs of the FPGA. The objective is to meticulously assess the performance distinctions among various tile types within each CR.

3   AMD-Xilinx UltraScale+ Architecture

The design of AMD-Xilinx UltraScale+ devices adheres to a hierarchical structure [11]. At the topmost level of single-die UltraScale+ devices, the fabric is segmented into a two-dimensional grid of CRs, depicted in Fig. 1. In contrast to previous AMD-Xilinx FPGA families where CRs covered half the device's width, UltraScale+ devices can accommodate over two CRs per row. Each CR encompasses a clock network routing that consists of 24 horizontal and vertical routing tracks along with 24 horizontal and vertical distribution tracks, ensuring low skew, minimal duty cycle distortion, and enhanced jitter tolerance in clock distribution [15]. As shown in Fig. 1, a Horizontal Clock Spine (HCS) runs through the center of each CR, containing 24 horizontal routing and distribution tracks, leaf clock buffers, and the necessary interconnects between horizontal and vertical tracks.

Every CR comprises several vertical columns of tiles, with each column exclusively featuring tiles of the same type. However, different columns within a CR may have diverse tile types, resulting in a pattern of vertical homogeneity and horizontal heterogeneity spanning the entire chip. The assembly of CRs forms a tile coordinate system originating at the device's lower-left corner. Every coordinate accommodates an INT tile, flanked by two other tiles on its east and west sides. One of these is invariably a Configurable Logic Block (CLB), while the other might be a CLB, Digital Signal Processing (DSP), or Block RAM (BRAM) tile.

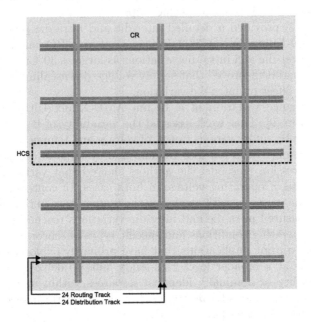

Fig. 1. Horizontal and Vertical Clocking in UltraScale+ Devices [15]

In the UltraScale+ architecture, each CLB encompasses a single site consisting of eight 6-input Look-Up Tables (LUTs), sixteen Flip-Flops (FFs), a dedicated fast lookahead carry logic, and various MUXes. Each LUT is connected to two FFs, and the eight LUT-FF pairs are labelled A to H. These FFs require specific control signals like clock, clock enable, and set/reset, which are not universally shared across all FFs in a site. Instead, FFs are split into two groups: the lower group (labels A-D) and the upper group (labels E-H), as illustrated in Fig. 2. Each group receives its own dedicated clock, set/reset signal, and two clock enable signals shared among its FFs. As shown in Fig. 2, each primary and secondary FF, marked as "Q" and "Q2", has a unique clock enable signal within a group. This clocking scheme's significance is especially pronounced in designs with multiple clock domains, where assigning a FF to a particular clock domain necessitates that other FFs in the same group align with the same domain.

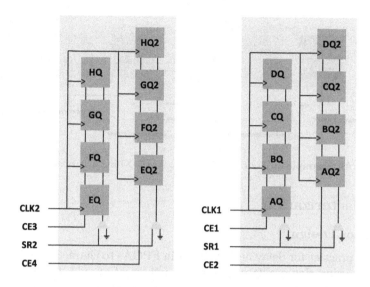

Fig. 2. Control Signals Entering a CLB [14]

Each INT tile contains a single slice, which is referred to as a Switch Matrix (SM), providing a set of local and global Programmable Interconnect Points (PIPs) for connecting various tiles together. Local PIPs make connections between tiles within a specific coordinate, while global PIPs connect tiles from different coordinates.

In AMD-Xilinx terminology, a connection between two tiles is called a Node, which is nothing but a collection of wires, as shown in Fig. 3. In UltraScale+ devices, global nodes connecting two INT tiles together are classified under single (S), double (D), quad (Q), and long (L) nodes, which span over one, two, four (or five), and twelve coordinates, respectively. However, as each INT tile acts as two back-to-back INT tiles for its surrounding tiles [19], these nodes travel one, one, two, and six coordinates in the horizontal direction, respectively. While individual PIPs have been dedicated to S/D/Q nodes interacting with each of the east and west tiles, the long nodes and clock-related nodes are shared among both tiles.

All the routing resources required for routing a design can be described by PIPs and nodes, in which the nodes are fixed resources while PIPs could be programmed and provide flexibility in routing. Accordingly, the FPGA's routing resources can be modelled as a graph, where nodes act as vertices and PIPs are modelled as the edges of this graph.

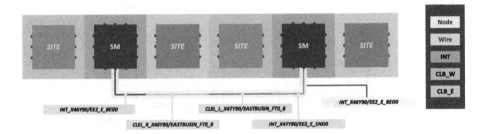

Fig. 3. An Example of Node and Wires in AMD-Xilinx UltrScale+ Devices

4 Characterization

4.1 Sensor Design

A common practice for delay measurement in FPGAs to characterize the process variation is using ring oscillators. ROs are a chain of an odd number of inverters in which the output is directly fed into the input, as shown in Fig. 4. The frequency of the RO (f_{RO}) is measured by feeding its output into one counter, while another counter simultaneously runs with a reference frequency to measure the RO frequency. Both counters keep counting for a certain amount of time t_c. Since the product of the frequency and the count value is roughly equal to t_c, the RO frequency can be calculated according to (1):

$$f_{RO} \approx C_{RO} \frac{f_{REF}}{C_{REF}} \tag{1}$$

where C_{RO} and C_{REF} are the count values corresponding to the RO and reference frequencies.

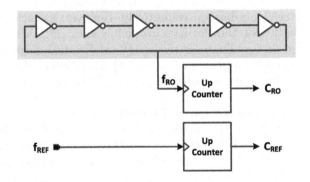

Fig. 4. A General Delay Measurement Setup Using an RO

The popularity of using RO-based sensors is due to their simplicity, which occupy a small area and are easy to be populated across the chip. The output frequency of ROs is determined by the delay of the loop (primitives and interconnects), and it can reach up to 6 *Ghz* in modern FPGAs [6]. However, no counters are capable of working with such a high frequency. Therefore, ROs with longer lengths are deployed in practice, which leads to higher inaccuracy in measuring individual logic or routing resources (e.g., the latency of an individual wire or a short path). Besides, the employment of multiple RO-based sensors oscillating at high frequencies at the same time could lead to voltage drop [9] and self-heating [12] phenomena. To tackle these issues, all sensors are clustered into multiple groups, and each group is activated sequentially. Moreover, practical ROs need to be implemented over multiple CLBs, and they occupy only specific resources in FPGAs, which could constitute biased results and conclusions.

In this paper, we have used the Cascaded Phases Shifting (CPS) technique introduced in [3]. Since this method is based on phase shifting, the frequency could be set low enough to avoid voltage drop and self-heating effects. Moreover, this method can characterize pure interconnect paths with sub-picosecond resolutions, which could provide more reliable results.

The characterization circuit is demonstrated in Fig. 5. This circuit contains a T-FF as a Test Pattern Generator (TPG), which is responsible for generating rising and falling transitions, which are propagated through a Circuit Under Test (CUT). This CUT is a combinational circuit comprising numerous logic gates and interconnections, or in its simplest form, it consists solely of a set of interconnects. A D-FF samples the propagated transitions, and then the launched and sampled transitions are compared using an XOR gate. A test clock generator is used to gradually shift the phase of one clock relative to another until the Sample FF starts getting metastable. Due to clock uncertainty, the metastability does not take place at a certain point, so multiple transitions must be launched at each phase. Therefore, a counter is employed to count the number of mismatches asserted by the XOR gate and report an error probability for each phase. Considering the uncertainty of the exact metastability occurrence, we need to define a threshold to consider it as the moment the setup time fails, and we will report this value as the CUT delay. For the sake of simplicity, we consider the mid-point of counter's value corresponding to the CUT delay. It is simply the point at which the counter's MSB experiences a rising transition.

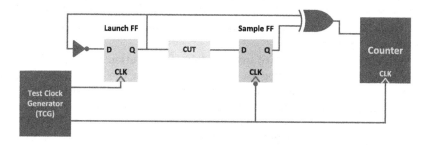

Fig. 5. Delay Characterization Circuit in the Phase Shifting Method [2]

The Test Clock Generator (TCG) structure is shown in Fig. 6, in which three Clock Managers (CMs) are cascaded. The CMs participating in the phase shifting along with the shift directions are denoted in Fig. 6. Unlike [3], which uses multiple sets of sampling to measure the CUT delay, we have employed a slightly different strategy. The end resolution equals the absolute difference of the CM_1 and CM_2 phase shift steps. Thus, we could conduct both incremental and decremental phase shifts simultaneously for each phase, enabling the sampling process to be carried out within a single set.

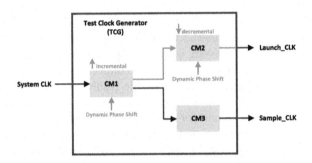

Fig. 6. TCG Structure of the CPS Technique

4.2   Characterization System Architecture

In RO-based characterization systems, an array of ROs are distributed around the chip while sufficient gaps are preserved between adjacent ROs. This distribution is deployed primarily due to the footprint of large sensors or as a means of preventing the self-heating effect of ROs. Although this arrangement extracts useful delay information at the implementation site, it does not provide fine-grained information about the latency of resources located in every coordinate of an FPGA chip. Moreover, the extracted delay values correspond to a limited number of resources, which are considered representatives of a large amount of other resources. For instance, the implemented RO sensor in [7] occupies at least five INTs and CLBs. Each INT consists of thousands of PIPs and wires, while each RO only utilizes a few tens of routing resources, which leads to poor coverage.

In comparison, our goal is to extract delay information of all possible local routing resources corresponding to each coordinate in the chip. Therefore, we need to cover as many routing resources as possible that could form a path (CUT) collectively and fit into a single pair of CLB-INT tiles. Obviously, performing variation characterization with such elaboration constitutes a larger set of CUTs, even in a single CR of the FPGA. In this way, these CUTs must be grouped in different configurations and loaded into the chip.

Our proposed characterization system is shown in Fig. 7, which automatically loads different configurations into the FPGA and receives the corresponding results to rising and falling transitions independently. Due to the extent of CUTs in each configuration, the CUTs, along with their associated test circuitries, are grouped into multiple segments as Characterization Units (CU). Each CU consists of the TPG, the CUT, and the sample FF, as shown in Fig. 8a. Segments are activated one at a time, and all N_P CUs in the segment are tested in parallel. To cut down on the number of primitives used by the XOR gate and the counter for each CUT in Fig. 7, a local TPG has been built inside the Output Response Analyzer (ORA) block, as demonstrated in Fig. 8b. For the sake of simplicity, the XOR gates are removed from Fig. 8b. This local TPG is synchronous with other TPGs in each CU, and its output is used for N_P XOR comparisons in the ORA block. N_P counters inside the ORA count the error occurrences for each CU and transfer the results to the transmitter block. The transmitter includes a First-In First-Out (FIFO) buffer to store the received data from the ORA and transmits the data over the UART to the host PC at the same time. The controller in the system is in charge of performing phase shifts and providing the required control signals to different blocks in the system. The host loads the appropriate bitstream in the FPGA and initiates the experiment by setting the mode of the experiment (rising or falling transition). Shifting the clock phases for half of the clock period, the controller stops the experiment and waits for the FIFO to become empty. After receiving all data from the chip, the host PC repeats the whole process until all configurations are tested.

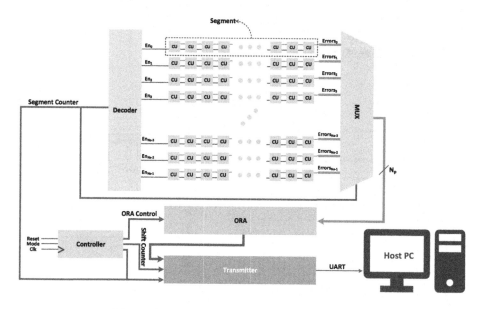

Fig. 7. Architecture of the Segmented Structure

It must be noted that TPGs launch multiple transitions at each phase, and depending on the experiment mode, only a particular transition is considered for comparison and counting. Furthermore, each counter transfers only one value to the transmitter for its corresponding CU in each segment. As mentioned before, the clock phases are shifted half the clock period for each segment. In the beginning, the setup slack of the sample FF is large enough, so the counters do not count any errors. However, after a certain number of phase shifts, the sample FFs become metastable, and the counter values start increasing until the timing is violated, at which point the counter values reach the maximum. When a counter value surpasses the mid-value relative to its value in the preceding phase, it is sent to the transmitter, and no further transfers occur for that counter until the end of the phase shift cycle for the current segment.

5   Experiment

All experiments have been conducted on a Trenz TE080-03 MPSoC equipped with AMD- Xilinx ZYNQ UltraScale+ XCZU9EG-FFVC900, which contains 25 CRs. The workflow of our automated test, covering the construction of the architectural model to the generation of the bitstream, is illustrated in Fig. 9.

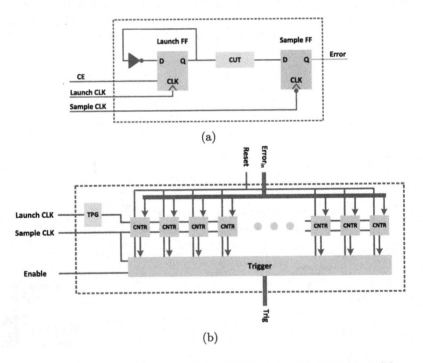

Fig. 8. The internal Structure of the CU Block (a) the ORA block (b)

As we aim to measure the variability of all coordinates independently, we need to fit each and every characterization circuit (Fig. 5) in only one coordinate. In this way, we refer to all routing resources (Nodes and PIPs) that could be covered by a path between two local launch and sample FFs as local routing resources. To put all local routing resources under test, we need to find paths including these resources. The first step in finding these paths is modelling the FPGA under test as a graph, which is referred to as the architecture graph and can be directly extracted from AMD-Xilinx Vivado. Having modelled the architecture graph, we find all the required paths for covering the local routing resources with the help of a Python script and partition them into multiple configurations.

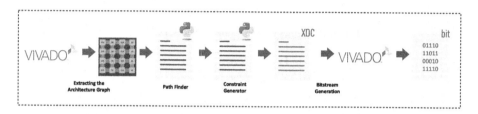

Fig. 9. Workflow of Test Configuration Generation

In the next step, the physical constraints, including placement and routing constraints, are generated for all paths of every configuration by a Python script. The placement constraints for cells (here, FFs or LUTs) are described by two *LOC* and *BEL* properties [18]. The *LOC* property specifies the site in which the cell is located, while the *BEL* property specifies the exact utilized primitive (here, FFs or LUTs) among all available primitives in a site. In addition to these properties, the *LOCK_PINS* property must also be specified for LUTs. This property specifies the mapping of logical LUT inputs, denoted by I0, I1, I2, ..., to physical LUT inputs, denoted by A1, A2, A3, ..., in AMD-Xilinx FPGAs [16]. The routing constraints must be located after the placement constraints in an XDC file. These constraints set the *FIXED_ROUTE* property for each net in the netlist, which must be described in a special format [17]. These physical constraints describe all placement and routing information corresponding to CUTs in the characterization system. However, there are extra blocks in the system that are placed and routed through Vivado prior to bitstream generation. Having generated all configurations' bitstreams, the host PC initiates the experiment by loading each configuration into the FPGA and receiving the corresponding delay value of each CUT in the design.

5.1 Resolution

CMs in UltraScale+ devices are called Mixed-Mode Clock Manager (MMCM) and are able to perform dynamic phase shifts with a $\dfrac{1}{f_{VCO} \times 56}$ step, where f_{VCO} is the Voltage-Controlled Oscillator (VCO) frequency of the internal MMCM's Phase-Locked Loop (PLL).

The CPS method enables us to tune the delay measurement resolution in a various range of subpicosecond values by setting the pre-divider (D), Multiplier (M), and post-divider (O) counters of MMCMs in Fig. 6. However, different settings can lead to different clock jitter. According to our observations of *Clocking Wizard* in Vivado, higher f_{VCO}, lower D, and higher $\frac{M}{D}$ result in lower peak-to-peak jitter. Therefore, iterating through all possible settings for the MMCMs in the TCG block of Fig. 6, we chose the values summarized in Table 1 for our experiments. According to [3] and selected settings of MMCMs, the timing resolution is calculated, as shown in (2).

Table 1. Settings of MMCMs in the CPS Method

MMCM	f_{in}	D	M	f_{VCO}	O	S_{PS}	f_{out}
MMCM1	100 MHz	1	15	1500 MHz	15	11.9 ps	100 MHz
MMCM2	100 MHz	1	16	1600 MHz	16	11.2 ps	100 MHz
MMCM3	100 MHz	1	16	1600 MHz	16	-	100 MHz

$$Resolution = |S_{PS_1} - S_{PS_2}| = 744 \; fs \tag{2}$$

5.2 Characterization Time

The contributing factors to the total test time are the number of configurations, the number of segments in each configuration, and the width of counters in the ORA block. We reached full coverage of all local routing resources in a CR with 60×14 dimension by packing 293,040 paths into 60 configurations. To decide on the counter width, we needed to make a trade-off between the accuracy of measurement and the execution time of the experiment. Generally, the total test time of a single configuration is calculated based on (3a):

$$t_{conf} = \frac{56 \times O_2 \times N_{Seg} \times n \times 2^W}{2 \times f_{out_2}} \tag{3a}$$

$$n = \frac{f_{VCO_1}}{f_{VCO_2} - f_{VCO_1}} \tag{3b}$$

Where O_2 is the post-divider of the MMCM2, N_{Seg} is the number of segments in a configuration, w is the counter width, f_{out_2} is the output frequency of the MMCM2 and MMCM3, and n is a coefficient calculated based on (3b).

It must be noted that $\frac{56 \times O_2 \times n}{2}$ is the total number of phase shifts performed during the testing of each segment, while N_{Seg} is determined by the total number of CUTs in a configuration and the number of Parallel CUTs (N_P) in a segment. Increasing N_P can reduce N_{Seg} and consequently t_{conf} dramatically; however, it causes more resources to be utilized by test circuitries and decreases the routability. Finding the optimum value for N_P needs further analysis, but we empirically found $N_P = 50$ as a good trade-off between routability and N_{Seg}.

Specifying the number of configurations and segments, we analyzed different widths for the counters and found $w = 10$ an optimum choice for balancing the accuracy and t_{conf}. To evaluate the precision of this counter width, we conducted 500 runs of the experiment for a single CUT. Subsequently, we generated histograms for the measurements of both rising and falling transitions independently. The resulting plots are illustrated in Fig. 10. As can bee seen, the chosen counter width provides a reliable accuracy over 500 iterations.

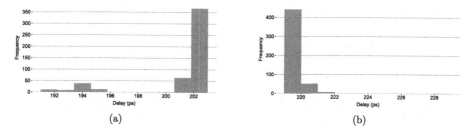

(a)   (b)

Fig. 10. Histograms of 500 Delay Measurements of an arbitrary CUT with $w = 10$ for Falling Transitions (a) and Rising Transitions (b)

5.3 Clock Region Variation Assessment

Our characterization efforts extended to multiple CRs, evaluating their behavior independently for both rising and falling transitions. Figure 11 displays heatmaps representing five CRs positioned in the four corners and the center of the chip. Given that each characterization circuit is tied to a specific coordinate, the measured delay of its CUT is only linked to that coordinate. Consequently, the value reported at each coordinate represents the average delays across the local routing resources of the CUTs situated within that specific coordinate. Notably, a comparative analysis between rising and falling transitions across various CRs suggests that the chip exhibits faster performance during falling transitions.

An intriguing insight emerges as we delve deeper into the heatmaps. Considering that each column comprises identical tile types, the anticipation was to witness consistent values across all coordinates within the column. However, a clear boundary has divided each column into two groups, with the lower half coordinates exhibiting faster performance. Upon comparing the observed results with the clock architecture of the UltraScale+ device, it became evident that this differentiation occurs precisely where the HCS is located within the CR.

Horizontal traversal across a CR reveals variances between different columns. This aligns with the columnar architecture of UltraScale+ devices, where all tiles within a column share the same type, while tiles within a row can encompass various types. A compelling observation arises when comparing the resultant heatmaps with the arrangement of tile types in the device under test. The pattern suggests that columns with two CLBs around the INT tile at each coordinate consistently demonstrate faster performance in contrast to columns with only one CLB at each coordinate. Among the latter, columns containing DSPs exhibit the slowest performance.

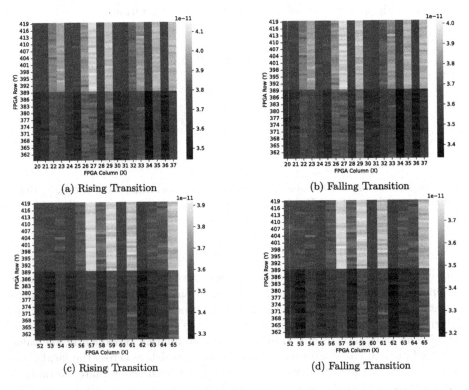

(a) Rising Transition

(b) Falling Transition

(c) Rising Transition

(d) Falling Transition

Fig. 11. Heatmaps of CR_X1Y6 (a, b) CR_X3Y6 (c, d) CR_X2Y3 (e, f) CR_X1Y0 (g, h) CR_X3Y0 (i, j)

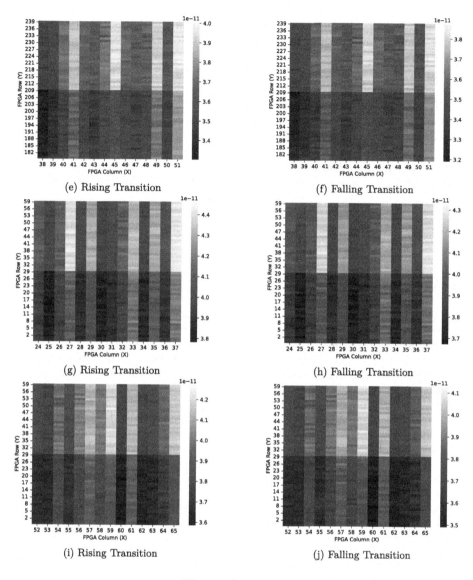

(e) Rising Transition

(f) Falling Transition

(g) Rising Transition

(h) Falling Transition

(i) Rising Transition

(j) Falling Transition

Fig. 11. (*continued*)

6   Conclusion

In this paper, we employed a distinctive approach to assess process variation within CRs of a ZYNQ XCZU9EG device. We measured the latency of all local routing resources within the CRs with a sub-picosecond resolution and conducted a comparative analysis across different tiles within the same CR. Our findings demonstrated a consistent trend among all CRs of the device under test, indicating that the lower half of the CRs, situated below the HCS, tends to exhibit faster performance.

Furthermore, we observed that the proximity of DSP and BRAM tiles could have a negative effect on the performance of routing resources within a column of CRs. In the Future, we plan to expand our characterization experiment to explore the impact of process variation on various types of routing resources, considering factors such as length and connectivity.

Acknowledgments. This project is supported by the UK EPSRC Project FORTE (EP/R024642/1). We also thank Carl-Zeiss-Foundation and AMD for supporting this work.

Disclosure of Interests. The authors have no competing interests to declare that are relevant to the content of this article.

References

1. Agarwal, K., Nassif, S.: Characterizing process variation in nanometer CMOS. In: Proceedings of the 44th Annual Design Automation Conference, DAC 2007, pp. 396–399. Association for Computing Machinery, New York (2007)
2. Babaei, B., Koch, D.: Precise characterizing of FPGAs in production systems. In: 2022 32nd International Conference on Field-Programmable Logic and Applications (FPL), pp. 464–465 (2022)
3. Babaei, B., Koch, D.: Tunable fine-grained clock phase-shifting for FPGAs. In: 2022 32nd International Conference on Field-Programmable Logic and Applications (FPL), pp. 384–390 (2022)
4. Baravelli, E., Dixit, A., Rooyackers, R., Jurczak, M., Speciale, N., Meyer, K.D.: Impact of line-edge roughness on FinFET matching performance. IEEE Trans. Electron Devices **54**, 2466–2474 (2007). https://api.semanticscholar.org/CorpusID:25864162
5. Dargar, S.K., Srivastava, V.M.: Performance analysis of 10 nm FinFET with scaled fin-dimension and oxide thickness. In: 2019 International Conference on Automation, Computational and Technology Management (ICACTM), pp. 1–5 (2019)
6. La, T.M., Matas, K., Grunchevski, N., Pham, K.D., Koch, D.: FPGADefender: malicious self-oscillator scanning for Xilinx UltraScale+ FPGAs. ACM Trans. Reconfigurable Technol. Syst. **13**(3) (2020)
7. Maragos, K., Lentaris, G., Soudris, D.: In-the-field mitigation of process variability for improved FPGA performance. IEEE Trans. Comput. **68**(7), 1049–1063 (2019)
8. Maragos, K., Lentaris, G., Soudris, D., Siozios, K., Pavlidis, V.F.: Application performance improvement by exploiting process variability on FPGA devices. In: Design, Automation Test in Europe Conference Exhibition (DATE), pp. 452–457 (2017)
9. Maragos, K., Taka, E., Lentaris, G., Stratakos, I., Soudris, D.: Analysis of performance variation in 16nm FinFET FPGA devices. In: 2019 29th International Conference on Field Programmable Logic and Applications (FPL), pp. 38–44. IEEE (2019)

10. Nawaz, S.M., Dutta, S., Chattopadhyay, A., Mallik, A.: Comparison of random dopant and gate-metal workfunction variability between junctionless and conventional FinFETs. IEEE Electron Device Lett. **35**(6), 663–665 (2014)
11. RapidWright: Xilinx Architecture Terminology. Accessed 08 Nov 2023
12. Sedcole, P., Cheung, P.Y.: Within-die delay variability in 90nm FPGAs and beyond. In: 2006 IEEE International Conference on Field Programmable Technology, pp. 97–104. IEEE (2006)
13. Tuan, T., Lesea, A., Kingsley, C., Trimberger, S.: Analysis of within-die process variation in 65nm FPGAs. In: 2011 12th International Symposium on Quality Electronic Design, pp. 1–5. IEEE (2011)
14. Xilinx Inc.: UltraScale Architecture Configurable Logic Block User Guide (UG574) (2017)
15. Xilinx Inc.: UltraScale Architecture Clocking Resources User Guide (UG572) (2023)
16. Xilinx Inc.: Vivado Design Suite Properties Reference Guide (UG912) (2023)
17. Xilinx Inc.: Vivado Design Suite User Guide: Implementation (UG904) (2023)
18. Xilinx Inc.: Vivado Design Suite User Guide: Using Constraints (UG903) (2023)
19. Zhou, Y., Maidee, P., Lavin, C., Kaviani, A., Stroobandt, D.: Rwroute: an open-source timing-driven router for commercial FPGAS. ACM Trans. Reconfigurable Technol. Syst. **15**(1), 1–27 (2021)

High Performance Connected Components Accelerator for Image Processing in the Edge

José L. Mira(✉)[iD], Jesús Barba[iD], Julián Caba[iD], José A. de la Torre[iD], Fernando Rincón[iD], Soledad Escolar[iD], and Juan Carlos López[iD]

Technologies and Information Systems Department, School of Computer Science, Paseo de la Universidad, 4, Ciudad Real, 13071 Castilla La Mancha, Spain
{joseluis.mira,jesus.barba,julian.caba,joseantonio.torre, fernando.rincon,soledad.escolar,juancarlos.lopez}@uclm.es

Abstract. In image processing, a connected components algorithm is a method used to identify and label the different objects or regions present in a digital image. This algorithm can be useful for a variety of image processing tasks, such as object recognition, image segmentation, and feature extraction. This work presents the implementation of a single-pass algorithm on an FPGA-based device suitable for high-performance edge computing vision applications, the Ultra96-V2 computing board. The design and implementation of the IP core have faced challenges using the AMD-Xilinx HLS workflow and tools, which require efficient and optimized use of resources, as well as the re-engineering of the algorithm to comply with the requirements imposed by the development framework. The performance of the proposed accelerator has been thoroughly analysed using the YACCLAB benchmarking framework against a high-end and a low-end CPU. The results show an expected loss in performance due to memory and clock frequency limitations. However, concerning energy efficiency, the hardware multicore architecture outperforms the software alternatives with an improvement between two and five times, depending on the size and complexity of the images.

Keywords: Connected Components · High Performance Edge Processing · Computer Vision · Field Programmable Gate Arrays

1 Introduction

Connected components (CC) analysis is a crucial step of many applications in computer vision, consisting of assigning unique labels to each region of an image that has been previously segmented by applying a thresholding process to differentiate objects from the background. Next, features of each region, such as area, centre of gravity, bounding box, and pixel value, are extracted based on their labels with the goal to classify each region into one of multiple classes.

Time complexity and intensive memory usage are two of the main problems to be faced when it comes to the development of a valid solution for embedded

I. Skliarova et al. (Eds.): ARC 2024, LNCS 14553, pp. 210–221, 2024.
https://doi.org/10.1007/978-3-031-55673-9_15

devices with a limited amount or resources or constraint power budget. Indeed, this is the context for image processing in the edge, a computing paradigm that performs image processing tasks locally, near the source of the data, rather than sending all the data to a centralized cloud or data center for processing. Image processing in the edge can also enable real-time or near-real-time analysis of image data, which can be critical in applications such as autonomous vehicles, surveillance systems, or medical imaging.

Despite the fact there have been multiple CC algorithms over time, only single-pass algorithms are actually suitable for FPGA-based implementations due to the reduction in memory bandwidth which represents the major bottleneck for such class of devices [10]. This class of CC algorithms are also suitable for stream image processing.

In the paper [7] the authors present a scalable architecture for efficient, parallel processing of connected components by optimising performance through the use of multiple processing units. However, it is important to note that the implementation of the algorithm was performed on a high-end FPGA, which may restrict its applicability on less capable devices. In addition, extensive testing with synthetic datasets was not carried out to obtain performance comparisons with other approaches. Therefore, further research is required to evaluate the effectiveness and scalability of the algorithm in different hardware configurations and conditions.

The paper [9] presents a novel hardware architecture for connected component labeling in embedded image processing systems. The proposed architecture achieves high processing speeds by effectively managing label collisions through an innovative design that combines collision resolution and DMA core configuration in parallel. However, the authors did not perform tests with synthetic images on their architecture.

In most works in the literature, only theoretical measures derived from architecture synthesis are taken into account, in this work, the modeling, design and implementation of the single-pass CC analysis algorithm originally proposed by Bailey et al. in [1] and later optimized in [8] is revisited and adapted to Xilinx-AMD Vitis design flow. The main goal is to evaluate the performance and energy efficiency of the FPGA implementation against state-of-the art software alternatives running on high-end and low-end processor platforms. It is out of the scope of this paper to compare our hardware solution in terms of resource usage (mainly BRAM memory) with other proposals due to the use of different FPGA architectures and synthesis tools. On top of this, the proposed HLS model of the core has been generalize to enable its benchmarking by means of YACCLAB [5] framework. The architecture allows multicore configurations, worst case label counter as well as resolutions beyond the common 640×640 resolution reported in the majority of the literature [8,9], which increases the demand of resources.

2   HW-CC Accelerator

Although the algorithm proposed by Bailey et al. [1] is designed taking into account FPGA-based computing devices avoiding, for example, the need to store the whole image in BRAM memories, it still presents challenges when it comes to pack it as a fully functional core for FPA-SoCs architectures such as the Xilinx ZynQ-UltraScale+. Also, limited performance and resource analysis have been made, limiting the validation to a specific size of input images and complexity. Therefore, a complete view of the actual development of a FPGA-based solutions is missing, preventing a fair benchmarking against software solutions. On top of this, facing the modeling of the architecture and logic of the algorithm using High-Level Synthesis (HLS) technology demands the re-engineering of the original design so as to make it compliant with the semantic and syntax constraints of HLS tools.

The main contribution of this work is the development of the HW-CC accelerator, a fully parameterized IP core ready-to-use in Xilinx's FPGA-SoC platform. Parameterization allows its use for a wide range of input images and scenarios (see Sect. 3) making it our solution flexible to adapt to different application and target platform requirements (memory availability, latency, etc.). This flexibility comes to a price, mainly due to the large memory needs for storing intermediate data when working with big images; for example, the *data table*, a data structure that holds statistics of the label regions, depends on the width (W) and the height (H) being $W/2 \times H/2$ the theoretical maximum. For this reason, in the proposed solution, mechanisms had to be developed to overcome this handicap, making an low-end FPGA-based platform suitable for CC algorithms.

With regard to the parameterisation mentioned above, this mainly deals with aspects related to the memory requirements of the system to guarantee its correct operation. Firstly, by parameterising the size of the image to be processed, the sizing of the necessary internal memory structures is crucially determined. This is of vital importance, as these structures are directly dependent on the size of the image. Another key aspect of the design is the possibility to parameterise the size of the cache system. This parameterisation is relevant in several aspects, such as the number of BRAMs used by this structure and the number of possible read or write misses that can occur. These factors, in turn, impact the performance of the algorithm. In addition, the system parameterisation also provides the option of using a one-way or two-way cache system, which may be of interest depending on the specific memory access patterns of certain types of images.

This architectural proposal represents an important contribution in addressing the challenges posed by the algorithm proposed above. By implementing an instance-based division of labour approach, a proper distribution of the workload in processing a complete image is achieved. This strategy allows harnessing the potential for parallelism inherent in processing image sections simultaneously, resulting in improved system performance and scalability. By splitting the overall task into smaller instances, greater flexibility is achieved by adapting to different applications and platform requirements. However, this division implies the development of mechanisms to maintain consistency in the algorithm's collection of statistics across instances.

Figure 1 sketches a high-level view of the HW-CC architecture which have been modeled in Vitis HLS C/C++. Memory interface uses both AXI-Stream

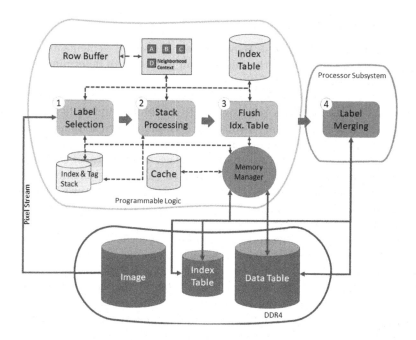

Fig. 1. Architecture of the HW-CC accelerator

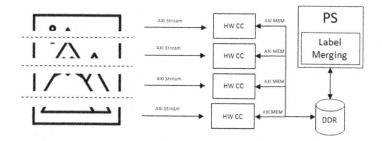

Fig. 2. High-level system composition

and AXI-Memory ports so the IP core can be easily integrated with the Processor Subsystem which runs the firmware for platform and peripheral configuration, DMA transfer management and execution of the *Label Merging* step. Figure 2 also shows the composition of the high-level system with the use of several instances of the accelerator working in parallel.

The HLS model defines the control and the memory elements, along with its mapping to FPGA resources, that realizes the algorithm in the most optimal way via the use of the appropriate pragmas and model parameters.

2.1 Memory Elements

- **Neigbourhood Context + Row Buffer**: These two elements are responsible for temporarily storing the information necessary to determine the labeling assignment for groups of pixels.

  On one hand, the row buffer temporarily stores the labels generated by the algorithm in the previous row, similar to a sliding window filter. The size of this row buffer in memory is directly determined by the number and size of the elements it will contain. In other words, the number of elements is directly related to the pixel width of the image, and the size of these elements coincides with the number of bits needed to encode the maximum possible number of labels. This, in turn, depends on the number of rows and columns in the image. This parameterization makes the size of this structure entirely customizable in the design.

  On the other hand, the neighborhood context is formed by the registers that spatially correspond to the pixels adjacent to the one being evaluated. These registers play a crucial role in selecting the value assigned to each pixel.

- **Index Table**: An array that holds the value of the tag to which a given index points. The size of this array can be parameterized in the model to fit the typical input image requirements. Another parameter of the model is the maximum number of labels, which determines the size of the word for the Index Table.

- **Index and Tag Stack**: This is a data structure used to merge two regions after each row is processed based on the values of their tags. In order to exploit the fact that index and tag information access is independent, it was decided to apply the pragma *ARRAY PARTITION* in order to allow parallel access to both values. The size of the stack is also a parameter of the model.

- **Memory Manager + Data Table + Cache**: The Data Table is the structure in which the statistics related to the labels are stored. In the proposed implementation the coordinates of the upper-left corner, width and height of each region is provided. The memory requirements of the Data Table would rapidly exhaust the available BRAMs in the FPGA fabric, specially for high resolutions. In order to make the HW-CC accelerator suitable for a variety of sizes and complexities, it has been decided to implement a simple cache system that allows the core handle large image sizes, without sacrificing the speed of access to the data. This module is also in charge of checking, reading and writing the blocks in the cache memory with respect to the on-board RAM when necessary. Given that during the algorithm's operation, it gradually assigns new labels to the new regions it passes through. In this process, space is occupied in the Data Table corresponding to these new labels. At the same time as this process is taking place, the merging of several previously assigned tags is also taking place. In this way, access to the entries in the table is usually done in an alternating manner. When implementing the cache, this memory access pattern is a problem because there are areas of the image in which data table entries belonging to different data blocks are accessed consecutively. This situation results in a high number of cache misses, with the respective execution time spent in having to replace the data block multiple times. Based on these characteristics of the memory access patterns, it was decided to implement a 2-way cache system in order to avoid unnecessary replacement of data blocks.

2.2 Algorithm Stages

Label Selection (HW). This stage is performed once for each pixel of the image, where the Neighbourhood Context is evaluated to determine which label will be generated in a given pixel. The following situations may arise in this process:

- Generate a new label, whereby a new record has to be created in the data table. To achieve this, a counter is employed, starting with the value 1, and it increments each time this operation is performed. This counter is responsible for being assigned to the label. In this process, the row and column values in which this label is contained are also stored.
- Assign an existing tag, which requires accessing the data table to update the statistics related to that tag. In this process, the parameters of the row and column in which the label is contained, as well as its area, are updated.
- There are two possible tags in the Neighbourhood Context so they are stored in the Index & Tag Stack to be resolved later, the smaller of the two is assigned to the pixel and the statistics are updated in the data table.

Stack Processing (HW). This stage is performed for each row of the image that has completed the algorithm. It accesses the Index & Tag Stack to perform the merge process between tags, which accesses the index table to update the corresponding indexes. Thanks to the implementation of this structure, potential conflicts that may arise in the resolution of labels that have been merged when consumed from the row buffer in the next row are resolved. When merging these labels, the values related to the rows and columns in which the new merged label is contained, as well as its area, are also updated.

Flush Index Table (HW). Once the algorithm has finished traversing the image, the cached data blocks are updated in DDR. Subsequently, the entire set of information generated by the algorithm needs to be transferred from internal memory to the DDR memory of the SoC. This step is essential for the data to be readily available and integrated into an image analysis system.

Label Merging (SW). Once the FPGA component is finished, the processor goes through the Index Table and the Data Table contained in the RAM memory to perform the final merging process between the different regions in order to obtain the final number of labels and their statistics. This step was moved to the software realm due to be a control intensive tasks with irregular memory pattern access, an scenario where the processor performs better than the FPGA.

3   Results

In this section, we present the results of our performance evaluation of various connected components labeling algorithms using the YACCLAB [5] benchmarking framework. Our evaluation aimed to compare the speed and energy efficiency of the proposed HW-CC accelerator IP against different algorithms on a set of test images provided by YACCLAB. Software benchmarks were run on: (1) a 12th Gen Intel(R) Core(TM) i7-12700K (3.6 GHz, 64 GB DDR5) executing an Ubuntu 20.4 GNU/Linux distribution; and (2) a Intel(R) Celeron(R) N5095 (2.0 GHz, 8 GB DDR4) executing an Ubuntu 22.4 GNU/Linux distribution. In both cases the test suite was compiled with GCC 11.3. By incorporating both a high-end workstation processor and a low-end CPU commonly present in commercial edge computing solutions, experimental validation can provide a better understanding of the proposed accelerator's capabilities.

The test suite comprised the out-of-the-box connected component algorithms that come with YACCLAB, namely: Scan Array-based with Union Find [11] (SAUF), Block-Based with Decision Tree [6] (BBDT), Pixel Prediction [4] (PRED), Directed Rooted Acyclic Graph [3] (DRAG) and Spaghetti Labelling [2].

The dataset used for experimental validation comprised a selection of the YACCLAB 2D subset which consists of binary images with labeled connected components. The dataset includes both synthetic images and real-world images from various sources. In this work, we test the HW-CC accelerator for edge image processing over the MIRflickr (25K images, average size and connected components: 0.17 megapixel and 495, respectively), Hamlet (104 images), Tobacco800 (1290 documents, 150–300 DPI and 1200×1600 to 2500×3200 resolutions), 3DPeS and synthetic random noise image subsets. A special note has to be made about the latter it allows to objectively test the scalability and efficacy of different algorithms. This subset provides ten images for each combination of size (32×32 up to 4096×4096 in steps of x2) and density (10% to 90%), resulting in a total of 720 images.

The Ultra96-v2 prototyping platform has been used to deploy and test the processing accelerator core. The Ultra96-v2 board is based on the Xilinx Zynq UltraScale+ MPSoC which integrates programmable logic and a four-core 64-bit Arm Cortex-A53 processor. The ZU3EG chip embedded in the platform is a low-end FPGA with modest capabilities and low power budget which makes it suitable for edge computing applications. Version 2021.1 of the Xilinx toolchain (Vitis HLS, Vivado and Vitis Unified Software Platform) has been used to model the HW-CC IP core, design and synthesize the platform and deploy the whole solution. No operating system support is required for running the firmware which executes on baremetal.

First, we evaluated the performance of the proposed solution against the real-world subsets selected. Though the architecture of the HW-CC accelerator is flexible and allows multiple parameter configuration, for this experiment an aggressive strategy was proposed in order to obtain the maximum performance. Therefore, row buffer size was established to 4K words, label data memory to 64K and cache block memory to 1K. The number of accelerator cores instantiated in the FPGA fabric is four, which raises the utilization of BRAM resources to 83% of the total available in the device. Post-synthesis results showed that it was possible to configure a 175MHz clock to drive the logic. However, we establish a conservative approach in this regard in order to avoid unexpected on-board behaviour. Thus, a safe 150MHz clocking configuration was set.

Table 1. Average run-time test (ms) for real-image subset

	MIRFlickr	3DPes	Hamlet	Tobacco	Avg. Gain
HW-CC-150	1.71	2.73	19.77	36.92	-
Intel i7-12700K					
SAUF	0.44	0.61	4.96	7.65	**−4.29x**
BBDT	0.36	0.35	3.44	4.93	**−6.45x**
PRED	0.54	0.72	6.92	10.52	**−6.33x**
DRAG	0.36	0.35	3.44	4.91	**−6.46x**
Spaghetti	0.2	0.18	1.89	2.68	**−11.99x**
Intel Celeron N5095					
SAUF	1.46	2.76	22.19	37.33	**−1.01x**
BBDT	0.88	1.33	13.86	22.96	**−1.76x**
PRED	1.49	2.87	22.96	38.69	**+1.02x**
DRAG	0.87	1.33	13.86	23.03	**−1.76x**
Spaghetti	0.41	0.53	5.16	7.89	**−4.46x**

Table 1 presents the average execution times for all the targeted image subsets. The results show a significant loss in performance compared to the i7 processor, and a moderate decrease in performance in the case of the Celeron processor.

The most attractive feature of the Zynq UltraScale+ architecture for edge computing applications is its efficiency in terms of power consumption. Average energy intake for our HW-CC has been measured using the interface provided by the on-board *Platform Management Unit* resulting in 3.74W during test execution. In the case of the i7 processor, *powerstat* command line tool has been used to monitor the increment in power consumption through the RAPL (Running Average Power Limit) interface; an average of 31.4W was observed. The Celeron-based computing platform had, however, to used a external energy consumption meter which reported a sustained increment of 10.3W during test execution.

Table 2. Gain in the average energy efficiency (J) for Real-Image Subset. HW-CC versus Intel i7 & Celeron.

	SAUF	BBDT	PRED	DRAG	Spaghetti
Intel i7	1.87	1.24	2.56	1.24	0.67
Intel Celeron	2.87	1.75	2.97	1.76	0.63

Table 2 shows the comparison of the efficiency, expressed as Joules, broke down by subset and algorithm. Average results expose a consistent cross-platform gain in all cases but the Spaghetti algorithm which outperform the rest due to its low execution time. It is important to note that all the algorithms evaluated achieve identical results in terms of region labelling. This observation demonstrates the consistency and accuracy of all the approaches analysed in this study in terms of their ability to identify and assign labels to the different regions present in the image.

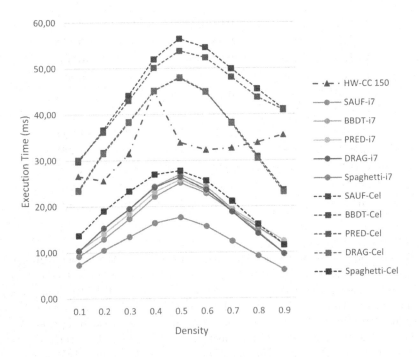

Fig. 3. Density test results.

In order to validate the performance and scalability of a solution, YACCLAB includes a set of random generated images that allows the execution of density and size tests. The density and size values mentioned above refer directly to the number of regions to be labelled in the image. These values are randomly generated and represent the granularity of the noise present in the image. The impact of this test is mainly evident in the total number of regions present in the image, as well as in the size of each region and the memory access pattern used by the algorithm. These aspects are important considerations as they influence the performance of the system. Figures 3 and 5 depict a comparison of run-times for each software algorithm and the 4-core 150 MHz version of the proposed HW-CC accelerator. In the Fig. 4, the difference between images with different density factors can be observed.

0.1   0.3   0.7

Fig. 4. Example of synthetic images in YACCLAB dataset with different intensities. It directly stresses the algorithm performance.

Average execution time is stable for HW-CC with slight higher values as the density increases broken by a peak on 0.4 foreground density images as it can be seen in Fig. 3. Comparison to i7 processor shows a performance degradation of $\approx -2x$ for all algorithms but Spaghetti which reaches $-3.03x$ with a maximum loss of $5.76x$ for 0.9 density images. However, HW-CC is faster than the Celeron processor in all cases - SAUF (35.9%), BBDT (4.2%), PRED (32.6%), DRAG (3.4%) - but, again, Spaghetti ($1.72x$ slower in average with a maximum loss of $3.07x$ for 0.9 density images).

Regarding size tests, the performance of the proposed accelerator maintains the same pattern across processors and algorithms. As it can be seen in Fig. 5, HW-CC core maintains the linear dependency of execution time as its software counterparts. Average performance loss versus i7 processor is $-2.14x$. Taking into account that Intel i7 processor power consumption is approximately ten times the energy the FPGA needs, it results in a $\approx 5x$ improvement in terms of energy efficiency while maintaining a fair computing capability for a device to be deployed at the edge of the computing infrastructure. As to the Celeron CPU, average loss in performance is -1.09, highly penalized by the efficiency of Spaghetti algorithm ($1.82x$ better). In the other cases, HW-CC is 10% faster. Overall, our FPGA-based solution is ≈ 2.5 times more efficient than the Celeron computing platform.

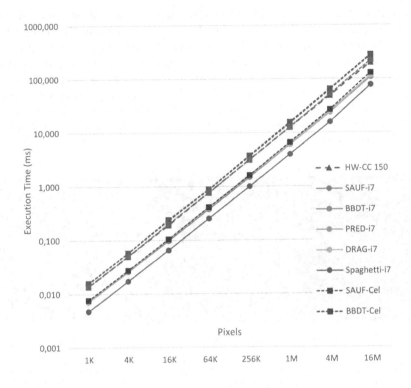

Fig. 5. Size test results.

4   Conclusions

In this work, the design and development of a hardware accelerator architecture for efficient analysis and labeling of components in images have been carried out, emphasizing the trade-off between computational power and energy consumption. Targeting embedded computing platforms deployed at the edge of information acquisition, processing, and transmission infrastructure (e.g., IoT platforms), the analysis of results considers not only performance but also the energy needs of the solution. Ultimately, the envisioned platforms for the final application involve a processing device based on an SoC-FPGA and powered by a battery, emphasizing the importance of energy efficiency.

Comparing with previous contributions in the state of the art is challenging as many works often lack necessary information, target FPGA devices from previous generations, and lack standardization in terms of conducted tests and utilized images, which directly impacts processing latency dependent on complexity and size. As a next step, we will work on developing a comparative framework and information compilation to objectively evaluate our solution in comparison to other state-of-the-art works.

Acknowledgment. This research has been funded by the European Union's H2020 programme under grant agreement no. 857159 (SHAPES project) and by the Spanish Ministry of Economy and Competitiveness (MINECO) under the TALENT project (PID2020-116417RB-C4, subproject 1) and the MIRATAR project (TED2021-132149B-C41).

Disclosure of Interest. The authors have no competing interest to declare that are relevant to the content of this article.

References

1. Bailey, D., Johnston, C.: Single pass connected components analysis. In: Proceedings of Image and Vision Computing (2007)
2. Bolelli, F., Allegretti, S., Baraldi, L., Grana, C.: Spaghetti labeling: directed acyclic graphs for block-based connected components labeling. IEEE Trans. Image Process. **29**, 1999–2012 (2020). https://doi.org/10.1109/TIP.2019.2946979
3. Bolelli, F., Baraldi, L., Cancilla, M., Grana, C.: Connected components labeling on drags. In: 2018 24th International Conference on Pattern Recognition (ICPR), pp. 121–126 (2018). https://doi.org/10.1109/ICPR.2018.8545505
4. Grana, C., Baraldi, L., Bolelli, F.: Optimized connected components labeling with pixel prediction. In: Blanc-Talon, J., Distante, C., Philips, W., Popescu, D., Scheunders, P. (eds.) ACIVS 2016. LNCS, vol. 10016, pp. 431–440. Springer, Cham (2016). https://doi.org/10.1007/978-3-319-48680-2_38
5. Grana, C., Bolelli, F., Baraldi, L., Vezzani, R.: Yacclab - yet another connected components labeling benchmark. In: 2016 23rd International Conference on Pattern Recognition (ICPR), pp. 3109–3114 (2016). https://doi.org/10.1109/ICPR.2016.7900112
6. Grana, C., Borghesani, D., Cucchiara, R.: Optimized block-based connected components labeling with decision trees. IEEE Trans. Image Process. **19**(6), 1596–1609 (2010). https://doi.org/10.1109/TIP.2010.2044963
7. Klaiber, M.J., Bailey, D.G., Simon, S.: A single-cycle parallel multi-slice connected components analysis hardware architecture. J. Real-Time Image Process. **16**(4), 1165–1175 (2019). https://doi.org/10.1007/s11554-016-0610-2
8. Ma, N., Bailey, D.G., Johnston, C.T.: Optimised single pass connected components analysis. In: 2008 International Conference on Field-Programmable Technology, pp. 185–192 (2008). https://doi.org/10.1109/FPT.2008.4762382
9. Spagnolo, F., Frustaci, F., Perri, S., Corsonello, P.: An efficient connected component labeling architecture for embedded systems. J. Low Power Electron. Appl. **8**(1), 7 (2018). https://doi.org/10.3390/jlpea8010007. https://www.mdpi.com/2079-9268/8/1/7
10. Walczyk, R., Armitage, A., Binnie, T.D.: Comparative study on connected component labeling algorithms for embedded video processing systems. In: International Conference on Image Processing, Computer Vision, & Pattern Recognition (2010)
11. Wu, K., Otoo, E.J., Suzuki, K.: Optimizing two-pass connected-component labeling algorithms. Pattern Anal. Appl. **12**, 117–135 (2009)

Spectral-Blaze: A High-Performance FFT-Based CNN Accelerator

Shine Parekkadan Sunny$^{(\boxtimes)}$ and Satyajit Das

Indian Institute of Technology (IIT) Palakkad, Palakkad, Kerala, India
112014002@smail.iitpkd.ac.in, satyajitdas@iitpkd.ac.in

Abstract. This paper presents Spectral-Blaze, a novel FFT-based CNN accelerator that effectively addresses computational and energy bottlenecks in spatial domain acceleration. The proposed architecture introduces Intra-Patch parallelization during the Hadamard product phase, which optimizes Complex MAC (CMAC) unit utilization and maintains consistent reuse patterns across multiple input feature map patches. This parallelization scheme simplifies the tiling, enabling independent selection of patch elements for efficient on-chip memory storage. Additionally, it leverages the Flex-Stationary dataflow to adaptively store tensors with high reuse opportunities in the on-chip memory, reducing the DRAM traffic. Spectral-Blaze also introduces an optimized FFT/IFFT process that integrates a modified row-column FFT, real FFT-based optimizations, and a vector-radix IFFT. The Spectral-Blaze prototype, implemented on the Zynq MPSoC (ZU7CG), demonstrates impressive performance gains, achieving a speedup of 4.98× for VGG-16 and 1.64× for AlexNet compared to baseline. The Energy-Delay Product (EDP) varies from 4.47× to 25.14×. Compared to flexible dataflow spatial accelerators, Spectral-Blaze achieves an average improvement of 8.82× over Eyeriss and 7.87× improvement over Flexflow in EDP while maintaining a comparable hardware setup. Spectral-Blaze also achieves a 4.59× reduction in MAC operations during convolution, even with VGG-16's compact filter sizes.

Keywords: FFT-based convolution · Tiling · DNN Accelerator · Intra-Patch Parallelization · Flex-Stationary

1 Introduction and Related Works

Popular deep learning accelerators [1–4] spatially unroll computations to achieve high throughput and energy efficiency. Most of the Deep Neural Network (DNN) inference models use convolution (CONV) layers as the building blocks that account for almost 90% of overall computations [5]. The convolution layers in CNN involve multiple levels of computational loops between the input feature map (ifmap) and weight (wt) tensors, as illustrated in Fig. 1. Traditional accelerators for CNN inference commonly rely on 2-D convolutions in the spatial domain. However, this approach has several significant drawbacks. One limitation is the requirement for separate 2-D convolutions to be performed for each

© The Author(s), under exclusive license to Springer Nature Switzerland AG 2024
I. Skliarova et al. (Eds.): ARC 2024, LNCS 14553, pp. 222–238, 2024.
https://doi.org/10.1007/978-3-031-55673-9_16

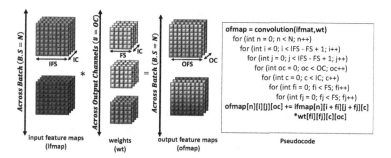

Fig. 1. Multi-loop Convolution Operation in a CONV layer

input and output channels, resulting in substantial Multiply and Accumulate (MAC) operations. Additionally, CNN acceleration typically relies on fixed parallelism across dimensions tied to the shape of the layer, such as the input/output channels in NVDLA-like accelerators [6] or the dimensions of the output feature map (ofmap) in ShiDianNao [4]. However, the effectiveness of this approach is highly dependent on the tensor dimensions within the layer. To illustrate, consider the 1st CONV layer of the VGG-16 network with 3 input channels and 64 output channels. Employing a spatial accelerator like NVDLA with a set of 8×8 Processing Elements (PEs), featuring $8\times$ input channel and $8\times$ output channel parallelization, results in a misalignment between the number of input channels and the degree of parallelization. Hence, nearly 62.5% of the PEs will remain idle. NVDLA specifically tackles this disproportion by incorporating an image input mode for the initial layer, but such imbalances can persist in other layers.

Due to limited on-chip storage, the tensors involved in convolutions are often partitioned or tiled, leading to redundant data movement between the accelerator and off-chip memory. Off-chip data movement represents the most energy-consuming aspect of DNN accelerators, estimated to be approximately $200\times$ more energy intensive than computation [7]. Therefore, an efficient tiling strategy that maximizes data reuse while minimizing off-chip data transactions is crucial. However, selecting an optimal tiling strategy is often challenging, given the vast search space and dependences on parallelization, memory hierarchy, and dataflow [8]. In addition, conventional spatial accelerators, such as NVDLA which employs weight stationary dataflow (WS), are required to maintain a fixed tensor (wt) in the on-chip memory. The NoC is designed to support this dataflow, by broadcasting ifmap and spatially accumulating psum. However, in deeper layers, the convolutional reuse of the wt tensor decreases significantly compared to ifmap reuse. Thus, a hard-wired dataflow generally results in suboptimal reuse behavior when considering the network as a whole.

The traditional approach of using 2-D convolutions in CNN accelerators in the spatial domain presents several challenges, including increased computational complexity, higher energy consumption, and limitations in the efficient handling of large-scale models. The hardwired dataflow in conventional accelerators restricts the flexibility necessary to optimize tensor reuse across layers. Therefore, it is imperative to address these limitations and explore alternative approaches.

Table 1. abbreviations table

Abbrev./term used	Definition
ifmap/ofmap, wt	Spatial domain - input/output feature map, weight
IFMAP, WT, OFMAP	FFT(ifmap), FFT(wt), FFT(ofmap)
psum, PSUM	partial sum, Partial OFMAP (without entire input channels)
patch	ifmap portion considered during OaD Convolution
PS^2, IFS^2, FS^2, N	patch size, ifmap size, weight size, batch size
PN, IC, OC	# of patches in an ifmap, # input channels, #output channels

1.1 Related Works

FFT-based CNN acceleration is an active area of research that aims to reduce the computational complexity and memory requirements of CNNs. Some terms used in this paper to describe FFT-based convolution are given in Table 1. The literature presented below is categorized to highlight the distinctions of the proposed work.

Several studies focus mainly on the 2-D convolution methodology rather than a comprehensive implementation of multichannel convolution. Consequently, they provide minimal discussion on tiling/reuse behaviors. [7] identifies FFT as one of the potential transform methods to speed up computations in a CONV layer. The authors have highlighted that FFT-based convolution reduces the number of multiplications from $\mathcal{O}(IFS^2 \times FS^2)$ to $\mathcal{O}(IFS^2 \times \log(IFS))$. Work by Abtahi et al. [5,9] explored trade-offs between different convolution techniques, namely Direct-Conv, FFTConv, and Overlap and Add (OaA), in multiple embedded devices. It showed that the OaA convolution outperforms Direct-Conv and FFT-Conv in terms of execution time and $(\frac{throughput}{watt})$ on all evaluated platforms. [10] proposes CirCNN, a principled approach to represent wt and process neural networks using block-circulant matrices. CirCNN utilizes FFT-based fast multiplication, simultaneously reducing computational and storage complexity. [11] proposes an FFT-based split convolution technique to accelerate CNNs. The proposed method splits ifmap and wt into smaller submatrices and then performs FFT-based convolutions on them separately. The results show that the number of multiplications was reduced to 1.5× over OaA.

Zhang et al. [12] propose a mechanism to accelerate state-of-the-art CNNs on a CPU-FPGA platform with coherent shared memory. This work maps the computations to a parallel OaA-based 2D convolver design. However, this design overlooks the reuse opportunities, making it memory intensive. Additionally, the CPU is involved in every data point operation, including overlap, ReLU, pooling, and depth concatenation, resulting in poor performance.

[13] discusses two forms of reuse in convolution calculations: OC-fold reuse for ifmap and N-fold reuse for wt. However,CNN computations offer more reuse opportunities and the adopted OaA convolution method is inferior [11]. Yixin [14] proposes an FFT-based kernel sharing technique called FS-Conv to reduce memory access. However, this approach focuses only on reusing the WT tensor,

ignoring other possibilities. Flexflow [3] is a spatial accelerator that features a PE capable of supporting three types of parallelism: feature map, neuron, and synaptic parallelism. Flexflow harnesses the combined benefits of these parallelisms to adapt to different CNN layers. Although FlexFlow discusses adaptive parallelization and spatial reuse, it does not propose a mechanism for temporal reuse and lacks the computational benefits of the frequency domain.

Complementary to our work, [15] proposes frequency domain quantization schemes to achieve CNN inference at high throughput in FPGAs. They analyze the impact of the quantization bit-width on the accuracy via signal-to-quantization-noise ratio. [16] shows an efficient approach that extends butterfly operations from the FFT algorithm to a general Butterfly Transform (BFT). By replacing pointwise convolutions with BFT, they reduce the computational complexity from $\mathcal{O}(n^2)$ to $\mathcal{O}(n\log(n))$ concerning the number of channels.

As seen, prior research predominantly focuses on the computational aspects of FFT, with limited exploration concerning the challenges encountered when devising end-to-end FFT-based CNN accelerators. This paper introduces the **Spectral-Blaze** framework, employing a comprehensive strategy to accelerate FFT-based CNNs, emphasizing the optimization of the binary computation phase (Hadamard product) through improved operand reuse.

1.2   Contributions

In this paper, we present a novel algorithm-architecture co-design approach that enhances the performance of CNN acceleration without affecting the accuracy of classification problems. Our contributions are summarized as follows:

1. An innovative parallelization scheme, called intra-patch parallelization, which effectively addresses the issue of underutilization of PEs, when parallelism is intricately linked with the layer shape.
2. Our intra-patch parallelization approach simplifies tiling in the frequency domain, and we propose a simple yet effective tiling approach that maintains a high average reuse factor.
3. A new dataflow scheme, named flex-stationary, is proposed for binary operations. It adaptively places operands in on-chip memory, resulting in improved operand reuse.
4. We introduce an optimized FFT/IFFT process that includes a modified row-column FFT, real-FFT-based optimizations, and a vector-radix IFFT.
5. We present an area-efficient RTL design of pipelined FFT/IFFT modules, along with an intra-patch parallelized Hadamard Product Generator, to enable high-throughput implementation.
6. Finally, we prototype our proposed approach on a Zynq MPSoC HW and benchmark it against state-of-the-art frequency domain and flexible spatial domain accelerators, in terms of throughput, energy, and EDP.

Experiments demonstrate that the Spectral-Blaze prototype implemented on the Zynq MPSoC (ZU7CG) demonstrates a remarkable acceleration, achieving a speedup of 4.98× for VGG-16 and 1.98× for AlexNet when compared to

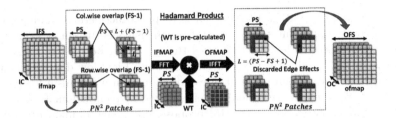

Fig. 2. Overlap and Discard method of 2-D convolution

the current state-of-the-art frequency domain accelerator. Notably, it attains an average improvement of 8.82× over Eyeriss and 7.87× over Flexflow in EDP, while maintaining a similar hardware configuration.

The rest of the paper is organized as follows. Section 2 provides algorithmic details of OaD Convolution and Vector Radix FFT (VR-FFT). Section 3 presents the proposed Algorithm-Architecture Co-Design. The experiments and results are discussed in Sect. 4. Finally, the paper concludes in Sect. 5.

2   Background

This section provides a concise overview of OaD convolution and VR FFT.

Overlap and Discard Convolution (OaD Conv). The split convolution method mentioned in [11], involves partitioning a single plane obtained from a channel of the spatial ifmap into 2-D patches of size PS × PS. Each patch is formed by taking data points from the last (FS − 1) rows and columns of the previous patch, followed by (PS − FS + 1) × (PS − FS + 1) new data points. For each channel, the wt is resized by appending (PS − FS) × (PS − FS) zeros, and a PS × PS point 2-D FFT of the wt patch is computed and stored. The Hadamard product is taken between the ifmap and the WT patch as in Eq. 1. After IFFT, the first (FS−1) points of output are corrupted by aliasing and must be discarded, while the last (PS − FS + 1) × (PS − FS + 1) points of output are identical to the result from linear convolution. The process is depicted in Fig. 2. Equation 2 represents the case of hadamard product when tiling is applied, with the subscript t signifying the tensor size considered in each tiling step.

$$\forall oc \in [1, OC] \text{ and } \forall pn \in [1, N * PN^2],$$

$$OFMAP[oc][pn] = \sum_{ic=1}^{IC} (IFMAP[ic][pn] \cdot WT[oc][ic]) \tag{1}$$

$$\forall oc \in [1, OC_t] \text{ and } \forall pn \in [1, N_t * PN_t^2],$$

$$PSUM_{out}[oc][pn] = PSUM_{in}[oc][pn] + \sum_{ic=1}^{IC_t} (IFMAP[ic][pn] \cdot WT[ic][oc]) \tag{2}$$

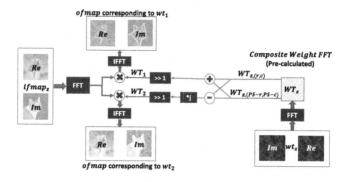

Fig. 3. Real FFT-based convolution process

Vector-Radix FFT (N×N-Point 2D FFT). The VR-FFT is an extension of Cooley-Tukey FFT that efficiently performs multidimensional FFTs by breaking down the DFT into smaller ones. The 2-D DFT, as shown in Eq. 3, represents the transformation of a spatial input $S(x, y)$ into the spectral domain $X(u, v)$, where (x, y) represents the spatial positions and (u, v) represents the spectral bins. The VR-FFT algorithm can be realized using a 4-input butterfly unit, as described in Eq. 4.

$$X(u,v) = \sum_{x=0}^{N-1} \sum_{y=0}^{N-1} S(x,y) \cdot e^{-j2\pi\left(\frac{ux}{N} + \frac{vy}{N}\right)} \tag{3}$$

$$X(u,v) = \text{EE}(u,v) + \omega_N^v \cdot \text{EO}(u,v) + \omega_N^u \cdot \text{OE}(u,v) + \omega_N^{u+v} \cdot \text{OO}(u,v)$$

$$X(u,v+\frac{N}{2}) = \text{EE}(u,v) - \omega_N^v \cdot \text{EO}(u,v) + \omega_N^u \cdot \text{OE}(u,v) - \omega_N^{u+v} \cdot \text{OO}(u,v)$$

$$X(u+\frac{N}{2},v) = \text{EE}(u,v) + \omega_N^v \cdot \text{EO}(u,v) - \omega_N^u \cdot \text{OE}(u,v) - \omega_N^{u+v} \cdot \text{OO}(u,v)$$

$$X(u+\frac{N}{2},v+\frac{N}{2}) = \text{EE}(u,v) - \omega_N^v \cdot \text{EO}(u,v) - \omega_N^u \cdot \text{OE}(u,v) + \omega_N^{u+v} \cdot \text{OO}(u,v)$$

$$\tag{4}$$

It expresses the combination of the output coefficients X through the even-even (EE), even-odd (EO), odd-even (OE), and odd-odd (OO) groups. The EE group corresponds to the $(\frac{N}{2} \times \frac{N}{2})$ DFT of the even-even elements, and similar definitions apply to the others. ω_N represents the Nth root of unity $(e^{-j\frac{2\pi}{N}})$.

3   Proposed Algorithm-Architecture Co-design

Spectral-Blaze adopts a novel algorithm-architecture co-design approach, leveraging algorithmic advancements to reduce operational counts, improve tensor reuse, and effectively harness these enhancements in architectural design. The combination of a compiler and a runtime driver serves as a bridge, seamlessly integrating optimal algorithmic settings with the chosen architecture. The subsequent sections delve into the specific details of this proposed design.

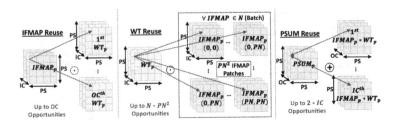

Fig. 4. Reuse Opportunities in the OaD Convolution

3.1   Algorithmic Improvements

Spectral-Blaze introduces an innovative approach to efficiently handle FFT-based convolution of real operands. In addition, the proposed intrapatch parallelization facilitates enhanced dataflow and tiling strategies, resulting in improved tensor reuse. Below, we discuss these algorithmic improvements.

Optimized Real-FFT. Within the CONV layers, the utilization of real numbers in FFT leads to conjugate symmetry, resulting in the inefficient utilization of nearly half of the storage and computational resources. To address this, we propose a novel scheme that simultaneously executes two real convolutions in a single step, as illustrated in Fig. 3. This is achieved by combining the two ifmap patches of the same batch, forming a composite patch (ifmap$_z$) as in Eq. 5. Similarly, the composite weight patch wt$_z$ is pre-computed by combining the weights of two distinct output channels. The FFT is performed on ifmap$_z$ and wt$_z$, the output is denoted as IFMAP$_z$ and WT$_z$. During runtime, pre-calculated WT$_z$ is partitioned into individual FFTs by leveraging the symmetry property, as in Eq. 6, where r and c represents the row and column positions.

$$\text{ifmap}_z = ifmap_1 + j \cdot ifmap_2, \quad \text{wt}_z = \text{wt}_1 + j \cdot \text{wt}_2 \tag{5}$$

$$\text{WT}_1(r,c) = \frac{\text{WT}_z(r,c) + \text{WT}_z(\text{PS}-r, \text{PS}-c)^*}{2}$$

$$\text{WT}_2(r,c) = \frac{j \cdot (\text{WT}_z(\text{PS}-r, \text{PS}-c)^* - \text{WT}_z(r,c))}{2} \tag{6}$$

Storing a symmetrical half of the WT coefficients for each output channel individually is possible. However, this method results in a slightly larger memory footprint ($\text{PS}*(\text{PS}+1)$ vs. PS^2) and creates nonuniformity in patch size between IFMAP$_z$ and WT$_z$. Recovering individual weights during run-time is found to be optimal considering high-energy DRAM access [7]. The composite OFMAP$_z$ is obtained by performing the hadamard product between IFMAP$_z$ and the split individual weights, as described in Eq. 7.

$$\text{OFMAP}_{z1} = \text{IFMAP}_z \cdot \text{WT}_1, \quad \text{OFMAP}_{z2} = \text{IFMAP}_z \cdot \text{WT}_2 \tag{7}$$

Table 2. determining stationary operand based on reuse opportunites

DATAFLOW	WS	IS	OS
Stationary Tensor	WT	IFMAP	PSUM
Reuse Opportunities	High for WT	High for IFMAP	High for PSUM
Condition with composite patch	$(\frac{N}{2} * PN^2) \geq IC \& (\frac{OC}{2})$	$(\frac{OC}{2}) \geq IC \& (\frac{N}{2} * PN^2)$	$IC \geq (\frac{OC}{2}) \& (\frac{N}{2} * PN^2)$
Tensors fetched b/w tiling iterations	PSUM & IFMAP	WT & PSUM	IFMAP & WT

Subsequently, the inverse FFT of $OFMAP_{z1}$ and $OFMAP_{z2}$ are computed to obtain $ofmap_{z1}$ and $ofmap_{z2}$. In these composite ofmaps, the real part corresponds to the convolution output of 1st ifmap, while the imaginary part represents the output of 2nd ifmap. This approach, which executes two real convolutions in a single step, achieves a $2\times$ improvement in storage and computational efficiency.

Data Reuse Opportunities/Reuse Potential. The inherent structure of CNNs provides several opportunities for data reuse, extensively discussed in [7]. However, the application of frequency domain convolution, specifically the OaD convolution, presents relatively unexplored prospects. These instances of data reuse are illustrated in Fig. 4 and can be categorized differently, deviating from spatial acceleration terminology, as follows: (a) IFMAP Reuse: IFMAP patches can be reused across multiple WT patches to compute all output channels. This is similar to Fmap reuse mentioned in [7] and can allow up to OC times the reuse of IFMAP patches. (b) PSUM Reuse: Modifying the PSUM patches as in Eq. 2 requires read and write in every tiling iteration. The buffering of PSUM enables maximum reuse of $2 * IC$. (c) WT reuse: WT patches can be reused across the $N * PN^2$ IFMAP patches. This includes the N-fold reuse across the elements in a batch and the PN^2-fold reuse in a single plane. This is similar to the filter and convolution reuse mentioned in [7].

Flex-Stationary Dataflow. In contrast to conventional dataflow approaches, the proposed architecture allows adaptive stationing of any operand in on-chip memory, enhancing reuse. In other words, it can function as Weight, Output or Input Stationary (WS/OS/IS), depending on the available reuse opportunities within a CONV layer. The selection of the appropriate dataflow scheme is determined by the relative reuse opportunities of the composite patches; the conditions are shown in Table 2. For example, if the reuse opportunities of WT outweigh those of IFMAP, the static compiler chooses the WS scheme and WT is updated least frequently. Generally, the initial layers favor the WS dataflow, while the latter layers tend to favor the IS dataflow due to reduced WT reuse and increased IFMAP reuse.

Proposed Tiling. Spectral-Blaze's tiling process is unique due to consistent reuse opportunities across patches and elements in the frequency domain with

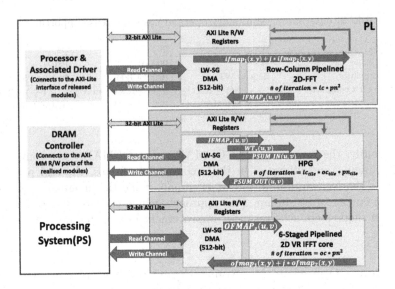

Fig. 5. MPSoC-based realization of Spectral-Blaze

intra-patch parallelization. Unlike traditional accelerators, Spectral-Blaze provides flexibility in dataflow, allowing a simple greedy algorithm-based tiling approach using Eq. 8. The subscript msp represents the memory size on the chip in terms of composite patches, and t is the size considered during the tiling. With one stationary tensor as per above, two tiling variables are fixed, making it easy to determine the size of the remaining tensors. If the stationary tensor cannot fit in the on-chip memory, it is tiled across the dimensions with the least reuse.

$$on\text{-}chip_{msp} \geq IC_t \times PN_t + IC_t \times OC_t + OC_t \times PN_t$$

$$Here, \ IC_t \leq IC, OC_t \leq \frac{OC}{2}, PN_t \leq \frac{N}{2} \times PN^2 \tag{8}$$

3.2   Proposed Accelerator Architecture

The schematic diagram of Spectral-Blaze, based on Zynq-MPSoC, is shown in Fig. 5. The associated Register Transfer Level (RTL) design is created employing the High-Level Synthesis (HLS) design methodology. This design uses a task-level pipeline, using DRAM as an intermediary for FFT, HPG, and IFFT operations, with an on-chip tile buffer to maximize tensor reuse during binary operations. DRAM access is via a lightweight scatter-gather (LW-SG) DMA. A 32-bit AXI-Lite interface interacts with the CPU driver for only control parameters, minimizing processor intervention in computation. Processing is divided into load, compute, and store tasks with a pipelined task-level approach for load and store tasks, reducing the impact of DRAM latency on performance. Data sharing among tasks is facilitated using on-chip PIPO (ping-pong) or FIFO mechanisms.

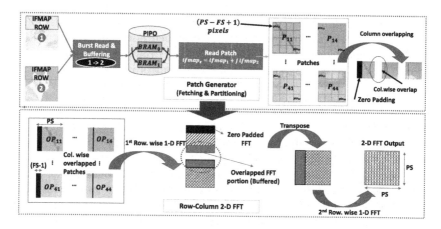

Fig. 6. Forward FFT Module

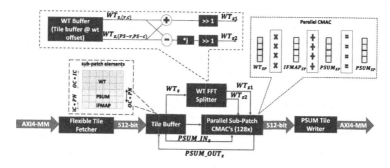

Fig. 7. Hadamard Product Generator

Internal caching structures are used to maintain data order to optimize DRAM accesses during ifmap fetching and ofmap writing, utilizing burst access.

Modified Row-Column Pipelined 2-D FWD-FFT. The FWD-FFT module computes the patch-wise 2-D DFT of the spatial ifmap. To avoid redundant computational and DRAM transactions for overlapping patches, we propose a new scheme called modified row-column 2-D FFT. This consists of a patch generator and a row-column 2-D FFT unit, as illustrated in Fig. 6.

- **Patch Generator:** It creates composite column-wise overlapping patches from ifmap with a fetcher and a partitioning unit. The fetcher unit retrieves $(PS - FS + 1)$ rows of pixels from 1st ifmap and 2nd ifmap. The partitioning unit divides these data into multiple ifmap patches, which later form a composite patch as in Eq. 5. Overlapped portions are buffered to avoid redundant DRAM access.
- **Row-Column 2-D FFT (RC-2D FFT):** This unit operates on overlapped patches generated by the patch generator. It performs 1-D FFT operations

in row and column directions on these patches using a 6-staged pipelined butterfly unit. To save on row FFT of overlapped portion, a buffer will store the FFT output coefficients of the last $(FS - 1)$ rows. The module performs 2-D FFT of $IC \times PN^2$ patches with a single control input.

Hadamard Product Generator (HPG). The HPG module is designed to compute the point-wise Hadamard product between the IFMAP and WT patches. The resulting product is accumulated across the input channels and subsequently fed into the IFFT module. In our proposed approach, the Hadamard product serves as a critical phase of binary computation that requires improvements in tiling and dataflow strategies. The total number of patches to be handled for a layer is $OC * IC * N * PN^2$. The HPG along with its interfaces is illustrated in Fig. 7. The detailed microarchitecture of the HPG module is not included in this paper. The following sections cover the key features of the HPG module.

- Intra-Patch Parallelization: The FWD-FFT and INV-FFT modules handle computations over IC and OC, while the HPG module is responsible for computations across both OC and IC, making it the most computationally demanding phase in the proposed architecture. To achieve high throughput, we introduce a novel parallelization scheme called *Intra-Patch Parallelization*. It operates across the elements of a subpatch (sp), wherein multiple Complex Multiply-Accumulate (CMAC) units work in tandem to perform the Hadamard product of a 2D patch. The complete utilization of CMAC units is attainable regardless of the layer size, as long as the number of units is a power of 2 and is less than PS^2. In practice, the majority of CONV layers satisfy this criterion. To enable intra-patch parallelization, the HPG module incorporates reshaped memory elements that provide concurrent access to all elements of a subpatch. The CMAC array fetches data from the on-chip memory, performs the Hadamard product computation, and aggregates (across the IC) the result with the previous partial sum in parallel. By avoiding dependencies and implementing instruction-level parallelism, an initiation interval of 2 cycles is achieved in this SIMD operation.
- Flex-Stationary Dataflow: To enable *Flex-Stationary dataflow* as explained in the Sect. 3.1, the HPG datapath includes an on-chip memory that allows partial updates as identified by the update flags of the control register. For example, in WS dataflow, the update flag of WT is disabled for a longer duration, while the tensors IFMAP and PSUM are frequently updated. This means that IFMAP and PSUM are streamed and WT is kept stationary in the on-chip memory.

Vector-Radix Inverse FFT (VR-IFFT). The Spectral-Blaze includes an Inverse FFT (IFFT) module that executes the IFFT on OFMAP patches generated by the HPG module. This module employs a Vector-Radix FFT unit consisting of six stages and an adapter unit that enables the IFFT through

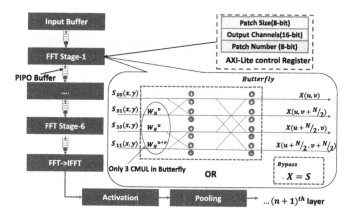

Fig. 8. Vector-Radix FFT

Fig. 9. Adaptor for realizing inverse FFT by forward FFT

forward FFT operations. To minimize DRAM transactions, the activation and pooling functions are implemented within the IFFT module.

The datapath of the VR-FFT module consists of an input buffer, six FFT stages, and an output buffer, as shown in Fig. 8. Each of these stages contains a VR-FFT butterfly unit, which can eliminate up to 25% of the multiplications required by the row-column 2-D FFT. The VR-FFT does not require a memory-intensive transposer stage, which is present in the row-column approach. Task-level pipelining allows concurrent reading of input patches from DRAM, computation of multiple stages, and writing of output patches to the DRAM enhancing throughput. Depending on the control signals, each FFT stage can either compute the butterfly or bypass the calculations allowing configurable FFT sizes. IFFT is computed using forward VR-FFT, employing coefficient interchange and scaling techniques as in Fig. 9. To process all patches in a layer, the INV-FFT module runs the FFT operation $OC \times N \times PN^2$ times continuously as programmed by the driver. Additionally, the output buffer uses the discard size to choose only the last $(PS - FS + 1) \times (PS - FS + 1)$ data points for the activation layer.

Activation and Pooling Layers. In Spectral-Blaze, multiple activation functions are implemented as combinational logic and selected by the selection bits of the control register. The output of the activation function is then directed to the pooling unit. This pooling unit maintains the necessary state information of ofmap to perform inter-patch pooling. Both the activation unit and the pooling

Table 3. Break-up of FPGA Resources in XCZU7CG

Module	BRAM(18k)	URAM	FF	DSP	LUT
HPG	80	96	32644	768	75233
FWD-FFT	132	0	33089	84	34094
INV-FFT	112	0	28257	88	29954
Total	324	96	93990	940	139281
% of utilisation	51.84	100	18.65	54.40	60.56

unit are internal components of the IFFT module, and the write transactions of this module to DRAM are limited to the output of the pooling layer. Fully connected layers are not considered in the scope of this work.

Static Mapper and Runtime Driver. The static mapper is used to determine the optimal FFT parameters and tiling schedules for a given CNN layer. The mapper computes the tile sizes for each operand with the stationary scheme and available on-chip memory. A runtime driver is developed to configure the relevant AXI-Lite control registers, enabling the transmission of the deduced control parameters to the HW blocks.

4   Results and Discussions

The experiments were carried out for the inference workflow of widely used CNN models such as VGG-16, AlexNet, ResNet, and ZFNet for comparison of performance/energy with state of the art spatial and FFT-based accelerators. Spectral-Blaze architecture is implemented in the Iwave Zynq MPSoC (xczu7cg) development kit with Float16 (FP16) arithmetic. Importantly, the convolution output of the proposed matches that of spatial convolution, limited only by the precision of FP16, and no accuracy loss is observed in classification problems with a subset of the Imagenet dataset. The architecture offers resource scalability, the current configuration features a 128-element CMAC array. Details of the distribution of resources between modules are presented in Table 3.

Table 4. Comparison against FFT-based baseline: Zhang et al. [12]

Layer	VGG-16 (5 layers) runtime (ms)		Alexnet runtime (ms)	
	Zhang et al.	Proposed	Zhang et al.	Proposed
CONV1	32.74	0.88	17.17	2.25
CONV2	46.48	9.74	7.94	0.93
CONV3	82.75	5.84	4.50	0.36
CONV4	82.90	11.20	6.71	0.46
CONV5	18.40	4.59	4.49	0.38
Total	263.27	32.26	40.81	4.39
Speed-up		8.16		9.30

Table 5. Comparison against FFT-based baseline: Yixin [14]

	Yixin		Proposed	
	VGG-16	Alexnet	VGG-16	Alexnet
Activity Count Based Energy Estimate (GLB+SPAD+NOC+MACS)				
nano Joules	1.20E+08	1.31E+07	2.37E+07	4.80E+06
Normalized	5.05	2.72	-	-
Performance				
Initiation Interval (Cycles)	1.39E+09	3.12E+07	2.80E+08	1.90E+07
Initiation Interval(Seconds)	6.97	0.16	1.40	0.09
Normalized	4.98	1.64	-	-
Energy-Delay Product				
In Joule*Sec	8.34E-01	2.04E-03	3.32E-02	4.56E-04
Normalized	25.14	4.47	-	-

4.1 Experimental Setup

Spectral-Blaze is compared with state-of-the-art FFT-based accelerator. Taking into account the scarcity of flexible dataflow architectures in frequency domain, state-of-the-art spatial accelerators such as Eyeriss, Flexflow and MAERI have been simulated within the MAESTRO [17] analytical tool. For a fair comparison, these simulated architectures have an equivalent number of MACs, L2, and L1 memory sizes to the combined requirements of FFT, IFFT, and HPG modules. (1 $CMAC \approx 3MAC$). With adequate pipelining, the designated device we've chosen enables Spectral-Blaze to achieve a maximum clock speed of 200 MHz. We have considered a batch size of 20 real frames in all our experiments.

4.2 Performance Benchmark-Frequency Domain Accelerator

As discussed in Sect. 1.1, most frequency domain accelerators consider only single channel convolution except [12–15]. The architectures mentioned in [13,15] use precision approximations and are not directly comparable to our work. Therefore, we have used the results reported by [12,14] for comparison with the proposed as given in Table 4 and 5. The proposed accelerator achieves a speed up of 8.16× and 9.30× over [12] while running inference on VGG-16 and AlexNet. Spectral-Blaze uses only 28.51% more equivalent Xilinx resources than [12]. Compared to a more recent work, Yixin, the proposed work achieves an improvement of 25.14× and 4.47× in the Energy Delay Product (EDP) for VGG-16 and Alexnet using equivalent area.

Table 6. Energy/Performance Comparison against flexible dataflow architectures

Eyeriss Like (w/o compress)				Maeri Like				Flexflow				Proposed			
VGG 16	Alex net	Res net18	ZF Net	VGG 16	Alex net	Res net18	ZF Net	VGG 16	Alex net	Res net18	ZF Net	VGG 16	Alex net	Res net18	ZF Net
Activity Count Based Energy Estimate in millijoules (GLB+SPAD+NOC+MACS)															
38.6	4.2	3.2	3.6	113	19.1	9.8	15.9	35.1	4.2	3	3.3	23.7	4.8	2.5	4.2
Performance (Initiation interval expressed in million clock cycles)															
4100	91.8	129	84.5	8290	206	283	196	3961	89.0	125	81.9	280	19	33.9	32.3
Performance (Initiation interval expressed in seconds)															
20.50	0.46	0.65	0.43	41.45	1.03	1.42	0.98	19.80	0.45	0.62	0.41	1.40	0.10	0.17	0.16
Energy-Delay Product (millijoule*Sec)															
790	1.9	2.1	1.5	4680	19.7	13.9	15.6	696.8	1.9	1.8	1.4	33.2	0.5	0.4	0.7
Normalized to the proposed (improvement in ×)															
23.8	4.23	4.98	2.26	140.92	43.05	33.39	22.86	20.98	4.05	4.52	1.98	-	-	-	-

4.3   Performance/Energy Benchmark- Flexible Spatial Accelerators

Table 6 presents performance and energy comparisons between the proposed and flexible dataflow spatial accelerators. In VGG-16, Alexnet, ResNet-18, and ZFNet, the proposed accelerator achieves an average speedup of 6.47×, 6.25×, and 13.71× compared to Eyeriss, Flexflow, and MAERI for various layers. As a result of reduced data traffic, the proposed accelerator achieves an average energy improvement of 1.17×, 1.09×, and 4.13× over the aforementioned. Notably, the proposed method greatly benefits from layers with ample reuse opportunities and large weight sizes. Spectral-Blaze attains an impressive 100% reuse for tensors with the highest opportunities for reuse. Tiling only impacts tensors with lower reuse potential, effectively leveraging most reuse opportunities across the entire network, resulting in reduced DRAM access.

5   Conclusion

Spectral-Blaze achieves a speedup of 4.98× for VGG-16 and 1.64× for AlexNet compared to the existing state-of-the-art frequency domain accelerator. The EDP varies between 4.47 − 25.14× compared to Yixin. It achieves an 8.82× average improvement over Eyeriss and an 7.87× improvement over Flexflow in EDP while having a similar hardware configuration. The proposed tiling scheme maintains reuse factors across dimensions, offering more opportunities for reuse, and only performs tiling in the dimensions with the lowest reuse.

Disclosure of Interests. The authors have no competing interests to declare that are relevant to the content of this article.

References

1. Chen, Y.-H., Krishna, T., Emer, J.S., Sze, V.: Eyeriss: an energy-efficient reconfigurable accelerator for deep convolutional neural networks. IEEE J. Solid-State Circuits **52**(1), 127–138 (2017)
2. Kwon, H., Samajdar, A., Krishna, T.: MAERI: enabling flexible dataflow mapping over DNN accelerators via reconfigurable interconnects. SIGPLAN Not. **53**(2), 461–475 (2018)
3. Lu, W., Yan, G., Li, J., Gong, S., Han, Y., Li, X.: Flexflow: a flexible dataflow accelerator architecture for convolutional neural networks. In: 2017 IEEE International Symposium on High Performance Computer Architecture (HPCA), pp. 553–564 (2017)
4. Du, Z., et al.: Shidiannao: shifting vision processing closer to the sensor. In: 2015 ACM/IEEE 42nd Annual International Symposium on Computer Architecture (ISCA), pp. 92–104 (2015)
5. Abtahi, T., Kulkarni, A., Mohsenin, T.: Accelerating convolutional neural network with FFT on tiny cores. In: 2017 ISCAS. IEEE (2017)
6. Zhou, G., Zhou, J., Lin, H.: Research on NVIDIA deep learning accelerator. In: 2018 12th IEEE International Conference on Anti-counterfeiting, Security, and Identification (ASID), pp. 192–195 (2018)
7. Sze, V., Chen, Y.-H., Yang, T.-J., Emer, J.S.: Efficient processing of deep neural networks: a tutorial and survey. Proc. IEEE **105**(12), 2295–2329 (2017)
8. Kao, S.-C., Krishna, T.: GAMMA. In: Proceedings of the 39th International Conference on Computer-Aided Design. ACM (2020)
9. Abtahi, T., Shea, C., Kulkarni, A., Mohsenin, T.: Accelerating convolutional neural network with FFT on embedded hardware. IEEE Trans. VLSI Syst. **26**, 1737–1749 (2018)
10. Ding, C., et al.: CirCNN: accelerating and compressing deep neural networks using block-circulant weight matrices, volume Part F131207, pp. 395–408. IEEE Computer Society (2017)
11. Chitsaz, K., Hajabdollahi, M., Karimi, N., Samavi, S., Shirani, S.: Acceleration of convolutional neural network using FFT-based split convolutions (2020)
12. Zhang, C., et al.: Frequency domain acceleration of convolutional neural networks on CPU-FPGA shared memory system. In: Proceedings of the 2017 ACM/SIGDA International Symposium on Field-Programmable Gate Arrays, FPGA 2017, pp. 35–44. Association for Computing Machinery, New York (2017)
13. Zeng, H., Chen, R., Zhang, C., Prasanna, V.: A framework for generating high throughput CNN implementations on FPGAS. In: Proceedings of the 2018 ACM/SIGDA International Symposium on FPGA, FPGA 2018, pp. 117–126. Association for Computing Machinery, New York (2018)
14. Liu, B., Liang, H., Wu, J., Chen, X., Liu, P., Han, Y.: Accelerating convolutional neural networks in frequency domain via kernel-sharing approach. In: 2023 28th Asia and South Pacific Design Automation Conference (ASP-DAC), pp. 733–738 (2023)
15. Sun, W., Zeng, H., Yang, Y.E., Prasanna, V.: Throughput-optimized frequency domain CNN with fixed-point quantization on FPGA. In: 2018 International Conference on ReConFigurable Computing and FPGAs (ReConFig), pp. 1–8 (2018)

16. Alizadeh Vahid, K., Prabhu, A., Farhadi, A., Rastegari, M.: Butterfly transform: an efficient FFT based neural architecture design. In: 2020 IEEE/CVF CVPR, Los Alamitos, CA, USA, pp. 12021–12030. IEEE Computer Society (2020)
17. Kwon, H., Chatarasi, P., Sarkar, V., Krishna, T., Pellauer, M., Parashar, A.: MAE-STRO: a data-centric approach to understand reuse, performance, and hardware cost of DNN mappings. IEEE Micro **40**(3), 20–29 (2020)

Special Session: Collaborative Research Projects

Trusted Computing Architectures for IoT Devices

An Braeken[1]($\boxtimes$)(iD), Bruno da Silva[1](iD), Laurent Segers[1](iD), Johannes Knödtel[2](iD), Marc Reichenbach[2](iD), Cornelia Wulf[3](iD), Sergio Pertuz[3](iD), Diana Göhringer[3](iD), Jo Vliegen[4](iD), Md Masoom Rabbani[4](iD), and Nele Mentens[4](iD)

[1] VUB, Brussels, Belgium
an.braeken@vub.be
[2] Institute of Applied Microelectronics and Computer Engineering, University of Rostock, Rostock, Germany
[3] Adaptive Dynamic Systems, TU Dresden, Dresden, Germany
[4] ES&S, COSIC, KU Leuven, Diepenbeek, Belgium

Abstract. Industry has been the tireless engine of prosperity. The introduction of the Internet acts as a booster to this engine, but, unfortunately, where money goes, crime follows. Big corporations spend a lot of money to secure their IT systems. Although Internet of Things (IoT) devices are not as big nor powerful as these IT systems, their power comes from their vast number. This is even more true if these devices are connected to the Internet. Industrial automation has adopted these IoT devices in the Industrial Internet of Things (IIoT), giving yet another boost to growth. However, the effort to secure IoT devices is nearly bleak in comparison to industry's IT infrastructure. This work has the aim to illustrate that this does not need to be the case. In Trusted IoT, existing ideas in academia are translated into concrete use cases. Four use cases are handled: Environmental monitoring, IIoT on Coarse-Grained Reconfigurable Architectures (CGRAs), mobile robots and RISC-V driven unmanned aerial vehicles. Details are provided on the proof-of-concept implementations and results, addressing the security threats identified in the adversary model. Our findings highlight that solutions for securing IoT devices are feasible and achievable by focusing on the architectural level.

Keywords: IoT · Security · Architectures

1 Introduction

The digital explosion has fundamentally changed our lives in just over two decades. The digital revolution changed communication, transportation, and healthcare drastically, among many other fields. In particular, the use and advent of Industrial Internet of Things (IIoT) devices propelled industrial automation exponentially. This advancement is driven not only by the interconnection of billions of devices incorporated in industrial networks but also by exchanging,

I. Skliarova et al. (Eds.): ARC 2024, LNCS 14553, pp. 241–254, 2024.
https://doi.org/10.1007/978-3-031-55673-9_17

analyzing, and utilizing information thereby building a holistic and interlaced environment for future industries. Thanks to the low cost of internet connectivity, every device will have access to the internet within the next decade[1]. This vast pool of interconnected devices broadens the opportunity for better business and ease of life but also attracts the attention of cybercriminals.

While big corporations spend billions of dollars for the security of their systems, small IoT infrastructures often face negligence in terms of security and privacy. However, these systems deal with sensitive, private data. Although these systems are not too powerful, there are many. Thus, cyber-attacks on these devices can lead to a catastrophe. In the past decade, we have experienced that hackers often target the IoT devices employed in smart home systems and turn them into cyber zombies to mount large-scale Distributed Denial of Service (DDoS) attacks on critical infrastructures of government sites. There is an adage saying that a chain is no stronger than its weakest link. This also holds for IoT devices. Therefore, it is of utmost importance that all devices provide a decent level of protection against cyber criminals.

In the TrustedIoT project, the focus lies on the hardware aspect of the security. The project innovation has two main focuses. One is integrating and evaluating existing hardware-assisted security solutions. The other is developing new solutions on various platforms to address the identified security requirements inherent in the application domain. As a result, the resulting devices can offer protection against different types of attackers, even with physical access to the devices. This is a realistic assumption, given that these devices are often in remote and potentially hostile environments. The use cases are chosen in different application domains and contain different architectural properties, such as intensive internal/external memory access, real-time processing requirements, computation-intensive algorithms, and specific interfacing requirements.

The four use cases and corresponding technologies being studied are as follows:

- Environmental monitoring based on low-end platforms.
- Industrial IoT on a platform of Coarse-Grained Reconfigurable Architectures (CGRAs). CGRAs are reconfigurable processing platforms that represent an intermediate solution between the highly efficient Field Programmable Gate Arrays (FPGAs) and flexible General Purpose Processors (GPPs).
- Mobile robots based on industry-related heterogeneous processing systems.
- Unmanned aerial vehicles using multi-core RISC-V platforms.

The remainder of this paper will first give a motivation for each use case in Sect. 2. Next, Sect. 3–6 will elaborate on each use case individually. Finally, conclusions are drawn, and a short glance at future work is given in Sect. 7.

---

[1] https://www.microsoft.com/en-us/research/uploads/prod/2017/03/Seven-Properties-of-Highly-Secure-Devices-1st-Edition.pdf.

2   Motivation

The project TrustedIoT focuses on ensuring the security of IoT devices by developing and demonstrating best practices for hardware-based security modules. We compare and evaluate existing solutions, including commercially available modules and academic proposals, to identify their shortcomings for resource-constrained IoT devices. Our approach involves building a hybrid architecture that addresses these shortcomings through a bottom-up approach to create a trusted computing architecture.

To this end, we highlight our findings based on four use cases that focus on:

1. Environmental sensing: exploiting the trusted executing environment (TEE) to implement a secure key agreement protocol and guarantee the authentication of the data from the platform's sensors (including GPS).
2. Industrial IoT: implementing an end-to-end flow for CGRAs with multi-tenancy, privilege separation and memory protection in mind.
3. Mobile robots: providing access control of software tasks to hardware accelerators on a shared FPGA.
4. Unmanned Aerial Vehicles: substituting all micro-controllers with open-source counterparts on one shared FPGA.

As part of the objectives of the CORNET (COllective Research NETworking) call, proof-of-concept implementations are developed for specific use cases. Knowledge is shared with our industrial partners, enabling them to stay at the forefront of cybersecurity research. In the next sections, we describe for each of the use cases the general concept, related work, adversary model, Proof of Concept (PoC) and results.

3   Use Case 1: Environmental Sensing

Environmental monitoring allows us to keep track of the current state of the environment and to draw trends spanning over a longer time frame. The sensing options include, among other things, temperature, humidity levels, acoustics, light irradiance, visual images, vibrations and air quality. Combining the current sensed values with the current location and time with an integrated GPS module offers location and time-aware monitoring, and thus a fine-grained analysis. Once captured, the samples are processed and transmitted to a remote server (Fig. 1). The capturing of the samples is typically obtained by means of low-power embedded devices with limited available memory and power. Therefore, these devices typically do not integrate the available security features present in nowadays modern computer technologies. However, data privacy and authenticity, and the ability to remotely update the firmware are playing an increasing role in remote embedded applications. Therefore, our aim is to investigate affordable hardware-assisted security mechanisms for secure remote monitoring applications.

Related Work. There are a lot of papers in the literature on building sensor networks for air quality and environmental monitoring. Some do not even include

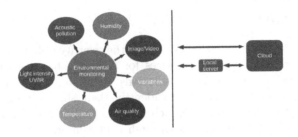

Fig. 1. Environmental monitoring system topology

security measurements [18]. In contrast, others implement only basic security, mainly on the application level, to ensure secure transmission of the IoT data over the network [12]. In [17], a flexible IoT middleware is proposed to offer end-to-end security and deal at the same time with session resumptions in case of intermittent network conditions. However, again the security is implemented at the application level.

As far as the authors are aware, we did not find any papers describing the development of a secure environmental monitoring platform, where security at the hardware level is included for establishing a secure connection. In particular, guaranteeing the authenticity of the GPS module at hardware level has not been described earlier.

Adversary Model. As the sensing devices are aught to be set out in unsupervised environments, there are several potential security risks:

- Attacks via the communication channel between the remote server and the sensing device. This includes reading the data by a third party, spoofing malicious data and jamming the communication means.
- Physical intrusion by opening the casing of the device and trying to derive the key material.
- Moving the device to another location and thus deceiving the GPS module.
- Reprogramming and/or reconfiguring the sensing device with malicious firmware.

Appropriate encryption and hashing are required to guarantee data privacy and authenticity between the sensing devices and the remote server. On the embedded device, the encryption key must be securely stored to avoid data spoofing. On the other hand, a sufficiently strong hashing mechanism needs to be provided such that data alteration between the two parties can be detected. Remotely placed embedded systems can also suffer from communication media operating improperly. Usually this could be the result of a broken channel, but also be the result of intentional jamming between the devices and the remote server. Storing the data locally onto non-volatile memory temporarily alleviates communication failure. However, embedded microcontrollers are typically constrained in available on-chip flash memory, resulting in the requirement of a secure, non-volatile off-chip memory. Also a mutual authentication and key agreement protocol is required to securely update the firmware.

Proof of Concept (PoC). The device we develop allows us to measure sound pressure levels (SPL), vibrations, temperature and humidity, and light irradiance. Besides the attached sensors, an onboard L96-M33 GPS module [19] allows us to compute the location and obtain an accurate time stamp. An SD-card module and a USB connector, respectively, allow the local storage of the captured samples and mimic the transfer of the processed samples to an attached computer. The embedded sampling and pre-processing are done via the PIC32CM5164LS0064 microcontroller manufactured by Microchip [16]. This microcontroller is based on the ARM-Cortex M23 and possesses many hardware-enabled security features such as (but not limited to):

- Data privacy via encryption methods, including AES-128/192 and 256, GCM and data authenticity via hashing methods such as SHA-128 and 256.
- A true random generator that is based on a silicon or device-specific entropy source and that is guaranteed to be unique and unclonable for each device.
- Trusted Execution Environment via TrustZone. TrustZone allows one to compartment the application in secure and non-secure code sections, mitigating the risks of malicious firmware execution.
- Trusted peripherals: many peripherals, including the many communication busses required by the sensors, the RTC, the different clock mechanisms, and some input-outputs (IOs).
- SHA or HMAC-based secure boot that allows authentication of the user boot loader image. When the authentication fails, the microcontroller re-initiates the boot process until successful authentication.

The devices are designed with custom printed circuit boards (PCBs), allowing us the full flexibility of peripheral selection. Moreover, the custom design allows the integration of a power measurement circuit for both the microprocessor and the attached sensors. Safe key storage for data encryption allows private communication between the embedded device and the remote computer. However, a key agreement scheme is required to safely operate remote updates onto the device, with new encryption keys being generated at regular intervals. Therefore, a crypto-authentication integrated circuit (i.e. ATSHA204A, [15]) from Microchip is attached to the microcontroller and allows the computation of a challenge-response for a secure key agreement protocol for symmetric keys used in AES-256. The trusted peripherals, and especially the trusted input-output (IO), allow to detect the physical intrusion on the embedded device in the secure code application. Once an intrusion is detected, the embedded devices are considered compromised and stop transmitting data to the remote computer.

Results. The communication between the embedded system and the remote computer requires between 34 and 80 bytes to transmit all sensory data. The AES-256 encryption and the SHA-256 hashing, respectively, require an additional 17 to 32 bytes and a fixed 32 bytes, totaling up to 64 bytes. Given the average of 64 data bytes, the data privacy and authentication requires, on average, 50% of the packet size transmitted between the microcontroller and the remote computer.

The ARM-Cortex M23 family implements the TrustZone functionality. The application code written in the non-secure part communicates with the code residing in the secure part via "veneer"-function calls. This function calls the secure code to verify many parameters, such as the validity of the arguments and the address space of the caller method. Only 3 different function calls of this type are implemented. The preliminary results show that the additional execution penalty for these function calls is limited between 100 and 1000 clock cycles and is negligible (1% to 3%) compared to the execution of the complete application.

However, the TrustZone requires the provision of enough memory space for both the secure and the non-secure application parts. The allocated memory space (flash and SRAM) usable by the application is thus much lower compared to the same application without TrustZone. In our implementation, 25% of the memory space (both flash and SRAM) is allocated to the secure code, while 75% is allocated to the non-secure part. The PIC32CM5164LS0064 micronctroller has the hardware-supported functionality to run code in a trusted environment. The MPLab X IDE toolchain provided by the manufacturer allows the configuration and programming of secure and non-secure application parts. The Harmony plugin, together with the Microchip Code Configurator, allows for fast application prototyping on the Microchip microcontroller. However, developing the application with TrustZone still has a steep learning curve associated with the trusted execution, impacting the development time of embedded applications.

4   Use Case 2: Mobile Robots

Mobile robots that exploit hardware acceleration while operating in an untrusted environment must prevent illegal access to their hardware accelerators. On the software side, hypervisors allow to isolate trusted from untrusted guest operating systems. On the hardware side, fine-grained isolation mechanisms that allow the shared usage of hardware accelerators are lacking. In this use case, we provide a mechanism that enables data isolation for the shared usage of hardware accelerators by software tasks and prevents unauthorized access from malicious software tasks. The proposed solution focuses on hardware accelerators that are used in a hardware/software co-design and are accessed via AXI memory-mapped interfaces.

Related Work. Many research works target the protection of hardware accelerators, e.g., against cloning attacks, reverse engineering, hardware trojans or side-channel attacks [23]. Equally important is the protection of the communication between processor and hardware accelerators. Huffmire et al. [10] propose logical and physical isolation between IP cores combined with an interconnect tracing technique. Deb Nath et al. [5] provide a centralized reconfigurable security policy engine in combination with security wrappers around each IP core and a design-for-debug infrastructure interface. Mbongue et al. [13] transfer the Mandatory Access Control (MAC) policy implemented in SELinux to hardware accelerators. A software security server is combined with a hardware controller added to each accelerator that manages the access permission. None of the presented works tackles data isolation of hardware accelerators shared dynamically by several software tasks.

Adversary Model. This use case targets adversaries in the form of malicious software tasks that invade the address space of a hardware accelerator assigned to a different task. The adversary can tamper with data, steal the results or impair the execution of a hardware accelerator and so pose a threat to the confidentiality, integrity, or availability of the associated data.

Proof of Concept (PoC). The concept of virtual FPGAs (vFPGAs) is introduced in order to control access to hardware accelerators. Each software task is given a virtual view of the FPGA that only includes the hardware accelerators required by the task. The realization of vFPGAs builds upon the isolation mechanisms provided by the L4Re operating system framework [1]. The IO server of L4Re is used to set up a virtual bus from each task to its vFPGA that includes a virtual memory-mapped I/O (MMIO) address range. The MMIO addresses contain address ranges for the data exchange with hardware accelerators as well as addresses to communicate with the hardware task scheduler.

The hardware task scheduler controls access to hardware accelerators in a dynamic way and so can react to changing requirements of software tasks. The hardware task scheduler is an IP core that operates within spatial and temporal constraints. When a task requires hardware acceleration, it sends a request to the hardware task scheduler. The hardware task scheduler identifies the requesting software task by its unique MMIO address. By considering available accelerators as well as their workloads, the scheduler maps the physical address of the chosen accelerator to a virtual address range of the software task. It adds this entry into the translation table of a custom memory management unit for the programmable logic (PLMMU). As demonstrated in Fig. 2, the PLMMU is inserted into the read and write address channels of the AXI4-Lite bus to translate virtual into physical addresses. As soon as an entry exists in the translation table, the software task can periodically use the assigned hardware accelerator without further requests from the scheduler. Shared usage of hardware accelerators is reached by assigning disjoint physical address ranges to software tasks. Priority

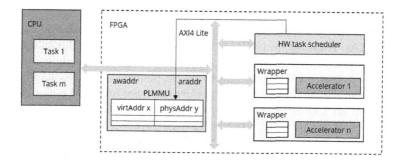

Fig. 2. Access control with the PLMMU and the hardware task scheduler

queues located in the wrapper of each hardware accelerator ensure compliance with the tasks' priorities.

If a task writes to an MMIO address that it has no access rights to, the task receives an exception. The same applies if a task is written to the scheduler's MMIO address assigned to a different task. In this way, unauthorized access of software tasks to hardware accelerators is prevented, ensuring the security of critical components.

Results. The virtualization layer was evaluated with encryption cores encrypting data of varying sizes. Figure 3 demonstrates that the PLMMU adds negligible overhead to the communication between software task and hardware accelerator (in the worst case 22 clock cycles, corresponding to 0.48%) compared to a system that does not provide any access control for the hardware accelerator.

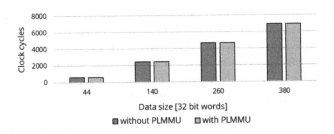

Fig. 3. Overhead induced by the PLMMU

5   Use Case 3: Industrial Internet of Things

The term "Industry 4.0" encompasses a range of modern digital technologies applied in industrial production. These technologies often involve the monitoring, aggregation, and analysis of sensor and process data, utilizing edge or cloud computing platforms. In many instances, local preprocessing of data is necessary to manage the bandwidth demands of sensors, especially in data-intensive scenarios like computer vision. This requirement underlines the need for computing architectures designed for high-volume data applications.

One such class of architectures are CGRAs. CGRAs consist of a grid of Processing Elements (PEs) connected through an interconnect, echoing the principles of FPGAs. However, in CGRAs, these elements offer less flexibility and are more coarse-grained. The specific functionalities and programmability of the PEs and the interconnect vary according to the implementation. CGRAs blend the adaptability of FPGAs with superior performance per area and power efficiency, making them an appealing choice for relevant tasks in Industry 4.0 settings. In Fig. 4, a block diagram is shown to highlight the structural differences. Industrial environments typically encompass a broad spectrum of security concerns, with key priorities being the availability of systems, the safety of operations, and the confidentiality of trade secrets. In our specific use case, we address the challenges

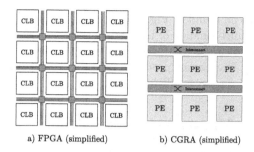

a) FPGA (simplified)   b) CGRA (simplified)

Fig. 4. Systematic comparison between FPGAs and CGRAs.

associated with multi-tenancy in connected systems that utilize CGRAs. This situation presents similar security concerns to those encountered with FPGAs in the same domain. Notable among these are the need for robust memory protection between firmware modules from different vendors, mitigation of potential side-channel attacks, and ensuring the consistent availability and reliability of the system. Addressing these issues is crucial for maintaining the integrity and security of CGRA-based industrial systems.

While CGRAs share some security concerns with FPGA systems, these aspects are not yet thoroughly explored in the context of CGRAs. A deeper investigation into these security concerns could provide valuable insights for the application of CGRAs in Industry 4.0.

Our focus is on heterogeneous data processing systems that typically incorporate a processor for control, monitoring, and connectivity functions. These systems often integrate a processor running system software alongside an accelerator for data processing.

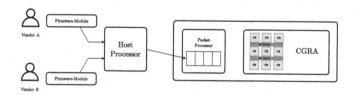

Fig. 5. Simplified block diagram of the HERA architecture design.

System Model. The architecture we employ is the VCGRA, an overlay architecture for FPGAs, developed by Fricke et al. [8]. This CGRA implementation has been selected for its alignment with our project's requirements. To enhance the security and ensure effective component isolation within such a system, we plan to adopt the HERA methodology, as introduced by Holzinger et al. [9].

In our system model, the HERA methodology is employed as a comprehensive end-to-end flow designed specifically for heterogeneous systems like ours. An overview of this can be found in Fig. 5. Central to this methodology is its capability to facilitate multi-tenancy of isolated workloads. This is achieved through the implementation of a hardware scheduling and dispatching unit, known as a "packet processor". The packet processor plays a crucial role in allocating and controlling access to resources efficiently.

6   Use Case 5: Unmanned Aerial Vehicles

Today's Unmanned Aerial Vehicles, commonly referred to as drones, contain multiple microprocessors with varying capabilities. The processor that runs the flight computer is much more potent than the one that is present in the electronic speed controller (ESC). The complete vehicle is as secure as its weakest link. Verifying the "health-status" of all these processors through attestation protocols is a cumbersome task, let alone the fact that it does not scale. In this use case, all processors are replaced by RISC-V alternatives and moved within a single FPGA. This substantially reduces the required effort for attestation.

Related Work. Typically, collective attestation employs a spanning tree overlay to propagate attestation requests and collect aggregated results at the root node [2,3]. However, this mechanism relies on centralized verification, which poses challenges. To address these challenges, researchers proposed a fair distribution of the verification process among different devices [7,14,20].

In order to achieve attestation of a single device, as part of these attestation schemes, we simplify collective attestation of multiple microprocessors hosted on an FPGA to a one-device-only attestation.

Proof of Concept (PoC). To strengthen the security of a drone, in this use case all microprocessors are moved within a single FPGA, as illustrated in Fig. 6. To keep the use case feasible within the project, three microprocessors are considered. For each of these three, a similar RISC-V implementation is sought. These implementations replace the existing microprocessor. This effort maximizes the compatibility with the already available solutions from the industry. The three selected processors are: 1) the flight controller, implemented on an ibex [11]; 2) the communication core, implemented on a NeoRV32 [22]; and 3) the ESC, implemented on a PicoRV32 [4].

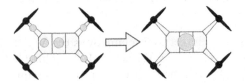

Fig. 6. Centralisation of microprocessors by replacing them with RISC-V implementations on an FPGA

With the entire design of the drone on a single FPGA, attestation is simplified. This is achieved by performing a readback of the configuration memory, as was discussed in earlier work [21].

The substitution of the three microprocessors by their RISC-V implementations is straightforward. To realize the intended protection, one additional, independent core is installed: the embedded hardware security module (eHSM). The latter contains a microprocessor for management and attestation functionality, a crypto coprocessor, and measures for multi-tenancy protection. As multiple parties are present on the same device, this could also introduce a new attack vector [6]. To protect the eHSM, lessons from cloud multi-tenancy are incorporated. These components are shown in Fig. 7.

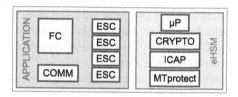

Fig. 7. Architecture of the FPGA implementation. The "Application" houses the Flight Computer (FC), the communication core (COMM) and the four ESCs. The "eHSM" includes a processor (μP), the crypto core, ICAP readback functionality and protection for Multi-Tenancy.

Adversary Model. We have considered an active adversary with the following capabilities.

- Software Adversary: A software adversary can inject malware into the system firmware and perform replay attacks by sending old attestation values to the verifier.
- Communication Adversary: A communication adversary can perform read/write on any data and perform read operation to the processor's instructions. Additionally, it can also forge communication data between different sensors.
- Hardware adversary: A hardware adversary can add or remove sensors on the FPGA platform, or tap signals outside of the FPGA. Nonetheless, while prevention or mitigation of the hardware adversary is out of the scope of this research, detection is the prime goal.

Assumptions. In this research, We do not consider stealthy, non-intrusive physical attackers, such as side-channel attacks. Additionally, we do not consider threats covering application software or its implementation or supply chain vulnerabilities.

Results. Table 1 shows the very preliminary and still incomplete resource usage. The application only houses the "COMM" core and a single "ESC" core, while the eHSM does not have the "MTprotect" in place. These numbers are generated with Xilinx Vivado v2020.2, targeting a VC707 development board.

Table 1. Preliminary and incomplete results of the FPGA implementation

	Slice LUTs	Slice registers	BRAM	ICAP
Application	1214	2788	9	0
eHSM	577	1524	5	1
Total	4966	4364	14	1

7   Conclusions and Future Work

Providing only security at the application layer is often insufficient to protect against challenging attack scenarios. In particular, when IoT devices are put in the field, one should consider the possibility that the attacker has physical access to the device and might be able to extract the key material, breaking the full security of the scheme. Therefore, it is of utmost importance to include a decent level of hardware protection for the devices.

Integrating hardware security is a challenging task. It requires in-depth knowledge of the underlying hardware structure, which is specific to each type of device. Often, information is missing about the tools and libraries required for addressing the specific security features present on the platform. Therefore, the learning curve for the developer is steep, increasing the time to market of a product. However, once acquired to the platform, a correct and effective use of the security features offered by the platform greatly contributes to the protection of the device.

In this work, four use cases have been presented. All of these share the goal of bringing trust to IoT devices. By translating and combining the knowledge that is present in academia, and porting it to industrial use cases, the industrial motor of our prosperity is more secured. This will boost progress as less money is lost due to criminal activities. Although, even more importantly, the lives of everybody are less vulnerable to threats. For the remainder of the project, all presented use cases will be finalized. Interesting results will be published, and demonstrators will be given on each use case.

Acknowledgements. This work is part of the COllective Research NETworking (CORNET) project "TrustedIOT: Trusted Computing Architectures for IoT Devices". The Belgian partners are funded by VLAIO under grant number HBC.2021.0895, while the German partners are funded by the BMWi (Federal Ministry for Economic Affairs and Energy) under IGF-Project Number 343 EBG.

References

1. L4Re - L4 runtime environment. https://os.inf.tu-dresden.de/L4Re/doc/index. html. Accessed 1 Dec 2023
2. Ambrosin, M., Conti, M., Ibrahim, A., Neven, G., Sadeghi, A.R., Schunter, M.: SANA: secure and scalable aggregate network attestation. In: Proceedings of the 2016 ACM SIGSAC Conference on Computer and Communications Security - CCS 2016 (2016)
3. Asokan, N., et al.: SEDA: scalable embedded device attestation. In: Proceedings of the 22nd ACM SIGSAC Conference on Computer and Communications Security, CCS 2015, pp. 964–975 (2015)
4. Claire Wolf: PicoRV32 - A Size-Optimized RISC-V CPU. https://github.com/ YosysHQ/picorv32. Accessed 1 Dec 2023
5. Deb Nath, A.P., Ray, S., Basak, A., Bhunia, S.: System-on-chip security architecture and cad framework for hardware patch. In: 2018 23rd Asia and South Pacific Design Automation Conference (ASP-DAC), pp. 733–738 (2018). https://doi.org/ 10.1109/ASPDAC.2018.8297409
6. Dessouky, G., Sadeghi, A.R., Zeitouni, S.: SoK: secure FPGA multi-tenancy in the cloud: challenges and opportunities. In: 2021 IEEE European Symposium on Security and Privacy (EuroS&P), pp. 487–506 (2021). https://doi.org/10.1109/ EuroSP51992.2021.00040
7. Dushku, E., Rabbani, M.M., Vliegen, J., Braeken, A., Mentens, N.: Prove: provable remote attestation for public verifiability. J. Inf. Secur. Appl. **75**, 103448 (2023)
8. Fricke, F.: A novel top to bottom toolchain for generating virtual coarse-grained reconfigurable arrays. In: 2021 31st International Conference on Field-Programmable Logic and Applications (FPL), pp. 267–268 (2021). https://doi. org/10.1109/FPL53798.2021.00051
9. Holzinger, P., Reichenbach, M.: The HERA methodology: reconfigurable logic in general-purpose computing. IEEE Access **9**, 147212–147236 (2021). https://doi. org/10.1109/ACCESS.2021.3123874
10. Huffmire, T., et al.: Moats and drawbridges: an isolation primitive for reconfigurable hardware based systems. In: 2007 IEEE Symposium on Security and Privacy (SP 2007), pp. 281–295 (2007). https://doi.org/10.1109/SP.2007.28
11. lowRISC: Ibex RISC-V Core. https://github.com/lowRISC/ibex. Accessed 1 Dec 2023
12. Malche, T., Maheshwary, P., Kumar, R.: Environmental monitoring system for smart city based on secure internet of things (IoT) architecture. Wireless Pers. Commun. **107**(4), 2143–2172 (2019)
13. Mandebi Mbongue, J., Saha, S.K., Bobda, C.: Domain isolation in FPGA-accelerated cloud and data center applications. In: Proceedings of the 2021 on Great Lakes Symposium on VLSI, pp. 283–288 (2021)
14. Mansouri, M., Jaballah, W.B., Önen, M., Rabbani, M.M., Conti, M.: FADIA: fairness-driven collaborative remote attestation. In: Proceedings of the 14th ACM Conference on Security and Privacy in Wireless and Mobile Networks, WiSec 2021, pp. 60–71. Association for Computing Machinery, New York (2021). https://doi. org/10.1145/3448300.3468284
15. Microchip: ATSHA204A, Fast, Secure, and Cost Effective Symmetric Authentication. https://www.microchip.com/en-us/product/atsha204a. Accessed 16 Oct 2023

16. Microchip: PIC32CM5164LS00064. https://www.microchip.com/en-us/product/ PIC32CM5164LS00064. Accessed 8 Dec 2023
17. Mukherjee, B., et al.: Flexible IoT security middleware for end-to-end cloud-fog communication. Futur. Gener. Comput. Syst. **87**, 688–703 (2018)
18. Ouni, R., Saleem, K.: Framework for sustainable wireless sensor network based environmental monitoring. Sustainability **14**(14), 8356 (2022)
19. Quectel: L96 Hardware Design. https://auroraevernet.ru/upload/iblock/36c/ 36c11c043ed14557903899eb54fc4657.pdf. Accessed 2 Oct 2023
20. Rabbani, M.M., Vliegen, J., Winderickx, J., Conti, M., Mentens, N.: Shela: scalable heterogeneous layered attestation. IEEE Internet Things J. **6**(6), 10240–10250 (2019). https://doi.org/10.1109/JIOT.2019.2936988
21. Vliegen, J., Rabbani, M.M., Conti, M., Mentens, N.: SACHa: self-attestation of configurable hardware. In: 2019 Design, Automation & Test in Europe Conference & Exhibition (DATE), pp. 746–751 (2019). https://doi.org/10.23919/DATE.2019. 8714775
22. Zephyr Project memberss and individual contributors: NEORV32. https://github. com/stnolting/neorv32. Accessed 1 Dec 2023
23. Zhang, J., Qu, G.: Recent attacks and defenses on FPGA-based systems. ACM Trans. Reconfigurable Technol. Syst. (TRETS) **12**(3), 1–24 (2019)

PROACT - Physical Attack Resistance of Cryptographic Algorithms and Circuits with Reduced Time to Market

Asmita Adhikary[1], Abraham Basurto[1], Lejla Batina[1], Ileana Buhan[1], Joan Daemen[1], Silvia Mella[1], Nele Mentens[2]([✉]), Stjepan Picek[1], Durga Lakshmi Ramachandran[3], Abolfazl Sajadi[2], Todor Stefanov[2], Dennis Vermoen[3], and Nusa Zidaric[2]

[1] Radboud University, Nijmegen, The Netherlands
[2] Leiden University, Leiden, The Netherlands
n.mentens@liacs.leidenuniv.nl
[3] Riscure, Delft, The Netherlands

Abstract. Electronic devices that populate the Internet of Things play increasingly important roles in our everyday lives. When these devices process, store, or communicate personal or company-critical data, digital security becomes a necessity. However, mechanisms to secure electronic systems have a significant influence on the cost of the system and come with an overhead in energy consumption, computational delay, and (silicon) chip area. Therefore, developing secure electronic systems is a balancing act between minimizing the overhead and maximizing the security. Moreover, in rapidly evolving markets, there is another parameter that can have a negative influence on the security strength of electronic devices, namely the time to market: it takes longer to bring a secure product to the market than to develop a product with no or little security measures in place.

In the PROACT project, we tackle the challenge of maximizing the security strength while minimizing the overhead w.r.t. energy consumption, computational delay, and hardware resources, as well as reducing the time to market of digital electronic systems. We specifically focus on the fast development of efficient cryptographic hardware with protection against physical attacks, i.e., attacks that exploit the physical implementation of cryptographic algorithms. Physical attacks are categorized into (1) side-channel analysis attacks that target the extraction of secret information by monitoring side-channels like the power consumption, the electromagnetic emanation or the timing of the device, and (2) fault analysis attacks that aim at introducing computational errors that lead to the leakage of secret information. Physical security is of vital importance when potential attackers can easily get in the vicinity of an electronic system. This is the case in, e.g., medical sensor devices, wearables and implants, which are typically constrained in energy budget, cost and form factor, and are therefore the perfect use case for the results of PROACT.

Keywords: side-channel analysis · fault analysis · cryptography · hardware security

I. Skliarova et al. (Eds.): ARC 2024, LNCS 14553, pp. 255–266, 2024.
https://doi.org/10.1007/978-3-031-55673-9_18

1   Introduction and Envisioned Contributions

As digital data are omnipresent in our daily lives, the need for digital security is growing rapidly. This is illustrated by popular media frequently reporting on attacks that expose the security flaws of real-life electronic systems. A very powerful type of attack is a physical attack, which exploits the physical implementation of a cryptographic algorithm, as shown in Fig. 1. The first category of physical attacks is side-channel analysis attacks [1], which analyze the information available through side channels, such as the power consumption, the electromagnetic (EM) emanation, or the timing behavior of an electronic system. Another type of physical attack is a fault analysis attack [2], which perturbs the system, e.g., through the injection of a laser beam, a clock glitch, or a power supply glitch, in order to retrieve secret information. Especially for Internet-of-Things (IoT) devices, physical attacks form an underestimated threat and must be dealt with through proper countermeasures.

To achieve the highest level of physical security, protection mechanisms must be foreseen throughout all steps in the knowledge value chain: in the design of cryptographic algorithms, the design of cryptographic circuits, and the physical implementation of cryptographic chips. Additionally, design choices made in one of these steps introduce constraints in other steps, such that interaction between the steps in the chain is indispensable. PROACT covers the entire knowledge value chain in the development of physically secure cryptographic hardware, from algorithms to fabricated chips.

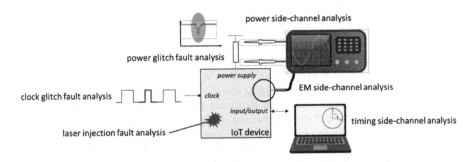

Fig. 1. Examples of physical attacks (i.e., fault analysis and side-channel analysis) on an IoT device.

Since many IoT devices are limited in energy/power consumption and computing resources, implementing countermeasures is challenging. Manual efforts by experienced designers can be effective but are prone to errors and do not lead to optimal results when the design space is large. Existing design automation tools can optimize towards low energy/power and low resources but do not take into account physical security. **PROACT develops design automation tools with low energy/power consumption, low computational resources, and high physical security strength as optimization goals.**

The IoT market consists of rapidly evolving applications. Therefore, minimizing the time to market of new products and services is crucial to survive for companies that operate in this market segment. However, evaluating the physical security of a cryptographic chip is typically something that is done after the (silicon) chip is fabricated. This makes the elapsed time between the design of a cryptographic algorithm/circuit and the physical security evaluation very long. A weakness detected in the evaluation phase leads to a re-spin of the chip, taking away the competitive advantage of the company that intends to be the first to bring a new IoT application to the market. **PROACT designs, implements, and validates a pre-silicon simulator for physical security to maximize the chances of first-time-right cryptographic chips.**

The aforementioned design automation tools and pre-silicon simulator facilitate our proposed modifications to the traditional design flow for cryptographic hardware as shown in Fig. 2. The physical security simulation becomes a new crucial step in the flow, just before the chip fabrication, because an early feedback on the security strengths of the chip could trigger important physical security related improvements on the cryptographic algorithm/hardware design, thereby significantly reducing the time to market of the chip.

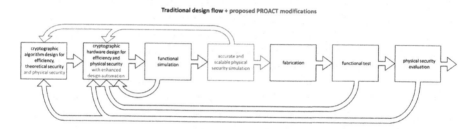

Fig. 2. Proposed modifications to the traditional design flow.

In PROACT we aim to answer the following research questions:

- What are the problems with respect to physical security in existing cryptographic algorithms, and how can we design algorithms that are resilient against physical attacks?
- Which cryptographic circuits have optimal physical security strength, energy consumption, resource occupation, and performance, or an optimal trade-off of these properties?
- How can we use design automation to improve the efficiency and the physical security of cryptographic circuits?
- How can we design a pre-silicon physical security simulator with optimal accuracy and simulation speed?
- How can we use artificial intelligence to improve the accuracy and simulation speed of the pre-silicon simulator?

– Which state-of-the-art and beyond-state-of-the-art analysis methods can be used to perform a systematic evaluation of the developed cryptographic chips and validation of the pre-silicon simulator?

2   Project Goals and Status of the Conducted Research

The research and development work in the PROACT project is divided across four work packages (WP1, WP2, WP3, and WP4), each having their own specific goals that jointly contribute to the main project objectives introduced in Sect. 1.

2.1   WP1: Algorithm Design

The goal of the first work package is to have a process allowing the feedback from the other work packages on the design of cryptographic algorithms and their implementation, in the form of requirements, restrictions and recommendations. Requirements we are thinking of are the following:

– Low latency: applications such as memory or pointer encryption [16] for protection against micro-architectural attacks require low latency: a very short time between the availability of specific inputs (plaintext, ciphertext, memory address, ...) and the output (plaintext or ciphertext). Moreover, the latency of a circuit is correlated to its energy consumption [2,10], so low latency is also a recommendation for lightweight use cases that run on battery power.
– Suitability for masking and threshold implementation: if side channel attacks such as power or electromagnetic analysis are a threat and countermeasures against these attacks at mode level are not an option or undesirable, masking or threshold implementations may be a cost-effective countermeasure. This requirement usually boils down to limiting non-linear operations in the round function to have low algebraic degree.
– Suitability for protection against sophisticated fault attacks like Statistical Ineffective Fault Attacks (SIFA) [13]. One very promising countermeasure is to implement the cipher using the combination of *toffoli* gates and masking as laid out in [8]. Clearly the cipher shall be suited to be implemented efficiently with those building blocks.
– Suitability for instruction/operation shuffling and having equivalent representations. When protecting against power or electromagnetic analysis but also faults, the ability to execute the operations in a round function in different orders, called *shuffling* provides an additional layer of protection on top of masking or threshold implementations. The suitability of a round function for shuffling is strongly determined by the amount of parallelism in the cipher. For example in AES [11] the 16 S-box computations can be done in any order. Equivalent representations are the result of symmetry and can be useful against fault attacks in the presence of redundant computations. The attack vector is then to force the same fault twice and the existence of equivalent representations allows randomizing the *location* where the computation takes place [17].

These are just a few examples and we expect a myriad of requirements, restrictions and recommendations to originate from the other work packages or more in general of the design flow.

2.2   WP2: Circuit Design and Design Automation

We are designing a circuit, nicknamed the PROACT chip, to obtain real measurements (e.g., circuit power consumption, timing performance, etc.) needed for the design of the pre-silicon physical security simulator, and for evaluation and validation of the simulator. Currently, we are designing and selecting benchmark circuits for the PROACT chip. The PROACT chip will allow side-channel analysis of cryptographic software executed on a general-purpose CPU as well as side-channel analysis of custom cryptographic hardware, i.e., cryptographic co-processors. We are also considering protected software and hardware implementations. This approach ensures a holistic evaluation of the security of a system on a chip.

The first version of the PROACT chip, shown in Fig. 3, is currently prototyped on a Field-Programmable Gate Array (FPGA) and will later be fabricated as a dedicated ASIC chip. This design leverages a RISC-V core (Ctrl-RV) and two 32-bit registers (Control Reg and Status Reg) to control the system. The main general-purpose CPU component is a second RISC-V core (SW-RV in Fig. 3) dedicated to executing cryptographic software. We selected the Ibex core for this project, an open-source 32-bit RISC-V CPU written in System Verilog [12]. Furthermore, the PROACT chip will include cryptographic co-processors, such as Ascon [7], Xoodyak [9], and AES [1].

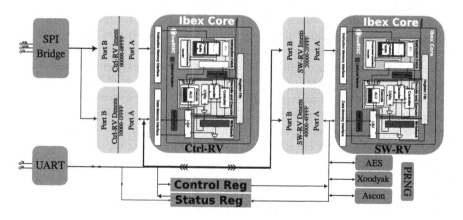

Fig. 3. The PROACT chip block diagram.

The controller (Ctrl-RV) is programmed using the Serial Peripheral Interface protocol (SPI Bridge in Fig. 3). Once initialized, this controller establishes a UART-based communication channel with a host computer for processing commands and controls. For instance, when loading the SW-RV instruction and data memories, the configuration commands need to specify the size and desired start addresses for the SW-RV instruction and data memory segments. When the SW-RV memories are loaded, the Ctrl-RV sets a flag in the Control Reg to activate SW-RV and waits for a specified flag in the Status Reg, indicating that SW-RV completed the execution. Similar control mechanism is implemented for the co-processors. The PROACT chip is designed as a cooperative target and sets appropriate triggers for precise power (or other) trace acquisition.

In parallel to the PROACT chip development, we are evaluating the accuracy and usefulness of power consumption estimation data, obtained from Cadence synthesis tools at different levels of abstraction, for the purpose of physical security evaluation of VLSI circuits. This includes selecting appropriate scope, e.g., circuit submodules and (interface) signals, and signals coverage of the circuit testbenches.

2.3 WP3: Pre-silicon Physical Security Simulator Design

Side-channel attacks that leak sensitive information through a computing device's interaction with its physical environment have proven to severely threaten the security of a device when adversaries have physical access to the device. Traditional approaches for leakage detection measure the physical properties of the device. Hence, they cannot be used during the design process and fail to provide root cause analysis. An alternative approach gaining traction is automating leakage detection by modeling the device. This work package aims to develop a simulator that takes a digital circuit design after synthesis, placement, and routing as input. The goal is to perform simulations of the physical security of the design, i.e., of the side-channel leakage and the effect of a fault injection. Artificial intelligence will enable the fast and accurate simulation of large circuit designs. The input for the training phase will consist of fabricated benchmark circuits and accompanying measurement data for physical security. These benchmark circuits will be selected based on a thorough analysis of the typical components of cryptographic circuits. The PROACT chip, discussed in Sect. 2.2, includes such benchmark circuits that will be measured. The goal is to determine which circuits are the most useful for training the simulator. At the end of the PROACT project, this will lead to guidelines for technology companies to generate the benchmark circuits and make the measurement data available. Following this approach, the technology can be characterized for physical security, and the simulator can be trained for this specific technology.

As a first step in the project, we investigated the state of the art for designing side channel simulators. In this study [6], we classify approaches to automated leakage detection based on the model's source of truth. We organize the existing tools on two main parameters: whether the model includes measurements from a concrete device and the abstraction level of the device specification used for constructing the model. We survey the proposed tools to determine the current knowledge level across the domain and identify open problems. In particular, we highlight the absence of evaluation methodologies and metrics that compare proposals' effectiveness across the field. Our results help practitioners who want to use automated leakage detection and researchers interested in advancing the knowledge and improving automatic leakage detection. In this study, we made an inventory of available tools[1], and we determined the methods for automating leakage detection and summarized open problems. One of the conclusions is that no side channel simulator is available for RISC-V architectures like the one we made in this project. One of our main findings shows that creating a side channel simulator is primarily based on manual work and prohibitively effort-intensive. Capturing microarchitecture events characteristic to complex processors, such as pipeline stalls or misprediction, is an open problem. We found no evidence that AI techniques have been used to automate the manual work required to build a side-channel simulator.

One challenge for using AI techniques is the availability of labeled datasets. The conventional side-channel analysis demands substantial manual effort for setup preparation and trace recording, rendering it more intricate during the dynamic design phase, where software alterations occur frequently. Additionally, limited hardware descriptions and restricted access to process technology information have hindered identifying the specific instruction(s) responsible for leakage. We introduce ABBY [5], an open-source side-channel leakage profiling framework that targets the microarchitectural layer. Existing solutions to characterize the microarchitectural layer are device-specific and require extensive manual effort. ABBY's main innovation is data collection, which can then automatically describe the microarchitectural behavior of a target device and has the additional benefit of being extendable to similar devices. Using ABBY, we created two datasets that capture the interaction of instructions for the ARM CORTEX-M0/M3 architecture. These sets are the first to capture detailed information on the microarchitectural layer. They can be used to explore various leakage models suitable for creating side-channel leakage simulators. These attributes encompassed instruction interactions, operand interactions, pipeline effects, and memory transaction interactions. We delved into linear and nonlinear (predominantly deep learning-based) leakage models with the datasets acquired. The effectiveness of these leakage models was subsequently evaluated and compared using evaluative metrics such as the adjusted R^2, F-test, and actual side-channel attack outcomes. A preliminary evaluation of a leakage model produced with our dataset of real-world cryptographic implementations shows performance comparable to state-of-the-art leakage simulators. To showcase the effectiveness of the ABBY framework and assess the quality of the dataset it produces, we constructed a leakage model based on the ABBY-CM0 dataset. Our comparisons between this model and ELMO yielded strikingly similar results, underscoring the high caliber of the ABBY-CM0 dataset. To examine ABBY's scalability, we curated the ABBY-CM3 dataset. Concurrently, we designed a side-channel power

---

[1] https://ileanabuhan.github.io/Tools/.

simulator targeting the ALU component, drawing insights from the ABBY-CM3 dataset. Compared with the actual board, the simulator's performance was on par, further attesting to the impeccable quality of the ABBY-CM3 dataset.

We performed a similar study considering tools for protecting implementations against fault injection attacks [3]. Fault injection attacks have caused implementations to behave unexpectedly, resulting in a spectacular bypass of security features and even the extraction of cryptographic keys. Developers want to ensure the robustness of the software against faults and eliminate production weaknesses that could lead to exploitation. Several fault simulators that promise cost-effective evaluations against fault attacks have been released. In [3], we set out to discover how suitable such tools are for a developer who wishes to create robust software against fault attacks. We found four open-source fault simulators that employ different techniques to navigate faults, which we objectively compare and discuss their benefits and drawbacks. Unfortunately, none of the four open-source fault simulators use artificial intelligence (AI) techniques. However, AI was successfully applied to improve the fault simulation of cryptographic algorithms, though none of these tools is open source. We suggest improvements to open-source fault simulators inspired by the AI techniques used by cryptographic fault simulators.

2.4   WP4: Evaluation and Validation

Millions of products undergo rigorous security evaluations every day in evaluation laboratories around the world [20]. Testing for side-channel resistance is a key aspect of security evaluations for implementations featuring cryptography. The effort involved in testing is considerable, and the stakes for companies are high [4]. Moreover, cryptographic implementations often go through multiple cycles of leakage evaluation, e.g., as specified in ISO/IEC 17825:2016. Such a process is costly because it requires a high level of expertise and significant manual labor, especially when considering resourceful adversaries [23].

In recent years, developments in deep learning-based side-channel analysis (DLSCA) have made it one of the obvious choices when evaluating/validating the security of devices. While this trend is mostly academic for now, we expect the industry will soon follow with developments of various standards; for instance, there is a new standard draft for minimal requirements for evaluating machine learning-based SCA resistance.[2] In the process of the DLSCA evaluation, there are a number of questions to consider. What AI technique to use? How to tune it? Do we need trace pre-processing or feature engineering? What are the appropriate metrics to evaluate the security? What threat model to assume? How many side-channel measurements are necessary? How does a neural network defeat an implementation with a countermeasure?

Hyperparameter tuning represents one of the central points to achieving powerful deep learning performance, and SCA is no exception, with several directions to follow:

---

[2] Minimum Requirements for Evaluating Machine-Learning based Side-Channel Attack Resistance.

1. Random/grid search. While random/grid search is easy to mount and can give excellent results (like in the current state-of-the-art), one still needs to define appropriate hyperparameter ranges that should be sufficiently small. Additionally, one commonly needs to evaluate many random models to improve the chances of obtaining good models.
2. Advanced tuning techniques. DLSCA investigated techniques like Bayesian optimization [26] and reinforcement learning [21], which exhibit excellent attack performance. Still, such techniques can be computationally expensive and have additional parameters to tune (shifting the problem from tuning the neural network hyperparameters to tuning the search technique parameters).
3. Methodologies. Methodologies can provide a systematic way to build neural networks that perform well in DLSCA. Unfortunately, it is difficult to design a methodology that is easy to follow and works for diverse targets/leakage models/neural network architectures.

It is also necessary to consider what features of side-channel traces will be inputted into neural networks. The first works on machine learning (and template attack) required a precise selection of features, making the effort in the feature engineering phase often much more significant than running the attack itself. Moving to the deep learning techniques brought promise that we require less feature engineering, allowing more time for hyperparameter tuning. As such, the common approach was to consider an interval of features that leaks the most [20]. Still, recent results showed that there is a further benefit when providing raw traces to neural networks, as it is possible to mount even optimal attacks (those that require only a single attack trace), but at the cost of more effort in hyperparameter tuning [18]. Thus, we reached a trade-off between the effort in feature engineering and hyperparameter tuning. Interestingly, the latest works showcased that it is possible to reach optimal attacks even if we provide "only" an interval of features, but then, the neural network architectures must be more complex, even using language models [15]. That being said, using all features is not possible for any profiling attack, as already discussed. Thus, it was shown possible to make a more powerful feature engineering phase based on a novel distance metric customized for SCAs, allowing the template attack to compete or even outperform state-of-the-art DLSCA [25]. Extending this concept further, it is possible to design custom loss functions for DLSCA that consider the most relevant features (e.g., features processed by the deep layers of neural networks) [30]. Finally, an important part of making the attacks more powerful is also understanding why the attacks work, as such knowledge can improve not only the attack perspective but also the future design of countermeasures [19].

Running supervised deep learning-based SCA is not ideal for any attack scenario. Often, it becomes necessary to relax the assumptions on the attacker power and not assume anymore that there is a clone device or that the leakage model is known. One example in that direction is when the adversary possesses a similar implementation that can be used as a white-box reference design [14]. Moreover, recent works show it is possible to move toward non-profiled DLSCA by using the bijective relationship between the plaintexts and a fixed key [27]. Then, by following this, it is possible to mount attacks that even rival profiling DLSCA. Still, this approach can be considered non-profiled but not unsupervised because we still build labels. Luckily, it is possible to move toward non-profiled DLSCA by using, e.g., the multi-regression output approach [22]. Such an approach can be further improved by using techniques like ensembles and data augmentation. On the other hand, it is possible to consider different SCA paradigms, like collision attacks in the DLSCA setting [28]. In settings where we cannot assume the knowledge of leakage models, it is possible to run the attacks in model-free settings [24]. Finally, for settings where the evaluator has only a limited number of profiling traces, it is possible to make such attacks more powerful by examining the relationship between all possible key candidates, which leads to a novel metric describing the generalization power of a profiling model [29].

3   Conclusion and Next Steps

PROACT aims at adding the physical security dimension to the design flow of ASICs, which typically only focuses on the optimization of energy consumption, computational delay and hardware resources. The achieved results so far include (1) the design of a system on chip that is prototyped on an FPGA and almost ready for tape-out, (2) a suitability analysis and comparison of existing physical security simulators, and (3) the improvement of physical attack strategies. Two tape-outs are planned within the project in order to validate the envisioned physical security simulator that will be built within the project.

Acknowledgements. This work was funded by the Dutch Research Council (NWO) through the PROACT project (NWA.1215.18.014).

Disclosure of Interests. The authors have no competing interests to declare that are relevant to the content of this article.

References

1. FIPS 197: Advanced Encryption Standard (AES) (2021). https://doi.org/10.6028/NIST.FIPS.197-upd1
2. Aagaard, M.D., Zidaric, N.: ASIC benchmarking of round 2 candidates in the NIST lightweight cryptography standardization process: (preliminary results). IACR Cryptol. ePrint Arch., p. 49 (2021). https://eprint.iacr.org/2021/049
3. Adhikary, A., Buhan, I.: SoK: assisted fault simulation - existing challenges and opportunities offered by AI. In: Zhou, J., et al. (eds.) ACNS 2023. LNCS, vol. 13907, pp. 178–195. Springer, Cham (2023). https://doi.org/10.1007/978-3-031-41181-6_10
4. Azouaoui, M., et al.: A systematic appraisal of side channel evaluation strategies. In: van der Merwe, T., Mitchell, C., Mehrnezhad, M. (eds.) SSR 2020. LNCS, vol. 12529, pp. 46–66. Springer, Cham (2020). https://doi.org/10.1007/978-3-030-64357-7_3

5. Bazangani, O., Iooss, A., Buhan, I., Batina, L.: ABBY: automating leakage modeling for side-channels analysis. In: Proceedings of the 2024 ACM Asia Conference on Computer and Communications Security (2024, to appear)

6. Buhan, I., Batina, L., Yarom, Y., Schaumont, P.: SoK: design tools for side-channel-aware implementations. In: Suga, Y., Sakurai, K., Ding, X., Sako, K. (eds.) ASIA CCS 2022: ACM Asia Conference on Computer and Communications Security, Nagasaki, Japan, 30 May 2022–3 June 2022, pp. 756–770. ACM (2022). https://doi.org/10.1145/3488932.3517415

7. Christoph Dobraunig, I.: Ascon-a submission to CAESAR. In: 15th Central European Conference on Cryptology, p. 23 (2015)

8. Daemen, J., Dobraunig, C., Eichlseder, M., Groß, H., Mendel, F., Primas, R.: Protecting against statistical ineffective fault attacks. IACR Trans. Cryptogr. Hardw. Embed. Syst. **2020**(3), 508–543 (2020). https://doi.org/10.13154/TCHES.V2020.I3.508-543

9. Daemen, J., Hoffert, S., Peeters, M., Assche, G.V., Keer, R.V.: Xoodyak, a lightweight cryptographic scheme (2020)

10. Daemen, J., Massolino, P.M.C., Mehrdad, A., Rotella, Y.: The subterranean 2.0 cipher suite. IACR Trans. Symmetric Cryptol. **2020**(S1), 262–294 (2020). https://doi.org/10.13154/TOSC.V2020.IS1.262-294

11. Daemen, J., Rijmen, V.: The Design of Rijndael - The Advanced Encryption Standard (AES). Information Security and Cryptography, 2nd edn. Springer, Heidelberg (2020). https://doi.org/10.1007/978-3-662-60769-5

12. Davide Schiavone, P., et al.: Slow and steady wins the race? A comparison of ultra-low-power RISC-V cores for internet-of-things applications. In: 2017 27th International Symposium on Power and Timing Modeling, Optimization and Simulation (PATMOS), pp. 1–8 (2017). https://doi.org/10.1109/PATMOS.2017.8106976

13. Dobraunig, C., Eichlseder, M., Korak, T., Mangard, S., Mendel, F., Primas, R.: SIFA: exploiting ineffective fault inductions on symmetric cryptography. IACR Trans. Cryptogr. Hardw. Embed. Syst. **2018**(3), 547–572 (2018)

14. Karayalcin, S., Krcek, M., Wu, L., Picek, S., Perin, G.: It's a kind of magic: a novel conditional GAN framework for efficient profiling side-channel analysis. Cryptology ePrint Archive, Paper 2023/1108 (2023). https://eprint.iacr.org/2023/1108

15. Kulkarni, P., Verneuil, V., Picek, S., Batina, L.: Order vs. chaos: a language model approach for side-channel attacks. Cryptology ePrint Archive, Paper 2023/1615 (2023). https://eprint.iacr.org/2023/1615

16. LeMay, M., et al.: Cryptographic capability computing. In: MICRO 2021, pp. 253–267. ACM (2021)

17. Miteloudi, K., Batina, L., Daemen, J., Mentens, N.: ROCKY: rotation countermeasure for the protection of keys and other sensitive data. In: Orailoglu, A., Jung, M., Reichenbach, M. (eds.) SAMOS 2021. LNCS, vol. 13227, pp. 288–299. Springer, Cham (2021). https://doi.org/10.1007/978-3-031-04580-6_19

18. Perin, G., Wu, L., Picek, S.: Exploring feature selection scenarios for deep learning-based side-channel analysis. IACR Trans. Cryptogr. Hardw. Embed. Syst. **2022**(4), 828–861 (2022). https://doi.org/10.46586/tches.v2022.i4.828-861. https://tches.iacr.org/index.php/TCHES/article/view/9842

19. Perin, G., Wu, L., Picek, S.: I know what your layers did: layer-wise explainability of deep learning side-channel analysis. Cryptology ePrint Archive, Paper 2022/1087 (2022). https://eprint.iacr.org/2022/1087

20. Picek, S., Perin, G., Mariot, L., Wu, L., Batina, L.: SoK: deep learning-based physical side-channel analysis. ACM Comput. Surv. **55**(11), 1–35 (2023). https://doi.org/10.1145/3569577

21. Rijsdijk, J., Wu, L., Perin, G., Picek, S.: Reinforcement learning for hyperparameter tuning in deep learning-based side-channel analysis. IACR Trans. Cryptogr. Hardw. Embed. Syst. **2021**(3), 677–707 (2021). https://doi.org/10.46586/tches.v2021.i3.677-707. https://tches.iacr.org/index.php/TCHES/article/view/8989

22. Savu, I., Krček, M., Perin, G., Wu, L., Picek, S.: The need for more: unsupervised side-channel analysis with single network training and multi-output regression. Cryptology ePrint Archive, Paper 2023/1681 (2023). https://eprint.iacr.org/2023/1681

23. Shelton, M.A., Samwel, N., Batina, L., Regazzoni, F., Wagner, M., Yarom, Y.: Rosita: towards automatic elimination of power-analysis leakage in ciphers. In: Proceedings 2021 Network and Distributed System Security Symposium. Internet Society, Virtual (2021). https://doi.org/10.14722/ndss.2021.23137. https://www.ndss-symposium.org/wp-content/uploads/ndss2021_4B-3_23137_paper.pdf

24. Wu, L., Ali-pour, A., Rezaeezade, A., Perin, G., Picek, S.: Breaking free: leakage model-free deep learning-based side-channel analysis. Cryptology ePrint Archive, Paper 2023/1110 (2023). https://eprint.iacr.org/2023/1110

25. Wu, L., Perin, G., Picek, S.: The best of two worlds: deep learning-assisted template attack. IACR Trans. Cryptogr. Hardw. Embed. Syst. **2022**(3), 413–437 (2022). https://doi.org/10.46586/tches.v2022.i3.413-437. https://tches.iacr.org/index.php/TCHES/article/view/9707

26. Wu, L., Perin, G., Picek, S.: I choose you: automated hyperparameter tuning for deep learning-based side-channel analysis. IEEE Trans. Emerg. Top. Comput., 1–12 (2022). https://doi.org/10.1109/TETC.2022.3218372

27. Wu, L., Perin, G., Picek, S.: Hiding in plain sight: non-profiling deep learning-based side-channel analysis with plaintext/ciphertext. Cryptology ePrint Archive, Paper 2023/209 (2023). https://eprint.iacr.org/2023/209

28. Wu, L., Tiran, S., Perin, G., Picek, S.: An end-to-end plaintext-based side-channel collision attack without trace segmentation. Cryptology ePrint Archive, Paper 2023/1109 (2023). https://eprint.iacr.org/2023/1109

29. Wu, L., et al.: Label correlation in deep learning-based side-channel analysis. IEEE Trans. Inf. Forensics Secur. **18**, 3849–3861 (2023). https://doi.org/10.1109/TIFS.2023.3287728

30. Yap, T., Picek, S., Bhasin, S.: Beyond the last layer: deep feature loss functions in side-channel analysis. In: Proceedings of the 2023 Workshop on Attacks and Solutions in Hardware Security, ASHES 2023, pp. 73–82. Association for Computing Machinery, New York (2023). https://doi.org/10.1145/3605769.3623996

A Flexible Mixed-Mesh FPGA Cluster Architecture for High Speed Computing

Sergio Pertuz(✉) ⓘ, Cornelia Wulf ⓘ, Najdet Charaf ⓘ, Lester Kalms, and Diana Göhringer ⓘ

Adaptive Dynamic Systems, TU Dresden, Dresden, Germany
`sergio.pertuz@tu-dresden.de`

Abstract. This paper focuses on integrating multiple FPGAs for High-Performance Computing (HPC) applications with a priority on computational capability and reliability. It introduces a reliable inter-FPGA cluster architecture, detailing experimental results of FPGA communication layer performance and hardware management using FreeRTOS on a TMR Microblaze processor. The communication layer features a hardware core for inter-FPGA communication performance, evaluated on a multi-FPGA cluster testbed. Results demonstrate high-speed data transfer and fault tolerance. The hardware manager enhances system flexibility, enabling dynamic task scheduling for hardware accelerators. The paper's benchmark application is an image-processing pipeline, showing practical applicability with data throughput exceeding 67.4 Gb/s and low latency of 288 ns.

Keywords: FPGA cluster · parallel processing · radiation hardening · FPGA-FPGA communication

1 Introduction

FPGAs enable rapid prototyping, fast emulation, and exploration of new architectures without ASIC production overhead [5]. They provide reconfigurability, flexibility, and cost advantages over ASICs for embedded and HPC systems, approaching GPUs in raw performance with greater energy efficiency [11]. Despite their computational power, combining multiple FPGAs in a system is essential for various applications, presenting scalability challenges.

Cluster-based solutions, comprising efficient interconnected computing devices, address scalability issues in FPGA systems [1,3,6]. The slowdown of Moore's Law and the growing data center size emphasize the value of specialized compute devices [3]. FPGA-based clusters offer a simple and effective way to achieve high computational performance through massive parallel processing, with their presence increasing in data centers [7,12,16]. Using clusters of commercial off-the-shelf FPGA boards, like Zedwulf [10] and ZCluster [8], proves cost-effective and enhances resource availability and expandability.

© The Author(s), under exclusive license to Springer Nature Switzerland AG 2024
I. Skliarova et al. (Eds.): ARC 2024, LNCS 14553, pp. 267–281, 2024.
https://doi.org/10.1007/978-3-031-55673-9_19

While master-slave designs simplify implementation, they lack fault tolerance, making them vulnerable to a master FPGA failure. A masterless design,
without a central authority, ensures fault tolerance and operational continuity in
case of a failure. Considering extreme scenarios, such as radiation-prone environments in aerospace, space exploration, and nuclear research, demands a robust
and dependable communication infrastructure. Standard protocols like Ethernet may not suffice, necessitating the choice of a radiation-resistant and reliable
communication protocol.

With that in mind, this paper proposes an extendable Commercial Off-The-
Shelf (COTS) Field Programmable Gate Arrays (FPGA)-based cluster architecture that enables processing between multiple FPGAs. The cluster architecture
must comply reliability requirements to enable its utilization in hostile environments [2]. This is as part of the EUFRATE project which aims to develop and
test radiation-hardening methods for telecommunication payloads deployed for
Geostationary-Earth Orbit (GEO) using COTS FPGAs. The primary contributions of this paper are listed as follows:

- A mixed-mesh topology for a cluster-based FPGA. In this architecture, the
  FPGA tiles (group of four FPGA nodes) are fully connected, while the extension to more tiles is connected in a mesh style.
- The development of a reconfigurable multi-FPGA interconnection infrastructure that allows data access among different FPGAs using high-speed
  transceivers. The results achieved are comparable to other solutions available
  in the state-of-the-art and have advantages over commercial solutions such as
  Xilinx's Chip2Chip core.
- At the intermediate layer, a cluster manager software based on a distributed
  "masterless" or "peer-to-peer" scheme that allows increased scalability and
  fault tolerance.

This paper is organized as follows: Sect. 2 introduces the state of the art
of related FPGA clusters and highlights their strong and weak points, Sect. 3
introduces the designed FPGA cluster architecture describing every component
and their advantages. Section 4 introduces the software overlay that manages the
FPGA cluster. Finally, Sect. 5 presents the implementation results followed by
the conclusions.

2   State of the Art

This section focuses on FPGA-based clusters, describing their characteristics
and advantages while looking at example applications and architectures going
through their topology, communication infrastructure, and management.

Bai et al. [1] proposed a low-cost cluster using 48 Xilinx Zynq-7020 ARM-
FPGAs-based SoCs. They use the ARM for node-to-node communication via
Message Passing Interface (MPI), while the FPGA is used for more complex
computations. The compute nodes are interconnected via a Gigabit Ethernet
switch to form a local area network.

Hernández et al. [6] proposed a low-cost cluster of low-end Cyclone-V FPGAs embedded in DE1-SoC boards and connected to an ARM dual-core. Two fast ethernet routers connect the ARM CPUs. They developed an operating system based on Debian 8, which runs on the ARM CPU for fast network communication and to provide OpenCL support. Several benchmarks have been parallelized for the cluster and a workstation to compare execution time and energy consumption. In addition, the cluster is more than five times cheaper than the workstation, which is an advantage of using low-cost FPGAs.

Caulfield et al. [3] describe an FPGA-based acceleration architecture for data centers that are both scalable and flexible. The FPGAs can communicate directly with each other over the network without going through a CPU. They developed a reliable inter-FPGA communication protocol that achieves comparable latency to the previous state-of-the-art while scaling up to a hundred thousand nodes.

Takano et al. [16] present a cluster of four compute nodes connected via Ethernet through a hub. Each compute node has an Intel Core-I7 CPU and a Xilinx Kintex KC705 FPGA connected via PCI-E. In addition, the FPGAs have a bidirectional connection with each other via SubMiniature version A (SMA) communication cables (4 Gb/s) in a ring topology.

Ueno et al. [17] presented a tightly coupled FPGA cluster. The host system consists of eight (Intel Xeon 5122×2) CPUs connected via a 16-port 100 Gb/s fat tree network switch using Infiniband cables. In addition, the FPGAs are directly connected in a torus topology, which makes the system scalable. The system consists of a router, a flow controller [9], a serial transceiver, and a remote Direct Memory Access (DMA) controller. The remote DMA controller reads and writes from and to local memory(s) on any FPGA controlled by the servers using MPI. The router is connected to four bidirectional communication ports, adds header information to the message, and uses an X-Y routing algorithm. The measured payload bandwidth for a single FPGA-to-FPGA link is 32.2 Gb/s. On the other hand, the host network is more effective for collective communication, where performance is highly dependent on bandwidth. When only the FPGA or the host network is used, an input to the destination server becomes a bottleneck because there is no alternative route.

In [14], a Multi-FPGA framework for distributed processing is implemented together with a framework for task distributions. This work uses SMA cables to connect to the different FPGA nodes and reports a throughput of 5 Gb/s. Nevertheless, the scalability of this work could be improved due to the number of available connectors on the development board. A follow-up to this work is seen in [13], where SATA cables are used to avoid the previously claimed scalability problem. However, it includes an FPGA as a master node and considers the others as slave nodes. This fact, together with the usage of Zynq processing cores limits the readability and the fault tolerance of the system.

This paper introduces a FPGA-based cluster design with resource-efficient communication interfaces and tailored protocols. In contrast to previous approaches using generic bus protocols like PCI-E or Ethernet, our work employs a physical channel that is less prone to environment effects, i.e., Aurora

Table 1. Comparison against the related works on the state of the art.

Author	Own	[13] (2022)	[1] (2017)	[6] (2018)	[3] (2016)	[16] (2019)	[17] (2019)
CPU	TMR MicroBlaze embedded	1x ARM Cortex-A9	1x ARM Cortex-A9	1x ARM Cortex-A9	2x Intel Haswell	1x Intel Core-i7 4770	2x Intel Xeon 5122
FPGA	4 x XILINX KCU105	4 x XILINX SoC ZC706	Cortex-A9	1x Intel Cyclone-V	1x Intel Stratix-V	1x XILINX Kintex-7	4x Intel Arria-10
CPU-CPU	n/a	n/a	48-port Gigabit ETH	2 x 4-port Fast ETH	40Gb QSFP+ (shared)	ETH HUB 1000 BASET	16-port 100Gb Infiniband
CPU- FPGA	AXI-MM	AXI-MM	yes	yes	PCI-E Gen3x8	PCI-E Gen2x4	PCI-E Gen3x8
FPGA-FPGA	Aurora + Mixed-Mesh	Aurora + Star	no	no	40Gb QSFP+ Ring	Ring Coaxial 4 Gbps	40Gb QSFP+ Torus
Compute Nodes	4 FPGA	4 FPGA	48 SoC	4 SoC	–	4	8
Fanout Channels	4 two-lanes	4 four-lanes	48 four-lanes	2 four-lanes	four-lanes	four-lanes	
Fault Tolerance	yes	no	no	no	no	no	no
Latency	288ns	200 ns	n/a	n/a	n/a	n/a	344 ns
Throughput	67.4 Gb/s	2.5 Gb/s	0.352 Gb/s	n/a	40 Gb/s	n/a	32 Gb/s

protocol over SMA cables. Additionally, while other designs often rely on ARM processors for communication, limiting the cluster reliability, we employ a Triple-Modular Redundant (TMR) MicroBlaze processor for enhanced fault tolerance. Finally, our mixed-mesh topology with Aurora facilitates high fault tolerance, low latency, and competitive throughput (67.4 Gb/s). These and other distinctions are summarized in Table 1.

3   Architecture

This section presents a comprehensive overview of the architecture of our extendable COTS FPGA-based cluster. The architecture is designed to leverage the benefits of combining multiple FPGAs in a scalable, fault-tolerant system catering to high-performance computing applications in hostile environments.

3.1   Inter-FPGA Architecture

The topology plays an essential role in scalability. A ring topology is often sufficient depending on the application's requirements [3,16]. If better scalability is needed, a mesh or torus can be used [17]. However, reliability is often not considered in their approaches. Therefore, we propose a tiled-based approach with a fully connected mesh for intra-tile communication to achieve reliability and a torus for inter-tile communication to achieve scalability.

The cluster can be scaled using different tiles. Figure 1 presents an example of how the cluster scales to 16 FPGA nodes. When extended to multiple tiles, the nodes extend the network to the outside to one or multiple tiles.

Each FPGA node in the cluster requires four full-duplex lines from the Aurora links. Three of these links are used for intra-tile communication, while the fourth link is used to scale the system and connect it to other tiles (as seen in Figs. 1 and 2). The forwarding RRX and RTX use a specialized XY routing algorithm that is deadlock-free.

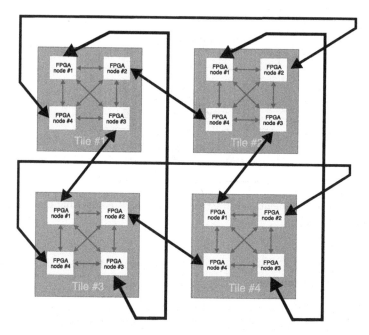

Fig. 1. Inter-tile communication infrastructure topology. The depicted example features a cluster of four tiles, each consisting of four interconnected FPGA nodes. The cluster employs a mixed-mesh topology, where the individual tiles are fully connected, and additional tiles are seamlessly integrated using the extra Aurora connector.

To connect the different nodes, it needs a communication network. In detail, the used approach, schematized in Fig. 2, involves fully connecting each FPGA node within a tile. Each link employs an Aurora full-duplex protocol through an SMA coaxial cable. Additionally, each FPGA node has a fourth Aurora port which can be used if multiple tile exits, creating a network of tiles. This allows scalability without needing more Aurora ports.

The advantage of this design is that no global address space would be needed. The nodes processing system would determine the exact destination. Due to its scalability, this design could also be more easily adapted to a multi-tile design. The possibility of using FIFOs can also be evaluated to increase throughput due to reduced waiting times on the sender's side. For the tile-based design (Fig. 2), adjustments would have to be made to the RRX and RTX blocks that affect the routing algorithm.

Deadlock is not a problem within a tile because all nodes are directly connected. Another characteristic of this design is that one node per tile may fail without affecting the cluster reliability because of the direct connections. It must be adaptive and take an alternative path if a connection fails.

3.2   Intra-FPGA Architecture

Figure 3 describes a high-level block diagram of the developed FPGA node architecture, where it is possible to see all the main building blocks to be implemented

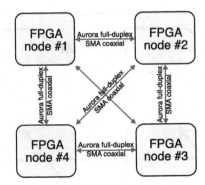

Fig. 2. Intra-tile communication infrastructure topology, comprising four FPGA nodes that are fully connected.

on the FPGA. All the listed components are further discussed in the following subsections of this document.

- The MicroBlaze (MB) TMR Processing System, consisting of the node's general purpose domain composed of a hardened microprocessor running the main reliability, cluster management services, and application-specific computations and main node data-flow management.
- Array of accelerators for benchmarking that are easily exchangeable and consist of programmable functional units in charge of accelerating applications parallel and compute-intensive tasks.
- Network Adapter (NA), consisting of dedicated hardware cores in charge of managing the exchange and flow of data across nodes and within the node itself, according to the processing system requests.
- Double Data Rate (DDR)4 Memory Controller enables access to the on-chip external memory from the processing system and NA.
- Interface with the accelerators, consisting of a dedicated infrastructure to feed and harvest data from it, according to the application requirement.
- Aurora Interface for the Data Link. At least three are envisioned to form a tile with a full-mesh topology, while four should be present for the nodes interfacing with the outside and have a network of 4 tiles.

This interconnecting cluster design allows the data-flow independent from the processor core, allowing the NA to move and copy data within the cluster while the processing elements on the FPGA continue doing other operations.

3.3   MicroBlaze Triple Modular Redundancy

One of this work's architecture objectives is to meet system availability and reliability requirements, which is why the TMR method is chosen for the software processor of the nodes. The overall processing system for the FPGA cluster node consists of a Xilinx MB soft-core TMR subsystem that runs the critical reliability

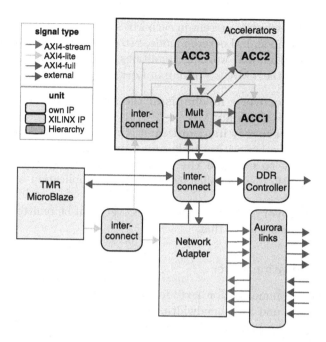

Fig. 3. FPGA node architecture overview. This figure presents an example design show-casing the utilization of the NA in an FPGA node architecture. The NA is directly connected to the DDR, enhancing communication efficiency without involving the processor, thereby freeing up application processing resources. Additionally, the accelerators are depicted to illustrate their potential inclusion in the design.

and cluster management services to support the core software services related to cluster management, system state allocation, and compute allocation.

This implementation enables both redundancy failure masking and system recovery. The MB TMR subsystem is fault-tolerant and can nominally operate after a failure. Together with the ability to detect and recover from an error, the implementation ensures the reliability of the entire subsystem.

Different options for implementing the MB TMR subsystem emphasize fault tolerance. All variants do not provide scrubbing methods or recovery mechanisms out-of-the-box. Instead they only protect the design from a single fault. Therefore, it is necessary to include a combination of the TMR subsystem with software scrubbing to avoid fault accumulation.

Fail-safe mode, on the other hand, further improves the operation of the two remaining healthy MB sub-blocks after the first failure and performs a recovery mechanism to repair the faulty MB. The fail-safe mode includes two additional hardware cores: the TMR Manager, which provides a recovery mechanism, and the TMR Soft Error Mitigation (SEM), which performs scrubbing.

The recovery in fail-safe mode work as follows: the MB subsystems run in normal mode when no fault occurs; this mode is called voting, and all outputs are majority-voted. When a fault is detected in one of the blocks, the status of the TMR manager, which is present in each MB subsystem, changes from Voting mode to Lockstep mode. In Lockstep mode, two of the three MB subsystems are considered to be in normal working conditions. Four possibilities or decisions can be made when the TMR is working in Lockstep mode:

- **Execute the recovery mechanism:** the software will handle the break signal and restore the faulty MB.
- **Postpone the recovery mechanism:** it is possible to postpone the recovery mechanism until other critical tasks are completed.
- **Not necessary to execute the recovery mechanism:** the system does not need to perform an explicit recovery if the application allows periodic reset of the MB.
- **Omit the recovery mechanism:** the recovery can be omitted if the application requirements allow that.

3.4   Communication Layer

In designing the communication layer for our cluster architecture, we aimed to ensure low latency and high bandwidth. A key consideration was to avoid data traffic bottlenecks by implementing a communication model that bypasses the host CPUs. To achieve this, we opted to utilize routers, which effectively manage inter-FPGA communication and facilitate seamless data flow.

Considering the diverse communication scenarios that can arise in distributed computing clusters, we identified three primary cases: scatter, point-to-point, and gather. Data must be transferred from one compute unit (CU) to multiple other CUs in scatter scenarios. Point-to-point cases involve transferring intermediate results generated by one CU to another CU. Lastly, partial results must be merged and submitted to the application software in gather scenarios.

Given the importance of bandwidth and latency between distributed nodes, we selected the Aurora 64B/66B protocol IP provided by Xilinx to support our cluster architecture. The Aurora protocol offers several advantages, including scalability, lightweight design, high data rate, and simplex and full-duplex communication support. The core also provides easy-to-use AXI4-Stream-based framing and flow control interfaces, streamlining the integration process.

The protocol's throughput depends on the number of transceivers and the target line rate of these transceivers. For our project, we chose a configuration with a single full-duplex lane per link, allowing us to achieve the desired balance between high-speed communication and resource utilization.

While other works in the field, such as the ones presented in [4,15], have demonstrated impressive throughput and low latency for inter-FPGA communication, it is crucial to emphasize that our research addresses a distinct set of challenges and requirements. These works and many others use Ethernet as the physical layer for intercommunication, which excels in standard environments but may not offer the desired reliability under extreme radiation conditions.

In contrast, our proposed architecture leverages SMA cables over the robust Aurora protocol to facilitate inter-FPGA communication. This intentional choice

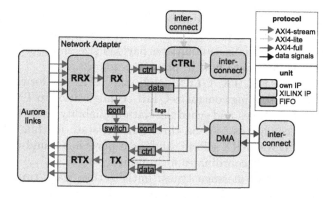

Fig. 4. The network adapter. It showcases a combination of custom-designed blocks and standard Xilinx IPs. The design includes a Xilinx DMA controller block which manage communication tasks and facilitate seamless handshakes, freeing up the processor from communication overhead.

aligns with the crucial need for radiation resistance and reliability in specific applications. By optimizing for such radiation-prone environments, we make a unique and valuable contribution to the field of high-speed inter-FPGA communication.

In the following sections, we present the details of our cluster's architecture and the experimental results, demonstrating the effectiveness of our approach for achieving high-speed data transfer and fault tolerance in radiation-prone environments.

3.5 Network Adapter

Figure 4 gives an overview of the NA, which connects the internal communication infrastructure with the Aurora links. All cores implemented in this research are realized using High-Level Synthesis (HLS). Most buffers (ctrl and conf) are small (e.g., 16 elements) to improve overall throughput and prevent waiting cycles. Only the data buffer between RX and DMA is more significant (512 elements) to prevent deadlocks and increase the overall throughput.

The communication protocol comprises three layers: flit, package, and message. A flit, transmitted in a single clock cycle through AXI4-stream, is the basic unit. A package, including a header flit for routing and data flits (payload), is identified by the last signal in AXI4-stream. Messages can be split into multiple packages to prevent blocking, with the header flit indicating the first (Start-of-Frame (SoF)) or last (End-of-Frame (EoF)) package.

Three buffer types exist: control, data, and configuration. Control buffers facilitate data exchange between CTRL units of different nodes. Data buffers handle data flits for DMA units, ensuring readiness before initiating a transfer. Configuration buffers handle flit exchange for synchronization, forwarding, and port configuration.

Five configuration flit types are present: header, start, initialization, pause, and resume. Header flits set package routes, start flits configure TX for data or control messages, and initialization flits set payload size and coordinates. Pause and resume flits manage data flow to prevent deadlocks.

Five cores include RX, TX, CTRL, RRX, and RTX. RX forwards packages based on header flits, sending control to CTRL, configuration to TX, and data to DMA. TX creates packages and schedules data availability using a round-robin scheduler. CTRL configures NA via three parallel state machines for control, configuration, and DMA. RRX selects valid input ports in a round-robin manner, and RTX uses header flit coordinates for routing.

The NA handles five message types: initialization, data transfer between DDR memories via DMA, and smaller control messages between CPUs of different nodes. Configuring CTRL registers initiates message transmission.

4 Management Software

The management software serves functions of monitoring execution, controlling data flow, and responding to disruptions and errors. Concurrent task execution is facilitated by FreeRTOS. In a one tile configuration (i.e., four FPGAs), two FPGAs are connected to the host PC or CPU, as illustrated in Fig. 5. The FPGA cluster operates on a master-less scheme, where one FPGA assumes the role of managing cluster tasks and resource scheduling, referred to as the FPGA leader, while the remaining FPGAs act as followers. The leader role is dynamically assumed by the first FPGA that is ready to do so, and this leader FPGA is specifically tasked with communication responsibilities with the Host PC or CPU.

When a hardware accelerator does not give a live signal within a given period, the management software re-executes the task on a different hardware accelerator on the same FPGA. If no suitable accelerator is available, it determines the FPGA within the tile with the most free accelerators. This requires the information about functioning and free accelerators within the node. Therefore, the FPGA nodes exchange control messages with directly linked nodes whenever

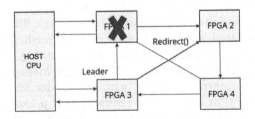

Fig. 5. Fault response mechanism: The leader FPGA establishes a primary connection to the host PC, with a secondary link available within the cluster. A backup FPGA, connected to the secondary link, stands ready to assume leader role in case the initial leader fails.

the state of an accelerator changes. In the case that a complete FPGA fails, the leader redirects the hardware tasks of this FPGA. The management software checks the availability of hardware accelerators on the own FPGA as well as on neighboring nodes. It redirects the hardware tasks to the nodes with the highest capacity in order to reach a balanced load distribution within the FPGA cluster. If the failing node was the leader of the cluster, the second node with a link to the host CPU takes over control. This scenario is depicted in Fig. 5.

5 Evaluation

5.1 Test Application

The node design is tested and evaluated on four AMD Kintex™UltraScale™FPGA KCU105 Evaluation Kit running a test application and the test architecture introduced on Fig. 3. The boards are connected as described in Fig. 2. The physical links are SMA cables connected to an 8-Port SMA/34 Differential Pair FPGA Mezzanine Card (FMC) module extension board. The testbed contains then four nodes, which build a full tile. It is intended to test the various functions of the network adapter. However, it can also receive and send control and data messages in parallel. The test application designates the leader and the node currently managing the cluster, which can be described as follows.

0. All nodes initialize their network adapter.
1. The leader requests if it can send data to a follower.
2. The follower gives a grant to the leader to send data.
3. The leader sends data to the memory of the follower.
4. Repeat steps 1–3 [x2] to the other two followers.
5. The follower requests to send processed data to leader.
6. The leader gives a grant to the follower to send data.
7. The follower sends processed data to leader's memory.
8. Repeat steps 5–7 [x2] from the other two followers.

The following further settings are used for the test application:

– All logical components' frequency is set to 100 MHz.
– The DDR controller frequency is set to 300 MHz
– The Aurora's physical layer's frequency is 157 MHz.
– The bitwidth of all AXI4-stream (Fig. 3) is 64-bit.
– The message size sent are in a range from 32 kB to 35 MB.
– The maximum package size is set to 32 flits.

Finally, the AXI performance monitor was used for measuring the performance of the intra-FPGA AXI and AXI-Stream interfaces.

To cover a wide range of data sizes and assess performance under varying conditions, this test procedure was repeated 32 times for 11 different data sizes. A comprehensive set of performance measurements was obtained by executing the test procedure multiple times with varying data sizes. The results of these

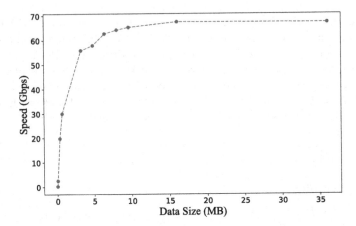

Fig. 6. Data Size vs. Throughput. Each point represents the mean value between read and write operations, which exhibit similar performance. Each data point also represents the mean value obtained from 32 different experiments.

evaluations, showcasing the relationship between data size and system speed, are detailed in Fig. 6. This graph illustrates the cluster's performance, achieving speeds ranging from 0.257 Gbps for small data sizes up to 67.473 Gbps for larger data loads. Noteworthy speed improvements were observed across various data sizes, demonstrating the network adapter's efficiency in managing high-speed data transfer between the interconnected FPGAs.

5.2   Performance and Resource Utilization Analysis

From the application test, the measured throughput at the output of the sender's DDR FIFOs is 67.4 Gb/s. The data transfer takes 70 clock cycles. 3 additional clock cycles are needed between each burst read of the DMA. The burst size of the DMA has been set to 256 bytes. Therefore, a total of 3×3 clock cycles are added by the DMA.

The maximum throughput measured at the input of the receiver's DDR is 67.4 Gb/s. The data transfer from this side required 3 additional clock cycles added by the NA.

The measured latency of the system was 85 clock cycles (288 ns). This latency is added for two reasons: after the manager configures the CTRL unit, the flits are read from its DDR, and the second is the latency added by the Aurora cores. Other reasons for the latency mainly come from (1) the manager setting the registers in the CTRL unit, (2) the CTRL unit reading this data and configuring the DMA, and (3) for the CTRL unit to create a control message for the receiver node.

From the sender's perspective, the transfer had 72 clock cycles (240 ns) overhead after reading the first data flit from the sender's DDR. The first data flit is written in the DDR of the receiver. This is the time it takes for the data to pass through two network adapters and two routers.

Table 2. Device utilization report summary of the network adapter depicted in Fig. 4.

	LUT	LUTRAM	BRAM	DSP
Utilization	9964	1299	28	0
Utilization [%]	4%	1%	5%	0%

The first flit of the DMA control message, which is needed to configure the DMA of the receiver, passes the NA 80 clock cycles before the first flit of the DMA data message.

Table 1 compares the proposed architecture against other works in the literature. Several advantages can be seen against other works, such as the throughput and fault tolerance features.

Table 2 shows the resource consumption of the node FPGA for the implementation described in Sect. 5.1. Table 2 depicts the overall resource utilization of the NA described in Fig. 4, including the Aurora core. It can be seen that the network adapter is lightweight in terms of resources, as the consumption of all resources does not exceed 5% of the available resources on the target device KCU040.

5.3 Microblaze Recovery Test

As mentioned, this work's cluster incorporates Xilinx MicroBlaze TMR, which employs a vector table to store interrupt handler addresses. These interrupts can pause the processor's execution, necessitating the handler to store critical state information such as the program counter, stack pointer, and register file. To introduce a controlled environment for error testing and evaluation, we integrate a specialized IP core that manipulates the instruction stream, allowing us to inject functional errors into the TMR subsystem's processor. This error injection capability enables us to assess the system's robustness and fault tolerance in the presence of faults or transient errors.

During the error injection process, the TMR subsystem's processor undergoes a recovery procedure. The recovery process includes several steps, taking approximately 40 s to complete. Firstly, the processor's execution is halted, and its state is saved, capturing critical context information. Subsequently, a reset is initiated to restore the processor to a known state. After the reset, the processor's state is restored from the previously saved context information. Additional steps are carried out to ensure synchronization with peripheral devices, such as the UART (Universal Asynchronous Receiver/Transmitter).

6 Conclusions

In conclusion, the evaluated system achieved a high throughput of 67.4 Gb/s at the output of the sender's DDR FIFOs. The measured latency of the system was 288 ns, including the time it takes for the data to pass through two network adapters and two routers. The node FPGA's resource consumption was shown to be lightweight, using less than 5% of the available resources on the target device (without considering the accelerators or MB). These results demonstrate that the proposed architecture can achieve high throughput using significantly less resources, while also providing fault tolerance features thanks to its masterless topology. Overall, the evaluated system shows promising potential for high-performance data transfer applications in FPGA-based clusters.

Future work for the cluster architecture includes adapting the RRX and RTX blocks to support the proposed mixed-mesh topology for cluster extension. Additionally, testing the cluster with diverse applications that stress the internal connections between accelerators is also planned. Furthermore, incorporating dynamic partial reconfiguration for the TMR subsystem will enhance the cluster's adaptability and resource utilization. This feature will enable on-the-fly reconfiguration of individual FPGA nodes, leading to improved system performance and fault tolerance in radiation-prone environments.

Acknowledgements. The EuFRATE project is financially supported by the European Space Agency (ESA) in response to the call ESA AO/1-10240/20/UK/ND within the ARTES 4.0 CORE competitiveness generic programme line Component A: Advanced Technology, Activity Reference 5C.416.

Disclosure of Interests. The authors have no competing interests to declare that are relevant to the content of this article.

References

1. Bai, X., Jiang, L., Dai, Q., Yang, J., Tan, J.: Acceleration of RSA processes based on hybrid ARM-FPGA cluster. In: 2017 IEEE Symposium on Computers and Communications (ISCC). IEEE, July 2017
2. Bozzoli, L., et al.: EuFRATE: European FPGA radiation-hardened architecture for telecommunications. In: 2023 Design, Automation & Test in Europe Conference & Exhibition (DATE), pp. 1–6 (2023)
3. Caulfield, A.M., et al.: A cloud-scale acceleration architecture. In: 2016 49th Annual IEEE/ACM International Symposium on Microarchitecture (MICRO). IEEE, October 2016
4. Ewais, M., Vega, J.C., Leon-Garcia, A., Chow, P.: A framework integrating FPGAs in VNF networks. In: 2021 12th International Conference on Network of the Future (NoF), pp. 1–9 (2021)
5. Gandhare, S., Karthikeyan, B.: Survey on FPGA architecture and recent applications. In: 2019 International Conference on Vision Towards Emerging Trends in Communication and Networking (ViTECoN), pp. 1–4 (2019)

6. Hernández, M., Del Barrio, A.A., Botella, G.: An ultra low-cost cluster based on low-end FPGAs. In: Proceedings of the 50th Computer Simulation Conference. Society for Modeling and Simulation International (SCS) (2018)
7. Hou, J., et al.: A case study of accelerating apache spark with FPGA. In: 2018 17th IEEE International Conference on Trust, Security and Privacy in Computing and Communications/12th IEEE International Conference on Big Data Science and Engineering (TrustCom/BigDataSE). IEEE, August 2018
8. Lin, Z., Chow, P.: ZCluster: a zynq-based hadoop cluster. In: 2013 International Conference on Field-Programmable Technology (FPT). IEEE, December 2013
9. Mondigo, A., Ueno, T., Tanaka, D., Sano, K., Yamamoto, S.: Design and scalability analysis of bandwidth-compressed stream computing with multiple FPGAs. In: 2017 12th International Symposium on Reconfigurable Communication-centric Systems-on-Chip (ReCoSoC). IEEE, July 2017
10. Moorthy, P., Kapre, N.: Zedwulf: power-performance tradeoffs of a 32-node zynq SoC cluster. In: 2015 IEEE 23rd Annual International Symposium on Field-Programmable Custom Computing Machines. IEEE, May 2015
11. Nurvitadhi, E., et al.: Can FPGAs beat GPUs in accelerating next-generation deep neural networks? In: Proceedings of the 2017 ACM/SIGDA International Symposium on Field-Programmable Gate Arrays. ACM, February 2017
12. Osana, Y., Sakamoto, Y.: Performance evaluation of a CPU-FPGA hybrid cluster platform prototype. In: Proceedings of the 8th International Symposium on Highly Efficient Accelerators and Reconfigurable Technologies. ACM, June 2017
13. Salazar-García, C., et al.: A custom interconnection multi-FPGA framework for distributed processing applications. In: 2022 35th SBC/SBMicro/IEEE/ACM Symposium on Integrated Circuits and Systems Design (SBCCI), pp. 1–6 (2022)
14. Salazar-Garcia, C., Garcia-Ramirez, R., Rimolo-Donadio, R., Strydis, C., Chacon-Rodriguez, A.: PlasticNet+: extending multi-FPGA interconnect architecture via gigabit transceivers. In: 2021 IEEE International Symposium on Circuits and Systems (ISCAS). IEEE, May 2021
15. Shen, Q.C., Zheng, J., Chow, P.: RIFL: a reliable link layer network protocol for FPGA-to-FPGA communication. In: The 2021 ACM/SIGDA International Symposium on Field-Programmable Gate Arrays. ACM, February 2021
16. Takano, K., Oda, T., Ozaki, R., Uejima, A., Kohata, M.: Implementation of distributed processing using a PC-FPGA hybrid system. In: 2019 International Conference on Field-Programmable Technology (ICFPT). IEEE, December 2019
17. Ueno, T., Miyajima, T., Mondigo, A., Sano, K.: Hybrid network utilization for efficient communication in a tightly coupled FPGA cluster. In: 2019 International Conference on Field-Programmable Technology (ICFPT). IEEE, December 2019

A Safety-Critical, RISC-V SoC Integrated and ASIC-Ready Classic McEliece Accelerator

Vatistas Kostalabros[1]($\boxtimes$)(iD), Jordi Ribes-González[2], Oriol Farràs[2],
Miquel Moretó[1], and Carles Hernandez[3]

[1] Barcelona Supercomputing Center, Barcelona, Spain
`vatistas.kostalbros@bsc.es`
[2] Universitat Rovira i Virgili, Tarragona, Spain
[3] Universitat Politècnica de València, València, Spain

Abstract. Security is an integral part of ensuring the integrity of safety-critical systems. Safety-critical systems with extremely long-lifespan, such as the ones employed in the space and automotive industry, need additional security measures that can guarantee the thwarting of both current and future attacks. In that respect, the future advent of large-scale quantum computers, could potentially compromise the security of such systems leading to catastrophic consequences. To this end, in this paper we present the integration of the post-quantum cryptosystem of Classic McEliece (CM) in an open-source platform for high-performance safety-critical systems (SELENE). The SELENE project proposed a new family of safety-critical computing platforms, which builds upon open source components such as the RISC-V instruction set architecture, GNU/Linux, and the Jailhouse hypervisor. This work capitalizes on the modularity of the SELENE hardware platform and proposes a high-performance and constant-time HLS-based accelerator of the encoding and decoding subroutines of CM. We specifically present the first integration of a CM accelerator in a Linux-capable and RISC-V based System-on-Chip (SoC). Our experiments show significant speedups of up to 4.9× and 198× compared to a scalar software implementation of CM encoding and decoding subroutines respectively, executed on an x86 core. We additionally showcase a successful implementation of our accelerator in an ASIC context using the Global Foundries 22 nm technology node operating at >1 GHz frequency.

1 Introduction

The rapidly evolving scientific research of quantum computing [6,9,10,29] is striving towards the development of a fully-fledged, large scale quantum computer. Such a technological leap could not only accelerate computationally demanding tasks, but also break currently used asymmetric cryptographic algorithms within a short amount of time. To this end, post-quantum cryptography (PQC), has risen to meet the challenge posed by the quantum threat.

© The Author(s), under exclusive license to Springer Nature Switzerland AG 2024
I. Skliarova et al. (Eds.): ARC 2024, LNCS 14553, pp. 282–295, 2024.
https://doi.org/10.1007/978-3-031-55673-9_20

One exemplary secure PQC algorithm is Classic McEliece (CM), which has a long-standing history, as its security has withstood the test of time since its invention nearly 40 years ago [4]. CM also shows relatively fast execution times for its encoding and decoding subroutines, compared to other PQC schemes [7]. In the context of safety-critical systems, the effective deployment of PQC schemes becomes mandatory to ensure their integrity. However, traditional safety-critical hardware does not usually provide enough computing capabilities. At the same time, these computers have to meet stringent timing performance constraints (e.g. Vehicular communication, VPNs). Therefore, the evident need for additional performance gains justifies the use of dedicated hardware accelerators.

To this end, our proposal bridges this gap, by proposing the integration of a CM accelerator in a safety-critical, and Linux enabled RISC-V SoC. We explicitly target the acceleration of the encoding and decoding subroutines. Specifically, with this paper we make the following contributions:

- We present the first CM accelerator integrated in a Linux-capable RISC-V SoC. The accelerator is programmed using a standard Linux driver and API.
- We showcase a hardware solution for the CM encoding that leverages streaming architecture to eliminate the need to store the PK at the accelerator.
- We show the ASIC-readiness of our accelerator on the Global Foundries (GF22nm) technology node operating at >1 GHz frequencies.
- We demonstrate speedups of up to 4.9× and 198×, to the encoding and decoding subroutines respectively, compared to a scalar x86 software baseline.
- We grant public access to the developed source-code repository.

This paper has the following structure. Section 2 introduces the CM cryptosystem. Section 3 presents the hardware accelerator design. Section 4 gives specific details on the experimental methodology and the RISC-V SoC integration. Section 5 evaluates the performance of our proposal. Section 6 compares with the state-of-the-art work on CM acceleration, and Sect. 7 concludes this work.

2   Background

SELENE Project: The SELENE SoC has been developed in the context of the SELENE project [17] with the aim of providing a flexible and open-source computing platform that can be customized to different safety application domains such as automotive, space, or railway. In these domains, computing platforms need to last from years to decades and thus, it becomes mandatory to ensure their safe operation during the expected lifetime. Nowadays, the interconnectivity needs of many of these systems has forced the industry analysing the potential impact of security breaches in the functional safety of these products. In this context, efficient PQC computations are becoming a necessity in many safety-related applications too.

SELENE platform comprises a 64-bit RISC-V multicore with built-in support for safety, such as diverse redundant execution, and end-to-end contention monitoring support. Additionally, the SoC can be easily extended with hardware acceleration using the provided AXI interfaces and can be easily programmed using the available low-level software support. The SELENE platform source code is open and publicly available in the following repository.

Key-Encapsulation Mechanisms (KEM): The CM cryptosystem is a KEM. The main functionality of KEMs is to enable the secure establishment of a session key between a server and a client. KEMs consist of three algorithms: key generation, encapsulation, and decapsulation. Encapsulation and decapsulation further comprise encoding and decoding subroutines, respectively.

In brief, in a client-server communication scenario, the server initially generates a public-secret key pair (PK, SK) using the key generation algorithm. Then the client, which holds the server's PK, feeds it to the encapsulation algorithm to produce a session key in plaintext and ciphertext (CT) forms. Finally, the server receives the encrypted session key, and decrypts it using its own SK and the decapsulation algorithm. Upon successful completion of this protocol, both the client and the server have established a common session key in a secure way and they can go on communicating via symmetric cryptographic algorithms (e.g. AES). We note, that, due to its strong security properties, CM supports static keys. That means that the computationally intensive key generation is executed infrequently and therefore it is not a strong candidate for acceleration, in a safety-critical device scenario. Therefore, our proposal focuses on the design of an accelerator for the encoding and decoding subroutines, which encloses the majority of the encapsulation and decapsulation computational load, respectively.

Classic McEliece: CM core functionality is based on the classical cryptosystems of McEliece and Niederreiter [26,27]. CM shows fast encoding and decoding speeds and has very small ciphertexts that make it particularly appealing in some scenarios [21]. Its main KEM parameters are:

- Three integers $m, n, t > 0$ satisfying $n \leq 2^m$ and $m \cdot t < n$. Also, denote $k = n - m \cdot t$ and $q = 2^m$.
- Two monic irreducible polynomials f, F, defining the finite fields $\mathbb{F}_q = \mathbb{F}_2[z]/(f(z))$ and $\mathbb{F}_{q^t} = \mathbb{F}_q[y]/(F(y))$.

CM defines five parameter sets, which correspond to five different security levels. These parameter sets modify the inner workings of the scheme in order to trade off security for efficiency, affecting the size of the PK, SK, CT, and the overall KEM performance. Table 1 presents the basic CM parameters, along with their respective values.

In the following listing, we briefly describe the encoding and decoding subroutines of the CM KEM.

Encoding:

[1] Let $e \in \mathbb{F}_2^n$ a random vector with exactly t ones.
[2] Compute $C_0 = (I_{n-k}, T) \cdot e \in \mathbb{F}_2^{n-k}$.

Table 1. CM parameter sets and sizes of the PK, SK, and CT [4].

Security level	Parameter set	m	n	t	PK size [KB]	SK size [KB]	CT size [Bytes]
L1	mceliece348864	12	3488	64	255	6.3	128
L3	mceliece460896	13	4608	96	511.8	13.2	188
L5$_1$	mceliece6688128	13	6688	128	1020.5	13.56	240
L5$_2$	mceliece6960119	13	6960	119	1022.2	13.58	226
L5$_3$	mceliece8192128	13	8192	128	1326	13.75	240

Decoding:

[1] Let $v \in \mathbb{F}_2^n$ be C_0 padded with k zeros.

[2] Compute the $2t \times n$ matrix $\left(\alpha_j^i / g^2(\alpha_j) \right)_{i,j}$.

[3] Extend this matrix to a $2mt \times n$ matrix $H^{(2)}$ by writing elements as column m-bit vectors.

[4] Compute the syndrome $H^{(2)} \cdot v$.

[5] Find the error locator polynomial $\sigma(x)$ of the syndrome, using Berlekamp-Massey decoding.

[6] Let $c = (c_i)_i \in \mathbb{F}_2^n$ with $c_i = 1$ if and only if $\sigma(\alpha_i) = 0$, and $c_i = 0$ otherwise.

3   Accelerator Design

The overall accelerator design comprises the encoding plus random error-vector generation and the decoding hardware modules, merged under a common interface. We term the respective accelerator modules as Enc and Dec. Encoding poses a hardware implementation challenge due to the high memory bandwidth requirements that arise from the large size of the PK, which can be of up to 1.3 MB [4,11]. Decoding, on the other hand is a computationally intensive function, dominated by Galois Field (GF) arithmetic primitives.

HLS-Design Approach Motivation: We follow an HLS-design approach on the proposed CM accelerator and its Enc and Dec modules. HLS methodology offers us the ability to design the whole Enc and Dec in a time-efficient manner. Moreover, in the context of the evolving landscape of PQC, a versatile design methodology like HLS, is crucial for the timely adaptations to emerging attacks. The ability to provide updated cryptosystem specifications and accommodate respective changes in an already functional accelerator, is superior to that offered by a fully-RTL design, which is arguably less flexible.

Encoding Module: Enc comprises a syndrome encoding function, and a random error-vector generator. The large size of the PK, which is used in the syndrome encoding, makes the acceleration of the encoding function challenging, as traditionally the whole PK has to be loaded from the main memory and stored

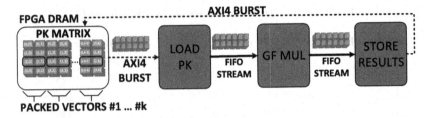

Fig. 1. Example of multiple PK values vectorization, AXI burst loading and intra-accelerator data-movement using FIFOs.

in the accelerator private memories for further computation. Nevertheless, our proposal combines a streaming data communication paradigm, together with a task level parallelization technique, thus eliminating the need to store the PK in the accelerator premises.

HLS Optimizations: Due to the large PK size, the data movement between the core and the accelerator accounts for a significant part of the execution time of Enc. Thus, our acceleration approach aims to efficiently hide the PK load latency by overlapping it with the execution of the syndrome encoding function and the random error-vector generation. This is realized using a dataflow programming model in the accelerator's code (i.e. task level parallelism).

Nevertheless, this technique alone was not able to provide substantial speedup, as the sheer time of sequentially loading all PK values overshadowed any potential acceleration. Thereby, we decided to pack together individual PK values into an n-byte wide vector, thus utilizing better the available AXI interface bandwidth. The vectorization factor n is user-configured, to provide the optimal performance solution for different PK matrix sizes. Our experiments show full utilization of the maximum available bandwidth (i.e. 1 kb) in the RISC-V SoC using the AXI interface. We note, that, if the user needs to perform loads exceeding the 1kb limit, each AXI load gets penalized with extra clock cycles. This is the case for the high-security levels (i.e $L5_1$, $L5_2$, and $L5_3$).

Once loaded, every instance of this wide vector is processed by the syndrome encoder module in a pipelined fashion. The data communication between the hardware sub-modules happens with the use of HLS streams, which are mapped to FIFO structures. The latter are automatically mapped to FPGA embedded memory elements. By achieving a constant flow of data through the accelerator's FIFOs we avoid any unnecessary stalls of the design. Moreover, we are able to instantiate the smallest possible FIFOs size (i.e. two), thus totally avoiding the use of private BRAM memories for the PK since the latter is entirely streamed through the accelerator. Figure 1 depicts the PK vectorization optimization.

Finally, for the random generation of the error-vector polynomial, we use an open-source Xilinx HLS version of the AES256 ECB function. We note that the use of this function is approved by the CM NIST submission making our accelerator fully compliant to the NIST specification.

Decoding Module: The decoding functionality consists mainly of arithmetic primitives, like GF arithmetic operations, as well as more complex functions that build on top of the GF arithmetic. Its successful hardware acceleration lies in the efficient application of HLS pragmas, to facilitate parallel memory accesses, unrolling of computational loops and successful pipelining. Hereby, we propose a Dec module that, taking advantage of the algorithm's computational intensive nature, provides significant performance speedups with straightforward-yet-effective HLS techniques.

HLS Optimizations: The decoding algorithm consists of the GF arithmetic primitives of multiplication, division and exponentiation, as well as the respective memory operations of loading and storing GF elements. It also comprises Berlekamp-Massey decoding, syndrome decoding, matrix transposing, support vector computation, and error locator polynomial computation algorithms, along with the Benes network and its respective layers' computation. The aforementioned functions further consist of multiple calls to GF arithmetic primitives.

The acceleration potential of Dec lies in its computational part, since its inputs are rather small, but it performs numerous and complex computations over them. Specifically, the CT matrix ranges up to a few hundred bytes, while the SK size is an order of magnitude smaller than the respective PK (Table 1). For this reason, we focus on the optimization of Dec through accelerating its most computationally intensive functions. These are namely the syndrome decoding and the error locator polynomial computation: they account for ≈70% of the decoding total execution time. In particular, we pipeline and unroll the computational loops of these primitives maximizing their acceleration potential. Moreover, we also optimized the GF arithmetic functions, which are used by the syndrome and error locator polynomial generation, as well as the matrix transpose primitive, which is used by the support generation. To take fully advantage of loop pipelining, we use a partial array partitioning HLS directive on all the involved matrices, according to the rate to which we need to concurrently load/store values of the respective matrices. With the use of array partitioning, we manage to load and store elements of the same matrix, which are specifically partitioned in different memories, in a single clock cycle. For the larger arithmetic functions, we choose to only fully pipeline their computational loops, as any further loop unrolling blows up the resource consumption without much performance optimization. In this way, we maximize the achieved throughput and enhance the performance of Dec. To further optimize the performance and resource consumption of the Dec accelerator, we create multiple hardware instances of the GF arithmetic modules whose concurrent execution enhances the yielded acceleration (i.e. multiplication, inversion, etc.).

4   Implementation to SELENE SoC

Experimental Setup: The SELENE SoC uses the VCU118 FPGA board [2], where a RISC-V ISA softcore is implemented alongside the CM accelerator. The

VCU118 platform is a Xilinx board featuring the Virtex Ultrascale+ XCVU9P-L2FLGA2104E FPGA device. The RISC-V ISA core is based on the NOEL-V processor design [13] provided by Cobham Gaisler, and implements the RV64GC RISC-V ISA. NOEL-V is an in-order and dual issue core which is coupled with two external DDR4 memory banks, configured as 2 GB each. We used an FPGA emulation frequency of 100 MHz for both the accelerator and the core. Figure 2 provides a high-level overview of the most important core and accelerator modules, as well as their respective SoC interconnects.

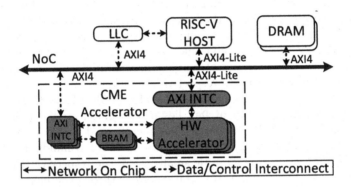

Fig. 2. High-Level overview of the RISC-V core, the CM accelerator and their interface. Blue color hardware blocks belong to the accelerator. (Color figure online)

Interfacing with the RISC-V Core: In the SoC, we make use of the AXI interface to couple the CM accelerator with the RISC-V core. Specifically, we use an AXI4-Full interface for the CPU-accelerator data transfer part, while the AXI4-Lite interface is used for the control and configuration part of the accelerator by the core. The AXI4-Full is handling the bandwidth-demanding input/output data movement from the external DRAM, using dedicated channels for every parameter and high-performance features like AXI bursts (shown in Fig. 1). On the other hand, AXI4-Lite, with its minimal hardware overhead, configures the accelerator's functionality using memory-mapped registers from the interconnected core without wasting valuable bandwidth.

Development Tools and Operating System Integration: The CM accelerator is developed using the Xilinx Vitis HLS EDA tool (version 2020.1) and integrated into the NOEL-V based SoC as a standalone IP. Specifically customized Vitis library functions facilitate the core-accelerator parameter passing. We initially used the VCU platform as a prototype board to verify our accelerator's correct functionality and also test the interfacing with the RISC-V core. A debian-based Linux image [1] boots on top of the RISC-V core that exposes the accelerator as a device driver. The OS driver provides capabilities to the user such as functionality configuration (choosing between Enc and Dec), input/output data loading and execution initiation/halting of the CME accelerator.

Towards the ASIC-SoC: Apart from our SELENE integrated accelerator, we decided to move towards implementing our proposal in an ASIC. In order to produce ASIC-grade RTL, we used our specifically refactored HLS source code with custom generated SRAMs, as an input to the Siemens Catapult EDA tool. At the HLS level, we migrated Xilinx specific pragmas, interface definitions and libraries (e.g. FIFO streams), to the respective Catapult ones. We used Cadence's Genus and Innovus EDA tools for the RTL synthesis and the Place and Route (PnR) process, respectively We targeted the GF22nm technology node using a 10 metal layers stack. We managed to achieve 1.13 GHz operating frequency in the typical corner with an area of 0.59 mm^2 after PnR using the CM accelerator for security level 1. We can safely assume that our accelerator can achieve at least a 1 GHz operating frequency on all security levels, since we keep the loop pipelining and unrolling analogous to the parallelization potential offered on each level. In order to foster a fair comparison between our proposal and the state-of-the-art counterparts, we extrapolate our execution time using the FPGA SoC execution time in clock cycles at the 1 GHz frequency (see Sect. 6). We note that since the actual ASIC frequency is faster, our approximation is underestimating the performance of our accelerator, thus providing a lower limit for our performance. We leave the actual performance optimization of the CM accelerator in all security levels with the Catapult ASIC toolflow as future work.

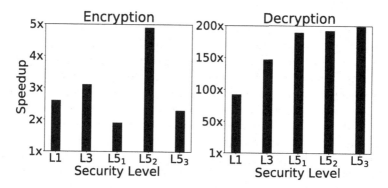

Fig. 3. Speedup provided by Enc (left) and Dec (right) at all security levels and for the encryption and decryption functions, respectively. Baseline=x86 executed CM software version

5   Performance Evaluation

In this section, we present the performance evaluation of the proposed CM accelerator in the context of the SELENE SoC. More ASIC related results are presented in Sect. 6.

Speedup: Since the NOEL-V core residing at the SELENE SoC is a resource-constrained RISC-V core, we refrained from comparing to a CM software executed at NOEL-V as a software baseline. Instead, we decided to provide a more fair performance comparison of our RISC-V integrated accelerator with a CM software executed at a COTS x86 core. For this reason, we picked the i7-5th generation CPU, which operates at 2.9 GHz frequency. Figure 3 presents the speedup provided to the encryption and decryption functions of CM, by Enc and Dec, compared to the software version of CM executed on a single core of the x86 processor without any special vectorization support. We note here, that, the execution time measurements of our proposal include the timing overhead for the data movement from the DRAM to the accelerator.

Figure 3 shows that Dec provides performance speedups between 92× and 198×. Dec being computationally intensive gains its speedup largely from the acceleration of the GF arithmetic primitives.

Enc shows performance speedups ranging from 1.9× up to 4.9×. The encoding function and its respective acceleration is heavily dependent on the efficient loading and subsequent processing of the PK values from the accelerator. In the current RISC-V SoC implementation the PK is stored in the external DRAM, which adds significant data communication overhead, especially for the PK data. Nevertheless, the design of Enc manages to effectively mitigate the large PK loading and high bandwidth challenge imposing minimal memory overhead and significance performance speedups.

Security-Performance Tradeoff: Figure 3 shows a steady speedup increase of Enc and Dec across the different CM security levels. In particular, when the CM security level increases, the accelerator handles larger matrices and therefore performs more computations. Both of the latter, give the accelerator more parallelization potential, thus enabling a higher performance yield. On the other hand, Enc shows a different speedup profile across the security levels. To elaborate, after an initial increase from L1 to L3, the speedup drops to around 2× for levels $L5_1$ and $L5_3$. This happens because for these levels Enc exceeds the 1kb limit per AXI burst, due to the bigger size of the respective PK matrix row. This results in penalization with extra clock cycles and consequently in a lower speedup. However, this does not hold for $L5_2$, since this level handles a smaller PK matrix row that does not exceed the 1kb threshold. Additionally, the respective baseline software implementation has to handle extra computations since the respective PK matrix row is not a Byte-multiple, while in our proposal this issue was easily handled, thus resulting in a higher relative speedup.

Table 2. Experimental platform FPGA resource consumption for `Enc` and `Dec`.

Accelerator	Security level	Resource Consumption [%]				Speedup [x]
		LUT	BRAM	DSP	FF	
Enc	L1	90961	164	0	50820	2.6
	L3	96341	178	0	69029	3.1
	$L5_1$	114523	164	0	93469	1.9
	$L5_2$	408983	56	0	112890	4.9
	$L5_3$	122420	178	0	96035	2.3
Dec	L1	414473	94	0	57144	92.4
	L3	832344	127	0	83335	147.1
	$L5_1$	1055585	117	0	98025	189.5
	$L5_2$	996121	71	0	90940	192.5
	$L5_3$	1064951	145	0	101709	198.8

Resource Utilization: Table 2 presents the `Enc` and `Dec` FPGA resource consumption on the SELENE platform, along with the respective speedup[1]. For the `Enc` module, we see a gradual increase on LUTs, BRAMs and FFs along with the security level increase. The security level $L5_2$ is an exception, as it shows a relative higher speedup comparing to the rest of the security levels. The respective resource consumption is also increased accordingly with the exception of the BRAM resources. This is justified, since level $L5_2$ operates on smaller matrices than the rest of CM security configurations of the 5th level (i.e. $L5_1$ & $L5_3$) which means less data communication overhead while still providing an elevated acceleration potential. Moreover, the `Dec` accelerator experiences a gradual increase on the LUTs, BRAMs and FFs on all security levels, peaking at the $L5_3$ security level configuration. The BRAM resources show a decrease in $L5_2$ for the `Dec` module too for the exact same reason we mentioned above. We note, that, on both accelerator modules, the BRAM consumption is attributed solely to the AXI interface, since the streaming data communication employed at the accelerators completely avoids any private storage of values.

6 Related Work

Since their conception at 1974 and 1986, the McEliece [26] and Niederreiter [27] cryptosystems have been the subject of numerous hardware implementation studies, ranging from smart cards [32], to microcontrollers [12,15,18,25], and to reconfigurable hardware [3,14,16,19,20,23,24,31]. The announcement in 2017 of the CME participation at the NIST PQ contest has sparked the interest of many research teams, leading to novel and efficient hardware implementations. Roth et al. [30] and Chen et al. [7] targeted embedded applications and specifically

---

[1] ASIC results in GF22nm technology node are analyzed in Sect. 4.

the Arm Cortex M4 microprocessor. Pircher et al. [28] explored the impact of vector instructions on the acceleration of the Gaussian elimination algorithm, accelerating the CME Key Generation. Wang et al. [33,34] proposed a fully-RTL and open-source FPGA implementation of the Niederreiter cryptosystem in FPGA devices. An end-to-end implementation of the whole CME KEM has been recently proposed by Chen et al. [8] showing novel techniques to accelerate the Key Generation part. Basu et al. [5] presented an HLS acceleration of several 1th Round NIST PQ contest cryptosystems, including CME. Finally, Kostalabros et al. [22] presented an open-source HLS-based HW/SW co-design acceleration of the most critical functions of CME KEM algorithms (Key Generation, Encapsulation and Decapsulation) tailored for heterogeneous CPU+FPGA platforms.

Table 3. Hardware implementation feature comparison with state-of-the-art.

Proposal	Description Language	SoC Integrated	ASIC Ready	PK Memory Footprint	Open source
This work	HLS	✓(RISC-V)	✓	✗	✓
[33]/[34]	RTL	✗	✗	✓	✓
[8]	RTL	✗	✗	✓	✗
[5]	HLS	✗	✗	✓	✗
[22]	HLS	✓(Arm)	✗	✓	✓

Our proposal has several features that distinct it from the rest of the scientific works. Table 3 presents the major differences between this work and the main CME implementations in the state-of-the-art. Our proposal presents the first ASIC-ready CME accelerator integrated in a RISC-V SoC. Therefore our reported results reflect the execution time of the whole system including data communication from the core as well as the operating system execution time overhead. Other proposals (see Table 3) do not interface their accelerator with a core and therefore their results omit the CPU-accelerator data communication overhead, which in most cases is the bottleneck of the system. Moreover, the ASIC-readiness of our proposal showcases a robust design that can easily be integrated in a tapeout process decreasing significantly the time from design to an actual operating SoC. What is more, the versatility of our HLS-design methodology allows the incorporation of algorithmic changes to the actual hardware design at late stages of the tapeout process, which is a fundamental requirement in the standardization of a cryptosystem that evolves over time. In terms of hardware resource consumption, it is evident that an HLS-based acceleration cannot compete against a fully-RTL optimized implementation. Nevertheless, a major scope of our proposal is to provide a time-efficient CM acceleration, mitigating the huge PK size hardware implementation challenge of the CM cryptosystem. For the above reasons we chose to compare our proposal's performance against

Kostalabros et al. [22]. Table 4 showcases the superiority of our CME acceleration method with speedups ranging from 3.93× to 26.7× for the encoding part, and from 24.5× to 39.3× for the decoding part.

Table 4. Encoding/Decoding speedup comparison against [22].

Security level	Execution time [ms]									
	L1		L3		$L5_1$		$L5_2$		$L5_3$	
Algorithm	Enc	Dec	Enc	Dec	Enc	Dec	Enc	Dec	Enc	Dec
CME SoC	0.11	0.42	0.24	0.89	0.45	1.14	0.36	1.14	0.38	1.19
[22]	0.74	10.46	1.16	22.3	1.81	40.58	9.84	38	2.08	46.83
Speedup [×]	6.53	24.5	4.79	24.9	3.96	35.5	26.7	33.1	5.46	39.3

7   Conclusions

To the best of our knowledge, this paper proposes the first ASIC-ready accelerator for CM, integrated in a safety-critical and Linux capable, RISC-V SoC. The `Enc` and `Dec` accelerator modules provide speedups of up to 4.9× and 198×, respectively, compared to a scalar software baseline. Moreover, our proposal requires an area of less than $0.6\,mm^2$ and reaches frequencies above 1 GHz when synthesized in GF22nm technology node. The source code of our hardware design is open-source and publicly available at the following hyperlink.

Acknowledgements. This work has been partially supported by the European HiPEAC Network of Excellence, by the Spanish Ministry of Science and Innovation MCIN/AEI 10.13039/501100011033 (contracts ACITHEC PID2021-124928NB-I00, PID2019-107255GB-C21 and "Ramón y Cajal" fellowship No. RYC2020-030685-I), by the Generalitat de Catalunya (contract 2021-SGR-00763), by the Agency for Management of University and Research Grants (AGAUR) of the Government of Catalonia under "Ajuts per a la contractació de personal investigador novell" fellowship No. 2019FI B01274 and the grant 2021SGR 00115, by the European Union within the framework of the ERDF of Catalonia 2014–2020 under the DRAC project [001-P-001723], by the project HERMES funded by INCIBE, and by the European NextGenerationEU/PRTR.

Disclosure of Interests. The authors have no competing interests to declare that are relevant to the content of this article.

References

1. ISAR - Integration System for Automated Root filesystem generation. https://github.com/siemens/isar-riscv
2. Xilinx Virtex UltraScale+ FPGA VCU118 evaluation kit. https://www.xilinx.com/products/boards-and-kits/vcu118.html

3. Agrawal, R., Bu, L., Kinsy, M.A.: Quantum-proof lightweight McEliece cryptosystem co-processor design. In: 2020 IEEE 38th International Conference on Computer Design (ICCD), pp. 73–79. IEEE (2020)

4. Albrecht, M.R., et al.: Classic McEliece: conservative code-based cryptography (2020)

5. Basu, K., Soni, D., Nabeel, M., Karri, R.: NIST post-quantum cryptography-a hardware evaluation study. IACR Cryptol. ePrint Arch. (2019)

6. Castelvecchi, D.: IBM's quantum cloud computer goes commercial. Nature News (2017)

7. Chen, M.S., Chou, T.: Classic McEliece on the arm cortex-M4. IACR Trans. Cryptogr. Hardw. Embed. Syst., 125–148 (2021)

8. Chen, P.J., et al.: Complete and improved FPGA implementation of classic McEliece. IACR Transactions on Cryptographic Hardware and Embedded Systems (2022)

9. Choi, C.Q.: IBM's quantum leap: the company will take quantum tech past the 1,000-qubit mark in 2023. IEEE Spectr. **60**(1), 46–47 (2023)

10. Chow, J., Dial, O., Gambetta, J.: IBM quantum breaks the 100-qubit processor barrier. IBM Research Blog (2021)

11. Crockett, E., Paquin, C., Stebila, D.: Prototyping post-quantum and hybrid key exchange and authentication in TLS and SSH (2019)

12. Eisenbarth, T., Güneysu, T., Heyse, S., Paar, C.: MicroEliece: McEliece for embedded devices. In: International Workshop on Cryptographic Hardware and Embedded Systems (2009)

13. Gaisler, C.: NOEL-V Processor (2020). https://www.gaisler.com/index.php/products/processors/noel-v

14. Ghosh, S.: On the implementation of McEliece with CCA2 indeterminacy by SHA-3. In: 2014 IEEE International Symposium on Circuits and Systems (ISCAS) (2014)

15. Ghosh, S., Delvaux, J., Uhsadel, L., Verbauwhede, I.: A speed area optimized embedded co-processor for McEliece cryptosystem. In: 2012 IEEE 23rd International Conference on Application-Specific Systems, Architectures and Processors (2012)

16. Ghosh, S., Verbauwhede, I.: BLAKE-512-based 128-bit CCA2 secure timing attack resistant McEliece cryptoprocessor. IEEE Trans. Comput. **63**, 1124–1133 (2012)

17. Hernández, C., et al.: SELENE: self-monitored dependable platform for high-performance safety-critical systems. In: 23rd Euromicro Conference on Digital System Design, DSD 2020, Kranj, Slovenia, 26–28 August 2020, pp. 370–377. IEEE (2020). https://doi.org/10.1109/DSD51259.2020.00066

18. Heyse, S.: Low-Reiter: Niederreiter encryption scheme for embedded microcontrollers. In: International Workshop on Post-Quantum Cryptography (2010)

19. Heyse, S., Güneysu, T.: Towards one cycle per bit asymmetric encryption: Code-based cryptography on reconfigurable hardware. In: International Workshop on Cryptographic Hardware and Embedded Systems (2012)

20. Heyse, S., Güneysu, T.: Code-based cryptography on reconfigurable hardware: tweaking Niederreiter encryption for performance. J. Cryptogr. Eng. **3**, 29–43 (2013)

21. Hülsing, A., Ning, K.C., Schwabe, P., Weber, F., Zimmermann, P.R.: Post-quantum wireguard (2020)

22. Kostalabros, V., Ribes-González, J., Farràs, O., Moretó, M., Hernandez, C.: HLS-based HW/SW co-design of the post-quantum classic McEliece cryptosystem. In: 2021 31st International Conference on Field-Programmable Logic and Applications (FPL) (2021)

23. López-García, M., Cantó-Navarro, E.: Hardware-software implementation of a McEliece cryptosystem for post-quantum cryptography. In: Future of Information and Communication Conference (2020)
24. Massolino, P.M.C., Barreto, P.S., Ruggiero, W.V.: Optimized and scalable co-processor for McEliece with binary Goppa codes. ACM Trans. Embed. Comput. Syst. (TECS) **14**, 1–32 (2015)
25. Maurich, I.v., Heberle, L., Güneysu, T.: IND-CCA secure hybrid encryption from QC-MDPC Niederreiter. In: Post-Quantum Cryptography (2016)
26. McEliece, R.J.: A public-key cryptosystem based on algebraic coding theory. Coding Thv **4244**, 114–116 (1978)
27. Niederreiter, H.: Knapsack-type cryptosystems and algebraic coding theory. Prob. Contr. Inform. Theory **15**(2), 157–166 (1986)
28. Pircher, S., Geier, J., Zeh, A., Mueller-Gritschneder, D.: Exploring the RISC-V vector extension for the classic McEliece post-quantum cryptosystem. In: 2021 22nd International Symposium on Quality Electronic Design (ISQED) (2021)
29. Resch, S., Karpuzcu, U.R.: Quantum computing: an overview across the system stack. arXiv preprint arXiv:1905.07240 (2019)
30. Roth, J., Karatsiolis, E., Krämer, J.: Classic McEliece implementation with low memory footprint. In: International Conference on Smart Card Research and Advanced Applications (2020)
31. Shoufan, A., Wink, T., Molter, G., Huss, S., Strentzke, F.: A novel processor architecture for McEliece cryptosystem and FPGA platforms. In: 2009 20th IEEE International Conference on Application-specific Systems, Architectures and Processors (ASAP) (2009)
32. Strenzke, F.: A smart card implementation of the McEliece PKC. In: Samarati, P., Tunstall, M., Posegga, J., Markantonakis, K., Sauveron, D. (eds.) WISTP 2010. LNCS, vol. 6033, pp. 47–59. Springer, Heidelberg (2010). https://doi.org/10.1007/978-3-642-12368-9_4
33. Wang, W., Szefer, J., Niederhagen, R.: FPGA-based key generator for the Niederreiter cryptosystem using binary Goppa codes. In: Fischer, W., Homma, N. (eds.) CHES 2017. LNCS, vol. 10529, pp. 253–274. Springer, Cham (2017). https://doi.org/10.1007/978-3-319-66787-4_13
34. Wang, W., Szefer, J., Niederhagen, R.: FPGA-based Niederreiter cryptosystem using binary Goppa codes. In: International Conference on Post-Quantum Cryptography (2018)

Exploiting FPGAs and Spiking Neural Networks at the Micro-Edge: The EdgeAI Approach

Paolo Meloni$^{(\boxtimes)}$, Paola Busia, Gianluca Leone, Luca Martis, and Matteo A. Scrugli

Università degli Studi di Cagliari, Cagliari, Sardinia, Italy
{paolo.meloni,paola.busia,gianluca.leone,luca.martis,
matteo.scrugli}@unica.it

Abstract. This paper outlines the initial FPGA-centric endeavors within the EdgeAI project, targeting scenarios where extremely constrained power-energy parameters intersect with the demand for high performance and accuracy in executing Artificial Intelligence (AI) algorithms. Our discussion, after presenting the generalities of the EdgeAI project, revolves around the project objective of leveraging simultaneously event-based spiking neural networks and low-end FPGA chips for very-low-power near-sensor AI inference. We present the hardware/software implementation of this approach and the early results on the project use cases.

Keywords: FPGAs · Spiking neural networks · edge computing

1 At-the-Edge AI and the EdgeAI Project

At-the-edge Artificial Intelligence (AI) empowers Machine Learning (ML) and Deep Learning (DL) at the network's periphery, closer to sensors and actuators, for localized data collection and processing, reducing latency, enhancing data privacy and security, and diminishing the need for cloud connectivity.

However, this poses challenges related to the execution of a complex computing workload on resource-constrained platforms. Thus, it requires dealing with diverse technologies and optimizing energy usage.

The EdgeAI project [1], a joint effort of 42 partners, part of the Key Digital Technologies (KDT) Joint Undertaking (JU), aims to face such challenges, to play a pivotal role in Europe's digital evolution towards smarter processing solutions at the edge. It focuses on creating fresh electronic parts and systems, refining processing setups, improving connectivity, and developing software, algorithms, and middle-layer technologies.

EdgeAI -*Edge AI Technologies for Optimised Performance Embedded Processing*-project is funded by Key Digital Technologies Joint Undertaking (KDT JU) - grant agreement No 101097300.

I. Skliarova et al. (Eds.): ARC 2024, LNCS 14553, pp. 296–302, 2024.
https://doi.org/10.1007/978-3-031-55673-9_21

1.1 EdgeAI Applications

The main aim of EdgeAI is to advance solutions across various layers of AI technology, culminating in the creation of real-time performing multimodal edge AI implementations for diverse industrial sectors.

The EdgeAI project partners work to demonstrate the applicability of the developed approaches in 20 demonstrators across five industrial value chains:

- digital industry,
- energy,
- agri-food and beverage,
- mobility, and
- digital society,

considering performance, security, trust, and energy efficiency demands inherently in each of these demonstrators. EdgeAI is designed to provide benefits across industrial sectors, to significantly contribute to the ubiquitous adoption of at-the-edge AI in society.

1.2 Reconfigurable Computing in EdgeAI

The EdgeAI vision spans across the whole computing continuum [2], as represented in Fig. 1, comprising:

- the micro-edge (processing units in embedded microcontrollers, sensors, and actuators, etc.)
- the deep-edge (processing units providing extended processing power, in gateways, mobile phones, programmable logic controllers, etc.)
- the meta-edge (on-premises high-performance edge processing microservers combining different microcontrollers and processors for specific operations)

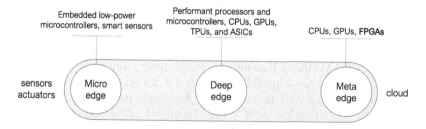

Fig. 1. EdgeAI vision of the computing continuum.

To this aim, different research tasks focus on a wide scope of heterogeneous processing platforms, aiming to amalgamate different computing solutions such as central processing units (CPUs), graphics processing units (GPUs), tensor processing units (TPUs), application-specific integrated circuits (ASICs), neuromorphic processing units (NPUs), system-on-chip (SoC) [2].

Moreover, since adaptability is one of the key requirements, and the possibility of reconfiguring the processing nodes and easily adapting them to different use cases and usage modes is of foremost importance, field-programmable gate arrays (FPGAs) are a main key enabling technology in the project and in the AI domain in general. Thus, numerous research efforts are spent by the community to optimize their use for the inference of AI algorithms in an edge computing protocol. To date, however, most approaches are focused on exploiting the parallelism of resources on FPGA fabric, for processing image streams with impressive data rates, tolerating power consumption figures compliant with the deep- or meta-edge, while how to use FPGAs for processing sensor data at the micro-edge is still an open question. In this area, in the initial phase of the project, two main research lines have emerged. On one hand, EdgeAI researchers have explored and confirmed the use of FPGAs at the meta-edge, focusing on tool-enabled workload reduction for Convolutional Neural Networks (CNNs), implementing techniques for hybrid quantization that have enabled mid-end FPGAs to outperform alternatives in energy efficiency [2].

On the other hand, we have studied the usage of FPGAs at the micro-edge, for the inference of more power-efficient event-based algorithms such as Spiking Neural Networks (SNNs), combining light-weight topologies with low-power reconfigurable devices, to enable inference in an envelope of few milliwatts.

In the rest of the paper, we focus on this latter effort, providing an overview of the hardware/software developed IPs and a glimpse on achieved results.

2   Background

SNNs emerge as a promising solution with energy-efficient, event-driven processing. However, exploiting the benefits of event-driven processing often requires specialized computational architectures.

FPGAs, due to their highly customizable hardware design, present themselves as suitable candidates for these computational tasks. Their design allows for the exploitation of sparse neuron firing patterns. The core Digital Signal Processor (DSP) slices are engineered to adeptly handle a suite of arithmetic operations including addition, multiplication, and multiply-and-accumulate. On another front, BRAM (Block Random Access Memory) units, due to their adaptable design and size, are especially suitable for integrating SNN models and facilitating data access and management. Although most effective pure-SNN processors are neuromorphic ASICs like Truenorth, Spinnaker, and Loihi, in related literature, some efforts concentrate on leveraging FPGAs to enhance flexibility and integration [3]. Some aim to simulate bio-realistic neural tissue [4], while others focus on processing event-encoded images via SNNs, relying on mid-to-high-end FPGA devices [5,6]. Other studies [7,8] target smaller devices, emphasizing spiking convolution layers for two-dimensional inputs, like images from DVS cameras. However, these implementations might not be suitable for low-power smart sensors due to their higher power/energy/cost requirements.

Within EdgeAI, we have explored SNN execution on low-power FPGAs, to demonstrate the practicality of such an approach within feasible power budgets for battery-operated and cost-effective sensor nodes.

3   Light-Weight SSNs for the Micro-Edge

We have created an architectural template, that we named SYNtzulu, and tested it across various near-sensor data processing scenarios. Figure 2 illustrates its system-level architecture. It is implemented on a Lattice iCE40UP5k FPGA and comprehends as main processing elements:

– a RISC-V core handling input/output data flow and configuring SYNtzulu;
– an 8-way SIMD SNN engine executing the inference of feed-forward SNNs composed of dense layers of LIF neurons.

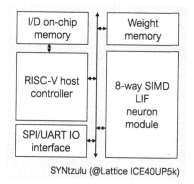

Fig. 2. Architecture overview of the low-power SNN engine developed within EdgeAI

The SNN engine comprises a configurable encoding slot preprocessing the sensor data to obtain spike trains, and a dual decoding slot translating output spike trains into classification outcomes. Moreover, it is tailored for executing SNN inference exploiting spike sparsity, and fostering low power consumption.

3.1   Capabilities and Constraints in Processing

The inference time of a specific SNN in SYNtzulu is directly influenced by the number of synapses and the time needed for computing the synaptic current. All other operations happen concurrently and overlap during execution. Since the SNN consumes 8 synapses per cycle, the inference throughput is thus given by the number of active synapses divided by 8, multiplied by the clock frequency, settable to up to 45 MHz.

The active synapse count is determined by the SNN topology and by the sparsity, since, thanks to a dynamic *spike stack* inside the SNN engine, inactive upstream neurons can be skipped during the computation of the LIF dynamics.

The primary limitation of `SYNtzulu` is the size of the weight memory, imposing a cap on the number of synapses in the executing SNN. While the memory composition can vary using on-FPGA storage macros, the default ICE40UP5k configuration can store 131,072 8-bit weights.

We have demonstrated that lightweight SNNs fitting within this limit can achieve top-tier accuracy in processing online sensor data, more specifically in ECG, EEG, and EMG [9–11]. Some example results are reported in Fig. 3 and Fig. 4.

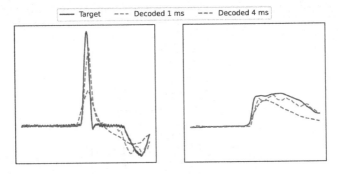

Fig. 3. View of example results on the EEG decoding dataset. The Figure shows two differently timed decoding experiments of the velocity of a macaque hand on the basis of the recorded intracranial EEG.

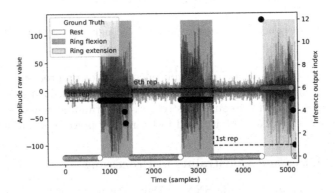

Fig. 4. Example result on the EMG classification datasets. Identification of rest and three gestures (two ring flexions and one ring extension from EMG)

Power consumption measured on the breakout board corresponds to around 12 mW during inference and around 1.2 mW during idle, when the system is acquiring input data and no events need to be processed. Considering the sparsity in the datasets mentioned above and the corresponding sampling times, average power consumption goes down to around 1.4 mW. Summarizing, in this use case, SYNtzulu consumes just 0.5 mW/MHz and shows energy efficiency corresponding to 136 pJ per synapse[1]. These measurements highlight that, when the task's nature (and consequently, the SNN algorithm) permits a lightweight approach, SYNtzulu can be utilized to develop highly efficient near-sensor processing nodes, resulting in substantial energy savings.

4   Conclusion and Future Work

The EdgeAI project is entering the second year of activities. FPGA-related activities will continue to improve accuracy and power efficiency in the project use case, focusing on improved training and quantization strategies, as well as on testing novel architectural template features and alternative FPGA devices for implementation.

Disclosure of Interests. The authors have no competing interests to declare that are relevant to the content of this article.

References

1. EdgeAI website. https://edge-ai-tech.eu/. Accessed 10 Jan 2024
2. Vermesan, O., Marples, D.: Advancing Edge Artificial Intelligence: Systems Contexts. River Publishers, Aalborg (2023)
3. Isik, M.: A survey of spiking neural network accelerator on FPGA. In: arXiv preprint arXiv:2307.03910 (2023)
4. Leone, G., Raffo, L., Meloni, P.: A bandwidth-efficient emulator of biologically-relevant spiking neural networks on FPGA. IEEE Access **10**, 76780–76793 (2022)
5. Li, S., et al.: A fast and energy-efficient SNN processor with adaptive clock/event-driven computation scheme and online learning. IEEE Trans. Circ. Syst. I Regular Papers **68**(4), 1543–1552 (2021). https://doi.org/10.1109/TCSI.2021.3052885
6. Panchapakesan, S., Fang, Z., Li, J.: SyncNN: evaluating and accelerating spiking neural networks on FPGAs. ACM Trans. Reconfig. Technol. Syst. **15**(4), 1–27 (2022)
7. Liu, H., et al.: A low power and low latency FPGA-based spiking neural network accelerator. In: 2023 International Joint Conference on Neural Networks (IJCNN), pp. 1–8 (2023). https://doi.org/10.1109/IJCNN54540.2023.10191153
8. Carpegna, A., Savino, A., Di Carlo, S.: Spiker: an FPGA optimized hardware accelerator for spiking neural networks. In: 2022 IEEE Computer Society Annual Symposium on VLSI (ISVLSI), pp. 14–19. (2022). https://doi.org/10.1109/ISVLSI54635.2022.00016

---

[1] Based on worst-case power usage and minimal performance due to worst-case pipeline imbalance.

9. Leone, G., Martis, L., Raffo, L., Meloni, P.: On-FPGA spiking neural networks for multi-variable end-to-end neural decoding. In: Palumbo, F., Keramidas, G., Voros, N., Diniz, P.C. (eds.) ARC 2023. LNCS, vol. 14251, pp. 185–199. Springer, Cham (2023). https://doi.org/10.1007/978-3-031-42921-7_13 ISBN 978-3-031-42920-0

10. Scrugli, M.A., et al.: On-FPGA spiking neural networks for integrated near- sensor ECG analysis. In: 2024 Design, Automation Test in Europe Conference Exhibition (DATE) (2024)

11. Scrugli, M.A., et al.: sEMG-based gesture recognition with spiking neural networks on low-power FPGA. In: Design and Architecture for Signal and Image Processing. Springer (2024)

Author Index